THE CAMBRIDGE
CLASSICAL LIT

General Editors
P. E. EASTERLING
Regius Professor of Greek, University of Cambridge
E. J. KENNEY
Emeritus Kennedy Professor of Latin, University of Cambridge

Advisory Editors
B. M. W. KNOX
formerly Director of the Center for Hellenic Studies, Washington
W. V. CLAUSEN
Emeritus Pope Professor of the Latin Language and Literature, Harvard University

VOLUME I   PART 1
Early Greek Poetry

THE CAMBRIDGE HISTORY OF CLASSICAL LITERATURE

VOLUME I: GREEK LITERATURE

PART 1   Early Greek Poetry
PART 2   Greek Drama
PART 3   Philosophy, History and Oratory
PART 4   The Hellenistic Period and the Empire

THE
CAMBRIDGE HISTORY
OF
CLASSICAL LITERATURE

VOLUME I   PART 1

Early Greek Poetry

Edited by

P. E. EASTERLING
Regius Professor of Greek, University of Cambridge

and

B. M. W. KNOX
formerly Director of the Center for Hellenic Studies, Washington

CAMBRIDGE
UNIVERSITY PRESS

Published by the Press Syndicate of the University of Cambridge
The Pitt Building, Trumpington Street, Cambridge CB2 1RP
40 West 20th Street, New York, NY 10011–4211, USA
10 Stamford Road, Oakleigh, Melbourne 3166, Australia

First published 1985 and reprinted 1986, 1987, 1988 as chapters 2–8 of
The Cambridge History of Classical Literature, Volume 1
First paperback edition 1989
Reprinted 1995

Printed in Great Britain by Athenæum Press Ltd, Gateshead

Library of Congress catalogue card number: 88–6123

British Library cataloguing in publication data
The Cambridge history of classical literature.
Vol. 1 [Greek literature], Pt 1, Early
Greek poetry.
1. Classical literature, to c. 500 –
Critical studies
I. Easterling, P. E.   II. Knox, Bernard M. W.
(Bernard MacGregor Walker)
880'.09

ISBN 0 521 35981 3

CONTENTS

CONTENTS

ABBREVIATIONS

BT	Bibliotheca Scriptorum Graecorum et Romanorum Teubneriana (Leipzig & Stuttgart)
Budé	Collection des Universités de France, publiée sous le patronage de l'Association Guillaume Budé (Paris)
Bursian	Bursian's *Jahresbericht über die Fortschritte der klassischen Altertumswissenschaft* (Berlin, 1873–1945)
CAF	T. Kock, *Comicorum Atticorum Fragmenta* (Leipzig, 1880–8)
CAH	*The Cambridge Ancient History* (Cambridge, 1923–39)
*CAH*²	2nd ed. (Cambridge, 1961–)
CHCL	*Cambridge History of Classical Literature* (Cambridge, 1982–5)
CGF	G. Kaibel, *Comicorum Graecorum Fragmenta* (Berlin, 1899)
CGFP	C. F. L. Austin, *Comicorum Graecorum Fragmenta in papyris reperta* (Berlin, 1973)
CIL	*Corpus Inscriptionum Latinarum* (Berlin, 1863–)
CVA	*Corpus Vasorum Antiquorum* (Paris & elsewhere, 1925–)
Christ–Schmid–Stählin	W. von Christ, *Geschichte der griechischen Literatur*, rev. W. Schmid and O. Stählin (Munich, 1920–24) 6th ed. (Cf. Schmid–Stählin)
Diehl	E. Diehl, *Anthologia Lyrica Graeca* I (2nd ed. 1936); II (3rd ed. 1949–52)
DTC	A. W. Pickard-Cambridge, *Dithyramb, tragedy and comedy.* 2nd ed., rev. T. B. L. Webster (Oxford, 1962)
DFA	A. W. Pickard-Cambridge, *The dramatic festivals of Athens.* 2nd ed., rev. J. Gould–D. M. Lewis (Oxford, 1968)
DK	H. Diels–W. Kranz, *Die Fragmente der Vorsokratiker.* 6th ed. (Berlin, 1951–2)
EGF	G. Kinkel, *Epicorum Graecorum Fragmenta* (Leipzig, 1877)
FGrH	F. Jacoby, *Fragmente der griechischen Historiker* (Berlin, 1923–)

ABBREVIATIONS

FHG	C. Müller, *Fragmenta Historicorum Graecorum* (Berlin, 1841–70)
FYAT	(ed.) M. Platnauer, *Fifty years (and twelve) of classical scholarship* (Oxford, 1968)
GLK	H. Keil, *Grammatici Latini* (Leipzig, 1855–1923)
GLP	C. M. Bowra, *Greek lyric poetry*, 2nd ed. (Oxford, 1961)
Gow–Page, *Hell. Ep.*	A. S. F. Gow–D. L. Page, *The Greek Anthology: Hellenistic Epigrams* (Cambridge, 1965)
Gow–Page, *Garland*	A. S. F. Gow–D. L. Page, *The Greek Anthology: The Garland of Philip* (Cambridge, 1968)
Guthrie	W. K. C. Guthrie, *A history of Greek philosophy* (Cambridge, 1965–81)
IEG	M. L. West, *Iambi et Elegi Graeci* (Oxford, 1971–2)
IG	*Inscriptiones Graecae* (Berlin, 1873–)
Kai	G. Kaibel, *Comicorum graecorum fragmenta*, 1 fasc. 1 *Doriensium comoedia mimi phylaces* (Berlin, 1899)
KG	R. Kühner–B. Gerth, *Ausführliche Grammatik der griechischen Sprache: Satzlehre.* 4th ed. (Hannover, 1955)
Lesky	A. Lesky, *A history of Greek literature*, tr. J. Willis–C. de Heer (London, 1966)
Lesky, *TDH*	A. Lesky, *Die tragische Dichtung der Hellenen*, 3rd ed. (Göttingen, 1972)
LSJ	Liddell–Scott–Jones, *Greek–English Lexicon*, 9th ed. (Oxford, 1925–40)
Loeb	Loeb Classical Library (Cambridge, Mass. & London)
OCD²	*Oxford Classical Dictionary*, 2nd ed. (Oxford, 1970)
OCT	Scriptorum Classicorum Bibliotheca Oxoniensis (Oxford)
Ol	A. Olivieri, *Frammenti della commedia greca e del mimo nella Sicilia e nella Magna Grecia* (Naples, 1930)
Paravia	Corpus Scriptorum Latinorum Paravianum (Turin)
PLF	E. Lobel–D. Page, *Poetarum Lesbiorum Fragmenta* (Oxford, 1963)
PMG	D. L. Page, *Poetae Melici Graeci* (Oxford, 1962)
PPF	H. Diels, *Poetarum Philosophorum Graecorum Fragmenta* (Berlin, 1901)
Pfeiffer	R. Pfeiffer, *A history of classical scholarship* (Oxford, 1968)
Powell	J. U. Powell, *Collectanea Alexandrina* (Oxford, 1925)
Powell–Barber	J. U. Powell–E. A. Barber, *New chapters in the history of Greek Literature* (Oxford, 1921), 2nd ser. (1929), 3rd ser. (Powell alone) (1933)
Preller–Robert	L. Preller, *Griechische Mythologie*, 4th ed., rev. C. Robert (Berlin, 1894)

RAC	*Reallexikon für Antike und Christentum* (Stuttgart, 1941–)
RE	A. Pauly–G. Wissowa–W. Kroll, *Real-Encyclopädie der klassischen Altertumswissenschaft* (Stuttgart, 1893–)
Roscher	W. H. Roscher, *Ausführliches Lexikon der griechischen und römischen Mythologie* (Leipzig, 1884–)
SEG	*Supplementum Epigraphicum Graecum* (Leyden, 1923–71; Alphen aan den Rijn, 1979–)
SH	P. J. Parsons and H. Lloyd-Jones, *Supplementum Hellenisticum* (Berlin & New York, 1983)
SLG	D. L. Page, *Supplementum Lyricis Graecis* (Oxford, 1974)
SVF	H. von Arnim, *Stoicorum Veterum Fragmenta* (Leipzig, 1903–)
Snell	B. Snell, *Tragicorum Graecorum Fragmenta* (Göttingen, 1971–)
Schmid–Stählin	W. Schmid–O. Stählin, *Geschichte der griechischen Literatur* (Munich, 1929–48)
Spengel	L. Spengel, *Rhetores Graeci* (1853–6); I ii rev. C. Hammer (Leipzig, 1894)
TGF	A. Nauck, *Tragicorum Graecorum Fragmenta*, 2nd ed. (Leipzig, 1889)
Walz	C. Walz, *Rhetores Graeci* (Stuttgart, 1832–6)

EDITORIAL NOTE

Updating of bibliographical material in the paperback edition has been undertaken where possible in references to recently published texts and commentaries. This edition also incorporates corrections received by the editors after the 1986 reprinting of the one-volume hardcover edition.

1

HOMER

I. THE POET AND THE ORAL TRADITION

What would the world be like if the *Iliad* and *Odyssey* had utterly perished, or been preserved only in fragments? The question hardly bears thinking about. Yet only a fraction of Greek tragedy has survived – why then are we so fortunate in the case of Homer, who lived and worked some three hundred years earlier than the great tragedians, long before the era of libraries and a developed book-trade, probably even before writing itself was seriously applied in Greece to the composing and recording of works of literature? The main reason is that Homer was from the beginning the most admired poet of Hellenic and Hellenized antiquity, and remained so until near its end. He seemed to embody the spirit of an age of heroes, yet never looked old-fashioned like Aeschylus or morally dubious like Euripides. Learning his poetry by heart was an essential part of ordinary education, and that, more than anything, is what saved it from fragmentation and decay in the first centuries after his death. Once consigned to writing, the text gradually achieved a standard form. The written versions ran wild at first, but were slowly reduced to order by scholars and librarians in Athens, Alexandria and Pergamum from the fifth to the second centuries B.C.[1] For hundreds of years even after that, as is shown by the ruins of Graeco-Roman settlements along the Nile, on the dry escarpments where papyrus books happen to survive, the *Iliad* and *Odyssey* were still widely read, more popular even than the lowbrow and more modern works of Menander. Many of the papyrus fragments of Homer come from school copies, but many are from finely-written rolls that were the treasured possession of educated men. Six or seven hundred years before, closer to the time when the poems were made, things were not very different. Even the philosophers Plato and Aristotle dropped quotations from Homer into their lectures and treatises, perpetuating (and in Plato's case also criticizing) the traditional idea of him as fountain-head of wisdom and expert on such diverse matters as medicine, military affairs and popular morality. If their quotations were not always quite accurate, that was

[1] Mazon (1948) 7–38; J. A. Davison in Wace and Stubbings (1962) 221–5; Kirk (1962) ch. 14.

not because the epics were obsolescent or no reasonable texts available. Rather they were too available for their own good; one carried much of the text in one's head and did not bother to unwind the awkward papyrus volumes to check a reference or an exact context.

This orality of Homer is of prime importance not only as a factor in the transmission and survival of his work but also in determining its true quality. For it is imperative to understand about the *Iliad* and *Odyssey* that they were composed wholly or substantially without the help of writing, by a poet or poets who were effectively illiterate, and for audiences that could not (or at least for literary purposes did not) read. So much can be discovered simply on internal evidence from the style of the poems, and in particular from their dependence on a great mass of standardized phrases or 'formulas' that could be fitted together to cover many of the common actions and events of heroic experience. Both the broad scope of this coverage and its surprising economy (for there was usually just one phrase for the expression of a single idea within the limits of a given portion of the hexameter verse) are proof that Homer made use of a *traditional* diction, evolved over several generations by a whole sequence of singers. In other words, his was a special kind and degree of what most poets employ, an artificial – because a poetical – language. His verses were sung, with some help from the lyre, and as an *aoidos* or singer he had to be able to produce them fluently – not exactly spontaneously, but by a kind of instinctive yet controlled release of phrases, verses and ideas that he had absorbed from other singers and made part of his own artistic personality. 'Memorizing' and 'improvising' are misleading, if much-used, terms for what he and the other heroic singers did, although his activity entailed elements of both. For the oral poet has heard many songs in his time; he assimilates their form and substance and much of their exact expression, adjusting them continuously to his own special repertory of favourite plots, phrases and motifs. When he sings a song he has heard before, it tends to emerge always slightly differently, stamped with his immediate range of theme and vocabulary, lengthened or shortened or otherwise varied according to audience and circumstance, as well (of course) as to his personal capacities, ambitions and inclinations.

The consequence is that each singer was at the same time a representative of the tradition of heroic poetry – and therefore a transmitter – and a unique shaper of the songs, language and ideas he had acquired from the tradition – and therefore an innovator. Many singers must have been less than brilliant, and their innovations would be neutral at best; at worst they would tend to corrupt the songs learned from others, either by truncating and deforming them or by relatively tasteless and incompetent elaboration. Other singers would be able to combine and extend their acquired materials in ways that amounted to important new creation. Homer must have been one of these; and yet *his* mode of creation obviously went far beyond what was normal, or ordinary. It was, in a valid sense, unique.

This can be clearly demonstrated in at least one respect. For oral poetry works fairly strictly within certain functional limitations, and one of these is length – a limitation imposed by what an audience can reasonably absorb and enjoy on a single occasion. Most oral heroic poems could surely be heard in an afternoon or evening, or part of one. The singers Phemius and Demodocus who are shown in action in the *Odyssey* sing songs that occupy some, but only some, of the time after the evening meal. We may guess that most ordinary songs varied from about a hundred verses (the length of the self-contained and apparently unabbreviated song about the unfortunate love-affair of Ares and Aphrodite that is placed in the mouth of Demodocus in *Odyssey* 8) to about five or six hundred verses – the extent, say, of many of the twenty-four books into which each great epic is divided. This was something like the norm of length, determined by what an audience would tolerate and a singer could perform. Now clearly each of the great Homeric epics vastly exceeds this norm: by a factor of something approaching twenty-four, if it is indeed the case that many of their single books approximate to the functional length. Therefore Homer (if he may be allowed for the time being to be the indisputable composer of both) was an absolutely *abnormal* oral poet. We know of none other like him. Even his imitators in the post-oral period, for instance the almost unknown composers of the 'Epic Cycle' who wrote poems designed to fill the gaps or exploit the omissions of Homer's narration of the war against Troy and its aftermath, operated on a far smaller scale. As for possible predecessors, we know of none by name or repute. At the same time it is certain that many predecessors existed, precisely the founders and developers of the oral heroic tradition; and we have no reason to suspect any of them of inordinate scale or ambition. There is every likelihood that the *Iliad* was the first very long, or monumental, poem and the *Odyssey* the second. The *Iliad*, then, would be Homer's own invention and conception, and in elaborating and agglomerating many of the ordinary songs from his repertoire and making them into a unified whole he would have been exemplifying a kind of monumental aspiration that seems to have been in the air in the eighth century B.C., and was paralleled in the appearance at precisely that period of colossal temples and enormous funerary vases. As for his audiences, they would just have had to tolerate the inconvenience of several performances in sequence, and would perhaps be most likely to do so in response to a unique reputation and genius – as much as through the provision of some specially suitable occasion like a religious festival, as has often been supposed.

Virtually all the lesser hexameter poetry vanished into thin air, destroyed in different ways by mediocrity and by literacy. Everything that was not an *Iliad* or *Odyssey* must have seemed, by comparison, both brash and thin. It was both

3

the special *réclame* of the two great epics and their persistent orality that probably maintained them until they were first written out in a complete form (although no doubt with many inaccuracies) for the purposes of the 'rhapsodic' contests that became popular as part of the Panathenaic Games in the sixth century B.C. Yet one of the curious things about Homer is his appearance on the scene just at the end of the oral period – at the exact epoch in which writing, through the introduction from the Levant of a practicable alphabetic system in the ninth or early eighth century B.C., began to spread through Greece. The earliest alphabetic inscriptions to be found there (as distinct from the vague and cumbrous syllabic documents of the Mycenaean age) date from shortly after 750 B.C. and are both brief and informal.[1] A verse or two of poetry could be scratched or painted on a perfume-pot or drinking-cup, but it is improbable that writing was used for the recording, let alone the composing, of anything resembling continuous literature until almost a century of further development both of the script itself and of the form and material of books. The first distinguishable figure of the era of literacy is Archilochus, the warrior-poet of Paros and Thasos, who referred to an eclipse of the sun in 648 B.C. and certainly composed his poems in writing, replete though they still were with the diction of the old epic.[2]

It is tempting to wonder whether Homer was able to assemble his complicated and monumental poems simply because of the recent availability of writing. The idea cannot be excluded that he somehow made use of written notes or written lists of themes and episodes. Yet it would be surprising if the new technique were to be applied so quickly as an essential element of such a massive undertaking. Scholars differ about this. Those who feel that Homer must have been literate in some sense (if only by dictating to a literate assistant) are motivated by their conviction that such long and subtle poems could not be composed by heart and ear alone. Close examination of the techniques of oral diction and analogous thematic construction suggests that their incredulity could be misplaced. But in any event there are important considerations of a different kind that are regularly overlooked. The primary one seems to be this: that Greece acquired a fully practicable writing-system uniquely late in its cultural development. Admittedly Egypt and Mesopotamia were technically quite advanced when they developed the art of writing ages before, back in the third millennium B.C. But the Achaean kingdoms of the second millennium, if they lagged behind in engineering and building (through the accidents of geography for the most part), were little less sophisticated in most other cultural matters than their Near-Eastern contemporaries and neighbours. In politics and religion, indeed, they clearly outstripped them. Yet they still lacked a script suitable for literature;

---

[1] Heubeck (1979) 109ff.; Kirk (1962) 69f.
[2] Kirk (1976) 197–9.

the Linear B syllabary was evidently confined to basic documentary uses, whereas cuneiform and hieroglyphs had long been used for historical, religious and even purely artistic literature.

In many respects, obviously, this strange backwardness of the Greeks over writing, their insistence on clinging to the worst available system – and then dropping it without immediate replacement – was disadvantageous to them. It must have been largely responsible, for example, for their historical naivety down to the time of Thucydides. In respect of poetry, however, it had some paradoxical merits. For the oral tradition (and such traditions are normally killed off by widespread literacy) continued and expanded far beyond the stage at which the requirements of either village or baronial entertainment might still be quite modest. Admittedly the heroic tradition (already well established, in all probability, in the late Bronze Age) ran into the 'Dark Age' that followed the Mycenaean collapse, but it was nevertheless still going strong in the new expansionist era of the tenth, ninth and eighth centuries B.C. – the era of colonizing and of political, social and economic stabilization. How far the range and techniques of oral poetry benefited is a matter for speculation. It is a likely guess that they did so considerably, and that the heroic poetry of the eleventh century (for example) had been much simpler, and in particular consisted for the most part of short sentences confined, as in other oral cultures, to the whole verse. If so, then the 'Dark Age' may not have seriously inhibited the development of relatively sophisticated techniques, like that of the expanded simile, in traditional poetry.

Even the creation of the monumental poem, more or less without warning, was now made possible. What had hitherto kept heroic poems short had presumably been not one but two main causes: not only function but also tradition itself. The functional desirability of shorter poems still applied, but tradition had already been broken in many important aspects of the cultural environment. Oral poetry originates, and is most conservatively maintained, in a traditional society – but Greek society in the eighth century B.C. was no longer that. Economic change, colonizing and exploration, the growth of urban life and the decline of kingship: these and other factors must have seriously disrupted a traditional way of life that had persisted (with some interruption at the end of the Bronze and beginning of the Iron Age) for many centuries. Largely through the failure to develop the technique of writing, traditional poetical methods survived into an age when traditional restraints on the scope and form of oral verse had virtually disappeared.

Thus the monumental epic was made feasible through a spirit of cultural experimentation that was still compelled to operate within the limits of non-literacy. In an important sense, therefore, the alphabet and Homer are likely to have been not so much cause and effect as parallel products of the new expansionism. A generation or so later the impulse had gone. Writing had spread too far for the creative oral genius to flourish much longer; one result was the derivative Cyclic poems and the *Homeric Hymns* (on which see pp. 69ff.), even the earliest and best of which, like the *Hymn to Demeter* or the *Hymn to Apollo*, show signs of self-consciousness and laboured imitation. The eighth century B.C. was exactly the period during which conditions were best for the production of a monumental epic; and that is the century to which the *Iliad* and *Odyssey* – the former near its middle, the latter near its end – most probably belong.[1]

How can one be so confident over this question of chronology? There is little enough help to be had from the ancient biographical tradition itself. The Greeks remained excessively vague about the person of Homer. Admittedly Herodotus got his date roughly right, for he placed Homer and Hesiod not more than ten generations before his own time, his source presumably being some genealogical tradition; yet we cannot expect too much accuracy from people who, even after Herodotus, persisted in ascribing the poet's birth to a river-nymph.[2] One consoling feature is that there existed in the Ionian island of Chios a guild of rhapsodes, or professional reciters, who called themselves the Homeridae or 'Descendants of Homer' and can be traced back into the sixth and perhaps even the seventh century B.C.[3] They failed to convince their contemporaries either that Homer was certainly a Chiote or that they had special rights to the correct text of his poems. Yet the claims of Chios over most of its ancient competitors are considerable, and the Homerids were perhaps not so much fraudulent as naive in thinking they could continue to control an oral tradition in an age of literacy. In any event Homer must have lived before the mid-seventh century, when we find unmistakable allusions in Callinus, Semonides and the *Hymn to Apollo* and when the spread of writing was putting an end to oral poetry as a living tradition.[4] At the other end of the scale he must have worked after the date of the Trojan War that provided his subject, and that took place, in one form or another, in the thirteenth century B.C.

The earliest and latest conceivable dates for Homer are, say, 1200 and 650 B.C., but several factors combine to suggest a date closer to the end than to the beginning or even the middle of this long period: the lifetime of Hesiod, for instance, who is probably later than Homer but not by much, and who seems to fit best, by other criteria, into the early seventh century. More specific indicators are the objects, practices and beliefs described in the Homeric poems themselves. Admittedly the poems are an artificial amalgam, both in language and in cultural content, of elements derived from different periods: from the poet's own time, from that of his closer predecessors in the oral tradition, and indeed from all the

[1] Kirk (1962) 282–7.   [2] Herodotus 2.53; *Certamen* 10.
[3] Pindar *Nem.* 2.1f., with scholium; Kirk (1962) 272 and (1976) 140f.; Wade-Gery (1952) 19–21.   [4] Kirk (1962) 283; Mazon (1948) 264.

centuries back (in theory at least) to the Trojan War itself. If we can identify some of the latest of these elements then we have an approximate lower limit for the composition of the poems – provided always that the elements are integral and not later accretions. A few are probably datable after about 900 B.C.: the pair of throwing-spears as standard armament (conflated in the *Iliad* with the single Mycenaean thrusting-spear), the use of large tripod-cauldrons (described among the Phaeacians' gifts to Odysseus), Phoenician ships trading widely in the Aegean (in the *Odyssey* again, prominently in Odysseus' false tales and Eumaeus' account of his childhood). Still fewer elements point to the eighth century, including perhaps the occasional description of what amounts to 'hoplite tactics', that is, fighting in close-packed ranks as opposed to the heroic system of duel and free-for-all. One or two objects, especially in the *Odyssey*, can be paralleled by archaeological finds from the early seventh century and not from the eighth: for example the gorgon-head as decorative motif. All this suggests about 700 B.C., or conceivably just a decade or two later for the *Odyssey*, as *terminus ante quem*. The development of language points in the same direction; for example the *w*-sound represented by the old letter digamma had disappeared from spoken Ionic Greek by the seventh century but was still observed more often than not by the Homeric singers. This is a precarious criterion, admittedly, for an oral tradition; so is the appearance on vases of figure-scenes apparently derived from one or other of the poems – they occur increasingly from about 675 B.C. onward, but that could be the result of new artistic fashion as much as of the spread of the Homeric epics.

Only a handful of passages prevent one from arguing Homer back into the late ninth century rather than the middle to late eighth; but those passages look organic, and in any event that would be the furthest one could reasonably go. Naturally, since his poetry was largely traditional, it contained elements that were created long before that: archaic phraseology (βοὴν ἀγαθός 'good at the war-cry', ἀνὰ πτολέμοιο γεφύρας 'along the bridges of war', ἐν νυκτὸς ἀμολγῶι 'in the milking-time of night'), archaic names of people and places, archaic objects (silver-studded swords, a boar's-tusk helmet – this in an episode developed relatively late, the night-expedition of *Iliad* 10).[1] Indeed a fair amount of both the incident and the expression of each poem could be derived from centuries before Homer's own time. Parts could go back close to the time of the Trojan War itself, and fragments to an even earlier period of the late Bronze Age. A recent linguistic argument suggests that the Homeric modes of separating adverbial and prepositional elements that were later combined into compound verbs belong to a stage of language anterior to that represented in the Linear B tablets.[2] If so, that would take elements of Homer's language back

---

[1] Swords, e.g. *Il.* 2.45, 14.405; helmet, *Il.* 10.261–71.
[2] Horrocks (1981) 148–63.

more than 500 years before his time – not impossible in an oral tradition, but unlikely for more than sporadic relics of morphology or syntax. The contribution of, say, the tenth and ninth centuries B.C. remains even more problematical. It was probably considerable, presumably larger than that of the late Mycenaean age. Even so Homer himself, as monumental composer, can plausibly be credited with everything that accompanies great scale. That may include the more highly elaborated similes, much of the more complex (and often more felicitous) language, including the longer and more complicated sentences, and most of the crucial and elaborate episodes: for example the deaths of Patroclus and Hector in the *Iliad* and the careful plotting against the suitors in the *Odyssey*.

Chios, Smyrna, Colophon, Ephesus: the cities that seriously claimed Homer for their own were at least all in Ionia, directly across the Aegean from mainland Greece. Moreover the dialect of the poems is predominantly Ionic (although there is a substratum of Aeolic forms, from the region just to the north of Ionia, that were retained for primarily metrical reasons); and there are a few signs in the *Iliad* of personal knowledge of the country round Troy and of the whole east-Aegean seaboard.[1] That all adds up, at any rate for the *Iliad*, to the conclusion that Homer was an Ionian singer, that he lived and worked primarily in Ionia. One is reluctant to conclude anything strikingly different for the *Odyssey*. Admittedly its main scene, the island of Ithaca, lies over on the far western side of Greece, and Telemachus' journey takes him down into the southern Peloponnese, still a good way from Ionia and Troy. Yet such geographical details as are provided, for example about the exact position and terrain of Ithaca itself, contain just that mixture of fact, distortion and fancy that we might expect of a tale whose elements had been widely diffused – right across the mainland and to the further side of the Aegean in this case, to be developed and elaborated there by the Ionian school of singers.[2] Moreover the dialect of the poem is no less strongly Ionic in colouring than that of the *Iliad*. That might conceivably be the result of literary convention, which ensured that all subsequent epics should approximate to the dialect of Homer; but such a convention is unlikely to have worked so strongly within the oral period itself.

The regional affiliations of the two poems raise directly at last the question of the specific authorship of the *Iliad* and *Odyssey*, one that has proved notoriously beguiling and intractable over the ages – although it is hardly one of the more productive questions either about the poems or about Homer, whose biography remains remarkably bare in any event. Even the purely poetical questions that might be thought to depend on authorship can be almost as well answered by the assumption of earlier and later stages in the working life of a single main

[1] *Il.* 2.144ff., 459ff., 9.5, 13.12f.; cf. Kirk (1962) 272f.
[2] E.g. *Od.* 9.21–7, 13.344–51.

8

composer as by that of separate composers. At least it seems probable that the earlier poem was known to the composer of the later one.

More interesting are the differences between the poems themselves, whatever their external implications. The first task is to distinguish differences that could be caused merely by different subjects. The predominantly martial poem will obviously be rich in martial vocabulary and, in spite of occasional scenes by the ships or in Troy, short of domestic language. The *Odyssey*, on the other hand, being a combination of picaresque or fantastic adventure with the peacetime life of Ithaca, and to a lesser extent of Pylos and Sparta, will be short of martial language and have much more about travelling, storms at sea, palace life and so on. Actually the language, which in broad terms is remarkably consistent between the two poems, varies in certain detailed respects quite independently of subject, and this may be significant. The *Odyssey* has a number of exclusive formulas, among them the following: κακὰ βυσσοδομεύων 'pondering evils', τετληότι θυμῶι 'with steadfast spirit', μεταλλῆσαι καὶ ἐρέσθαι 'to question and ask', κατεκλάσθη φίλον ἦτορ 'dear heart was broken', δύσετό τ' ἠέλιος σκιόωντό τε πᾶσαι ἀγυιαί 'the sun set and shadowed were all the streets'. All these occur five times or more. The last instance, a whole verse, is admittedly inappropriate to all except the Troy-scenes of the *Iliad*, but the rest are of general application. One can add the whole verses that occur frequently in the *Odyssey* but only rarely in the *Iliad* – and then in parts (like Book 24) that are least traditional and show some degree of relatively late development: ἀλλ' ἄγε μοι τόδ' ἔειπὲ καὶ ἀτρεκέως κατάλεξον 'but come, tell me this and truthfully declare it' (thirteen uses against four) and the famous ἦμος δ' ἠριγένεια φάνη ῥοδοδάκτυλος Ἠώς 'when early-born rosy-fingered Dawn appeared' (twenty uses against two). Conversely the following among others are exclusive to the *Iliad*: ἐρεβεννὴ νύξ 'dark night', μοῖρα κραταίη 'mighty destiny', ὄσσε κάλυψε 'covered his eyes', and (only four times, but useful as one might think for describing Odysseus) φρεσὶ πευκαλίμηισι 'with subtle mind'. As expected, there are fewer exclusive general phrases in the earlier and therefore imitable poem, but some exclusive Iliadic single words, even though subject-conditioned in varying degrees, are striking: χραισμεῖν 'to help' (19 times), λοιγός, λοίγιος 'destruction, destructive' (25 times), κλόνος 'rout' (28 times), ἕλκος 'wound' (22 times). The *Odyssey* can counter with δέσποινα 'mistress' (10 times) as its most strikingly exclusive word – again subject-conditioned to some extent, but a conspicuous absentee from the *Iliad* none the less.

Changes in vocabulary, especially in formular vocabulary, are more suggestive in an oral than in a literate context. They tend to imply a different repertoire, and hence a different singer or even a different regional tradition. This last possibility cannot apply in the Homeric case; the similarities and interdependence of the two poems are too conspicuous for that. Different singers are a

HOMER

stronger possibility, and nothing in particular, except perhaps the phenomenon of two such great poets so close together, excludes it. Yet we still cannot overlook 'Longinus'' conception of the *Odyssey* as the work of Homer's old age (*Subl.* 9.13), for the same singer can develop or curtail his formular apparatus to a limited extent over a period of years, not least with poems of differing tone or genre.

In general the language and style of the two poems are not dissimilar. It is important to recognize, nevertheless, that broad stylistic differences do exist and may be significant. They can be summed up as amounting to a decline in vigour of expression in the later poem – again, that is not inconsistent with 'Longinus'' judgement. Even more significant, perhaps, is what appears to be a subtle but important alteration in the view taken of the gods: not so much that their messenger is Iris in the *Iliad*, Hermes in the *Odyssey* (although the completeness of that change is odd in itself) as that the gods of the later poem care for overall justice among mortals and not simply for the preservation of heroic decorum and the natural order as in the *Iliad*. The Zeus of the *Odyssey* begins (1.28–47) by expressing concern because men blame the gods for evil, whereas it is really their own fault, and he is periodically envisaged as sending blessings on the virtuous and punishment on sinners. The seeds of that attitude are admittedly present in the *Iliad*, but in the later poem they have grown into something more like a developed theology.[1] Again, the subject of the *Odyssey* might be held to lead more naturally to moral reflection, what with the wicked suitors and the paradigm of Orestes as avenger. Yet on the whole it seems reasonable to conclude that the theological presuppositions of the *Odyssey* are indeed the more developed, and imply a rather more sophisticated stage of the whole oral heroic tradition. Its language, even apart from formular vocabulary, is consistent with that, being slightly freer of archaisms and more generous with developed forms from the era of monumental composition itself. Other differences, especially in the redeployment, with slight variation, of basic characters and themes, will emerge in the pages that follow. On the specific question of authorship the most probable conclusion is perhaps that the *Odyssey* is the product of a separate main composer, although one cannot be certain that it is not indeed the work of 'Homer's' old age. In any case his name will continue to be used in the following pages for the monumental composer of each epic. But what really matters is that two poems of genius, so complementary and yet so distinct, appeared in the eastern half of Greece at the very dawn of the full historical age, to impose their stamp on almost every aspect of culture in the splendid civilization that followed.

[1] Lloyd-Jones (1971) ch. 2.

2. THE *ILIAD*

This grand and complex composition, surely the greatest of all epics, can be treated by the critic on many levels. Present readers will probably have read much of the poem for themselves, so that a mere paraphrase would be otiose. Yet in the end it has seemed best to base the discussion on a critical survey of the poem's main themes, book by book, and on translated passages chosen to illustrate the interlocking aspects of action and language. For the basic structure of the *Iliad*, though straightforward in itself, is often obscured by massive elaborations and digressions; and one must experience the whole in due order if the resulting impression is to be unified and monumental rather than merely chaotic. In the pages that follow the aim is gradually to build up a view not only of the narrative plan and its implications but also of the qualities of expression, style and feeling on which any refined appreciation of the poem must depend.

The epic opens with a short invocation to the Muse to sing of the 'wrath of Achilles'. That, with its immediate consequences, is to be the central narrative theme, although in different ways the entire *geste* of Troy, and the tensions inherent in the heroic code itself, are no less important. Prince Achilles' wrath is provoked by his quarrel with Agamemnon, leader of the Achaean – the Greek – forces encamped before Troy. Indirectly it is started by the god Apollo; he has sent a plague on the besieging army because, as the seer Calchas reveals, Agamemnon refuses to restore his prize of war, the girl Chryseis, to her father Chryses who is Apollo's priest. Already the poem has moved from its lapidary prologue to the heart of a tense debate among the Achaean leaders; already it displays the scale and detail of a work that is to be uniquely long and ambitious. Agamemnon is regally annoyed and insults first Calchas and then, more dangerously, Achilles who comes to the seer's defence. Achilles replies in vicious terms that challenge the honour and authority of the king to whom the expeditionary force has sworn allegiance – both as elder brother of Menelaus and so responsible for avenging Helen's abduction by the Trojan prince Paris, and as the uniquely powerful ruler of 'Mycenae of much gold'. In his disaffected words to Agamemnon Achilles already reveals the envy and discontent that were implicit not only in his particular role but also in the whole heroic scale of values:

'Yet my prize never equals yours, whenever the Achaeans sack a populous city belonging to the Trojans. It is my hands that perform the greater part of grievous fighting, but if ever a share-out is made then your prize is much greater, and I have to be content with something small to rejoice in when I return to the ships, exhausted though I am by fighting. But now I shall go back to Phthia, since it is obviously better by far to return home with my curved ships. I do not propose to win affluence and riches for you, here, while I myself suffer dishonour!' Agamemnon, lord of men, answered him: 'Be off, then, if that is your heart's wish. I do not ask you to stay for my sake; I have others to pay me honour, counsellor Zeus most of all. Of all the god-reared kings you are the most hateful to me; quarrelling, wars and battles are what you always like. Strong as you may be, it is a god, I imagine, that has made you so. Be off with your ships and comrades and rule over the Myrmidons; I care nothing for you, and do not mind if you *are* in a rage. But I give you this warning: since Phoebus Apollo wants to take my Chryseis, I shall send her back with my ships and comrades; but I shall go in person to your hut and fetch fair-cheeked Briseis, *your* prize, so that you can appreciate to the full how much more powerful I am than you – and anyone else may recoil from claiming to be my equal, and setting himself up against me as my peer!' These were his words, and grief came upon Achilles son of Peleus, and inside his shaggy chest his heart debated two separate courses; whether to draw the sharp sword from his thigh and stir up the others and kill the son of Atreus, or to put a stop to his rage and restrain his anger. While he pondered this in his heart and mind, and was drawing the great sword from its scabbard, Athena came from the sky; for white-elbowed goddess Hera despatched her, because she loved and cared for both men alike in her heart. And Athena stood behind Peleus' son and seized him by his brown hair, appearing to him alone. None of the others saw her, but Achilles was amazed, and turning round he instantly recognized Pallas Athena, and her eyes looked terrible to him...(1.163–200)

Agamemnon is to display a curious lack of confidence later in the poem, but here he is dangerously assertive of his rights and the honour due to him. He has been accepted by all the others, for the purposes of the expedition at least, as supreme *basileus* or king, and Achilles had better not go back on that. For a *basileus* derives his authority direct from Zeus – Zeus who asserts his own power over the other gods by right of ancestry and sheer strength and who supports an analogous but infinitely lesser power in human 'Zeus-reared kings'. The concept is ultimately derived from ancient Mesopotamia, where kingship was 'lowered from heaven' and devolved on the first generation of priest-kings on earth. Its logic is far from clear in the derivative and slightly confused Greek version, but the existence of a kind of divine right of kings is most plainly expressed in Book 2, where Agamemnon's sceptre, the symbol of kingly office (and, at the king's will, of a hero's right to speak in assembly), is described as having been made by the smith-god Hephaestus for Zeus, who gave it to the messenger-god Hermes to pass on to Pelops of Argos; and from Pelops it descended to his Argive successors, Atreus, Thyestes and then Agamemnon himself, who was also king of Mycenae (2.100–8).

The gods' involvement in the human quarrel is confirmed by the intervention of Athena. Naturally Achilles could not be allowed to kill the great king. That would have led to anarchy, and in any case the traditional tale made it plain that Agamemnon lived to sack Troy and be murdered on his return home by

Clytemnestra. Equally naturally, it is a god that has to prevent the chaotic deed – although as it happens Athena acts not as the agent of her father Zeus protecting the institution of kingship, but rather as the dedicated supporter of the Achaean army and implacable enemy of Paris (who had earlier offended her by his famous Judgement) and the other Trojans. No other passage in the *Iliad* describes a theophany so starkly. Usually the gods, when they intervene in human affairs, do so either invisibly or disguised as humans. Here Athena comes as a goddess, but acts with human tangibility by pulling Achilles' hair; she is invisible to the others but concretely and frighteningly deterrent to Achilles himself (1.193–200). And yet her intervention, although striking, is not especially stressed. It is just one of many ways (decisions taken in divine assembly on Olympus being the commonest) in which the singers of the Homeric tradition express the extreme interest they envisage the gods as taking in human affairs.

Chryseis is escorted back to her father by ship – the description is an exceptionally conventional one, formular almost to the point of staleness – and Apollo calls off the plague. Agamemnon reacts by depriving Achilles of Briseis, although he does so by sending heralds to fetch her and not, as he had threatened, in person. Achilles prays for revenge to his mother, the sea-goddess Thetis; she appears before him on the sea-shore in another remarkable epiphany and promises to try and persuade Zeus to favour the Trojans, and so make Achilles' withdrawal from the fighting all the more disastrous for Agamemnon. Her supplication of Zeus, his solemn oath of approval as he nods his great brow and shakes Olympus, and Hera's rage as she spies on the scene and guesses what it portends for the Achaeans, bring this exceptionally varied and dramatic book to a close.

At the beginning of the second book Zeus decides to send a misleading dream to Agamemnon, promising him imminent victory. Before joining battle the king has the bizarre idea of testing morale by proposing that his troops give up and go home – which they instantly try to do, being restrained with the greatest difficulty by Odysseus and the other leaders. No wonder the bitter and unheroic Thersites, 'the ugliest man to come to Troy', rails against authority; but the Achaeans only laugh delightedly as Odysseus lays into him with his staff – weakness and deformity were proper causes for heroic amusement, which is partly why the gods themselves had laughed at 1.599f. as they watched the crippled Hephaestus hobbling around in emulation of young Hebe or Ganymede. A great march-out from the naval camp is made both vivid and portentous by a string of no less than six successive similes that illustrate the gleam of weapons, the noise of thundering feet and hooves, the size of the Achaean army and the proficiency of its leaders (2.455–83). The march-out is also the pretext for a long poetical muster of contingents from the different regions of Greece – the 'Catalogue of Ships', so called by ancient scholars, which is seemingly based on an old list of the naval forces that assembled at Aulis at the start of the campaign and carefully records how many ships each leader had with him. This Achaean catalogue fills no fewer than two hundred and sixty-six verses (thereby revealing a good deal about the capacity of oral audiences) and is followed by a list of Trojan allies that is much shorter – a relief in a way, for it also betrays a certain jejune quality in both artistic and historical terms.

The flavour of the Achaean catalogue, with its careful recording of sometimes obscure settlements (which are probably never fictitious, however) and its imperfect fit here and there with the rest of the poem, is given by the description of Agamemnon's contingent centred on Mycenae:[1]

> Those who possessed Mykenai the well-built town
> and rich Korinthos and well-built Kleonai
> and who dwelt in Orneai and lovely Araithurea
> and Sikyon, where Adrastos was once king,
> and those who possessed Hyperesia and steep Gonoessa
> and Pellene, and who dwelt round Aigion
> and all along Aigialos and around broad Helike –
> of their hundred ships Agamemnon was commander,
> son of Atreus. With him by far the most numerous and best
> host followed; and among them he himself had donned flashing armour,
> exulting, and stood out among all the heroes
> because he was best and led by far the most numerous host. (2. 569–80)

The plain and factual, if slightly repetitious, style is relieved by the euphony of the place-names themselves. Their epithets sometimes seem derived from a different poetical tradition from that of the main poem, and a similar independence may account for the eulogy of Agamemnon, which is in sharp contrast with the ambivalent picture of him elsewhere as indecisive, torn by doubt, an erratic warrior. At least this extract deals with an important commander and some well-known cities; others, for example those listing the Thessalian contingents, contain few familiar names or none at all. And yet they have their own fascination, not only an antiquarian one but also through the impression they give of an utterly diverse yet ultimately Panhellenic army.

Book 2 ends with the list of Trojan allies, and Book 3 resumes the general description of the approaching armies. The book-division, incidentally, is fairly typical – organic in a way, a convenient enough place for a mild break, but no necessary indication that Homer himself composed in these book-units, or that they were not systematized and extended to twenty-four by later scholars

---

[1] Here and elsewhere, where it seems appropriate, I have varied the translation by dividing it into verse-lengths corresponding closely with the Greek, and also retained a closer transliteration of proper names.

and librarians. The expected clash of armies does not, however, take place. It is prevented when Paris (whose other name in the poem is Alexandros) runs ahead of the Trojans and issues a challenge to single combat. The challenge is instantly accepted by Menelaus, the prince whose wife Paris had enticed away. Helen herself joins King Priam and the Trojan elders on the wall above the Scaean gate of the city to watch the ensuing duel. The old men comment on her almost divine beauty, and the king asks her to identify for him some prominent Achaeans – a request notoriously more apt to the first than to the tenth year of fighting, but one that can be accepted in the loose framework of an ambitiously compendious poem. He begins by enquiring about Agamemnon himself:

'Come here, dear child, and sit by me, so that you can see your former husband and your relations by marriage and your friends – I don't blame you, but rather the gods, for bringing grievous war upon me from the Achaeans; and name for me this mighty man – tell me who this Achaean is, so noble and great. Others are taller in stature, but I never yet saw with my eyes anyone so handsome or dignified. He looks like a king.' Helen, divine among women, answered him: 'What reverence and awe I have for you, father-in-law! I wish I had been content to die in dishonour, when once I followed your son here and left my marriage-chamber and relatives and new-born child and delightful friends of my own age. But that did not happen, and I waste away in tears because of it. But I shall tell you what you ask and enquire about. This is the son of Atreus, Agamemnon ruler of broad domains, both good king and strong spearsman, and again, brother-in-law of my bitch-faced self – if these things ever really happened!' (3.162–80)

It is important for the *Iliad* that both Priam and Helen should be sympathetic figures, even though neither can have been entirely so in the ordinary heroic tradition. This passage serves to establish them as civilized and humane, as well as to restore, temporarily, the more imposing aspect of Agamemnon. Some of its plethoric phraseology ('saw with my eyes', 'ask and enquire') literally reproduces the Greek. These are formulas, standardized phrases, in this case probably quite ancient ones deriving from a stage when the diction was not so highly refined as it came to be by Homer's time – although he, of course, still retained much of the traditional language. The concluding phrase, εἴ ποτ' ἔην γε, is also a formula, but a more brilliant one; its literal meaning, 'if I ever was', conveys in so few words the mixture of incredulity and nostalgia with which Helen suddenly sees her own strange circumstances.

In the remainder of the episode known to the ancients as the 'Viewing from the Walls' she identifies for Priam first Odysseus, then Ajax and Idomeneus. Ajax is dismissed in a summary and off-hand way, even though he is an important and striking figure and Priam had specifically asked about him. Perhaps this is a rare piece of psychological subtlety (since Homer normally depicts the heroic character with broader strokes); for Helen seems to become increasingly distracted as she searches the battlefield for her own brothers, the Dioscuri, and concludes that they must either have stayed behind in Greece or be ashamed to appear among the others on account of their sister. But in reality, as the poet comments in a famous couplet, 'the life-giving earth already held them, back in Lacedaemon, in their own dear country' (3.243f.).

Paris and Menelaus now begin their duel in the space left clear for them between the two seated armies. Paris is soon in great danger, but Aphrodite snatches him away and hides him in a thick mist, then sets him down in his bedchamber back in Troy and summons Helen to join him. He is quite beautiful, she tells Helen, as he sits there on the fine bed, as if fresh from a dance rather than from the battlefield. But Helen sees through Aphrodite's disguise – she had taken the shape of Helen's old serving-woman – and accuses her of ruthlessly manipulating her in order to gratify the goddess's own wishes. '*You* go and sit by his side', she says; 'abandon the paths of the gods and never again return with your feet to Olympus, but fuss round him and take care of him till he makes you his wife – or his slave! As for me, I refuse to rush into his bed; it would be shameful, and the women of Troy would reproach me for it later. I have a heap of troubles already in my heart' (406–12). That is too much for a goddess to tolerate, even a Homeric one, and Aphrodite warns Helen not to make of her as violent an enemy as she had formerly been friend and protector. Helen is afraid, and follows meekly as the goddess leads her to make love with her paramour – the scene is a brilliant and extraordinary one, not only for its clarity and concision but also for its violent juxtaposing of love and war, of male voluptuousness and complacency and female indignation and subjection, and for its startling suggestion, more Mesopotamian than typically Greek, of the uses to which gods might put their mortal worshippers.

In the fourth book another and less mockable goddess, Athena, descends like a comet to the battlefield and takes the form of a warrior who persuades the archer Pandarus to shoot at Menelaus and so violate the truce made with solemn oaths before the duel. He inflicts a bloody but superficial wound which breaches the agreement and therefore allows the preparations for full-scale fighting to continue. In a formal and rhetorical episode King Agamemnon rallies his contingents and dispenses praise and blame to his princes. Rebuke, even if undeserved, is part of the heroic posture, but Agamemnon, true to his ambiguous status in the poem, turns out to be unusually bad at it; Diomedes especially has to show great patience with his tactlessness. After all the delays, battle is at last joined. A short generic account of the collision of armies is brought to life by an elaborate simile, and the poet passes to the first of the long series of individual encounters that form the constant background and typical material of the poem:

. . . Then at once came groaning and boast of men
slaying and slain, and the earth ran with blood.
As when winter torrents running down the mountains
throw together their heavy water into a valley bottom
from great springs, within a hollow gorge,
and from far in the mountains a shepherd hears their roaring,
so as they joined battle was their shouting and toil.
Antilochus was first to take a helmeted Trojan warrior,
a good man among the front fighters, Thalysias' son Echepolus.
He got in first with a blow to the ridge of the horse-plumed helm
and pierced his forehead, and the bronze spear-point
penetrated the bone; and darkness covered his eyes
and he toppled like a tower in the strong turmoil.
Powerful Elephenor seized him by the feet when he fell,
Chalcodon's son, leader of the great-hearted Abantes,
and dragged him out from beneath the missiles, keen to hasten
and plunder his armour, but his effort was short-lived;
great-hearted Agenor saw him dragging the body
– saw his flanks showing outside his shield as he bent over –
and struck him with bronze-tipped spear-shaft and loosed his limbs.
So the life-spirit left him, and over him grievous action was wrought
of Trojans and Achaeans. Like wolves
they sprang at each other, and man toppled man. (4.450–72)

The simile of the mountain torrents is typically Homeric in its leisurely development of detail, but also in its subtle complexity. The explicit point of comparison
is sheer noise and confusion; of mass fighting on the one hand, thunderous
water on the other. The roar of the torrent comes from far off in the hills, yet is
heard by a man, a solitary shepherd, who makes a poignant link between the
world of raw nature and that of men but who also leads on ingeniously from
mass fighting to the first individual combat of the poem. Admittedly the
Homeric style only rarely needs such devices; usually it moves from scene to
scene with simple directness; but here the simile serves this special purpose as
well as others. The fight itself contains elements that we shall see to be standard
in such individual encounters, although the elements are almost never used
in exactly the same combination. The mortal blow is traced in detail, the
victim's fall is marked by a striking phrase or simile, he is carefully identified by
patronymic and city. In the present episode there is, as often, a secondary victim
on the other side, and we are told precisely how he made himself vulnerable
and was killed. The sequence is rounded off by a reversion to general
fighting, less abstract than before only in that the Trojans and Achaeans are
now likened to wolves.

The series of individual fights is instantly resumed, first by an encounter whose

17

obscure young victim acquires an anecdotal pathos that renders him temporarily heroic, something more than a routine target for the irresistible Ajax:

> Then Telamonian Ajax struck Anthemion's son,
> handsome young Simoeisios, to whom his mother
> gave birth by the banks of Simoeis as she came down
> from Ida – she had accompanied her parents there to watch over the flocks.
> That was why they called him Simoeisios; but he did not pay back
> to his dear parents the cost of upbringing, but his lifetime was short,
> subdued as he was with the spear by great-hearted Ajax.
> For as he first came on, Ajax struck him in the chest by the right
> breast, and straight through his shoulder the bronze spear
> went, and he fell to the ground in the dust like a poplar
> that grows in a broad water-meadow,
> smooth, but with branches growing out from its top;
> a chariot-maker with shining iron
> has cut it down to bend a wheel-rim for a fine chariot
> and it lies weathering by the river's banks.
> Such was Anthemion's son Simoeisios, slain
> by Ajax of divine ancestry . . . (4.473–89)

Simoeisios' unusual name is explicated in progressive and lingering verses. Not much is disclosed apart from these details of his birth, but they, with the rustic naturalism of his mother's going up into the hill country with the family flocks and the pathetic comment about his frustrated upbringing, make the occasion a touching one. The fight itself is over almost as soon as begun; youngsters like Simoeisios make easy victims for great professionals like Achilles, Hector or Ajax. The wound is simple but immediately fatal, and he falls, not like a tower this time, but with stronger pathos like a tall and elegant tree that takes shape before our eyes in an image that is also a little confused (is it the falling or the fallen tree that matters most?) as detail after detail is added by the singer with effortless but also relentless virtuosity. And so the man-slaying continues, more rapid now, for a further sixty verses to the book's end.

By this point the modern reader is tending to look for relief from the bare fighting, for some further diversification by speeches at least, or by an episode at the ships or in the beleaguered city. He will have to wait until the sixth book for that; meanwhile the fifth opens with Athena inspiring Diomedes to special deeds of valour and destruction, and the whole of this very long book of over nine hundred verses continues to explore the theme of fighting, with only the encounters with gods, Ares and Aphrodite, to provide a lighter tone quite near the end. For the *Iliad* is as much a massive celebration of heroic struggle as anything else; and the delays over opening the battle were not because the poet kept putting off an evil but necessary moment and dwelling on more interesting matters, but in part, at least, to make an appropriately portentous preparation for the central business of warfare.

Diomedes is the dominant figure, but the impression òf violent and wide-spread battle is reinforced by typical encounters between lesser fighters. Here are two of them:

> Meriones ṣlew Phereclus, son of the joiner
> Harmonides, who knew how to make all cunning things
> with his hands; for he was a special favourite of Pallas Athena;
> it was he that made the balanced ships for Alexandros,
> the ones that began the trouble, that were an evil for all the Trojans
> and for himself, since he paid no heed to the divine decrees.
> Meriones pursued and overtook him,
> struck him in the right buttock, and the spear-point
> went right through under the bone and into the bladder;
> and he fell to his knees groaning, and death covered him over.
> Then Meges killed Pedaeus, Antenor's son –
> his bastard, but lady Theano carefully brought him up
> equally with her own dear children to please her husband.
> Phyleus' son, famed with the spear, came close to him
> and struck him with sharp spear on the bone behind the head,
> and the bronze cut through, along by the teeth and under the tongue,
> and he collapsed in the dust, gripping the cold bronze with his teeth. (5.59–75)

Again these two deaths illustrate several of the standard and recurrent devices and motifs of the minor battle poetry: the brief but often poignant biographical detail of the victim or his parents, the graphic and sometimes horrifying descrip-tion of the wound, the conventional but not entirely monotonous phrases for the death itself. In these two encounters (as indeed in the one that follows) there is an additional motif, for in each case the father surpasses his son in interest – the builder of the fatal ships that carried Paris to Lacedaemon, then the re-spected Antenor, an important Trojan prince. Pedaeus' stepmother, moreover, is the very Theano that appears as Athena's priestess in Troy in the next book. The audience is pretty well acquainted with heroic genealogy, so an allusive patronymic like 'Phyleus' son' presents no difficulty; it simply adds another piece of information about Meges, not essential but comforting to have, as well as permitting the singer to name him in a different part of the verse. As for the wounds, their description is alarming and heroic, as often, rather than clinically precise, even though in these two cases the anatomical details, including Pedaeus' teeth clenching on the spear-point, are just possible. It is an odd fact that the Cretan princes, of whom Meriones is second to Idomeneus, inflict crueller deaths than almost any other warrior on either side, as upon Phereclus here – something that might reflect the special taste of specifically Cretan poems that were then absorbed into the general heroic repertoire.

Even the war-god Ares, an almost barbaric import who remained an awkward appendage to the Olympian family, is wounded by Diomedes in the end. The wound is healed by Apollo and the blood thickens like curds; undismayed by his degrading position or Zeus's obvious dislike he sits by his father's side exulting, as complacent among the gods as Paris among mortals. So the fifth book ends. The sixth continues with no organic break as the fighting in the plain continues, but Diomedes' *aristeia*, his interval of special glory and invincibility, peters out on a recurring note of mild levity when he challenges the Lycian Glaucus to fight, but then discovers him to be an old family friend. The tale, with its detailed personal reminiscences and its parody of heroic boast and counter-boast, is told at length and may be a version of a once-independent song.

Meanwhile Hector returns to the city to organize prayers to Athena for the hard-pressed Trojans. Most of this sixth book consists of scenes in Troy brought about by this convenient, if slightly improbable, device; first with his mother Hecuba, then with Paris whom Hector rebukes for his slackness, then with Helen to whom he is kind and understanding, and at greatest length with his own wife Andromache. She implores him to be prudent, to play safe, not to risk her and her son as well as himself; Hector replies with full heroic severity, but also with unusual compassion and vivid imagination:

'I too am concerned about all this, Andromache; but I am terribly ashamed of what the Trojans and their wives with trailing gowns will think if I skulk like a coward away from the fighting. Moreover my own spirit forbids me to do so, since I have learned to be always valiant and to fight among the first of the Trojans, winning great glory for my father and myself. Well I know in my heart and mind that a day will come when holy Ilios is destroyed, and Priam of the strong spear and all his host. Yet I am not so concerned for the suffering of the Trojans... as I am for you, and the time when one of the bronze-corsleted Achaeans will lead you away in tears, depriving you of the day of freedom; and you will be in Argos, working at the loom under another woman's orders, and carrying water from some spring, some Messeis or Hypereia, much against your will, but strong necessity will lie upon you. And some day someone will say as he sees you weeping, "This is the wife of Hector, who used to be champion among the horse-rearing Trojans when they were fighting around Ilios."...But may the earth be poured over my dead body and conceal me, before I hear your cries as you are dragged away!' (6.441–65, with omissions)

Shortly afterwards compassion is replaced by sheer domestic tenderness, for as Hector stretches out to pick up his baby son Astyanax the child is frightened by his father's flashing helmet and waving plume and leans back into his nurse's bosom, 'and his dear father and lady mother burst out laughing, and at once glorious Hector took the helmet from his head and placed it shining on the ground...' (6.471–3). Stricter heroic standards are restored as Hector prays to

Zeus for the child to grow up to be even better than his father, 'and may he bring back bloody armour after slaying an enemy, and may his mother rejoice in her heart' (480f.). The whole scene is an extraordinary mixture of tragic irony – for the audience knows the child is to be brutally murdered when the Achaeans break into the city – and heroic cruelty and magnanimity. Hector shows no weakening of his resolve, but his words and actions illustrate the terrible confusion at the heart of the heroic ideal: the belief that a warrior's honour is paramount, that wife and even son must be risked for it, even if one recognizes as wrong the public opinion on which heroic honour depends. The moral balance of the whole epic is affected by the deliberate ambiguity and destructive undertones of this unusual scene. The note of domesticity is rarely sounded in this poem; here it is conspicuous, and not only renders Hector himself more solid as a foil for the stronger but harsher Achilles but also emphasizes for the listener the life of the beleaguered city and its impending doom, to give point and poignancy to the battle surging over the plain below.

Until now everything in the poem has been germane to the development of the wrath-plot or the purpose of displaying widespread warfare; moreover, there has been an engrossing variety of episodes, from the quarrel itself to the catalogue and march-out and eventual joining of battle, leading to Hector's brief return to Troy. Through the seventh and eighth books, by contrast, the intensity of poetic imagination and the sense of formal unity both decline. There are magnificent details, even whole scenes, but Book 8 in particular carries the action almost no further and seems to lack purpose, except as mere elaboration. It is true that oral poets are always concerned with that, and the gradual development of a basic narrative is what ultimately led to the great poem we possess. Even Homer, its monumental composer, must occasionally have succumbed to elaboration of a more or less routine kind. Pointless embroideries would usually, no doubt, be censored soon enough – dropped, that is, from the poet's working repertory and excluded from the plan of the larger poem to which that repertory was leading. At any rate the seventh book opens with Athena and Apollo agreeing, untypically, to stop the general fighting by inspiring Hector to issue a challenge to a duel. This has all happened before, or something very like it, in Book 3. The present duel is between different principals – it is Ajax that draws the lot for the privilege of standing up to Hector – and considerably more elaborate than before. No reference is made to its predecessor or its awkward consequence in the treacherous breaking of the earlier truce, an omission curious in itself. Yet it is not inconsistent with a probability that emerges on other grounds: that the second duel is a more detailed and deliberately different elaboration of the first – or of some simpler archetype of both.

The sequence of blow and counter-blow is certainly more ambitious than elsewhere. Hector throws his spear first (by a common Homeric confusion over armament, for the single spear should properly be used for thrusting and not for throwing); it almost but not quite penetrates Ajax's massive and unique shield; Ajax in turn pierces Hector's shield and breast-plate but just fails to touch flesh as Hector swerves aside; they regain their spears and Hector thrusts at Ajax, but once again the great shield frustrates the blow. Again Ajax's spear penetrates, this time to graze Hector's neck – he can nevertheless hurl a huge stone, but Ajax's shield (seven ox-hides thick, tower-like and faced with bronze) once again wards off the missile. Ajax replies with an even bigger stone and lays his opponent flat. Apollo intervenes and sets him on his feet – 'and they would have smitten each other at close quarters with swords had the heralds not come, messengers of Zeus and men, Talthybius and Idaeus, the one Achaean, the other Trojan...' (7.273–6); and in such bland innocuous terms the heralds stop the fight. On what excuse? On the ground that 'night is already coming on; it is good to obey night' (282)! It seems an abrupt and pointless anticlimax, and the exchange of gifts that follows makes the episode resemble even more closely an almost playful encounter like that of Glaucus and Diomedes in Book 6, or an event in a warrior's funeral games like the contest-in-armour in Book 23; which may indeed be where part of the elaboration originated. Admittedly the heralds have a point when they declare that Zeus loves both men; and the poet, of course, loves his plot and cannot have the war brought to a premature end. But he could have arranged things differently and ended the duel in some other way – even the way adopted in Book 3, where the losing party is rescued by a god. It is a role that is hinted at for Apollo, but perhaps at the last moment the poet recoiled from the repetition.

Nothing else in the duel is strikingly unusual. Ajax's impenetrable shield is the decisive factor, but in other important combats, too, the dice are loaded, unfairly by modern standards, against one or other fighter. Yet the dénouement *is* unsatisfactory as it stands, and no amount of stress on the inevitable untidiness of oral poetry (which is particularly prone, and even more so when it is on a monumental scale, to minor inconsistencies) can adequately explain the anomaly. This is not to claim that the episode is an interpolation or post-Homeric addition, or that its inclusion was the responsibility of any but the main poet. Rather it seems to demonstrate that the re-use of standard themes, elaborated or otherwise deliberately varied, can sometimes lead even a great poet into temporary difficulties. Yet there are fine things, too, in this book. Ancient Nestor, survivor of an older generation of heroes, indulges at length in one of his famous reminiscences ('Would that I were young as I was when Pylians and Arcadians fought by swift-flowing Celadon...', 133f.) when he tells of a local war in which he killed Ereuthalion, who wielded the unconventional club of mace-man Areïthous – events and people derived from some minor regional tradition of heroic, or near-heroic, warfare. It is Nestor's plan, too, that dominates the end of the seventh book: to call a truce for the cremation of the dead and during it to build a great trench, protected by a wall, in front of the naval camp (327–43; 433–41). This major military obstacle is sometimes overlooked in the remainder of the poem, and both ancient and modern critics have been tempted to call it an intrusion. Yet it was probably Homer's own idea, after all – or the theme was an ancient one that was only sporadically observed in the developing tradition. The book ends unusually and vividly with the arrival of wine-ships from the neighbouring island of Lemnos.

The eighth book opens with a divine assembly at which Zeus bans the gods from helping either side. On the battlefield Diomedes rescues Nestor in a not very powerful episode. Hector carries all before him, but Zeus, contrary to his main purpose of helping the Trojans, accedes to Agamemnon's prayer for relief. The archer Teucer has a brief run of success but cannot hit Hector, and Zeus sets the Trojans on the offensive once more. Hera and Athena prepare to defy the ban, but are deterred by savage threats from Zeus. Night falls with the Trojans encamped in the plain threatening the ships, and so rounds off a book that is replete with divine decision and counter-decision, with rapid changes of fortune on the battlefield, but is formless and confused in its total effect.

The ninth book, by contrast, provides one of the central pivots of the wrath-plot. An embassy is despatched to Achilles to convey Agamemnon's change of heart and offer lavish gifts, with the intention of inducing Achilles to come to the rescue of the hard-pressed Achaeans. But he violently rejects the offer – threatens to leave for home forthwith, but later softens this by declaring that he will not lift a finger till Hector attacks his headquarters and sets fire to the ships. This second threat, which is quoted below, foreshadows the series of attacks by Hector that dominates the central part of the epic. The whole proceedings, both the preparations for the embassy and the speeches of persuasion and rejection that follow, are described with great virtuosity. Agamemnon begins characteristically by publicly urging the immediate abandonment of the expedition (in a variant of a theme already used of him in Book 2); Diomedes censures him firmly, though without the provocative insolence that Achilles had displayed: 'Zeus gave you contradictory gifts: he gave you honour above all others because of your sceptre, but fortitude in battle he gave you not' (9.37–9) – let him leave if he wishes, the rest will stay and complete their task. Nestor tactfully intervenes and suggests a dinner and a council of war for the chieftains; only then, when Agamemnon has had time to calm down, does he suggest that the moment has arrived for an apology. The king agrees and suggests generous compensation: treasure, slaves, his daughter for bride, whole cities. But when Odysseus repeats all this to Achilles, word for word in the oral manner, he is almost swamped by a long speech of rejection that is pathetic and near-hysterical by turns. Its argument is logical enough: why should he, Achilles, do the lion's share of the fighting and see Agamemnon keep all the best prizes? And why should the king and his brother be allowed to love their women, and not Achilles to love Briseis and resent her being snatched away out of pique? This suggestion of romantic attachment for a concubine is in itself rather unheroic, stimulated, no doubt, by the demands of rhetoric; but the underlying concern is with *timē*, honour:

> My heart is swollen with rage whenever I remember
> how the son of Atreus has made me look foolish
> among the Argives, as though I were some migrant devoid of honour.
> But go off and give him this message:
> I shall not for a moment turn my mind to bloody war
> until god-like Hector, martial Priam's son,
> reaches the huts and ships of the Myrmidons,
> killing Achaeans, and sets the ships ablaze. (9.646–53)

Phoenix tries to moderate his charge's anger with a parable about the Prayers healing the damage done by Infatuation, and by the more enthralling cautionary tale (which looks like a summary version of a complete song) about Meleager, who took umbrage and withdrew from his martial duties after killing the Calydonian boar. All is of no avail, and Odysseus and Ajax return alone to report Achilles' obduracy to their anxious comrades.

The fulfilment of Achaean fears is delayed by another independent episode during the same night: the spying expedition in which Odysseus and Diomedes first seize the Trojan spy Dolon, then slaughter the Thracian king Rhesus, newly arrived to help the Trojans, and capture his horses. These events occupy the tenth book, which has often been suspected of being a post-Homeric addition made, perhaps, by a brilliant and ambitious rhapsode – a professional reciter – in the seventh century B.C. The suspicion may be unjustified, although the events of the book, which are not referred to elsewhere in the poem, are sometimes odd in themselves and are expressed in language that occasionally seems to lie outside the usual formular repertoire. The behaviour no less than the clothing of the protagonists is certainly untypical; yet a night patrol does not call for day-time tactics or indeed apparel, and many readers, at least, find this book especially dramatic and enjoyable. As for language, we may be surprised (for example) by the simile at 5–8, in which Zeus flashes lightning 'making either an awful rainstorm or hail or snow... *or in some place the great mouth of piercing war*' (ἠέ ποθι πτολέμοιο μέγα στόμα πευκεδανοῖο). The oddity here is confined to a single verse which could be an intrusion; but then Agamemnon is said to groan as frequently as these lightning-flashes 'from the bottom of his heart, and his lungs trembled within' (τρομέοντο δέ οἱ φρένες ἐντός, 10), a unique

24

phrase; and a little later he 'drew many hairs by the roots from his head to Zeus on high' (πολλὰς ἐκ κεφαλῆς προθελύμνους ἕλκετο χαίτας | ὑψόθ' ἐόντι Διί, 15f.), again a bizarre expression far from the regular epic language for signs of grief. And yet the following, eleventh book, which is crucial to the main plot and is certainly by Homer, opens with a no less unique idea whereby Zeus, wishing to inspire the Achaean chieftains, 'sent grievous Strife to the swift ships of the Achaeans *holding a portent of war in her hands*' (πολέμοιο τέρας μετὰ χερσὶν ἔχουσαν, 11.3f.). The expression of the idea is admittedly more felicitous than that of the simile in Book 10, but even so we are reminded that Homer can sporadically and at any time use language and concepts unparalleled in the rest of the poem. That is especially so where the general circumstances of the action are irregular or unusual. It is only in a normal or regular context that unusual language and the apparent abandonment of the formular style give good grounds for suspicion of post-Homeric elaboration.

Book 11 brings a critical change in Achaean fortunes with the wounding of Agamemnon (after an interval of unusual martial prowess on his part) and then of Odysseus and Diomedes, and begins a sequence of no less than seven books devoted with great severity to the description of tense and desperate fighting. The delays and diversions over joining battle in the open plain lie far behind. If the reader had begun to expect that the monotony of hundreds of individual combats would be constantly relieved for him by viewings from the walls, scenes in Troy, night expeditions and the like, then his expectations must now fade almost away as he is driven to understand that warfare, subtly varied but relentless and massive in effect, is a dominant theme of the poem. It is true that close attention to language and detail reveals this poetry of warfare as brilliant and enjoyable in its own way; Homer is a master of variation, and the endless extension of formular situations brings its own pleasures. Nor is the poetry heartless; the succession of victories and victims, of turns of fortune as the battle moves to and fro, has its regular moments of pathos, sympathy, profound insight, even satire. Yet ancient listeners – ordinary people, surely, to a large extent, and not just an audience of military-minded aristocrats – must have had special motives and interests to enable them to follow attentively and appreciatively over the long hours of singing that this huge and austere central section required. The cardinal considerations may be these: that many men (not women) enjoy descriptions of fighting for its own sake; that this was a national epic in which every village and city in Greece could share (although it remains odd that the Athenian contingent had such a feeble role); that the audience must have known something about many of the families and individuals mentioned, and could appreciate sheer invention when it occurred; that in any event the poem could only be rendered in separate sections, over several days or parts of days; and that its remarkable author must have had a unique reputation, as well as unique gifts, and could thus compel attention to material that might have seemed too gargantuan and repetitive when presented by a lesser singer.

Of course there are still occasional diversions – several lesser ones and one major one. The wounded chieftains worry and confer behind the fighting, and that forms a new theme for variation, with much carrying of messages to and from and within the Achaean camp. The gods are repeatedly revealed in conclave, their minds on the progress of the war, either on Olympus or more frequently now on Mount Ida overlooking the battlefield itself. Poseidon and Apollo descend to inspire either side; among the human contestants there are special phases of triumph, for Agamemnon before he is wounded, for Idomeneus the Cretan leader, for Ajax as he dourly defends the ships, and for Hector almost throughout. The major diversion is the Deceiving of Zeus in the latter part of 14 and the beginning of 15: Hera, in order to give Poseidon greater freedom to help the Achaeans, and with the aid of Sleep and the girdle of Aphrodite, overwhelms Zeus with desire so that he makes love to her and then falls into a deep slumber. The episode is light-hearted and amusing (as Zeus recites to Hera a list of his mistresses whose charms she seems to him at that moment to surpass), but also touching and lyrical in tone:

> ...and the son of Kronos took his wife in his arms
> and the divine earth made fresh grass grow beneath them,
> and dewy lotus and crocus and hyacinth,
> thick and soft, which kept them high above the ground.
> In that they lay, and clothed themselves in a cloud
> that was fair and golden, and glistening drops of dew fell from it.
> So the Father slept, quite still, on the ridge of Gargarus
> subdued by sleep and love, and held his wife in his arms. (14.346–53)

Meanwhile Poseidon inspires Ajax to wound Hector, and the Trojans are driven back across the trench; but then Zeus wakes up, is furious at what he sees and decisively asserts just what is to happen. Apollo is to revive the stunned Hector and fill the Achaeans with panic, so that

> in flight they fall among the well-benched ships
> of Peleus' son Achilles; and he shall send into action his comrade
> Patroclus; and glorious Hector shall slay him with the spear
> in front of Ilios, once Patroclus has destroyed many young men
> – others, too, but among them my son, divine Sarpedon.
> In anger for Patroclus, divine Achilles shall slay Hector...(15.63–8)

We are reminded sharply by these words that, despite the occasional unexpected twist in the action, the general outcome of the war is not the object of suspense and was perfectly known to the audience. It is the exploration of detail, of exact motive and circumstance, that maintained the intensity of interest needed to carry listeners on through the dense concentration of this poetry – that, together with the progressive unfolding of the wrath-plot itself, which now takes a crucial step forward in the sixteenth book, perhaps the finest of the whole poem.

Book 15 had ended with Hector about to fire the ships. Ajax resists desperately, and then at the opening of 16 Patroclus carries the news to Achilles and begs to be allowed to join the fighting. Achilles not only consents but even lends him his own armour; Patroclus marches out with the Myrmidons and brings swift relief, then surges to the very walls of Troy, borne on against Achilles' instructions by triumph and destiny. First he kills Sarpedon, as Zeus had predicted or rather ordained – he was tempted when the time came to overrule destiny, but was dissuaded by Hera and the other gods (16.432–58). The encounter with Sarpedon is told at greater length than any of its predecessors (save for the formal duels of 3 and 7); it is important because it establishes Patroclus as truly magnificent and renders his own death at Hector's hands more awful, but also because the ascending series of tragic and exceptional deaths – Sarpedon, then Patroclus in 16, finally Hector in 22 – shows the special art and taste of Homer, the monumental composer, himself.[1] Each has significant elements of language and content in common with one or both of the others; each is an essential component of the monumental wrath-plot. Sarpedon, admittedly, is only preparatory in this respect, but he introduces a continuing note of pathos, accentuated by Zeus' grief and the shower of bloody rain he sends to do macabre honour to his son before he dies. Patroclus with his first throw hits Sarpedon's charioteer, not Sarpedon himself, just as he is later to hit Hector's charioteer Cebriones; here is no fighting over the charioteer's body, but Cebriones will be the object of a bitter struggle presaging the fight over Patroclus' own corpse that will occupy the whole of Book 17. The second spear-throw mortally wounds Sarpedon, whose concern that his body shall not be mutilated foreshadows that of Hector later. These three death-scenes are the only ones in which dying men speak, and the same verse is used in each instance: 'when he had thus spoken the end of death covered him'. So too the idea of the release of the *psyche* or life-spirit is common to all three; with Patroclus and Hector, and nowhere else, the soul is described as flitting mournfully down to Hades, but Sarpedon's body is to be carried to his homeland in Lycia by Sleep and Death, since as son of a god his soul might be expected to have a special fate.

The three scenes are closely related, and Homer seems to be developing them serially until he reaches the great climax of Hector's death. But the death of Patroclus is dramatically almost as important; in its preliminaries it is linked with that of Hector both by its strong pathos and by the fact that a god joins in on the other side and makes defeat inevitable. Patroclus as he faces Hector is

---

[1] Kirk (1976) 209–17.

struck from behind and dazed by Apollo, who remains invisible, and then his armour is stripped from him to render him helpless before a minor assailant and then Hector (16.787ff.). Hector, too, will be deceived by Athena, who will disguise herself as his brother Deiphobus and so persuade him to stand up to Achilles, and then will return Achilles' spear to him after his first throw has missed (22.226–77). Here, indeed, divine intervention seems gratuitous, for the audience knows that, strong as Hector may be, Achilles is the better man. Yet Homer is not so much interested in skill and physique and the actual exchange of blows (which are described in a standardized and almost perfunctory way) as in whether one or other combatant has been made irresistible by an upsurge of valour and heroic self-confidence that is the direct reflection of divine favour and even destiny. For Patroclus must die to bring back Achilles to the fight, and Hector must die to restore Achilles' bruised honour and make way for the fall of Troy, itself the punishment for Helen's abduction and the violation of the laws of hospitality that were Zeus's special concern.

A bitter struggle for possession of Patroclus' body occupies the 761 verses of the seventeenth book and marks the exceptional importance of his death. The tenseness of fighting as it surges back and forth, with first one side and then the other gaining the upper hand, is both emphasized and relieved by similes that reach a climax as the Achaeans finally prevail:

> Thus they eagerly carried the body out of the fighting
> toward the hollow ships; and war was stretched over them
> like fierce fire that speeds upon a city of men
> and, suddenly springing up, sets it burning, and the houses crumble
> in a great flame; and the force of the wind makes it roar.
> Just so, as they made their way, the unceasing din
> of chariots and fighting men beset them;
> but like mules that exert mighty strength
> and drag from the mountain over a rugged track
> either a beam or a great ship's timber, and their spirit
> is worn down by toil and sweat as they make haste,
> just so eagerly did they carry the body. And behind them
> Ajax and his brother held back the foe, as a wooded promontory
> holds back water by projecting into the plain
> and restrains the destructive streams even of mighty rivers
> and at once directs all their flow into the plain,
> baulking them, and the force of their stream makes no impression on it –
> just so did Ajax and his brother always hold off in the rear
> the Trojan attack...(17.735–53)

The almost abstract points of comparison, the naturalism of the scenes of power or violence in nature or in peacetime life and the piling of one comparison on another are typical of the Homeric use of developed similes, often imitated but never equalled. Each simile stands up to careful consideration in its accurate observation and brilliant expression, and in the comment it implicitly makes on the main action. Even the river-and-promontory simile, which seems to be drawn on and on in an effort to elicit the precise effect from an obdurate vocabulary, reproduces by its leisurely emphasis the solid and unremitting resistance of Ajax and Teucer.

Patroclus' corpse is firmly in Achaean hands, and now at last, at the start of the eighteenth book, Achilles learns the bitter news and rolls in the dust in his agony of heart. His mother Thetis arrives with her nymphs to try and comfort him; she can at least see to the making of new armour by Hephaestus to replace that of Achilles that had been wrenched from the body of his friend; meanwhile Hera sends Iris to persuade him to paralyse the Trojans with fright by appearing and shouting terribly by the trench. The poet turns for a significant interval to show Hector heroically but imprudently rejecting Polydamas' advice to retreat within the walls. The last 130 verses of the book are devoted to a splendid diversion, the description of the armour made by Hephaestus, above all of the great shield decorated with scenes of peace and war, all depicted in a compressed but evocative style akin to that of the similes, with dancing and harvesting, judgement in the market-place, ambushes and, as a sinister echo, the dragging away of corpses slain in battle.

Before Achilles can return to the fight there must be a formal reconciliation with King Agamemnon. It occupies much of the nineteenth book and is complemented and a little weakened by an argument about whether or not Achilles shall take food before going into action. From now until Hector's death there is a series of deliberate delays and diversions, comparable with those at the beginning of the poem, whose purpose is to heighten the audience's sense of Achilles' anger and determination and of the close concern of all the gods with what is happening. As Achilles drives out in his chariot, his horses, by a rare mixture of natural and supernatural, predict his death (19.397–424). Then in Book 20 the gods (apart from Zeus, who is too august for such sport) descend to the plain and prepare to fight each other in support of Trojans or Achaeans. The divine battle is abruptly broken off, and Achilles engages Aeneas after some lengthy and curiously rhetorical preliminaries; but Aeneas, like Hector a little later, is divinely whisked out of harm's way. In the next book, 21, the Theomachy or Battle of the Gods is resumed, but fizzles out without result; Poseidon and Apollo see that it is undignified, and an episode that is never handled with much confidence, and has surely been heavily distorted at some stage in the process of composition and development, is gradually allowed to rest (21.385–514).

Earlier in the twenty-first book, and before the resumption of the interrupted Theomachy, come two far more powerful scenes. The second is Achilles' fight with the river Scamander who resents being blocked and defiled with the corpses of his victims, and it is developed by Homer into a chilling and fantastic *tour de force*. The first is briefer and more ordinary in that it is simply another killing, but it brings out to an extraordinary degree the ruthlessness and pathos of heroic action as the poet focuses on the details of a single hopeless encounter (21.34–135). Achilles intercepts young Lycaon, one of Priam's many sons, whom he had captured not many days before and sent across to Lemnos to be ransomed. He expresses ironical surprise at seeing him back so soon, and then as the boy clutches Achilles' great spear with one hand and his knees, in a ritual gesture of supplication, with the other, addresses him in these words:

> 'You fool, do not speak to me of ransom or mention it. Before Patroclus drew on himself the day of destiny, then it was more congenial to me to spare Trojans, and I took many alive and despatched them across the sea. But now there is no one that shall escape death, of those that god casts in my hands before Ilios – of all the Trojans, but especially Priam's children. But you, too, friend, must die now; why do you lament so? Patroclus also died, and he was far better than you. Do you not see the kind of man I am in beauty and stature – son of a valiant father, and a goddess bore me and was my mother? But death and strong fate stand over me too; a dawn or evening or midday will come when someone will take away my life-spirit, too, in war, hitting me either with spear or with arrow from the bow-string.' So he spoke, and Lycaon's knees and dear heart were dissolved. He let go of the spear and sat with both arms spread out, and Achilles drew his sharp sword and struck him on the collar-bone beside the neck, and the two-edged sword sank right in, and he lay stretched out, face down on the earth, and the black blood flowed and wet the earth. (21.99–119)

At the end of 21 Apollo has disguised himself as Agenor and lured Achilles into chasing him, so allowing the Trojan army to retreat to the safety of the walls. Only Hector, driven by pride and destiny, remained out there in the plain, and the twenty-second book, in the great climax of the poem, describes his death, with the events leading up to it, on a larger scale than any other heroic encounter. His parents beseech him from the walls, and their despairing words are given in full. Hector remains adamant, and when Achilles draws near he tries to steel himself to face him – but fails, and starts running (22.90–144). Zeus pities him, not least as a faithful and regular sacrificer, but is deterred from sparing him by Athena in words similar to those used earlier by Hera about Sarpedon. Three times they circle the walls with Achilles close behind. Some of the landmarks they pass are described with painful and dramatic realism, like the hot and cold springs that are mentioned now for the first and last time. They run like race-horses, although the prize is no casual one but Hector's life; Zeus weighs the fates and Hector's sinks downward (22.208–13). Apollo abandons the doomed man, and Athena is sent exulting to help Achilles – as if he really needed it! She does so in two ways, both of them unfair by chivalrous standards: she appears at Hector's side as his brother Deiphobus, so that Hector thinks he has an ally, and then she gives back Achilles' spear to him when he misses with his first throw. Hector's return shot strikes Achilles' shield but bounces off (naturally, since the shield was made by Hephaestus); he calls for Deiphobus' spear, but the bogus ally has disappeared and Hector understands his true predicament:

> 'Alas! Assuredly the gods have called me toward death,
> for I said that hero Deiphobus was by my side –
> but he is within the walls, and I am deceived by Athena.
> Now evil death is close by me, no longer distant,
> and there is no avoiding it. In the past my safety was of concern
> to Zeus and his far-shooting son, who, before,
> were eager to protect me; but now destiny has come upon me.
> Yet let me not perish without effort and without glory,
> but after accomplishing some great deed for future men to hear of.' (22.297–305)

So Hector draws his sword and rushes at Achilles, who, however, has his spear back and is thus able to pierce his enemy's throat almost at leisure. The 'great deed' of Hector's words has amounted to little or nothing in effect, but it is the words themselves and the spirit behind them that matter most. Dying though he is, he still can speak; once again he implores Achilles not to maltreat his body – it is his special obsession – but hears in reply the reiterated cruelty of the threat to throw him to the dogs and birds. Once again Hector is forced to recognize the bitter reality, and he faces it with courage and a final threat:

> 'I recognize you well as I look upon you, and would never
> have persuaded you. Truly your heart in your breast is made of iron.
> Now is the time for you to consider whether I may not be a cause of
>   divine anger against you
> on the day when Paris and Phoebus Apollo
> destroy you, good fighter though you are, at the Scaean gates.'
> As he spoke these words the end of death covered him
> and his life-soul sped from his limbs and went toward Hades
> groaning over his fate, leaving his manliness and youth.
> God-like Achilles addressed him, even though he was dead:
> 'Die! My own doom I shall receive at the moment when
> Zeus and the other immortal gods wish to accomplish it.' (22.356–66)

With these assertions of inexorability and resignation, of divine control over men and the future fate of Achilles and of Troy, the martial part of the *Iliad* is done. Hector's is the last death in battle of the entire poem; what follows is concerned with the glorification, through proper burial, of Patroclus and Hector himself and with the resolution of Achilles' unnatural anger. But first comes the mutilation of his enemy's corpse as Achilles pierces Hector's ankles and drags him round the walls behind his chariot in an unparalleled parade of savagery that reduces Hecuba and Priam to total despair (22.395–415). In the twenty-third book Achilles turns to the overdue burial of his friend, whose ghost appears before him and demands to be released to the world below. Prisoners are sacrificed at his pyre in another act of pathological barbarism, but after that the singer turns to gentler pursuits, the funeral games held by Achilles to honour the dead man. The chariot-race and its consequences are lavishly evoked in over four hundred verses whose vivid detail and humour brilliantly suggest the lighter side of the heroic character, and are free from the ponderous touch of other partly humorous set-pieces – the chastisement of Thersites, the abortive Theomachy, or even the love of Ares and Aphrodite in the eighth book of the *Odyssey*. Subsequent contests in the funeral games are entertaining on a smaller scale, except for two or three (the fight in armour and the archery-contest in particular) that must have been elaborated by plodding rhapsodes.

The final, twenty-fourth book turns from Patroclus back to Hector and resolves the remaining issues, both narrative and moral, of the poem. Achilles is still periodically dragging the corpse behind his chariot, and the gods as they see it are affronted; not always Sunday-school characters in Homer, they are nevertheless determined guardians of the basic rules of order and respect. Zeus decides that Thetis shall instruct her son to surrender the corpse to King Priam, and Iris, the gods' messenger who is also the rainbow, is sent to tell Priam to set off at dead of night, with a cart and much ransom, for Achilles' hut. This strange adventure, which has sometimes been seen as a symbolic representation of a descent to the world of the dead, becomes less dangerous when he encounters Hermes, the god who escorts both travellers and souls, disguised as a young Myrmidon; he leads the old man across the battlefield and toward Achilles' encampment (24.349–447). Achilles receives the king magnanimously and looks after him (though not without moments of dangerous impatience) for much of the night in a hut that is now seen almost as a palace. The corpse has been divinely preserved from decay; it is placed on the cart and driven back to Troy, where the proper laments are sung for it by the women. A truce is made for the gathering of wood for the funeral pyre, and 'thus they saw to the funeral of Hector, tamer of horses', the closing verse of the poem.

It is in many ways an extraordinary ending. The whole book is punctuated by phraseology that reminds one of the *Odyssey* rather than the *Iliad* – partly because the events are closer to those of the non-martial poem and partly, perhaps, because these closing episodes, like those of the opening book, were favourite ones with audiences and singers, including Homer himself, and so acquired a veneer of more highly developed, or at least slicker, language. The events of the book, too, have something of the fantastic and mysterious quality of parts of the *Odyssey*, with the night journey, the divine young helper in disguise, the other-worldliness (Odysseus landing in Ithaca), the intimate conversations (as in the swineherd's hut) between Achilles and the old man who reminds him of his father. Yet all this complexity serves as a perfect culmination of the whole poem: a pathetic yet noble end to all the fighting, an unsentimental restitution of Achilles to the more admirable side of hero-hood with the final obliteration of his destructive wrath, and an overwhelming demonstration of the respect owed by men to destiny, to death and to the gods.[1]

3. THE *ODYSSEY*

The *Odyssey* belongs to the same epic tradition as the *Iliad* and shares with it much in the way of formular language and thematic material. But it is a different kind of poem, and for this and other reasons it warrants a rather different treatment – an attempt not to analyse it progressively, but rather to isolate its methods of construction and its unifying poetical aims. The two approaches complement each other, and the reader who engages directly with either poem will find himself applying both at once. If he starts with the *Odyssey*, he will be tempted to judge it independently and not in comparison with the *Iliad*. That has its advantages, but it remains true that a reasonable understanding of the *Odyssey* – which as we saw is likely to be subsequent in composition to the *Iliad* – can only come if the other poem is seen as its model in certain formal respects (for example scale, and the use of speeches and similes), and as an illustrious predecessor to be emulated or, at times, studiously ignored.

It is helpful, therefore, even if it might seem unimaginative, to consider how the *Odyssey* differs from the *Iliad* and in what respects it falls short of it or surpasses it. Clearly the subjects of the two poems impose their own special qualities. The *Iliad* is relentlessly martial in tone and detail; it contains, as we saw, important digressions, some of them with their own peculiarities of language, but the style as a whole, together with the treatment of situations and characters, remains severe and dignified, as might be considered appropriate to a heroic age and a heroic standard of values. The *Odyssey*, on the other hand, concerns a time of uneasy peace – the near aftermath of the Trojan War, admittedly, when some of the heroes have only recently reached home and when Odysseus himself is still lost and wandering, but when the main issue is personal, political and economic survival rather than mass fighting, public heroism, the acquisition of booty or manifest loyalty to friends and class. And there are other quite different issues that hardly belong at all to a nostalgically heroic conception of life: issues of love and respect between men and women, of devotion on the part of son, wife or servants, of hospitality in its less ostentatious forms, of the proper retribution for crime, even of the apportioning of divine and human responsibility for hardship and misfortune. None of these is

[1] Griffin (1980) is illuminating on the underlying concerns and emphases of both poems.

entirely unforeshadowed in the *Iliad*, but none becomes a dominant theme there as it does in the slightly later poem.

These broader and indeed more abstract topics do not of themselves require the hard concentrated language of Iliadic combat and endurance. Much of the formular phraseology remains common to the two poems, but the *Odyssey* extends the range of standardized phrases to cover fresh subjects. It also has several new and conspicuous locutions for common events or sequences, as was shown on p. 9. Somehow the language of the later poem is not only more relaxed but also blander and less vivid, more fluent but also occasionally more flaccid than that of the *Iliad*. Direct speech is no less important than before, but the speeches tend to be less dramatic, more leisurely and wordy, sometimes rather insipid even when no effect of that kind can have been intended. At their best, it is true, the conversations of the *Odyssey* achieve a degree of civilized subtlety that exceeds anything in the *Iliad*. When the gods decide to bring about Odysseus' release from the island of Calypso they send Hermes to instruct her, and as a consequence the nymph, reluctant but resigned, brings up the subject after dinner with her desirable guest:

> But when they had enjoyed food and drink, then Calypso, lady goddess, began their conversation: 'Lordly son of Laertes, Odysseus of many devices, so it is your desire to go home this very moment to your dear native land? Well, I wish you joy of it. Yet if you knew in your heart how many cares you are destined to fulfil before you reach your native land, you would stay here with me and keep to this house and be immortal, even though you long to see your wife for whom you yearn all your days. Yet I know that I am not her inferior in either body or stature, since it is in no way fitting for mortal women to vie in body and appearance with immortal goddesses.' Then in answer Odysseus of many counsels addressed her: 'Mistress goddess, do not be angry with me. I, too, am well aware that prudent Penelope is less than you in appearance and in stature when one looks upon her; for she is mortal, and you are deathless and free from old age. But even so I wish and yearn all my days to go home and see the day of my return. If once again some god strikes me down in the wine-dark sea, then I shall endure it and keep in my breast a steadfast spirit. For I have already suffered much grief and toil in waves and war; let this, too, be added to them.' These were his words, and the sun set and darkness came over them, and the two of them went into the inner part of the hollow cave and enjoyed themselves in love and stayed by each other's side. (5.201–27)

There is so much here that is lightly touched on and yet left inexplicit: the nymph's disappointment and surprise, Odysseus' tact and homesickness and determination to stick to what is properly human. The poet has already shown him as tired of Calypso, yet here at the end the passion revives itself as dutiful affection – well outside the range of normal heroic lust and proprietary interest in beautiful, efficient and valuable women. There is a quiet philosophy in this passage, a resigned insistence on human values, that is not uncommon in the *Odyssey* but that strips the gentle verses of taut heroic vigour as surely as it fills them with an insistent and almost urbane melancholy.

Speeches in the *Iliad* are hurled to and fro like weapons; in the *Odyssey* they are the ingredients of strangely placid conversations that surprise us only occasionally and then, for the most part, through the accidents and limitations of oral technique. In the opening book, which sets out the position in Odysseus' palace in Ithaca, with Penelope resigned and beset by suitors and Telemachus immature and powerless until he is stiffened by the disguised Athena, Penelope hears the court-singer Phemius as he sings of the return of various heroes from Troy. She is distressed because it reminds her of her own husband, apparently lost for ever, and asks the singer to choose another song. She is at once rebuked by her son, who treats her with a quite unexpected sternness that is the product (as the audience is meant to feel) of the new grown-up determination the goddess is instilling into him. That sternness raises the conversation above the usual unemphatic level and gives an urgency to the proceedings which, even with Athena's presence, they have strikingly lacked so far. Yet the tone of the boy's words is somehow odd, too bitter and sneering to be easily understood – precisely because they are not created for this particular occasion, but adapted from other contexts and compounded with minor motifs about the technique and status of singers (a recurring subject in this poem) and the proper place of women in the home:

'It is no reproach for this man to sing of the evil doom of the Danaans, for men assign greater glory to the song that is newest to its hearers. Let your heart and spirit endure hearing it; for Odysseus was not the only one to lose in the land of Troy the day of his return, but many other men perished. Go into the house and see to your own business, the loom and distaff, and tell the servants to get on with their work. Talking shall be the concern of men – of all of us, but of me most of all; for a man has the power in the home.' She was dumbfounded and went back into the house, for she took to heart her child's wise saying. She ascended to the upper storey with her serving-women and then wept for Odysseus, her dear husband, until grey-eyed Athena cast sweet sleep upon her eyelids. But the suitors made a din through the shadowy halls, and all of them desired passionately to sleep by her side in bed. Wise Telemachus began to address them as follows: 'Suitors of my mother, you whose arrogance is un-bridled, now let us take our pleasure at dinner; and let there be no shouting, since it is fine to listen to a singer such as this one, god-like in his utterance. And at dawn let us all go to the place of assembly and take our seats, for me to tell you this message outright – to get out of my halls! Concern yourselves with different kinds of feast; eat up what belongs to you, taking turns in each other's houses! But if this seems to you preferable and better, for one man's livelihood to be consumed without payment, then go on and devour it; but I shall call upon the eternal gods to see if Zeus may in the end grant that works of vengeance come to pass. Then would you perish, likewise without payment, in my house.' These were his words, and they bit their lips with their teeth as they marvelled at how confidently Telemachus addressed them. (1.350–82)

'Talking shall be the concern of men', says Telemachus to his mother here, adapting Hector's statement to Andromache in the sixth book of the *Iliad* (492f.) that warfare shall be the concern of men. Penelope retires with surprising meekness, not so much because the poet wants to make her into an enigmatic figure (which she nevertheless becomes, through similar manipulations, as the poem progresses) as because the stage must be left clear for a further demonstration of the young man's new confidence. But is it part of the poet's design that Telemachus should now speak out so spasmodically in an uneasy succession of threats against the suitors, a plea for better table-manners and renewed praise of singers before he comes to the real point – that he will give them an important message the next day? And is his anticipatory summary of this message, with its apparently mistimed threat of counter-action, a telling sign of passion and immaturity, or is it the result of a complicated adaptation of motifs and formulas that slightly outstrip the singer's complete control at this point? Perhaps the disjunction is unjustified and both causes are at work simultaneously; for part at least of the effect of an impassioned young man is presumably deliberate. But in this kind of context one can never be entirely sure; for if the Nausicaa-conversations of Book 6 show how delicate are the effects the poet of the *Odyssey* can achieve, there are many other cases where the inherited language and thematic material prove mildly intransigent, so as to impose a complexity that was probably not initially intended.

Not only speech but also narrative is generally smoother and less strongly expressive than in the earlier epic – unless what needs expressing is something outside, or on the edge of, the ordinary range of heroic language and tradition, like the delicate feelings of a young girl. It is significant that the *Odyssey* has far fewer similes than the *Iliad*. Admittedly its action is so complex and varied that it rarely calls for the diversionary element that similes, in one of their roles, can supply. When it does drag or falter it is usually because conversation has run riot (as it does between Odysseus and Eumaeus in the fourteenth book), and similes can do nothing to help. Where they occur is often in passages of Iliadic tone, as at the end of Book 21 where Odysseus, still disguised as a beggar, is handling the great bow that the suitors have failed to string:

But Odysseus of many counsels weighed the great bow and closely examined it. As when a man expert in the lyre and in singing easily stretches a string about a new peg, fitting the twisted sheep-gut from both sides, so without effort did Odysseus stretch the great bow. Then he took it and with his right hand tested the string, and it gave forth a beautiful singing note like the voice of a swallow. Great grief came upon the suitors, and all of them changed colour. Zeus

thundered loudly, revealing signs of what was to come; then much-enduring
noble Odysseus rejoiced, because the son of crooked-counselled Kronos had
sent him a portent; and he took a swift arrow that lay ready uncovered on the
table – but the others lay inside the hollow quiver, and the Achaeans were
destined soon to test them. He took the bow by the handgrip and drew the
string in the arrow-notches, there from the seat where he sat, and shot the arrow,
aiming straight ahead, and did not miss any of the axes – the first part of their
shaft – and the arrow with its heavy bronze tip went right through them to the
doorway. He said to Telemachus: 'Telemachus, your guest does not bring you
disgrace in your halls, seated though he is; I neither missed the target nor took
time or effort to string the bow. My strength is still firm, and not as the suitors
disparage it to dishonour me.' (21.404–27)

The details of this scene, with its careful description of the act of drawing the
bow-string (which is not exactly paralleled even in scenes concerning the
archers Teucer and Pandarus in the *Iliad*), and of the row of axes and the shot
itself, are peculiar to the *Odyssey*, as indeed is the subject of the brilliant simile
that typically concerns a singer once again; but the tone and style are nevertheless Iliadic, and they accord perfectly with the suddenly martial and heroic
subject matter.

Sometimes that kind of Iliadic energy is released in a scene that is not martial
but domestic and almost lyrical, and there the effect, 'Odyssean' now at its best,
is remarkable:

But when Nausicaa was about to turn back home again after yoking the mules
and folding the fair clothes, then grey-eyed goddess Athena had another idea,
that Odysseus should wake up and see the lovely girl, who should lead him to
the town of the Phaeacians. Then the princess threw a ball to one of her attendants;
she missed the attendant but threw it into the deep swirling water, and the
women gave a great shriek, and noble Odysseus awoke and sat up and debated
in his heart and spirit: 'Ah me, whose land have I come to this time? Are they
violent and fierce and without justice, or hospitable and with a god-fearing mind?
For a female cry came about my ears, as though of maidens – nymphs that possess
the steep mountain peaks and streams of rivers and grassy meadows. Or am I
perhaps close to men with human speech? Come, let me make trial and see for
myself.' So saying noble Odysseus emerged from the bushes, breaking off with
his thick hand a leafy branch from the dense undergrowth to keep from sight
his bare male genitals. And he went like a mountain-reared lion, confident in his
prowess, that goes through rain and through wind, and his eyes flash out, and
he comes upon the cattle or sheep, or goes after wild deer, and his belly urges
him to make trial of the flocks even to the point of entering a well-made fold.
Just so was Odysseus about to come among the fair-haired girls, naked though
he was, for necessity beset him. Terrifying he appeared to them, befouled with
brine, and they ran in panic in every direction over the jutting headlands.
Alcinous' daughter was the only one to stand firm, for Athena put courage in

her mind and took the fear from her limbs. And she stood facing him; and Odysseus wondered whether to grasp her knees and beseech the lovely girl, or to stand apart as he was and beseech her with soothing words to point out the town and give him clothes. (6.110–44)

There is so much here that is typical of the *Odyssey*: Athena determining the course of events, the charming accident with the ball, Odysseus' suspicions and tactful prudence in a fresh situation of potential danger. Yet as he rushes out like a ravenous lion he assumes an Iliadic role and posture, and Nausicaa, too, becomes heroic in her god-given imperturbability; and it is just this tension of roles and styles that gives the scene its special power and magic.

Yet the *Odyssey* as a whole is not really a heroic poem, and that tells us much about its limitations, especially in style and language, when compared with the *Iliad*. It has important qualities the *Iliad* does not possess, but if one wants to understand it properly then its diction, relaxed and at times almost nerveless, at other times strangely prosaic, has to be taken into account – not least because it is used in the service of an unusually complex and carefully constructed plot. An important consideration here is that the oldest parts of the narrative tradition to have left their mark on the language of Homer were probably martial and heroic in character. The system of standardized poetical phraseology that permitted the tradition to spread so widely in time and space grew up in the first instance to describe the actions, words and interests of aristocratic fighting men, on the battlefield or on raids or encamped round plunderable cities. This cannot be proved, but it is some indication that the most archaic-looking phrases (those for example with clustered Mycenaean elements) tend to be martial rather than domestic or picaresque in reference. 'Martial' is perhaps too narrow; among these older materials of oral poetry would be descriptions of seafaring, feasting and sacrifice, concomitants of fighting and the heroic life-style. Even the scenes behind the lines or in Troy could be based on archaic materials. Their assumptions and the language used to express them are still heroic, although one has a sense at this point of brilliant new singers carrying the old poetical equipment into fresh territories. In the *Odyssey* the exploration is carried still further. The scenes of conversation and feasting, of singers at work and of the finer nuances of encounters between men and women, depend on a vocabulary and phraseology that, although still formular, are sophisticated extensions rather than direct descendants of the severer language of strictly heroic poetry.

It is, of course, a mistake to treat the *Iliad* as a very ancient poem and the *Odyssey* as a very modern one. Little more than a generation's span, if that, separates them, and they might still be the work of the same main composer. That cannot be excluded. Yet they are different in essence, the one inclining to be archaistic and conservative, the other innovative and eclectic. The extension of its hero's (in the modern sense) values from honour, courage, success and love of showy possessions to resignation, endurance, plotting and humble disguises; of its lesser characters from minor warriors to magicians, one-eyed monsters, herdsmen and serving-women; of its locations from camp, battlefield and besieged city to Peloponnesian palaces, Ithacan countryside and the fantastic lands of Odysseus' adventures, does much for the variety of possible feeling and action, but at the same time stretches the resources and slightly dims the vigour of the oldest language of poetry. The capacity for adapting formulas to new uses can be carried almost too far, and the tight concrete phrases and verses of the *Iliad* tend to become abstract and imprecise in many parts of the *Odyssey*. That can be seen even from some of the passages which have been selected for translation in this account (although their primary function is to illustrate different and more positive qualities); and particularly from the description of the islet off the land of the Cyclopes (pp. 42f. below), where the subject is pastoral and lyrical but the language becomes at times curiously vague and repetitive, relying too heavily on conventional epithets (or other standardized devices) for the rich texture such a description needs. It is far superior to most oral poetry, and indeed most written narrative poetry; most oral poetry tends, like the Yugoslav, to be redundant and drab; but it falls below the exceptional standard of the *Iliad*, whose traditional timbre and constantly varied exploitation of a limited range of actions are particularly well suited by the taut expressiveness of familiar verse-components.

The widening of the traditional heroic ambience leads to a complementary result in a different sphere. For those Iliadic characters that recur in the *Odyssey* tend to become a little lifeless and indefinite, as if the poet did not quite know what to make of them. That does not apply to Odysseus himself, whose bravery -and resourcefulness are developed in the later poem into a touching and often witty amalgam of trickster-like ingenuity and over-confidence. But Nestor, Menelaus and Helen, as they are described at length in the third and fourth books when young Telemachus visits them in their palaces at Pylos and Lacedaemon, turn out to be disappointingly awkward and undramatic. Their chief interest lies in their accounts of the aftermath of the *Iliad* – the fate of Agamemnon, the Trojan horse, adventures in Egypt on the way home. Nestor is even wiser and more fatherly than in the other poem, but his modified prolixity is matched by that of too many other characters to be (as it was in the *Iliad*) both idiosyncratic and amusing. Menelaus is proud of his rich palace in an almost humble and completely unheroic way (4.78–99); his wife Helen, her ambivalent past glossed over by unconvincing professions of mixed feelings while in Troy, assumes some of the less dangerous characteristics of Circe as she spikes the drinks with an anodyne drug (4.219ff.). These are figures that are the product not of the heroic age of which they are the ostensible survivors, nor even of any depressed and diminished successor, but rather of poetic imaginations moving a little unsurely in what has become an artificial, almost a patchwork landscape.

To counterbalance these weaknesses the *Odyssey* possesses strong positive qualities peculiar to itself. The variety of its action, the simple but effective transitions from place to place, the ingenuity with which the main components of a complicated plot are interwoven – these required elaborations of planning greater than those needed for the *Iliad*, skilful and complicated though the man-oeuvres of the poetic battlefield had to be. Then there are special supernatural elements beyond the activities of the anthropomorphic gods themselves – who, although slightly different in character from those of the *Iliad*, for instance in their heightened moral sensibility and the increased role of the guardian deity, still belong to the same genre. The *Iliad* is almost free of complex omens once the famous manifestation at Aulis has been recalled by Odysseus in the second book. The *Odyssey* is full of them. Along with Odysseus' fictitious tales and the songs of Demodocus and Phemius they constitute the characteristic diversion of this poem, much as the developed simile and Nestor's reminiscences are typical diversions of the *Iliad*. Sometimes, as with the early appearances of the fugitive seer Theoclymenus, they are cursory and thin. If the monumental composer was aiming at a sense of the numinous and mysterious, then he achieved it more successfully in the fantastic and atmospheric passages to be mentioned shortly. And yet the idea of gods sending special signs to men – Odysseus at one point asks for, and gets, two kinds of sign at once, both a divine clap of thunder and a propitious saying by a human bystander (20.98–121)– accords well with the magical adventures that are an essential component of the poem, and even with Athena's almost doting protection of her favourite Odysseus. In its turn that protection seems consequently less pantomime-like when she transforms him back and forth from his own shape to that of a battered old beggar, or beautifies him at a touch to impress Nausicaa or Penelope. There are supernatural tricks by gods in the *Iliad* – Poseidon flicks Aeneas through the air at one point (*Il.* 20.325–9) – but they are rare and alluded to only in passing. The poets of the Odyssean side of the tradition evidently liked this sort of thing better, or, a fairer statement perhaps, found it more appropriate to the aura of fantasy that can surround even the most realistic scenes of the *Odyssey*.

This combination of fantasy and naturalism gives the poem one of its most powerful and unusual qualities. The minute detail of Odysseus shooting a stag in Circe's island is closely associated with an odd passage in which he surveys the landscape from a peak and (as later transpires) is mysteriously lost, so much so that he cannot distinguish east from west (10.145–97). When he awakes in Ithaca after being landed there from the Phaeacian ship he finds everything shrouded in mist by Athena so that he cannot recognize where he is (13.187ff.).

His subsequent encounter with the goddess is charming and etherial, until she suddenly discloses the familiar landscape and they settle down at the foot of an olive-tree, like a couple of peasants, to plan Odysseus' revenge. And as he sets off for that last journey home – last, except for the mysterious trip predicted by Tiresias to the place where men use no salt and mistake an oar for a winnowing-fan – his Phaeacian hosts carry both gifts and provisions down to the seashore:

> But when they came down to the ship and the sea
> immediately the illustrious escorts received the things
> and stowed them in the hollow ship, all the food and drink.
> Then they spread for Odysseus a rug and a sheet
> on the platform of the hollow ship, where he might sleep without waking,
> at the stern. He himself boarded and lay down
> in silence, while they sat each on his thwart
> in order, and loosed the stern cable from the pierced stone.
> Then they leant forward and churned the sea with their oars,
> and sweet sleep descended on Odysseus' eyelids,
> unwaking sleep, sweetest of all, nearest to death.
> The ship – as in a plain four-yoked stallions
> all leap forward together under the blows of the whip
> and rearing high swiftly accomplish their course,
> so did the ship's stern rear up, and behind it the wave
> seethed, the great purple wave of the boisterous sea.
> And the ship ran on very surely and steadily, nor would a hawk
> have kept pace with it, swiftest of flying creatures.
> So it ran on swiftly, cleaving the waves of the sea,
> carrying a man possessed of god-like intelligence
> who earlier had suffered very many griefs in his heart
> cleaving his way through wars of men and waves of the sea;
> but now he slept without stirring, forgetful of all he had suffered. (13.70–92)

The transition is from the distant and magical country of Scheria back to the realities of the suitors in Ithaca, and the poet creates an entrancing effect of timelessness as the hero lies on the stern-platform in the sleep that is almost indistinguishable from death, while the ship (which in truth needs no rowing, as the poem reveals elsewhere) cuts majestically through the waves – in unmistakable contrast to Odysseus' earlier struggles with storms and shipwreck. The close of this remarkable passage, which deliberately recalls the words of the poem's prologue, forms a coda to the foreign adventures of the 'man of many turns', and the death-like sleep imposes a kind of sacral interlude between them and the trials to come in Ithaca.

This particular sense of the mysterious is not entirely novel – one recalls Priam's nocturnal journey in the last book of the *Iliad*, which has, admittedly, been worked over here and there with the *Odyssey* in mind – but is sharpened by the poet's preoccupation with the idea of place. There is nothing quite like it in the *Iliad*, although its similes can evoke a scene in nature with spectacular economy and force. The poet of the *Odyssey*, on the other hand, evidently enjoyed the elaborate description of palaces (those of Odysseus, Menelaus and Alcinous), countryside (Scheria, Circe's island, Ithaca) and seascapes (Odysseus' shipwrecks, the voyage back from Scheria). In particular he developed the theme of the *locus amoenus* or 'delightful spot' that was to become so important in Latin and European pastoral. Calypso's cave is beset with verdant trees that are carefully named, and with water flowing from springs that nourish the wild vines there (5.63–71). When Odysseus goes to see his father Laertes in the last book of the *Odyssey* he finds him tending his garden out in the country, and its plants and trees are lovingly noted in the course of the complex recognition-scene (24.241ff.). The shape and feeling of Ithaca itself are conveyed as Odysseus walks over the rough tracks from the harbour of Phorcys to Eumaeus' hut, near Raven Rock and the spring Arethusa, and then back into the city past another spring surrounded by poplars.[1] The exotic places he visits in his wanderings are sometimes dealt with more cursorily, but Circe's island, as well as Calypso's, and the seashore scene with Nausicaa at the river's mouth are carefully evoked; and so are the harbours, sanctuary and market-place of the city of Scheria as Odysseus enters it in disguise.[2]

Landscape is not a naturally heroic topic – it is too liable to be inhabited by peasants and other mundane creatures – yet the singer of the *Odyssey* has made it into an important ingredient of his poem. 'The sun set and shadowed were all the streets' – even this repeated phrase, peculiar to the *Odyssey*, suggests a kind of visual imagination which, if it works sporadically through the whole heroic tradition, finds its fullest expression in the romantic and mysterious settings of this poem. Consider the leisurely detail of the description, not so much of the land of the Cyclopes itself, but rather of the small island that lies just off its coast where Odysseus and his companions beach their ship in the depths of night:

> From there we sailed onward, grieved in our hearts.
> We came to the land of the Cyclopes, overbearing
> and lawless, who trusting in the immortal gods
> neither plant anything with their hands nor plough
> but everything grows for them without sowing or ploughing –
> wheat and barley and vines which produce
> wine from fine grapes, and rain from Zeus gives them increase.
> They have neither laws nor decision-making assemblies
> but dwell on the peaks of high mountains
> in hollow caves, and they each make laws
> for children and wives, and take no heed of each other.

[1] *Od.* 13.345, 14.1–4; 13.408; 17.204–11.
[2] *Od.* 6.291–4, 7.43–5.

Then there is an island stretched out beyond the harbour
of the land of the Cyclopes, neither near nor far,
a wooded one. In it live numberless goats,
wild ones; for the tread of human feet does not keep them away
neither do hunters track them down, who suffer hardships
in the thickets as they roam over mountain crests.
Nor is the land given over to flocks or ploughed fields,
but unsown and unploughed for all its days
it is bare of men, but nurtures bleating goats.
For the Cyclopes have no crimson-cheeked ships,
neither are there ship-builders among them who could build
well-benched ships which could produce all those things,
by travelling to the cities of men, that in profusion
men carry to each other across the sea in ships.
Ship-builders would have made that island a prosperous possession;
for it is not a bad one, and would bear all things in season,
for there are meadows by the shores of the grey sea
that are soft and well watered; vines there would never fail.
There is smooth ground for ploughing; they would always reap
a deep harvest in season, since the soil beneath is very fertile.
And there is a safe harbour where there is no need of cable,
neither of casting out anchor-stones nor of tying on stern-ropes,
but only of beaching the ship and remaining for as long as the sailors'
spirit urges them and the winds blow.
But at the head of the harbour runs shining water,
a spring from the foot of a cave, and poplars grow round;
there we sailed in, and some god was leading us
through the dark night...(9.105–43)

Sometimes an important episode is marked out at its beginning by an elaborate description, of armament or locality for instance; but that does not entirely account for the depiction of the island at such length. The mainland that needed 'no planting or ploughing' seems to have triggered off the description of an ideal landscape awaiting development, but also solitary and therefore a little mysterious, because undefiled by men. Certainly the verses are cumulated one upon another almost too casually, and the sense begins to falter with those non-ships of the Cyclopes. It steadies itself again with the development of the ideal-harbour theme that recurs elsewhere and must have been a persistent dream of Homeric audiences and their colonizing predecessors; and the cave seems to prefigure the cave of the Nymphs at the head of the harbour of Phorcys in Ithaca, where Odysseus stores his treasure and where likewise a deity leads the way.

That kind of redeployment and careful variation of themes leads back to a question that has already been touched on. How can a poem so long and complex as this have been composed orally, without the aid (except perhaps in a minor way) of writing? Part of the answer is undoubtedly given by the observation that Homeric verses are made to a considerable extent out of standardized phrases designed to fill the three or four main segments of the hexameter verse. That gives the clue to the effortless composition of verses and distinct passages; but how were the passages put together to form such a large and complicated whole, and in general with such impressive consistency? Here the answer must be that the large-scale narrative is for the most part composed out of standardized narrative elements analogous to the small-scale formulas or fixed phrase-units. These larger components are motifs or themes, and they range from minor sequences of action or concept (as at the beginning of the passage just quoted, where 'we sailed on, and then came to another landfall' is a repeated motif of the sea-adventures) to broader topics like that of the unknown island in the same passage, or throwing oneself on the mercy of strangers as in the passage on pp. 37f., and basic narrative patterns like that of a human loved by a god or goddess who is rejected by him, as in the Calypso passage on p. 34. Themes of varying scope and content can of course be detected in the *Iliad* also; but the overall action is more restricted there, and the wide proliferation of themes is less important than the variation of a limited number, notably those concerned with single combat (including the hurling of weapons that miss or hit in turn) or the fortunes of massed battle. In the *Odyssey* the greater complexity and variety of action depend on an even more highly developed deployment of themes, together with a more sophisticated application of the arts of repetition and variation – or, to express it more accurately, repetition disguised by variation. It is by such means that the main poet of the *Odyssey* was able to build up his enormous structure, which can now be more easily seen to lie within the capacities of a single gifted singer – and later, and in a rather different way, of substantially illiterate reproducers. Determining these means is more than a merely technical or historical matter, for the poetry can be more exactly appreciated as the poet's resources, both in language and in his power to repeat, extend and vary a limited range of narrative themes, are better understood. This is the kind of approach (rather than by the establishment of the special 'oral poetics' that some critics hanker after) by which we can reach a fuller appreciation of the shape and construction of the *Odyssey*.

Above the level of minor motifs, the poem's major themes can be divided into several overlapping categories. First, in an arbitrary order, are the folktale themes. It is obvious to everyone who reads them that Odysseus' sea-adventures, which occupy from the fifth to the twelfth book or nearly a third of the poem, belong to the genre of popular story-telling known as folktale; and that many of their narrative ideas (like escaping from a one-eyed or blind giant, or the bag of winds, or the beautiful princess who helps the hero as Nausicaa helped Odysseus) are common to different popular traditions the world over. Folktales overlap myths and take many forms. Certainly this class of theme operates outside, as well as within, the strict limits of the sea-adventures. Success against apparently impossible odds is a conspicuous element of folktales, and is exemplified not only in Odysseus escaping from the Cyclops but also in his triumph over the suitors back in the everyday world. A popular folktale figure is the trickster, and Odysseus, more than Hermes, Sisyphus or Autolycus, is the main Greek exemplar. Ingenious ideas, like the No-man motif of the Cyclops episode or, more feebly, that of concealing the death of the suitors by pretending that a dance is in progress in the palace, are one speciality of the trickster, while disguise, which plays so prominent a part in the second half of the *Odyssey*, is another. The wife beset by suitors when her husband is thought to be dead is a popular folktale theme; it is often elaborated by the idea of putting off the suitors by a trick, as Penelope does with the shroud she weaves by day and unweaves by night, or alternatively by a test (here, of the bow and axes) or a quest. Finally the husband returns in the nick of time and deals with the suitors in various ways; this central theme belongs to many different cultures, and is so popular because it is piquant and dramatic and yet has a footing in real life, as well as because of its capacity for elaboration by the attachment of various ingenuity-motifs.

An important way of deploying these folktale themes, which applies to other types as well, is by repeating them in different forms and with varying degrees of elaboration. Many of the themes of the *Odyssey* are used over and over again in slightly different guises – we can see that most easily in some of the character-doublets. The good swineherd Eumaeus has a lesser male counterpart in the good cowherd Philoetius, and a female counterpart in the nurse Eurycleia, who in turn has a lesser shadow, Eurynome the keeper of the bedchamber. But Eumaeus also has an opposite counterpart in the form of the evil goatherd Melantheus, who has a sister of almost the same name, Melantho, who is equally evil and balances the good female servants, Eurycleia among them. For the principle of theme-duplication includes that of reversal; so Odysseus has a guardian angel in Athena and a corresponding divine enemy in Poseidon, who in turn is briefly paralleled by Helios, the sun, when Odysseus' companions slaughter his cattle. The theme of the nymph or goddess who detains the hero in her island and makes love to him is used first with Calypso and then with Circe, and the poet applies his arts of variation to make their episodes seem distinctively different, although they are in fact structurally almost identical.

Another category of Odyssean themes consists of universally dramatic actions or sequences of action; in a sense this category subsumes the folktale one, but without laying special stress on fantasy or ingenuity. The surmounting of apparently insuperable difficulties is such a theme (to put it in its most general and abstract form), and Odysseus exemplifies it repeatedly. Sometimes it is preferable to talk of narrative devices rather than themes, as when the singer inserts a long diversion at a critical moment (as Eurycleia's recognition of her master is tantalizingly interrupted for no less than seventy verses by the tale of how Odysseus got the revealing scar in the first place, 19.392–466) or turns unexpectedly to a different scene of action, for example from the palace in Ithaca back to Telemachus in the Peloponnese. Recognition in the broad sense is another narrative idea of wide application. It is at the heart of *Oedipus tyrannus*, but equally underlies the thoughts and behaviour of Telemachus and Penelope in their confusion about Odysseus, of Menelaus and Alcinous as they wonder on different occasions who their unknown guest might be, or of the suitors as they face the former beggar and discover their destiny.

A third overlapping category contains themes that doubtless came in other oral poems but were specially developed for the purposes of the *Odyssey*. Telling a false tale to keep one's identity concealed must have been used elsewhere, but with Odysseus it is almost a fetish, and his fictitious wanderings as Cretan refugee, or a Phoenician captive or passenger, become an important and recurrent element of the poem. Complementing this is the theme of disbelief in the face of his claims to know that the 'real' Odysseus is on his way home or already in Ithaca. Eumaeus in the fourteenth book (115–408) and Penelope in the nineteenth (508ff.) carry caution and incredulity to almost irritating extremes. Of course they have been misled by false claimants before, and Penelope's scepticism is in addition an aspect of the distrust she has to show toward the suitors; but clearly the singer of the *Odyssey* found this idea very much to his taste as a subject for variation and elaboration, and used it in the service both of suspense and of character-drawing.

Arrival in a strange land is another common theme, one bound to occur in folktales like the sea-adventures but developed in a special way in the *Odyssey*, where arrival in disguise is repeatedly followed by careful attempts to establish one's worth and gain status before the final revelation of identity is made. The theme occurs both when Odysseus reaches the land of the Phaeacians (with both Nausicaa and her father Alcinous) and in Ithaca itself (with both Eumaeus and Penelope); but in a truncated form it determines the delay in establishing Telemachus' identity when he arrives at the palace of Menelaus and Helen in the fourth book (20–170) – a scene that cannot be properly understood without knowledge of this general theme and its overall deployment. In this case it seems to be shyness rather than cunning that prevents him from saying who he is; when his father is mentioned he covers his face with his cloak to hide his tears, and that again is a motif that is re-used, not once but twice, when Odysseus is obstinately concealing his identity from the Phaeacians. As a final example of this category, the poet constantly uses the idea of individuals disclosing their steadfast loyalty to the lost Odysseus by breaking into a lament for him as soon as he is mentioned; that happens with Telemachus in the presence of Athena, and with Eumaeus, Telemachus and Philoetius, each in different ways, in the presence of the disguised Odysseus himself.[1]

It is precisely by using and re-using such themes as these that the main composer of the poem succeeded in constructing an apparently very complex plot out of a relatively small number of elements constantly varied and re-deployed. As a further kind of theme-ingredient he had at his disposal the whole tradition of the fall of Troy and its immediate aftermath – a kernel of historical fact, probably, remembered with increasing inaccuracy and then elaborated in prose stories and, soon enough no doubt, in short poems. The poet of the *Odyssey* carefully avoids repeating any of the content of the *Iliad* itself, but uses tales of Odysseus' spying expedition to Troy, of the city's fall, of the quarrel of Ajax and Odysseus and of the varying fortunes of the Achaean survivors as they return home. Above all, the death of King Agamemnon at the hands of Clytemnestra and Aegisthus is mentioned in detail both early and late in the poem (although the context in Book 24 involves one of the rare instances of post-Homeric elaboration).[2] Orestes is repeatedly held up to Telemachus as an example of youthful steadfastness and determination, just as Odysseus is warned not to return home openly and risk the fate of Agamemnon. The *exemplum*, the cautionary tale, is a recurring motif of the *Iliad* (notably in the story of the wrath of Meleager told to Achilles, *Il.* 9.527–605) as well as the *Odyssey*, and was doubtless a common element of much or most oral heroic poetry.

The practice of thematic variation could be an encouragement to secondary expansion as well as an aid to large-scale composition in the first place. There are sections of the *Odyssey* that are more certainly the result of rhapsodic elaboration than anything (beyond the occasional single verse) in the *Iliad*. Odysseus' journey to the world of the dead in the eleventh book embodies a probably familiar and traditional theme; but his meeting with Tiresias, his mother and certain dead companions takes a distinctly peculiar turn when he is envisaged as strolling in the underworld itself and watching its great sinners undergoing punishment (*Od.* 11.568–600) – and that is preceded by a catalogue of famous heroines that is highly inappropriate if not definitely suspect (11.225–329). The underworld theme is used again, once more probably by an imitator, in the curious 'Second Nekyia' that opens Book 24, when the souls of the dead suitors are led down by Hermes past scenery that is wholly alien to the usual Homeric view of Hades. But then most of that twenty-fourth book has evidently been heavily reworked and expanded from a smaller nucleus, probably by rhapsodes in the seventh or early sixth century B.C., who unleashed

[1] *Od.* 1.158–68, 14.61–71, 16.112–20, 20.185–210.
[2] *Od.* 1.35–43, 298–302; 24.19–22, 96 f., 191–202.

their virtuoso abilities on the most popular parts of the text before it was recorded complete in writing, at some time in the sixth century, to control the competitions in recitation at the Panathenaic games.

So much for the mechanics of construction and progressive elaboration. What can be said of the poem as a whole, considered as a work of the imagination – for that, whatever its pre-existing materials and techniques of repetition, it undoubtedly remains? It can be judged on two levels. On the first and more superficial one it is clearly a rich and engaging story, fluent and adroit in expression and rising at times to high poetry. Occasionally the momentum falters, especially in the conversations and plottings of the second half; but the skilful varying of basic themes and the combining of folktale adventures with Trojan memories and special ideas like Telemachus' trip to the Peloponnese enable the central plot of Odysseus' return and vengeance to sustain the weight of its massive treatment. On a second and deeper level the poem is sharply focused on its central character, Odysseus. That is what it professes in its opening words:

> Tell me, Muse, of a man, a man of many turns, who underwent many wanderings when once he had laid waste Troy's sacred city; he saw the towns and learned the mind of many men, and many were the griefs he suffered in his heart at sea, striving for his own life-soul and his comrades' return.

His release from Calypso is the first topic to be discussed among the gods, directly after this prologue, and although he is formally absent from the scene until the fifth book he is present in everyone's thoughts and words. Thereafter he is almost continuously the centre of attention.

'Seeing the towns and learning the mind of many men' has sometimes persuaded critics that the main composer is claiming Odysseus' experience to be both spiritual and intellectual. Actually the expression probably means no more than that between Troy and Ithaca he visited many places and often had occasion to ask himself whether the inhabitants were 'arrogant, wild and unjust or hospitable and of god-fearing mind' (for example at 6.120f.). Yet the poem does, in the end, reveal things about him that raise him above the level of a determined, resourceful and picaresque character. Admittedly some of its episodes do no more than that; whoever was hero of the sea-adventures in earlier versions, or of simpler tales of the return home of a long-lost king, we can be fairly sure that his role was simply to succeed – to be heroic but little more. The impression given by our *Odyssey* in its entirety is rather different. Is it simply the multiplicity of his successes that raises him to another plane? Surely not; it is something to do, rather, with the interplay of the different circumstances in which he finds himself, together with his responses to them and the effects he thereby has on others.

For it is a sign of the strong central conception of the monumental poem that all its characters (except for a few probable additions in the underworld scenes) are so powerfully affected by Odysseus. None of them is otiose in this respect, and none is treated as a mere mechanism for triggering off new events. Telemachus' journey is prompted by his determination to discover his father's fate, and his hosts, Nestor and Menelaus, are themselves almost obsessed with memories of the man. The suitors repeatedly try to convince themselves that he is dead, and the whole situation in the palace, not least the despondency and confusion of Telemachus and Penelope, depends on the dilemma created by Odysseus' long absence. Calypso 'the concealer' is necessary to initiate that dilemma; Odysseus himself is bored, but she is nonetheless devastated by the thought of losing him. In rejecting her offer of immortality Odysseus prudently decides in favour of common sense and humanity; but even being offered the choice makes him a little more than human, as we should remember when he finally does return, almost too coolly, to the wife and home and possessions he had claimed to love beyond all else. The Phaeacians, a half-magical people related to the gods and remote from ordinary men, are no less strongly affected by their shipwrecked guest. Nausicaa is fascinated by him, and so in a different way is her father Alcinous, a model of hospitality but also at times bluff, bumbling and comically obtuse. The eliciting of Odysseus' reminiscences is one purpose of the episode, but another is surely the placing of the hero in a kind of limbo between the open fantasy of Circe and Calypso and the erratic but intense realities of Troy and Ithaca. In that limbo he, and the audience with him, draws together the strands of past and future as the disparate elements of the plot are cunningly connected.

Once again Odysseus emerges larger than before, not only materially (he had arrived in Scheria naked, battered, a suppliant, and left with gifts worth more than his lost share of the booty from Troy) but also – much as one hesitates to use the expression – spiritually. Odysseus' spirit is not only his *thymos*, that part of him that is the passionate will to survive and that also suffers grief, and that in Greek literally means 'breath' or 'spirit'; it is also something for which Greek had no proper expression, the whole of man's experience reflecting itself in his personality and behaviour. Are we meant to sense that special aspect of Odysseus, his experience of most things human and some divine, once he has regained the familiar landscape of his native island? One wonders – for in some ways the action of the second half of the poem is too concentrated to let this side of him appear with great clarity, at least after his revelation of himself to Eumaeus and Telemachus. Those conversations of the fourteenth and fifteenth books were the obvious opportunity for the poet to make his point about Odysseus, if it were a point to be openly made; either then, or when Penelope is finally permitted to accept him as her husband. The poet certainly did not take

49

the first opportunity. Caution, and repeated false tales including hints that Odysseus is close at hand, are the main elements of those former scenes. As soon as the hero reveals his identity, and after a brief moment of hugging and rejoicing, the plotting continues. With Penelope it is almost the same, at least to begin with. But then, as they go to bed, he summarizes all his hardships and adventures and outlines Tiresias' prediction of a last journey to be made and a peaceful death from the sea (23.248–343).

That, perhaps, is the clue we need. For in most of his behaviour, both before and after his triumph, he has resembled an ordinary hero, fierce and cruel with the suitors and disloyal servants, generous and just with his friends. So far, then, an Iliadic figure. It is in his private demeanour with his wife, in the emphasis on his wanderings and sufferings, his encounters with divine beings, his happy but indefinite future, that Odysseus' role as the man of more than human experience is underlined. Boastful, erratic, morose and unfaithful he had been, at one time or another in the twenty years since he left home; but also brave, resourceful and passionate, a connoisseur of circumstances and of persons, of women no less than men; above all god-guided by Athena, with the blessing of all the Olympians save Poseidon (whose anger against Odysseus had been aroused by the blinding of his son Polyphemus) – not because he was of divine descent like Aeneas, Achilles or Sarpedon in the *Iliad* but because in the last resort he was *polymetis*, 'of many counsels'. Resourcefulness, the ability to assess and deal with things as they are, were qualities admired and rewarded by the gods, by Athena above all. In allowing Odysseus to experience grief, frustration and minor successes without for a moment being distracted from his ultimate aim, in making him the omnipresent figure who, whether lost or disguised or completely revealed, brings both truth and fantasy to the heroic past and the unsettled present, the poet of the *Odyssey* exhibits the touch of genius that his traditional materials did not necessarily contain or indicate.

2

HESIOD

'Who could speak highly enough of training in the art of writing?' asks the historian Diodorus (12.13.2). 'By this means alone the dead speak to the living, and through the written word those who are widely separated in space communicate with those remote from them as if they were neighbours.' The quarter-millennium from *c.* 730 to *c.* 480 in Greece was a period in which literacy came to have far-reaching effects on literature, making possible an infinitely complex network of relationships between authors remote from one another in time or space or both, and allowing the development of a single unified literary culture, to which local differences only added richness. For it is no coincidence that as literacy spread there came a growing consciousness of national identity, the universal Greekness of all who spoke and wrote the common tongue. This capital event, the re-invention of writing, was itself, moreover, only one element among many in the great renaissance of Greece which came from the rediscovery of the wider world after centuries of isolation – centuries in which, following the collapse of the literate Mycenaean culture between 1200 and 1100, all the fine arts and delicate skills of the Bronze Age had been forgotten and all that remained was the memory of great deeds and great heroes, enshrined in the traditional forms of oral poetry and chanted to precarious settlements of refugees on the coastal fringe of Asia Minor.

It makes sense to begin a discussion of the period of Greek literacy with Hesiod, not because there is any certainty that he was a literate poet – in fact there is much to be said for the view that he worked in a tradition of formular oral poetry which was fairly closely akin to Homer's – but because he was doing something new and individual which pointed the way that subsequent Greek poetry was to take. For while Homer keeps his own personality entirely separate from his poetry and gives no clue to any datable event with which he might be associated, Hesiod is the first European poet who introduces himself into his work as an individual with a distinctive role to play. And in *Works and days* he takes the important step of abandoning traditional narrative with its stock of set themes and scenes in favour of a poem with an argument, perhaps using models from Near-Eastern culture as his inspiration (though

51

we cannot be sure that Greek poets had not already taken to composing wisdom literature of this kind). In combining traditional form and style with a highly individual 'tone of voice' and in extending the range of the poet's functions Hesiod set the pattern for what we misleadingly call 'archaic' Greek poetry, the literature of a period of territorial expansion through colonization, of rapid social change and of sophisticated artistic experiment.

The date of Hesiod's poetic activity is disputed, but there can be little doubt that this was some time in the latter part of the eighth century. He tells us himself[1] how he won a prize for poetry in a competition in Chalcis at the funeral games of Amphidamas, a Chalcidian killed in a naval battle in the Lelantine War. This famous war, which drew so much of Greece into alliance that it is excepted from Thucydides' general disparagement of the campaigns of archaic Greece (1.15.3), was fought between the Euboean cities Chalcis and Eretria for the possession of the plain of Lelanton which lies between them. An upper limit for its date should therefore be provided by the presumably amicable colonial enterprises on which the two cities embarked jointly in Chalcidice and in the west at Pithecusae and Cumae, c. 750. The lower limit is indicated by the fact that it is said by Aristotle to have been an old-fashioned cavalry war (*Pol.* 1289b36–9); it must therefore predate the coming of hoplites and the tactics of the phalanx, c. 700–680. There is now archaeological confirmation of this date: the settlement on the ridge of Xeropolis, near Lefkandi in Euboea at the eastern (Eretrian) end of the plain of Lelanton, was destroyed without reoccupation shortly before 700, after continuous habitation since the Late Bronze Age. Amphidamas' funeral and Hesiod's victory belong therefore to the last third of the eighth century.

His father, he tells us, left the Aeolian city of Cyme for mainland Greece:

> Your father and mine, foolish Perses, used to go to sea in search of a good livelihood. One day he came here over a great expanse of sea, leaving Aeolian Cyme in a black ship. What he fled was not riches, wealth and prosperity, but evil penury, which Zeus gives to men. And he settled near Helicon in a miserable village, Ascra, which is bad in winter and unpleasant in summer, never any good. (*W.D.* 633–40)

That Hesiod's father should have left Asia for the less fertile and apparently overpopulated mainland is unexplained. But it is to be noticed that the date of his removal, which must have been about 750 or a little later, falls within the very period when others, themselves sea-going merchants, were leaving Cyme to share with Euboeans in the colonization of Cumae in Campania. Hesiod's father evidently became a farmer, for the poet and his brother fell out over an agricultural inheritance. The scale of their farming has sometimes been romantically disparaged. In fact the *Works and days* presupposes yeomen rather than

---

[1] *W.D.* 654–9 with schol.; Plutarch, *Mor.* 153f.

peasants. The farmer does not work alone but can employ a friend (370), as well as servants (502, 573, 597, 608, 766), has a lively forty-year-old free labourer to follow the plough and a slave-boy to turn in the seed (441–6, cf. 469–71), together with a female servant at home (405, 602). Of draught animals he has plough oxen and mules (405, 607f.). On the other hand he cannot afford merely to oversee the work of others: he must take his share too (458–61). For all Hesiod's harping on poverty (638, cf. 376f.), life at Ascra cannot have been too uncomfortable.

Three poems survive in Hesiod's name, together with a host of fragments of other works attributed to him in antiquity; all are composed in dactylic hexameters and in the conventional language of epic. Of the three survivors, one, the *Shield of Heracles*, is undoubtedly spurious and probably belongs to the sixth century.[1] Of the other two, the severest of ancient critics allowed only the *Works and days* to Hesiod (cf. Pausanias 9.31.3). But the poet is named in *Theogony* 22, and it requires some perversity to interpret the context in such a way as to deny that the author is here naming himself. Moreover, despite the general disparity of their subject matter the two poems offer versions of the Prometheus myth which, as Vernant has shown,[2] interlock with one another, and their close relationship in language, metre and prosody sets them apart from Homer on the one hand and the *Shield* on the other.

If both are indeed the work of Hesiod, the priority of the *Theogony* is easily established. For the opening of the *Works and days*, 11–23, appears explicitly to modify a doctrine of the *Theogony*: there is not after all only one kind of Eris (contention), as had been said at *Theog.* 225f.; there are two, beneficial competition as well as destructive strife. The same conclusion is suggested by Hesiod's treatment of the story of Prometheus and Pandora in the two poems. In the *Theogony* we read in detail of the sin of Prometheus and of the creation and adornment of Pandora (501–616), whereas in the *Works and days* Hesiod passes over the early part of the story in two lines (47f.), and dwells at length on the subsequent history of Pandora and the jar[3] (49–105). In the *Works and days*, in fact, Hesiod seems to presuppose knowledge of the *Theogony*. The latter may indeed be the very poem to which Hesiod looks back in *W.D.* 654ff., the prize-winning entry at Amphidamas' funeral. For the competition-piece was a *hymnos*, and the prize tripod was dedicated by the poet to the Muses of Helicon on the very spot where they had inspired him first. The *Theogony*, addressed to the Muses of Helicon, describes that first inspiration (22–35), and is itself characterized as a *hymnos* (33, cf. 11, 37, 51).

---

[1] Cook (1937) discusses its possible date.

[2] Vernant (1980) 184–5.

[3] A jar (*pithos*), not the box familiar in later European tradition, which derives from Erasmus; cf. Panofsky (1962) and West (1978a) on *W.D.* 94.

The poem begins with a long invocation of the Muses (1–115), itself of the nature of a 'Homeric' hymn, celebrating their power as well as their piety in singing of the generations of the gods. They are the daughters of Zeus by Memory, a parentage which recalls the long tradition of oral recitation, when a bard's skill did indeed depend on memory, his own and his forerunners'. It was they who 'once taught Hesiod beautiful song, as he tended his sheep under holy Helicon' (22–3) and 'they gave me a staff, plucking a fine branch of flourishing bay, and breathed in me a divine voice, so that I might sing of what was to come and what had been. And they commanded me to hymn the race of the blessed immortals and always to sing of themselves first and last' (30–4).

So Hesiod begins his account of creation and of the succession of divinities who have presided over it since the beginning. Partly a narrative of development, partly an account of the theological *status quo*, it is constructed loosely, with passages in which some three hundred gods are classified according to genealogy, interspersed with a number of more leisurely stories. The Creation itself is given no cause: Chaos, the yawning void, merely 'came into existence', followed by Earth, Tartarus and Eros (Love). From Chaos came Erebus and Night to become the parents of Aether (the clear upper air) and Day; from Earth came Heaven (Uranus), Mountains and the Sea. Then creation is filled with three main lines of descent, from Night, from Earth and Heaven, from the Sea. The main line is that of Earth and Heaven, leading through the generations of the Titans and Cronos to Zeus himself. The first extended myth (154–210) describes the dethronement of Uranus, castrated by Cronos, and the birth of Aphrodite from his severed genitals; the second (453–506), after another long section of genealogies, tells the story of Cronos, who determined to eat the gods, his children, in order to forestall his overthrow by one of them, but was tricked into swallowing a stone instead of Zeus and was supplanted in his turn.

By this time Hesiod has lost interest in cosmogony, and says no more of the way in which things came to be. The remainder of the poem is concerned to explain the world as it is rather than to identify stages in its development. So the rise of Zeus is followed by a list of the sons of the Titan Iapetus, which serves as an introduction to the story of Prometheus and Pandora[1] and the invention of woman, and the phenomena of sacrifice and fire (507–616). Here the scene is broadened again to present a resurgence of the Titans and their final overthrow by Zeus (617–720). There follows an account of Tartarus, where Zeus imprisoned them, the haunt of Sleep, Death, Cerberus and Styx (721–819). This is a prelude to the struggle between Zeus and the monster Typhoeus, the youngest child of Earth (820–80); when Zeus is victorious he

---

[1] For the fundamental significance of this myth see Vernant (1980) 168–85.

is elected king of the gods and gives to each of the immortals his or her sphere (881–5). From this point the poem tails off into an extended series of marriages and love-affairs, beginning with those of Zeus himself, then those of the other gods, goddesses, and nymphs, and ending with a transition to the *Catalogue of women*, a long poem of which only fragments survive.

In the *Theogony* there is much that successive editors have regarded as spurious,[1] but they disagree fundamentally in their choice of suspect passages, and it is hard to find safe criteria for judging interpolation in an author like Hesiod. Both his extant poems show a certain diffuseness, a tendency to be side-tracked from the matter in hand, which leads one to doubt whether they ever possessed any logical or rigorous arrangement. Nevertheless it may be agreed that the end of the *Theogony* is not as Hesiod left it: we might after all expect it to close with an invocation of the Muses, as promised at the beginning (34). There are some indications that the end of the poem was remodelled in order to smooth a transition to the *Catalogue of women*, which follows without a break in some of the manuscripts.

Herodotus regarded Homer and Hesiod as the founders of Greek theology (2.53), and the *Theogony* is the only coherent account of it to have survived from this early period. To the modern mind Hesiod's theology is bewildering: powers of nature are now conceived as geographical entities, as when Heaven's children are concealed in a hollow of the Earth (157f.), now made wholly anthropomorphic, as when Heaven himself suffers castration (178ff.). The Olympian gods, by contrast, are always anthropomorphic. Homer's beliefs were evidently similar. His gods are unfailingly human, but he alludes to the older powers in making Oceanus and Tethys the progenitors of the gods (*Il.* 14.201ff.). The creation myths of Homer and Hesiod soon came to seem unsatisfactory, and impersonal causes were adduced instead – either abstract, as when Alcman (*c.* 600) explained all in terms of End and Means (*Tekmor* and *Poros*, fr. 5.2.ii; fr. 1.14 schol.), or concrete, as when the sixth-century Ionian philosophers sought a primary substance among the four elements. Though the Olympians never lost their simple anthropomorphic nature, ridiculed as it was by Xenophanes as early as *c.* 530 (cf. frs. 21B 10–16 DK), the ambiguity of Hesiod's view of the powers of creation remained characteristic of much Greek religious thought even in the classical period, most obviously in relation to the powers which were essential to human life, Mother Earth as well as the river-gods and fountain-nymphs. In Hesiod these divinities rub shoulders with more abstract powers such as Toil, Famine, Sorrow and the other children of Strife, as well as with purely fantastic monsters, Chimaera, Sphinx and so on, any literal belief in whom was certainly abandoned by the Greeks of later days.

[1] Cf. Edwards (1971) 4–6.

Theological notions of such disparate kinds, it is clear, must have reached Hesiod from more than one tradition, to say nothing of his own invention. To what extent the cosmogony and theology which are unfolded in this poem would have appeared novel or exceptional to an eighth-century audience is hard to say; certainly, despite a general similarity of approach, not all is consistent in detail with Homer, and part of the material of the *Theogony* in fact shows close affinities with the theology of Egypt and the Near East. Striking parallels have been found in Hittite and Babylonian texts for the succession myth of Uranus–Cronos–Zeus and for Zeus's fight with Typhoeus.[1]

Hesiod's second poem, the *Works and days*, is like the *Theogony*, a celebration of the power of Zeus, to whom the Muses are invited to contribute a hymn. Zeus is the source of justice, and Hesiod will undertake to instruct his brother Perses in the truth (1–10). Though the instructions and the reflections which follow are mostly of very general application, Hesiod continually calls his brother to order with some sharply pointed moral.[2] The first truth is that there are two kinds of Contention (Eris): constructive competition and destructive rivalry (11–26). From this spring two of the poem's important themes, that Perses should give up the destructive strife which has marred relations between the two brothers – here Hesiod takes the opportunity to dilate upon the virtues of justice – and should instead let the spirit of competition direct him towards a life of honest labour on the farm. That it is a hard world, with toil and suffering as man's appointed lot, is illustrated by two myths. In the first, Hesiod resumes the story of Pandora, begun in the *Theogony* – her creation and adornment, and the jar out of which all evils flew to harass the world leaving only Hope imprisoned (42–105). It looks like a traditional tale, slightly clumsy in that no real reason is advanced for Hope's failure to escape. But what matters is the ambiguity of Hope's position: it expresses the essential ambiguity of human life, in which good and bad, happiness and unhappiness are inextricably intermingled.[3] The motif of the jar as prison is also found at *Iliad* 5.385–91, where Otus and Ephialtes are held in a bronze jar, but the closest parallel with Hesiod is at *Iliad* 24.527ff., where Achilles speaks of the two *pithoi* which stand at the entrance to Zeus's palace, the one containing good and the other evil, from which the god ladles out to men their combination of good and bad fortune in life. The second of Hesiod's myths designed to illustrate the hardness of life is that of the metallic ages of mankind, a gloomy tale of degeneration from Cronos' day, when the men of the golden race lived like gods without a care in the world, through silver and bronze to Hesiod's own race of iron (106–201). Here again we have an evidently traditional tale,

---

[1] Details in West (1966) 19–30, 106f., 379f.
[2] On the question whether Perses was real or fictitious see West (1978a) 33–40.
[3] Vernant (1980) 184–5.

somewhat crudely adapted. For Hesiod could not square this doctrine of progressive decline with his picture of the Seven against Thebes or the Achaeans before Troy. He therefore intercalated an age of heroes or demigods, non-metallic, between the bronze and the iron. A further, and surely conclusive indication that this myth is adapted from an alien source is its inconsistency with the *Theogony*, in which the time of Cronos is not at all paradisal, merely a stage on the road of progress towards the reign of Zeus.

His account of the iron race moves quickly from description of the present to prophecy of an even grimmer future:

> I wish that I had never belonged to the fifth race, but had either died earlier or been born later. For truly now it is a race of iron. Neither by day will men cease from toil and woe nor from suffering by night. And the gods will give them troubles hard to bear. None the less, even they will have some good mixed with their woes. But Zeus will destroy this race of mortal men too, when they come to have grey hair at birth. A father will not be in harmony with his children, nor the children with their father, nor guest with host, nor comrade with comrade, and a brother will not be dear to his brother as they were in the past. Men will dishonour their quickly ageing parents and will reproach them with harsh words of abuse, wicked men who do not understand the vengeance of the gods. They will not repay their aged parents the cost of their nurture, for might is their right, and one man will sack another's city. There will be no respect for the man who keeps his oath or for the just or the good; instead they will praise the man who does evil, insolence incarnate. And right and reverence shall depend on might. The bad man will harm the better, telling lies about him and confirming them with an oath. And ugly Envy, that causes uproar and delights in evil, will keep company with the whole of miserable mankind. Then Aidos and Nemesis[1] will wrap their fair bodies in white robes, and go from the earth with its broad paths to Olympus to join the race of immortals, forsaking men, and bitter sorrows will be left for mortal men, and there will be no help against evil. (174–201)

Hesiod now develops the theme of Justice, introduced by its opposite Hybris, the doctrine that might is right, which is embodied in the fable of the hawk and the nightingale. This, the earliest fable in extant Greek literature, points the path to be avoided by Perses, and by princes upon the seat of judgement, and the way of Justice to be followed (202–92). It is noteworthy that the somewhat radical view of the lawlessness and dishonesty of princes developed here runs counter to the favourable view of princes to be found in the *Theogony* (e.g. 80–93). It may be that Hesiod by now was older and wiser; it may be only that the flattery of princes matched the occasion of Amphidamas' funeral. Either way, it raises the question of the kind of occasion for which the *Works and days* was composed. Hesiod's preoccupation with ethics and with the justice of Zeus is a whole world away from the old aristocratic view of the

---

[1] Aidos = 'shame', 'reverence'; Nemesis = 'awe', 'public disapproval'.

divine right of kings, which is unquestioned in the *Iliad* and still largely prevails in the *Odyssey*, even if the self-condemning behaviour of Penelope's princely suitors marks the beginnings of doubt. In particular, it is noteworthy that in Hesiod's view injustice leads ultimately to war as the worst of evils (276ff.). War, of course, is the sport of princes, and in this passage above all Hesiod turns his back on Homer and the heroic tradition.

From Justice Hesiod turns to the broader theme of work: the attitude as well as the equipment of the farmer and householder is prescribed in the greatest detail, a calendar of the yearly round of toil (293–617). This whole section, the longest part of the poem, is of course invaluable for the insight it gives into the life and outlook of an ordinary Greek of the eighth century. There is no romantic view of country life such as Virgil was to import into his *Georgics*: the romantic approach is characteristic not of the countryman but of the city-dweller, and it is no accident that we first find it in the Hellenistic period, when truly urbanized society first began to emerge. Hesiod has no illusions about life on the farm. Here is his account of winter:

> Avoid the month of Lenaeon [late January/early February], wretched days, all fit to flay an ox, and the frosts, which are severe when Boreas blows over the earth. He blows across horse-breeding Thrace and on the broad sea and stirs it up, and the earth and woodlands roar. Often he falls upon oaks with their lofty foliage and thick pines in the mountain glens and brings them down to the bountiful earth, and then all the immense wood groans. And the beasts shiver and put their tails between their legs, even the ones whose hide is covered with fur. But his cold blasts blow through them despite their shaggy breasts. And he goes even through oxhide and it cannot resist him, and through the thin-haired goat. But the strength of Boreas does not penetrate the sheep, because their wool is abundant; yet it makes the old man bent like a wheel. (504–18)

And he goes on to give advice about the kind of boots and jerkin and felt cap that the farmer should wear against the bitter weather.

Farming, however, is not the only career Hesiod envisages. If, instead, the life of the merchant seaman seems to offer attractions, as it did to Hesiod's father, then words of warning and advice are in place (618–94). Whatever the means of livelihood, the indispensable basis is the family – even if financial prudence demands its strict limitation (376f.) – and this necessitates the choice of a wife. For Hesiod this seems to have been a matter for regret, and in his misogyny he anticipates Semonides (see pp. 112ff.). In the *Theogony* the creation of woman was the worst Zeus could do to plague mankind (570–612), and Love (*Philotes*) and Deceit are linked among the children of Night (224). In the present poem the need to choose a good wife and to treat her well serves largely as an occasion to warn of the havoc a bad wife can wreak (cf. 373ff.):

Bring a wife to your house when you are the right age, neither far short of thirty nor much older: this is the right age for marriage. The woman should be four years beyond maturity and marry in the fifth. Marry a virgin so that you can teach her proper conduct, and make a point of choosing someone who lives near, but take care not to make a marriage that will be a joke to your neighbours. For there is nothing a man can win that is better than a good wife, and nothing worse than a bad one – a parasite who scorches her husband without fire, however strong he is, and brings him to cruel old age. (695–705)

Finally, a few lines on friendship bring this part of the poem to a close (706–23).

The remainder of the *Works and days* has been thought spurious by many critics. Interesting as it is to the historian of religion, the detailed list of taboos it contains (724–64) has seemed to express a primitive narrowness of vision at odds with the broad and elevated concept of the justice of all-seeing Zeus. Yet it is common experience that in unsophisticated societies the most religious standards of probity in commercial dealings are in no way incompatible with the most elaborate web of superstition. A similar controversy has been waged over the last section of the poem – the *Days*, in fact (765–828) – which gives a list of days that are propitious or unpropitious for various undertakings. But the burden of proof is upon those who would declare the verses spurious.[1]

There is no doubt that as a whole the poem is lacking in that architectonic quality which strikes every reader of the *Iliad* and *Odyssey*. Those poems may sometimes seem to digress, sometimes dwell too long on one scene, sometimes repeat a theme a little tediously, but that they have a beginning, middle and end in the full sense of Aristotle's famous definition no one can doubt. About the *Works and days*, on the other hand, doubts have been expressed since Pausanias in the second century A.D. stated that according to the Boeotians the text of the poem began with our line 11 (9.31). One modern critic after another has condemned the end of the poem and even in the middle the apparatus criticus bristles with such words as *suspecta, damnavit, delevit, proscripsit, seclusit* – scholars have for years tried to make a logical discourse of the poem by cutting, rearranging and rewriting. The trouble is, they are asking too much of it. They are asking it to be a logical progression (as each of the Homeric poems is a narrative progression); they are treating it as if it were a practical handbook on agriculture or a poem about justice, with a continuous argument. Judged by that criterion it fails to live up to elementary standards of logic, consistency and structural coherence.

It must be judged, of course, by quite other standards. It is the first attempt in western literature to compose a large-scale work without the armature of a given narrative line. It is, in fact, an extraordinarily bold venture. In the

[1] For a review of the problems see West (1978a) 346–50.

Theogony Hesiod had a genealogical line to follow which was itself a sort of narrative thread; in the *Catalogue of women* he (or whoever was its author) simply added one story to another. The alternative title of the poem is Ἦ Οἶαι (*Ehoiai*); each fresh episode begins with ἣ οἷαι 'like those women who …' (or the singular ἣ οἵη 'like that woman who …'), followed by the tale of their loves, usually with a god, and the birth of heroes. Such a poem needed no structure and could obviously go on as long as anyone wanted to hear it; the episodes could be arranged in any order. But the *Works and days* has a purpose: to explain why life is a ceaseless round of labour and to offer advice which will make that labour profitable and tolerable. And it does this in a dramatic framework: Hesiod's quarrel with his brother Perses.

If the *Theogony* were not so plainly a farrago of Greek and oriental elements, the oriental character of much of the *Works and days* might have passed without notice, since it is in so many ways the fountain-head of an essentially Greek view of life. Yet it too has its antecedents in the east and in Egypt. The myth of the metallic ages of man, it has been noted, was not of Hesiod's own invention; exact parallels are wanting, but the closest analogies are with Zoroastrian myths.[1] The poem as a whole has many counterparts in Egypt and in the Near East, didactic works about life and behaviour which, however, typically enshrine the advice of a father to his son.[2] Hesiod's variant, the advice of brother to brother, is perhaps original, and no motive for the change need be sought beyond the poet's own circumstances. The Egyptian texts in this genre extend from the Old Kingdom to the Saïte dynasty beyond the lifetime of Hesiod, and include exhortations to agricultural toil in the context of a relationship between man and god that is not at all far removed in spirit from Hesiod's view of Zeus. Similar texts are found in the Near East, at Ugarit and elsewhere, and it is clear that the Sumerians (who loved animal fables similar to Hesiod's tale of the hawk and the nightingale), Hurrians and Babylonians all succumbed to the human temptation to seek to order the lives of others. In such a universal theme one must be careful not to rule out coincidence. Argument from such texts as the *Instructions of Ninurta* to his son, a Sumerian farmer's almanac, are particularly dangerous in view of the uniform demands of agricultural life. Yet there is enough in the Sumerian *Instructions of Šuruppak*, the Babylonian *Counsels of Wisdom*, and the Egyptian *Instructions* to locate Hesiod in the mainstream of a current of literature which enjoyed popularity in the orient (though not enough to identify a particular source or to establish a date for the arrival of this genre in Greece).

Some features of Hesiod's poetry may strike a modern reader as curiously quaint and 'archaic', by comparison even with Homer's. M. L. West has noted

[1] West (1978a) 172–7.
[2] For a survey of Near-Eastern wisdom literature see West (1978a) 3–15.

the difference between the expansiveness and eloquence of speeches in Homer and the brief, rather stiff utterances that Hesiod gives his characters: 'curt little affairs, devoid of Homeric rhetoric, and quaintly formal'.[1] So Hesiod's story-telling often seems comparatively naive and lacking in Homer's psychological depth, while his tendency to repetitiveness, and some tricks of style like his use of kennings (the 'boneless one" = the octopus, ἀνόστεος, *W.D.* 524; the 'five-branched thing' = the hand, πεντόζοιο, *W.D.* 742) may contribute to a certain impression of primitivism. But against this we should set the energy and vitality of his poetry and the authoritativeness of its tone, sometimes solemn, sometimes almost sardonic. There is an attractive robustness and absence of sentimentality even in his most idyllic passages, like the description of high summer in his directions for seasonal activities:

> When the golden thistle is in flower, and the chirping cicada sits in a tree and incessantly pours out its shrill song from under its wings in the time of exhausting summer heat, then goats are fattest and wine sweetest and women most wanton and men at their feeblest, for Sirius burns their heads and their knees and their skin is parched in the heat. Then is the right time for the shade of a rock and Bibline wine and milk bread and late-season goat's milk, and the meat of a heifer that has been put out to graze and has not calved, and of firstling kids. Drink the bright wine sitting in the shade when you have had your fill of food, turning your face towards the fresh Zephyr, and pour in three parts of water from a perpetually running, unmuddied spring, and the fourth part of wine. (*W.D.* 582–96)[2]

(This should be read without forgetting 500–3: 'Hope is not a good companion for a poor man, who sits around where people meet to chat when he has no decent livelihood. Tell your servants while it is still midsummer, "It won't always be summer: build yourselves shelters".')

There is real dignity in many passages: in the proem to the *Theogony*, or the picture of the just and unjust cities in *W.D.* (225–47), or the account of Hecate's honours in the *Theogony*, a passage which well illustrates how effective a rather simple use of repetition can be:

> ἣ δ᾽ ὑποκυσαμένη ῾Εκάτην τέκε, τὴν περὶ πάντων
> Ζεὺς Κρονίδης τίμησε, πόρεν δέ οἱ ἀγλαὰ δῶρα,
> μοῖραν ἔχειν γαίης τε καὶ ἀτρυγέτοιο θαλάσσης·
> ἣ δὲ καὶ ἀστερόεντος ἀπ᾽ οὐρανοῦ ἔμμορε τιμῆς,
> ἀθανάτοις τε θεοῖσι τετιμένη ἐστὶ μάλιστα.
> καὶ γὰρ νῦν, ὅτε πού τις ἐπιχθονίων ἀνθρώπων
> ἔρδων ἱερὰ καλὰ κατὰ νόμον ἱλάσκηται,
> κικλήσκει ῾Εκάτην· πολλή τέ οἱ ἕσπετο τιμὴ
> ῥεῖα μάλ᾽, ὧι πρόφρων γε θεὰ ὑποδέξεται εὐχάς·
> καί τέ οἱ ὄλβον ὀπάζει, ἐπεὶ δύναμίς γε πάρεστιν.

---

[1] West (1966) 74.
[2] This passage is imitated in the *Shield of Heracles* 393–7 and by Alcaeus (fr. 347).

ὅσσοι γὰρ Γαίης τε καὶ Οὐρανοῦ ἐξεγένοντο
καὶ τιμὴν ἔλαχον, τούτων ἔχει αἶσαν ἀπάντων·
οὐδέ τί μιν Κρονίδης ἐβιήσατο οὐδέ τ' ἀπηύρα
ὅσσ' ἔλαχεν Τιτῆσι μετὰ προτέροισι θεοῖσιν,
ἀλλ' ἔχει ὡς τὸ πρῶτον ἀπ' ἀρχῆς ἔπλετο δασμός·
οὐδ', ὅτι μουνογενής, ἧσσον θεὰ ἔμμορε τιμῆς,
[καὶ γέρας ἐν γαίηι τε καὶ οὐρανῶι ἠδὲ θαλάσσηι,]
ἀλλ' ἔτι καὶ πολὺ μᾶλλον, ἐπεὶ Ζεὺς τίεται αὐτήν.   (411–28)

And she [Asterie] became pregnant and gave birth to Hecate, whom Zeus son of Cronos honoured above all. He gave her splendid gifts, a portion to have as her own of the earth and the unharvested sea. She received honour too from the starry heaven, and she is exceedingly honoured by the immortal gods. For to this day whenever any mortal offers fine sacrifices and prays according to custom he calls upon Hecate; and great honour comes easily to him whose prayers the goddess receives favourably, and she grants him prosperity, for she has the power. For she has a portion among all those who were born of Earth and Heaven and obtained honour. The son of Cronos did her no violence and took nothing from her, of all the privileges that fell to her lot among the Titans, the former race of gods, but she continues to hold them just as she did when the distribution was first made. Nor, because she was an only daughter, did the goddess obtain a smaller share of honour [and privileges on land and in heaven and in the sea], but much more still, since Zeus honours her.

The individuality and power of Hesiod's imagination can best be seen from comparison with a work by one of his imitators, the short epic known as the *Shield of Heracles* (*Scutum* or *Aspis*), which is transmitted along with *Theogony* and *Works and days* in the medieval manuscripts. This is a weak and muddled account of the fight between Heracles and Cycnus, containing a long ecphrastic passage, modelled on Homer's accounts of the shields of Achilles (*Il.* 18.478–607) and Agamemnon (*Il.* 11.32–40), in which the shield of Heracles is described. It wholly lacks the strength and wit of Hesiod and depends for its effects on sheer accumulation of detail, preferably detail of a sensational kind:

By them stood Achlys [Woe, literally the mist that covers the eyes in death], gloomy and dreadful, pale, shrivelled, shrunken with hunger, with swollen knees and long fingernails. Mucus flowed from her nose, and blood dripped from her cheeks to the ground. She stood grinning horribly, and much dust, damp with tears, covered her shoulders. (264–70)

This is one of the less derivative passages; other less spine-chilling scenes are rather clumsily adapted from Homer. The work has no claim to be by Hesiod, though it shows close familiarity with his genuine work and was designed to fit into the *Catalogue of women*: it opens with a section on Heracles' mother Alcmena beginning ἢ οἵη (see above, p. 60).

Two main issues of Hesiodic scholarship remain unsettled: his relationship to Homer and his mode of composition. Although it now seems clear that Hesiod was active in the latter part of the eighth century, there is no consensus on the question of the relative dates of Hesiod and the *Iliad* and *Odyssey* respectively. All that can be demonstrated is that Hesiod and Homer are very closely comparable in language and manner: in essence they share the same dialect, and they have a large proportion of their vocabulary and formulaic phrases in common, though there are also notable differences,[1] and some of Hesiod's peculiarities of dialect are particularly hard to explain. G. P. Edwards, on the basis of a close study of Hesiod's language, arrived at the following conclusion:

Ionian epic poetry was known on the mainland in the time of Hesiod and was recited in its Ionic form even by mainlanders. The Homeric poems suggest themselves as the most obvious representatives of this Ionian tradition, but clearly they need not have been the only Ionian poetry which Hesiod could have known, nor can we assume that Hesiod knew them in the form in which they have survived in our written texts. At the same time, the most economical hypothesis may be that the *Iliad* and the *Odyssey* already existed and were known on the Greek mainland by Hesiod's time in a form recognisably the same as that in which we know them today...[2]

M. L. West, on the other hand, has argued that the *Theogony* is quite likely to be 'the oldest Greek poem we have',[3] on the grounds that both the *Iliad* and the *Odyssey* in their present form admit elements that cannot be dated earlier than *c.* 700 B.C. It is probably too risky to demand such precision from archaeological evidence, and in the end it may not matter that we cannot precisely date any of these poems; more important is the growing recognition by modern scholars that there was a common Ionian tradition of hexameter poetry in which both poets worked, despite their geographical separation.

Whether Hesiod was an oral or a literate composer is an equally controversial question; but here again there is an important area of agreement, namely that however Hesiod himself may have proceeded[4] the tradition in which he learned his craft was an oral one. It is probably impossible to prove one way or the other whether he used writing to compose his poetry, but there is perhaps some force in the consideration that a highly personal poem like the *Works and days*, which has no narrative thread to help the reciter, stood a better chance of surviving if it was committed to writing at a fairly early stage, that is, during the poet's lifetime. This is not to suggest that there was such a thing as a regular reading public at this date: the normal mode of communication

---

[1] West (1966) 77–91 and (1978a) 31f.; Edwards (1971) especially 140–65.
[2] Edwards (1971) 202f.
[3] West (1966) 46.
[4] West (1978a) 40–8 makes some interesting suggestions. Cf. Edwards (1971) 190–3.

between poets and their audiences was surely that of oral performance, whether at festivals or at some other kind of social gathering. But the wide acquaintance with *Works and days* that we can demonstrate for the archaic period[1] is difficult to account for without supposing that some use was made of written texts. As with the work of Archilochus and the early elegists and lyric poets, the possibility of long-term survival must have been enormously enhanced by the development of writing in Greek society.

[1] Tyrtaeus 12.43 may be an echo of *W.D.* 291; Semonides 6 is a reworking of *W.D.* 702f.; Alcaeus fr. 347 echoes *W.D.* 582–9; Ibycus 282 *PMG*, 18–24 may make use of *W.D.* 646–62.

3

THE EPIC TRADITION
AFTER HOMER AND HESIOD

I. THE CYCLIC EPICS

Homer and Hesiod, as the sole survivors of the earliest age of Greek literature, have conveyed such an impression of uniqueness that it requires some effort to recall that they were by no means without rivals and imitators. The formulaic nature of their verse, which implies a common bardic tradition, the recitations of Phemius and Demodocus in the *Odyssey*, and the occasion of Hesiod's competition at Chalcis all suggest that the eighth century was a period of lively poetic activity. When at *Od.* 12.70 the good ship *Argo* is said to be 'of interest to all', that surely alludes to some well-known treatment of the story of the Argonauts; and the brief résumé of Oedipus' story at *Od.* 11.271–80 must recall a more extended treatment elsewhere. We know that many early epic poems in fact survived from the archaic period alongside the works of Homer and Hesiod; at some (unknown) stage they were grouped into a sequence or 'cycle' starting at the remotest of beginnings with a *Theogony* and a *Battle of the Titans* and running through the legends of Thebes[1] and the Trojan War. They were performed by professional reciters (rhapsodes) in competitions at festivals, and must have been widely known until at least well into the fifth century. Probably the term 'cycle' was originally used of most epic narrative poetry, Homeric and non-Homeric alike; it was only after the time of Aristotle that 'cyclic' meant something essentially different from 'Homeric'.[2]

Of this enormous body of verse only a few brief quotations have survived – a mere 120 or so lines – but we have a helpful summary of the Trojan part of the Cycle (excerpted from a work of the fifth century A.D.,[3] the *Chrestomathia* of Proclus). This gives the whole story of the Trojan War, from the initial plan of Zeus to relieve the earth of excess population down to the death of Odysseus (and the final bizarre marryings-off: Penelope and Odysseus' son

1 The Theban epics were *Oedipodeia*, *Thebais* and *Epigoni*.
2 Pfeiffer (1968) 43f. and 230.
3 Unless a different Proclus is involved; cf. Severyns (1963).

Telegonus, Circe and Telemachus). The myths themselves must have been mainly very old, as we can tell from allusive references to them within the *Iliad* and the *Odyssey* (e.g. *Il.* 3.243f.: the Dioscuri, cf. *Cypria*; *Od.* 4.271–84: the Wooden Horse, cf. *Iliou persis*), but it is certain that many of the poems in the Cycle were composed later than the Homeric epics, probably in the seventh and sixth centuries, and many authors other than Homer are named (see Appendix).[1] According to Proclus the Trojan Cycle comprised *Cypria* (11 books); *Iliad*; *Aethiopis* (5 books); *Little Iliad* (4 books); *Iliou persis* 'Sack of Troy' (2 books); *Nostoi* 'Homecomings' (5 books); *Odyssey*; *Telegonia* (2 books). A glance at Proclus' summary at once suggests the importance of these epics for later Greek literature. The *Cypria*, for example, dealt with the following episodes: the judgement of Paris, the rape of Helen, the gathering of the Greek host, Achilles on Scyros, Telephus, the quarrel of Achilles and Agamemnon, Iphigenia at Aulis, Protesilaus. As Aristotle says in a critique of the formlessness of the cyclic poems, there is material here for many tragedies (*Poet.* 1459b1–7), and the same is true of most of the other works in the Cycle; their influence on lyric poetry, too, and on the visual arts must have been immense.

If our fragments were less meagre it would no doubt be possible to differentiate more sharply between the individual epics, which must have varied to some extent in quality and interest, as they did in date. A valuable attempt has been made by J. Griffin to characterize the cyclic poems by contrast with the *Iliad* and the *Odyssey*, with strong stress on the idea that the Homeric poems must have survived because they were better than the rest – more coherent and more amply detailed, more consistently serious, less sensational and romantic.[2] For example, the fantastic seems to have been more freely allowed by these authors: folk-tale motifs like the invulnerability of a hero (Ajax in the *Aethiopis*) or magic objects (Philoctetes' bow in the *Little Iliad*, the Palladium in the *Iliou persis*) and romantic incidents, like Achilles meeting Helen in the *Cypria* (a rendezvous arranged by Thetis and Aphrodite), suggest a very different tone from the severe world of the *Iliad*. The cyclic poets seem to have relished such pathetic and shocking episodes as the sacrifices of Iphigenia (*Cypria*) and Polyxena (*Iliou persis*) and to have been less discreet than Homer in the use of horrific stories of incest or kin murder. Of course such sensational material could be handled with great dignity and seriousness, as we know from plays like *Agamemnon* or *Oedipus tyrannus*, but from what little we have of the cyclic poems it does not seem likely that most of the authors had adequate poetic resources; certainly in later antiquity they are dismissed as formless, conventional, repetitive and flat. Aristotle's strongly expressed views in the

---

[1] Cf. Griffin (1977) 39 n. 9 for references.
[2] Griffin (1977).

Poetics (1459a30–b16) no doubt set the pattern for later criticism and ensured that the Cycle was no longer read: 'after Aristotle, compared with the two selected poems of Homer, everything "cyclic" was regarded as inferior, which meant at least conventional and often trivial'.[1] However, the tendency to neglect the cyclic poems may have begun earlier: we find Plato confining his quotation of epic to the *Iliad* and the *Odyssey*.[2] But by this time they had fertilized tragedy and provided the visual artists with an extremely rich and important body of source material.

Some of the epics composed in early times seem not to have been included in the Cycle (though our evidence is too meagre for certainty). Eumelus of Corinth, who was active in the latter part of the eighth century, may have been the author of the cyclic *Battle of the Titans* as some sources claim, but the rest of his work does not seem to have been treated as part of the Cycle. He is an interesting example of an epic poet who apparently chose and adapted his material with patriotic ends in view. He equated Corinth, which had no great past enshrined in legend, with the heroic but unidentifiable Ephyre, accounting for the change of name by a typical piece of invented genealogy (fr. 1). Thus armed with a corpus of mythology which included the tales of Sisyphus and Bellerophon, he proceeded to annex the Argonautic legend itself for Corinth under her new guise. To do this he made Aeetes an Ephyrean who ventured off into the unknown and settled in Colchis (fr. 2) and there received the Argonauts and Jason, whose adventures included the sowing of the dragon's teeth (fr. 9). We do not know the title of Eumelus' poem or poems: a later prose summary was entitled *Corinthiaca* or *History of Corinth* (Paus. 2.1.1). However named, Eumelus' work was one of the chief sources on which Apollonius of Rhodes drew for his *Argonautica* (see *CHCL* I, Part 4, 48), and it is in the scholia on Apollonius that the most notable fragments are preserved. The whole tenor of Eumelus' treatment of Ephyre and the Argonautic saga seems to have been propagandist, evidently designed to enhance the esteem of Corinth by giving her a rich epic tradition, and perhaps also providing in the story of Aeetes' emigration from Corinth an implicit historical argument which could be used to justify a Corinthian claim to territories on the Black Sea.

We can tell from the fragments of Eumelus, from what little is recorded about the work of the Cretan Epimenides, and from the allusive manner of Apollonius' epic that the Argonautic story continued to be a favourite subject for poetry. Another important corpus was the group of poems associated with Heracles, the most popular and most widely revered of all Greek heroes. Of these poems the oldest on record was the *Capture of Oechalia* (Οἰχαλίας ἅλωσις)

---

[1] Pfeiffer (1968) 230.
[2] Labarbe (1948) 410.

attributed to Homer himself or to Creophylus, though not, it seems, an original part of the Cycle. Peisander of Rhodes was the author (in the seventh or sixth century) of a more ambitious epic on the saga of Heracles which covered his whole career; this was followed by the much admired *Heraclea* of the Halicarnassian Panyassis, a cousin (or uncle) of Herodotus. Panyassis was active in the first half of the fifth century, and in the Alexandrian period he was esteemed as one of the finest epic writers; clearly ancient taste did not equate 'late' with 'bad' in the manner of modern scholarship.

Not all epic verse was devoted to heroic narrative: the form was clearly used also for classificatory, catalogue poetry: genealogies of the gods like Hesiod's *Theogony*, or the *Theogony* that stood at the beginning of the Cycle, or collections of human biographies like the *Catalogue of women* (see p. 60). And although *Works and days* seems to have been a poem of great originality, Hesiod was evidently not the only early Greek composer of didactic poetry. Among works doubtfully attributed to him we hear of the *Great works* (*Megala erga*), presumably another poem about farming, and the *Precepts of Chiron*, the advice purportedly given to Achilles by Chiron the Centaur. No doubt Hesiod, as the greatest poet in this field, attracted attributions of similar poems, just as Homer was reputed to have composed the *Thebais*, *Epigoni*, *Cypria*, and *Capture of Oechalia*, among others. In fact we should think of a large number of reciters, some of them composers as well, who performed and thereby helped to preserve a very substantial body of hexameter poetry.

There were also, it seems, attempts at self-parody within the tradition. Homer himself was credited with a curious piece of levity, the *Margites*. Its hero, if that is the word, is an archetypal village-idiot, unable to dig or plough or even to count beyond five. How, then, would such a simpleton fare amid the perils of matrimony? Not even knowing whether he was born from his mother or his father, afraid to sleep with his wife lest she complain to her mother of his inadequacy, he was at length tricked into it by her, and an account of their sexual relations evidently provoked great hilarity. A papyrus fragment, *P.Oxy.* 2309, may well preserve part of the poem; the scene is a bedroom equipped with chamberpot, and the action takes place in the 'black night'. The whole tale was evidently made more amusingly incongruous by being put into the mouth of a grave singer of epic in the manner of Homer's Demodocus or Phemius (fr. 1):

> ἦλθέ τις εἰς Κολοφῶνα γέρων καὶ θεῖος ἀοιδός,
> Μουσάων θεράπων καὶ ἐκηβόλου 'Απόλλωνος,
> φίλην ἔχων ἐν χερσὶν εὔφθογγον λύραν.

> An aged, divine minstrel came to Colophon,
> a servant of the Muses and Apollo the far-shooter,
> with his own tuneful lyre in his hands.

In Greek these three lines consist of two epic hexameters followed by an iambic trimeter, and the ancient metricians indicate that the poem as a whole consisted of blocks of hexameters alternating with blocks of trimeters in no discernible pattern. This is also the form of *P.Oxy.* 2309. A similar mixture of metres may already be intended in the light-hearted three-line inscription on a cup of the late eighth century found at Pithecusae,[1] where two hexameters are preceded by a line which can be scanned as an iambic trimeter. Although the attribution of *Margites* to Homer can be given no weight there is no reason to treat the poem as a late forgery; it could well belong to the seventh or sixth century and was widely quoted from the fourth century onwards.[2]

Another piece of epic parody, the *Battle of frogs and mice* or *Batrachomyomachia* (which seems to have been a great favourite as a school book in the middle ages and the Renaissance), is demonstrably later than the archaic period and most likely to be Hellenistic.[3] The main interest of this otherwise unexciting poem is that it does not seem to have been an isolated phenomenon but to have belonged to a genre of 'beast epics' – we hear of Battles of Cranes, Spiders and Starlings,[4] which may all have been in the same burlesque tradition.

2. THE HOMERIC HYMNS

Among the minor works often ascribed to Homer in antiquity were certain hymns, hexameter poems addressed to various deities. Thus Thucydides (3.104), citing Homer as the 'best evidence' for a historical judgement, quotes ll.145–50 of the *Hymn to Apollo* as from 'the prelude of Apollo'. The term 'prelude', *prooimion*, was a standard one for these hymns and probably implies that on occasions they were given as a preliminary to a longer epic recitation. At some time in later antiquity all the hexameter hymns not associated with other famous hymnodists (especially Orpheus, Musaeus, Olen and Pamphos) were gathered with those specifically attributed to Homer to form the corpus of 'Homeric Hymns' that has survived from the end of the medieval period. The truth is, however, that not a single one of these hymns, even the more imposing ones, can be by Homer, for their language and style are derivative, 'sub-epic', and in places clearly Hesiodic. The practice of ascribing to Homer a whole variety of poems in epic metres began quite early, whether through ambition, ignorance, piety or a sense of tidiness. It included a poem about Thebes, the *Thebais*, as well as unclaimed components of the 'Epic Cycle', those shorter and derivative epics that were designed to fill in gaps left by the *Iliad* and *Odyssey* and of which only plot-summaries and a few uninspired

---

[1] Page (1956).
[2] Testimonia in Allen (1912), *IEG* s.v. 'Homerus', West (1974) 190.
[3] See Wolke (1978) 46–70.
[4] Suda s.v. Ὅμηρος 45, 103.

fragments survive. So it is not surprising that Thucydides believed the Apolline hymn to be by Homer, or that other similar works were uncritically regarded as his. It is more puzzling, perhaps, that Hesiod was not occasionally chosen as their author, since at *Works and days* 656f. he claims to have won a contest with a hymn at the funeral games of Amphidamas in Euboea; and there was a well-known tradition that he and Homer sang a hymn to Apollo at Delos.

The corpus includes four long hymns (to Demeter, Apollo, Hermes and Aphrodite), of between 293 and 580 hexameter verses, and twenty-nine short ones, varying from three verses to fifty-nine in the case of Hymn 7, to Dionysus, which is probably truncated as it stands and looks relatively early on stylistic grounds. Hymn 1, also to Dionysus, may once, to judge by its position in the collection, have been a 'long' hymn, but only a twenty-one verse fragment, unimpressive in quality, survives. The long hymns and the short ones differ radically in intention and quality as well as in length; the latter are cursory eulogies addressed to a god or goddess with little or no narrative element, whereas the former narrate in a leisurely manner some central episode from the deity's mythical biography (so with the Hymns to Demeter, Hermes and Aphrodite) or attempt a broader coverage of his main aspects (*Hymn to Apollo*). There is another important difference: the long hymns seem to date from between 650 and 400 B.C. (to give broad but still ultimately conjectural limits), whereas many of the short ones are likely to be later. Indeed the latter are for the most part feeble and unimpressive, whatever their date, and it would hardly be an exaggeration to say that their chief interest is that, whether through sectarian zeal or through efficient libraries, they managed to survive at all. In fact even the long ones, judging by ancient references and quotations, seem to have made a rather slight impact in antiquity itself. Of these the Thucydidean quotation already noted is by far the most spectacular; otherwise there is a possible reference to the same hymn in Aristophanes (*Birds* 574), and Antigonus of Carystus in the third century B.C. quotes *Hymn to Hermes* 51. Other direct quotations are considerably later than that, but several echoes, at least, of the *Hymn to Demeter* are to be found among Hellenistic poets with their interest in the Mysteries.[1] This suggests that the Alexandrian Homerists did not consider the bulk of the corpus to be by Homer. Curiously enough the *Hymn to Demeter*, in spite of its relatively early though post-Homeric date, its superior poetical quality and its intrinsic religious interest, nearly passed into oblivion in the medieval period and survives only in a single manuscript (the early fifteenth-century Mosquensis, now in Leiden); whereas the remainder of the corpus was evidently much favoured by monks and copyists. The *editio princeps* by Demetrius Chalcocondyles, which appeared in Florence in 1488, was one of the earliest Greek texts to be printed.

[1] Richardson (1974) 68ff.

The *Hymn to Demeter* has considerable charm as well as religious and antiquarian appeal. It opens with the abduction, as she gathers flowers, of the young Persephone by Hades king of the underworld, who emerges from beneath the earth with his chariot. Her mother Demeter is heart-broken at the loss, and when she discovers from Helios, the Sun, that Zeus had condoned the abduction she abandons Olympus in disgust – the theme is an ancient Mesopotamian one – and wanders over the earth disguised as an old woman, until eventually she meets the daughters of King Celeus at Eleusis and is engaged to nurse the baby prince Demophon. She holds him in the fire each night to make him immortal, but is discovered by the child's mother; her identity revealed, she commands the building of a temple for herself there at Eleusis. Meanwhile the abandonment of her normal fertility functions has caused a famine, and Zeus is compelled to order Persephone's release from the underworld – where, however, she has been tricked into eating a single pomegranate seed and so is bound to return to Hades' realm for a third of each year (the time when the soil is infertile). But for the moment she is re-united with her mother and fertility returns to the stricken earth. Demeter instructs the Eleusinian princes in her rituals, which confer a better lot after death.

Little is revealed, or could be, about the secrets of the Mysteries themselves, but the Hymn is nevertheless a powerful piece of propaganda for Eleusis and the cult of the two goddesses. Athens, which took over Eleusis before 550 B.C., is not mentioned, which suggests that the poem was composed before this date. Other omissions, like the absence of reference to Iacchus, to the clan of Kerykes and to Triptolemus in his role of agrarian hero, are also unlikely to result from deliberate archaizing, and confirm that the hymn is indeed earlier than the mid-sixth century. Diction and style, which are still oral or nearly so, suggest a date toward the end of the seventh century, but here (as always with these poems) one is largely guessing. In any event the Hymn is no empty or artificial performance, but a religious document that provides an august aetiology of the foundation of the cult at Eleusis, as well as being a charter for the priestly administration of the Mysteries by the main noble families. In its emphasis on the fertility powers of Demeter and her daughter, specifically through Persephone's alternation between Olympus and the world below, it contrives to suggest a valid escape for initiates from the horrors of contemporary eschatology:

> And all the broad earth was weighed down with foliage
> and flowers; and Demeter made her way and revealed to the law-giving kings
> – to Triptolemus and Diocles, smiter of horses,
> and mighty Eumolpus and Celeus leader of the people –
> the performance of her sacred rituals, and declared her rites to all of them,
> her solemn rites, which are in no way to be transgressed, or learned by others,

or declaimed; for great reverence for the goddesses restrains the voice.
Blessed among men who dwell on earth is he who has seen these things;
but whosoever is uninitiated into the rituals, and has no share in them,
    nevermore
has a similar portion when he is dead, beneath the dank darkness. (472–82)

The *Hymn to Apollo* is artistically uneven, but only slightly less important
than the Demeter-hymn from a historical and religious point of view. It is
commonly regarded as a blend of two originally separate hymns, one to the
Delian, the other to the Pythian Apollo. The view has been disputed, but in
essence is probably correct.[1] Verses 1 to 178 tell of the goddess Leto's search
for a birthplace for Apollo, and of her eventually giving birth to the god in the
infertile little island of Delos. A rather odd prologue, perhaps added after
the main composition was complete, depicts the mature Apollo and the almost
excessive reverence paid him by the other Olympians. At the end of this
portion comes a *sphragis* or 'seal', a kind of signature by the composer, who
declares himself to be a blind man from rugged Chios (172). 177f. are a clearly
terminal formula: 'But I shall not cease from hymning Apollo of the silver·
bow, to whom fair-tressed Leto gave birth.' The three inconsequential verses
that immediately follow in our version connect the god with Lycia, Maeonia
and Miletus as well as with Delos (179–81); their purpose seems to be to widen
his range beyond the cult-place associated with his birth, and to provide a
transition to a distinct episode from which Delos is entirely absent. They are
followed, with no greater coherence, by the beginning, at least, of a loose
description of his progress down from Olympus to Pytho, the later Delphi.
Next the poet asks what aspect of the god he is to sing (207ff.); rejecting the
theme of his female conquests, he decides to relate how he passed through
many places in search of a site for his oracle.

This all looks like the start of a fresh hymn, or at least a separately-composed
episode designed to extend the Delian part. There is an obvious parallel with
the main theme of that part (the search for a site for his birth), which is reinforced by the catalogues of places visited in each case (216ff. and 30ff.). Such
themes presumably occurred in other hymns, too, but in the present case there
are signs of deliberate imitation and expansion, with the Delian part providing
the starting-point. For example the rhetorical enquiry about which aspect of
the god to celebrate appears in a simpler form in the Delian section (19–25),
and the more elaborate Pythian version (207ff.) also seems the more contrived.
Other thematic parallels are to be seen in Hera's wrath (95–101 and 305–55,
the latter an insertion of some kind) and in the barrenness of the chosen site
and the ability of the priests to live off sacrifices (54–60, developed in 529–37).

---

[1] Disputed most recently by West (1975) 161ff.; see further Kirk in Brillante, Cantilena and
Pavese (1981) 163–81.

Not even the Delian portion is a consistent and completely coherent composition; like most sub-epic poetry it uses pre-existing materials quite loosely at times. Its catalogue of places, for instance, begins as a list of Apollo's chief worshippers and turns into a gazetteer of Aegean promontories and islands; moreover, verse 81, with its mention of an oracle that can surely never have been an important feature of the early cult on Delos, is probably an intrusion from the Pythian part. Nevertheless the most probable conclusion is that the Delian part has provided the idea, and to a certain extent the model, for the Pythian.

Linguistically the Hymn is fairly homogeneous, except that the Pythian part observes the effects of the lost letter digamma more scrupulously than does the Delian.[1] That in itself suggests separate authorship, and on a simple view of linguistic and stylistic development could be held to indicate priority not for the Delian but for the Pythian hymn. But archaizing and imitative poems, which all the Homeric Hymns are in some degree, do not respond to this simple view, and the digamma criterion has been shown to be erratic in other respects also.[2] A broader and more important difference in style and intention appears in the emphatic interest of the Pythian composer in aetiology: the explanation of the curious ritual involving newly-broken horses at Poseidon's sanctuary at Onchestus (230–8); the origin of Apollo's association with Telphousa, implied in his traditional epithet Telphousios (244–77 and 375–87); the name of Pytho itself, emphatically connected with the rotting, *puthein*, of the corpse of the dragon slain by Apollo at the site of his oracular shrine (363–74); the explanation of Apollo's epithet Delphinios and the establishment of his priesthood, which occupies the last 150 verses of the poem and involves Apollo turning into a *delphis*, dolphin, and in this form diverting a Cretan ship to Cirrha, the port of Pytho – it being apparently known on the mainland that the god was worshipped as Delphinios in Crete. Several of these aetiological excursuses are in a crabbed and prosaic style distinct from the relaxed and ample expression of the Delian poem, with its simpler structure and more carefully limited intentions. Whether or not this suggests specifically priestly intervention, it is hard to believe that the Delian part would not have a much stronger aetiological tinge if it were the copy, in some sense, with the Pythian part as model.

There are at least three internal indications of date in the aggregated Hymn. First, the lively description of the festival at Delos is earlier not only than Thucydides (who as we saw quotes a part of it), but also than the Persian Wars, which interrupted this sort of gathering for a generation or so. Second, the informative scholium on Pindar, *Nemeans* 2.1 asserts that the blind Chian

---

[1] Janko (1982) examines this and other linguistic characteristics in detail.
[2] Allen, Halliday and Sikes (1936) xcviff.; Richardson (1974) 53f. and 334f.

singer of the Delian hymn was Cynaethus of Chios, a rhapsode who according to the same source was the first to perform Homer to the Syracusans in 504 B.C.[1] Third, the apparent prophecy after the event in verses 540–3 looks like a further reference to the re-organizing of the cult and games by the neighbouring states at the end of the First Sacred War in 586 B.C. The reference at 295–7 to the stone temple-floor of Trophonius and Agamedes might also be adduced, since that temple was burned in 548 (according to Pausanias 10.5.5); on the other hand deliberate archaizing is more likely with this well-known event than with the other and less conspicuous instances. Together, at least, these internal clues may be held to suggest a date later than 586 for the Pythian part. They do not, however, preclude a somewhat earlier date for the Delian portion, once we assume that the blind Chiote was not in fact Cynaethus (who may still have had something to do with the Pythian part) but, perhaps, the product of a pious effort to credit the hymn to Homer himself. On stylistic grounds it is tempting to push the Delian hymn back to the beginning of the sixth century, or less plausibly to the end of the seventh.

The *Hymn to Hermes* and the *Hymn to Aphrodite* must be dealt with more summarily, although they, too, are of interest for the history both of religion and of literature. The former relates how Hermes was 'born at dawn, was playing the lyre at midday and stole far-darting Apollo's cattle in the evening' (17f.). By far the greater part of the hymn is devoted to the theft of Apollo's cattle by the infant Hermes (68–507). It ends with Zeus and the now mollified Apollo agreeing on the young god's future prerogatives, but the tone throughout is one of ponderous irreverence and rustic humour rather than aetiological investigation. The language is more crabbed and difficult, containing fewer purely Homeric elements, than that of the other long hymns; it is notable for some conspicuous Attic and Boeotian forms. The tale of Apollo's cattle is at least as old as Hesiod's *Ehoiai*, but the style of humour (in which there is little that appears genuinely naive) and the obviously literate pastiche suggest as the general period of composition the late archaic or full classical age – some time, that is, between the late sixth and early fourth century B.C.

The *Hymn to Aphrodite* is shorter and structurally simpler, relating as it does the goddess' seduction of the young Anchises followed by her prediction of the birth and future of their child Aeneas. Linguistically it is the most Homeric of the long hymns – that is to say, of all of them; it is replete with Homeric verses, half-verses and formulas, very conventionally used, although like all the long hymns it also shows the influence of the Hesiodic tradition. Of itself that reveals little about the date of composition, but the sharing of a few unusual expressions with the *Hymn to Demeter*, together with at least one probable doublet-verse at 98 (which is more compatible with rhapsodic than

---

[1] West (1975).

with more fully literate techniques), suggests a relatively early date, say the early sixth century. Yet no period down to the end of the fifth century can be excluded; after that the production of this kind of straightforwardly archaizing imitation (at least at this relatively high poetical level) becomes improbable. For the Hymn is quite charming in places, especially in the sexual encounter itself (particularly 143–75) and in Aphrodite's description of the fate of Tithonus, which she adduces as reason for not making her own lover immortal. This last passage gives a taste of the Hymns at their best and may fittingly conclude the present brief account:

> Again, golden-throned Dawn ravished Tithonus away,
> another of your family, and like the immortal gods.
> She went to ask Kronos' son, of the dark clouds,
> for him to be immortal and live for the sum of days,
> and Zeus nodded and fulfilled her prayer.
> Foolish she was, lady Dawn, for she did not think in her heart
> of asking for youth, and stripping off destructive old age.
> So Tithonus, for as long as lovely youth possessed him,
> rejoiced in early-born, golden-throned Dawn
> and dwelt by the streams of Okeanos at the ends of the earth;
> but when the first grey hairs poured down
> from his beautiful head and noble beard
> the lady Dawn kept away from his bed –
> but cosseted him still, keeping him in her halls,
> with food and ambrosia, and gave him fair clothing.
> But when hateful old age hastened fully upon him,
> and he could not move or raise up any of his limbs,
> this seemed to her in her heart to be the best plan:
> she placed him in a chamber and closed the shining doors.
> His voice flows on unending, but there is no strength,
> such as was present before, in his gnarled limbs. (218–38)

4

ELEGY AND IAMBUS

I. ARCHILOCHUS

Archilochus is in many ways the focal point for any discussion of the development of literature in the seventh century, since he is the first Greek writer to take his material almost entirely from what he claims to be his own experience and emotions, rather than from the stock of tradition.

By a happy coincidence this central figure is also precisely datable. He was a contemporary of Gyges, king of Lydia *c.* 687–652 (fr. 19).[1] He alludes to the destruction of Magnesia by the Cimmerian Treres in or about the latter year (fr. 20), and seems himself to have been of military age at the time. In fr. 122 he speaks of the recent wonder of a total eclipse of the sun, which (despite recent attempts to revive the claims of 711 or 557) must be the eclipse of 6 April 648.

Archilochus the Parian presents himself as a man of few illusions, a rebel against the values and assumptions of the aristocratic society in which he found himself. A plausible explanation of this tension, to which we owe much of the interest of Archilochus' work, is to be found in the circumstances of his life. He came of a notable family. His grandfather (or great-grandfather?) Tellis had joined in taking the cult of Demeter to Thasos towards the end of the eighth century, and was to be immortalized in a great painting at Delphi by the Thasian Polygnotus (Paus. 10.28.3). The poet's father, Telesicles, also won distinction, as the founder of the Parian colony on Thasos. But if we may believe a passage (fr. 295) in which the fifth-century writer Critias is quoted as criticizing Archilochus for revealing damaging information about himself in his poetry, his mother was a slave, Enipo, and Archilochus was compelled by poverty to leave Paros and seek his fortune abroad. So Archilochus went to Thasos and served there as a soldier – we do not know whether he was actually a mercenary – and later, back in Paros, he helped to defend the island against attacks from neighbouring Naxos. In one such engagement he was killed by a Naxian named Calondas.

---

[1] Jacoby (1941) 99. All fragments in this chapter are numbered as in *IEG*.

ARCHILOCHUS

For all we know, Archilochus was a turbulent and even disreputable figure in his lifetime; but after his death his memory was treated with the religious veneration the Greeks gave to their writers of genius. There is ample evidence in the many references to him in later literature that he had achieved the status of a classic,[1] fit to be mentioned in the same breath as Homer and Hesiod, and from a text discovered on Paros in 1949 we now have detailed information about the kind of hagiography he inspired. The Inscription of Mnesiepes was set up in the mid-third century B.C. to record how Mnesiepes, on the instruction of Apollo's oracle, built a *temenos* (sacred precinct) for the worship of the Muses, Apollo, Dionysus and other deities, and in honour of Archilochus.[2] 'We call the place the Archilocheion and we set up the altars and we sacrifice both to the gods and to Archilochus and we pay him honour, as the god instructed through his oracle.' The text continues with the story of Archilochus' life and quotations from his works. Much is made of his miraculous meeting with the Muses, who gave him a lyre; in its essentials the story is reminiscent of Hesiod's encounter on Mt Helicon (see above, p. 53), but there is nothing to suggest that he told it himself.

Archilochus writes so vividly that critics have been inclined to treat his poetry as essentially autobiographical, on the assumption that the first person singular will normally refer to the poet himself 'in real life'. But we have the clear evidence of Aristotle (*Rhet.* 1418b23ff.) that he sometimes used dramatic *personae* – Charon the carpenter in fr. 19, a father speaking about his daughter in fr. 122 – and in any case, as K. J. Dover has pointed out, it is true of songs in general, and particularly of songs in pre-literate societies, that the first person may refer to any personality the composer chooses.[3] It is characteristic of songs to deal with the 'I' and the here and now, but there is no reason why they should be confined to the persons and situations of documentary reality. And M. L. West has argued that it may have been a particular feature of the type of poetry the ancients called 'iambus' to use imaginary characters and situations.[4] Since all the surviving work of Archilochus is in a fragmentary state it is difficult in many cases to be sure of the dramatic context of the poems; some of the apparently autobiographical avowals may well have been made by fictitious characters, and even when 'Archilochus' is the speaker there is no certainty that he was not assuming a role – Archilochus the mercenary soldier, the boon companion, the sexual adventurer, etc. On the other hand his addressees Glaucus and Pericles appear to have been real people,[5] and it would be absurd to claim that a poet composing songs for performance

[1] Cf. the list given by Tarditi (1968) 232–8.
[2] Text in Lasserre (1958); Tarditi (1968).
[3] Dover (1964) 199–212.
[4] West (1974) 22–39.
[5] For the monument on Thasos to Glaucus son of Leptines see Pouilloux (1964) 20f.

77

in a small community in which everyone knew everyone else would not exploit his audience's knowledge of that society and its relationships. For the literary critic, the historical questions are not the most important ones; it is possible to study – and enjoy – Archilochus' poetry without being able to ascertain the connexion between the poet's life and the picture he presents of it in the poems. But there may be great significance in the fact that he chose to make the individual's feelings and experiences the main subject matter of his poetry.

Formally Archilochus is an interesting mixture of the traditional and the radically new. In diction and phrasing he relies heavily on the epic,[1] but he also introduces a range of modern words and idioms, some of them quite earthy, and while he can hardly have invented his various metres from nothing – it is surely right to think of a flourishing tradition of popular song behind him – he seems to have been the major innovator who turned these every-day forms into an important literary medium. For, like Catullus, Archilochus makes a serious claim on our attention even when his subject matter is slight and trivial; his control over language and metre is so powerful that he forces us to respect his choices. Perhaps there is a special relevance to his times in the particular gestures he elects to make: the abandonment of grandly heroic attitudes in favour of a new unsentimental honesty, an iconoclastic and flippant tone of voice coupled with deep awareness of traditional truths. One of the most famous fragments (5) is his claim that he threw away his shield, a provocative rejection of one sort of image of 'the hero', but not in fact alien to some strands of thought in Homer (Odysseus might well have done the same):[2]

ἀσπίδι μὲν Σαΐων τις ἀγάλλεται, ἣν παρὰ θάμνωι,
ἔντος ἀμώμητον, κάλλιπον οὐκ ἐθέλων·
αὐτὸν δ' ἐξεσάωσα. τί μοι μέλει ἀσπὶς ἐκείνη;
ἐρρέτω· ἐξαῦτις κτήσομαι οὐ κακίω.

Some Saian prides himself upon my shield, a splendid piece of equipment, which I left by a thorn-bush – and I didn't leave it willingly. But I saved myself. Why should I mind about that shield? Let it go: I'll get another just as good.

Another piece (fr. 13), one of his most serious and dignified passages, which is usually cited as an example of the strong epic influence on his elegiac poems, still shows his distinctive qualities of directness and 'plain speaking', what G. S. Kirk has well described as his 'passionate and sardonic self-control':[3]

κήδεα μὲν στονόεντα Περίκλεες οὔτέ τις ἀστῶν
μεμφόμενος θαλίηις τέρψεται οὐδὲ πόλις·
τοίους γὰρ κατὰ κῦμα πολυφλοίσβοιο θαλάσσης
ἔκλυσεν, οἰδαλέους δ' ἀμφ' ὀδύνηις ἔχομεν

---

[1] Page (1964) 125–62.
[2] Lloyd-Jones (1971) 38–41; Seidensticker (1978).
[3] Kirk (1977) 41. For a similar ethos cf. frs. 11, 16, 17, 128, 131, 132.

ARCHILOCHUS

πνεύμονας. ἀλλὰ θεοὶ γὰρ ἀνηκέστοισι κακοῖσιν   5
ὦ φίλ' ἐπὶ κρατερὴν τλημοσύνην ἔθεσαν
φάρμακον. ἄλλοτε ἄλλος ἔχει τόδε· νῦν μὲν ἐς ἡμέας
ἐτράπεθ', αἱματόεν δ' ἕλκος ἀναστένομεν,
ἐξαῦτις δ' ἑτέρους ἐπαμείψεται. ἀλλὰ τάχιστα
τλῆτε, γυναικεῖον πένθος ἀπωσάμενοι.   10

No man in all our city, Pericles, will take pleasure in festivities as he mourns
these sad sorrows. Such were the men drowned by the waves of the surging sea;
and our lungs are swollen with grief. But, friend, the gods have given us a remedy
for desperate ills – endurance. First one man has trouble and then another:
now we are afflicted and grieve over the bleeding wound, but tomorrow it will
be someone else's turn. So now endure and put away feminine tears.

The thoughts as well as their expression are all traditional, but the image of
lungs swollen with grief is particularly telling in a context of men drowned
at sea, and the paradox of man's situation is finely brought out by 5–7, in the
contrast between the 'incurable' evils that he must suffer and the 'remedy'
the gods offer for them, which is entirely dependent on man's own will; the
enjambment of τλῆτε makes the point strongly.

The fragments of Archilochus are arranged by editors according to their
metrical form, the main divisions being elegy, iambic trimeter, trochaic tetrameter catalectic, and 'epodes' or repeating combinations of various iambic,
trochaic, and dactylic units in which the characteristic pattern is one longer line
followed by one (or two) shorter (e.g. iambic trimeter plus hemiepes, iambic
trimeter plus iambic dimeter).[1] This is convenient and orderly, but it may
imply greater distinctions between the different metrical patterns than were
felt by Archilochus and his contemporaries. In fact it makes sense to group
all the non-elegiac metres under the general heading 'iambus',[2] which seems
to have been the ancients' term for poetry of an informal every-day kind which
was designed essentially to entertain. The occasions on which iambus might
be performed must have overlapped to some extent with those thought appropriate for elegy, but the elegists seem to have sought some degree of decorum
in the poems they composed for performance at parties, on campaign, or in
public gatherings; they apparently avoided both obscene language and the
sort of topic that later belonged to the world of comedy – sex, food, violent
abuse of individuals – all of which are regular ingredients of iambus. In
Archilochus' rather scanty elegiac fragments we find no obscenity (though
this could be a matter of chance); what we do find is as much wit, vigour and
realism as in his other poems, and the homogeneity of tone and outlook
throughout his work is more striking than differences corresponding to

[1] See Metrical Appendix.
[2] West (1974) 22–39.

79

formal variations. Probably there was some difference in performance between elegy and iambus: elegy was commonly sung to the accompaniment of the pipe, *aulos*, whereas the iambic trimeters and trochaic tetrameters would be recited (or chanted?) and the epodes sung, presumably to an instrument, though we do not know which. Since for us as modern readers the similarities are greater than the differences, the poems will be considered by theme rather than according to formal criteria.

One important *persona* adopted by Archilochus is that of the professional soldier, full of the hard-bitten cynicism of his calling. There is little romance in the profession of a mercenary; he is valued only while the fighting lasts, as Archilochus tells his friend Glaucus (fr. 15: elegiacs). He has no time for the kind of commander whose pride is in his good looks: better a short, bow-legged figure so long as he has a stout heart (fr. 114: tetrameters). He looks at the casualty list with a knowing eye: seven dead, a thousand claiming the credit (fr. 101: tetrameters). For all we know some of the stray remarks quoted from Archilochus about Paros and Thasos could come from similar contexts: the tone is equally disenchanted and forthright. 'Goodbye to Paros and its figs and seafaring' (fr. 116); 'the woes of all the Greeks have come together in Thasos' (fr. 102); 'Thasos, thrice miserable city . . . .' (fr. 228); 'it stands like a donkey's back, clad in wild forests' (fr. 21, a view of Thasos).

The soldier must be tough, self-reliant, living for the present: this is the tone of several fragments which seem to come from songs designed for the military drinking party. In fr. 2 (elegiacs) he celebrates his self-sufficiency:

> In my spear is my kneaded bread, in my spear is my wine of Ismarus, and on my spear I lean to drink it.

Fr. 4 (again elegiacs) is more boisterous:

> Come on, take your cup; go over the swift ship's benches and wrench off the lids of the casks, take the red wine off the lees. We shan't be able to stay sober on this watch.

But the soldier could also offer exhortations to his comrades in more serious vein, as in fr. 128 (tetrameters), which though addressed to his own heart has obvious relevance for his audience. Its advice is 'nothing too much' – neither excessive exhilaration in victory nor excessive grief in defeat: 'understand the rhythm that controls men's lives' (γίνωσκε δ' οἷος ῥυσμὸς ἀνθρώπους ἔχει). Another tetrameter fragment (130) expresses the same traditional idea of mutability, again with Archilochus' distinctive vigour: 'often the gods raise up men prostrated on the black earth by their troubles, and often they knock flat on their faces men who've stood firm, on a sure footing – and then there is plenty of trouble for them and they wander, needy and robbed of their wits'. It may well be that the many fragments which refer to contemporary events come from similar poems of advice or exhortation to companions, pieces like fr. 105, which is quoted as a political allegory:

See, Glaucus. Already the deep sea is troubled with waves, and around the peaks of Gyrae the cloud stands upright, a storm-signal. From the unexpectedness of it, fear seizes me.

Many of the other fragments in tetrameters refer to the conflicts of the times (cf. 88, 89, 91, 93, 94, 96, 98), but they are too mutilated to give us a clear knowledge of the details. One common feature is clearly traceable: the poet is always committed, always expressing feelings and opinions about events, in a way that will influence an audience. Fr. 20 (iambic trimeters) is typical: 'I weep for the troubles of the Thasians, not for the Magnesians.'[1]

Fr. 1 sums up what is most remarkable about Archilochus, the fact that he presents himself as both man of action and poet: there is no suggestion that his poetic activity is a mere pastime for his moments of leisure.

εἰμὶ δ' ἐγὼ θεράπων μὲν 'Ενυαλίοιο ἄνακτος
καὶ Μουσέων ἐρατὸν δῶρον ἐπιστάμενος.

I am a servant of Lord Enyalios [Ares] and I understand the lovely gift of the Muses.

As Denys Page remarked, 'a social revolution is epitomised in this couplet':[2] it is inconceivable in Homer that the fighting man and the poet could be one and the same person. And it is typical that in expressing so novel an idea Archilochus should use language that is very closely modelled on the epic. He says very little elsewhere about his role as poet, though perhaps there is a hint of artistic self-consciousness in fr. 120: 'I know how to strike up the dithyramb, the lovely song of Lord Dionysus, when my wits are thunderstruck with wine.'

Archilochus the lover is another familiar figure in the poems (though 'lover' is too narrow a term for this frank celebrant of sex). The fragments on sexual themes range from the delicate and sensuous ('she rejoiced in the myrtle and the fair flower of the rose', fr. 30, cf. 31) to the coarsely explicit ('... as a Thracian or a Phrygian sucks his barley beer through a tube; and she was leaning forward, working', fr. 42; cf. 43, 119, 152, 252). Often his choice of expression is traditional: desire is the 'liquefier of the limbs' as eros is in Hesiod (*Theog.* 121) and it 'overpowers' him as eros conquered Zeus in the *Iliad* (14.315f.): ἀλλά μ' ὁ λυσιμελὴς ὤταῖρε δάμναται πόθος (fr. 196). His descriptions of the physical symptoms of passion owe their phrasing to the epic, but their intensity foreshadows Sappho's:

[1] For the historical background cf. Jacoby (1941) 104–7.
[2] Page (1964) 134.

ELEGY AND IAMBUS

δύστηνος ἔγκειμαι πόθωι,
ἄψυχος, χαλεπῆισι θεῶν ὀδύνηισιν ἕκητι
πεπαρμένος δι' ὀστέων.   (fr. 193)

I'm a helpless victim of desire, the life gone out of me, pierced through the
bones by the gods' bitter pains.

τοῖος γὰρ φιλότητος ἔρως ὑπὸ καρδίην ἐλυσθεὶς
πολλὴν κατ' ἀχλὺν ὀμμάτων ἔχευεν,
κλέψας ἐκ στηθέων ἀπαλὰς φρένας.   (fr. 191)

For such is the craving for love that has coiled itself up in my heart and dimmed
my eyes, robbing my breast of its tender senses.[1]

But he is very different, too, from Sappho and the other lyric poets – in form
(see p. 161), in range of subject matter and vocabulary, and in his apparently
exclusive concentration on heterosexual activity. The choice of a sexual theme
by Archilochus certainly does not imply a 'love poem': some of the verses
seem to come from the sort of entertaining narratives of low-life erotic adventure that we find in Hipponax (see pp. 117ff.), others evidently belong to poems
of violent invective, the lampoons which brought Archilochus his greatest
fame (or notoriety, cf. Pindar, *Pyth.* 2.54–6, where he is described as 'fattening
himself on hate and heavy words').

According to ancient tradition his favourite targets were a Parian called
Lycambes and his daughters, Neobule and her younger sister. The story went
that Lycambes promised Neobule to Archilochus as his wife, but then insulted
him by breaking the contract, and the poet retaliated with abuse so virulent
that the family (or some of them) committed suicide.[2] The evidence is bafflingly
difficult to assess, and the discovery of a new papyrus fragment which drama-
tizes the seduction of the younger daughter only adds to the complexity of the
problem.[3] The best known piece is fr. 172, the opening of a long attack on
Lycambes:

πάτερ Λυκάμβα, ποῖον ἐφράσω τόδε;
τίς σὰς παρήειρε φρένας
ἧις τὸ πρὶν ἠρήρησθα; νῦν δὲ δὴ πολὺς
ἀστοῖσι φαίνεαι γέλως.

Father Lycambes, what's this you've thought up? Who has relieved you of your
wits, which used to be so sound? Now you've made yourself a great laughing-
stock for the townsfolk.

In this poem (probably frs. 172–81) Archilochus used an animal fable, the
story of the fox and the eagle, to abuse the faithlessness of Lycambes, who

---

[1] The translation supplies the first person; the Greek does not make clear whose the feelings are.
[2] Evidence in West (1974) 26f.; *IEG* 1, 15 and 63f.
[3] *P.Colon.* 7511 = *SLG* 5478, West fr. 196A.

like the eagle has betrayed a friend and deserves the same hideous retribution. Evidently the poet shamed the daughters by describing in obscene detail an orgy in which he claimed they had taken part; some of the extant fragments (e.g. 48, 49, 51–4) may belong to this poem (or series of poems), but we have only teasing scraps of papyrus and very short quotations to judge from. The new fragment, the longest surviving piece of Archilochus, combines abuse of Neobule with a rather delicate description of how the younger daughter was seduced; it is difficult to see this as a purely defamatory poem,[1] though some degree of insult is clearly intended. An interesting approach to the story of Lycambes and his daughters has recently been made by M. L. West, who raises the possibility that they were 'not living contemporaries of Archilochus but stock characters in a traditional entertainment'.[2] The poet's freedom to assume different *personae* and to create fictitious situations needs always to be remembered; on the other hand we should avoid making the assumption that invective was never used by Archilochus in a direct and personal way. We know after all that the victims of Hipponax (and in a later age those of Catullus) were real enough.

The new fragment deserves quotation in full:[3]

> πάμπαν ἀποσχόμενος·
> ἶσον δὲ τολμ[
>
> εἰ δ' ὦν ἐπείγεαι καί σε θυμὸς ἰθύει,
> ἔστιν ἐν ἡμετέρου
> ἣ νῦν μέγ' ἱμείρε[ι   5
>
> καλὴ τέρεινα παρθένος· δοκέω δέ μι[ν
> εἶδος ἄμωμον ἔχειν·
> τὴν δὴ σὺ πένθ[
>
> τοσαῦτ' ἐφώνει· τὴν δ' ἐγὼ ἀνταμει[βόμην·
> ''Αμφιμεδοῦς θύγατερ   10
> ἐσθλῆς τε καὶ [περίφρονος
>
> γυναικός, ἣν νῦν γῆ κατ' εὐρώεσσ' ἔ[χει,
> τ]έρψιές εἰσι θεῆς
> πολλαὶ νέοισιν ἀνδ[ράσιν
>
> παρὲξ τὸ θεῖον χρῆμα· τῶν τις ἀρκέσε[ι.   15
> τ]αῦτα δ' ἐπ' ἡσυχίης
> εὖτ' ἂν μελανθῆ[

---

[1] As Merkelbach thinks it is (1974) 113.

[2] West (1974) 27. West also suspects (28) that Archilochus' presentation of himself as a bastard is similar role playing, noting that the name Enipo (see above, p. 76) 'with its connotation of ἐνιπαί ['abuse'] is suspiciously apt for an iambographer's mother'.

[3] Text from *SLG*; see Appendix for bibliography.

ἐ]γώ τε καὶ σὺ σὺν θεῶι βουλεύσομεν·
π]είσομαι ὥς με κέλεαι·
πολλόν μ' ε[20

θρ]ιγκοῦ δ' ἔνερθε καὶ πυλέων ὑποφ[
μ]ή τι μέγαιρε, φίλη·
σχήσω γὰρ ἐς ποη[φόρους

κ]ήπους. τὸ δὴ νῦν γνῶθι· Νεοβούλη[
ἄ]λλος ἀνὴρ ἐχέτω·   25
αἰαῖ πέπειρα δ .[

ἄν]θος δ' ἀπερρύηκε παρθενήιον
κ]αὶ χάρις ἢ πρὶν ἐπῆν·
κόρον γὰρ οὐκ[

..]ης δὲ μέτρ' ἔφηνε μαινόλις γυνή·   30
ἐς] κόρακας ἄπεχε·
μὴ τοῦτ' ἐφοῖτ' αν[

ὅ]πως ἐγὼ γυναῖκα τ[ο]ιαύτην ἔχων
γεί]τοσι χάρμ' ἔσομαι·
πολλὸν σὲ βούλο[μαι πάρος·   35

σὺ] μὲν γὰρ οὔτ' ἄπιστος οὔτε διπλόη,
ἡ δ]ὲ μάλ' ὀξυτέρη,
πολλοὺς δὲ ποιεῖτα[ι

δέ]δοιχ' ὅπως μὴ τυφλὰ κἀλιτήμερα
σπ]ουδῆι ἐπειγόμενος   40
τὼς ὥσπερ ἡ κ[ύων τέκω.'

τοσ]αῦτ' ἐφώνεον· παρθένον δ' ἐν ἄνθε[σιν
τηλ]εθάεσσι λαβὼν
ἔκλινα, μαλθακῆι δ[έ μιν

χλαί]νηι καλύψας, αὐχέν' ἀγκάληις ἔχω[ν,   45
δεί]ματι π..[.].μένην
τὼς ὥστε νέβρ[

μαჳ]ῶν τε χερσὶν ἠπίως ἐφηψάμην
ἧιπε]ρ ἔφηνε νέον
ἥβης ἐπήλυσις χρόα·   50

ἅπαν τ]ε σῶμα καλὸν ἀμφαφώμενος
λευκ]ὸν ἀφῆκα μένος
ξανθῆς ἐπιψαύ[ων τριχός.

'. . . but if you're in a hurry and can't wait for me
there's another girl in our house who's quite ready
to marry, a pretty girl, just right for you.'
That was what she said, but I can talk too.
'Daughter of dear Amphimedo,' I said,
'(a fine woman she was – pity she's dead)
there are plenty of kinds of pretty play

84

young men and girls can know and not go all the way
– something like that will do. As for marrying,
we'll talk about that again when your mourning
is folded away, god willing. But now
I'll be good, I promise – I do know how.
Don't be hard, darling. Truly I'll stay
out on the garden-grass, not force the doorway
– just try. But as for that sister of yours,
someone else can have her. The bloom's gone – she's coarse
– the charm too (she had it) – now she's on heat
the whole time, can't keep away from it –
damn her, don't let anyone saddle me with that.
With a wife like she is I shouldn't half
give the nice neighbours a belly-laugh.
You're all right, darling. You're simple and straight
– she takes her meat off anyone's plate.
I'd be afraid if I married her
my children would be like the bitch's litter
– born blind, and several months too early.'
But I'd talked enough. I laid the girl
down among the flowers. A soft cloak spread,
my arm round her neck, I comforted
her fear. The fawn soon ceased to flee.
Over her breasts my hands moved gently,
the new-formed girlhood she bared for me,
over all her body, the young skin bare;
I spilt my white force, just touching her yellow hair.

(tr. Martin Robertson)

The nearest parallel is fr. 23, another narrative (with reported conversation) of what appears to be a seduction scene; unfortunately the context here is not clear in detail.[1]

The aggressive tone adopted against Lycambes and Neobule is often heard in Archilochus' poetry directed against other (or no longer identifiable) targets: 'The hated babbler prowled about the house' (fr. 297); 'I long to fight you, as a man thirsts to drink' (fr. 125); 'One great principle I hold, to requite evil with terrible evil' (fr. 126); 'O Lord Apollo, do you also punish the guilty, destroy them as you know how' (fr. 26). The papyrus from Cologne that preserves fr. 196A also contains a short piece which amplifies fr. 188 and evidently was an important model for Horace (*Epod.* 8, *Odes* 1.25 and 4.13). It is an attack on an ageing woman (who may or may not be Neobule):

οὐκέ]θ᾽ ὁμῶς θάλλεις ἁπαλὸν χρόα, κάρφετα[ι γὰρ ἤδη
ὄγμοι]ς, κακοῦ δὲ γήραος καθαιρεῖ
.....], ἀφ᾽ ἱμερτοῦ δὲ θορὼν γλυκὺς ἵμερος π[ροσώπου

[1] Discussed by West (1974) 118–20.

85

πέπτω]κεν· ἦ γὰρ πολλὰ δή σ' ἐπῆιξεν
πνεύμ]ατα χειμερίων ἀνέμων ⟨　⟩ πολλάκις δε[

You don't bloom any more: your skin isn't soft, it's dried up with furrowing
wrinkles, and the...of nasty old age overpowers (you), and the sweet allure
has taken a leap and left your once alluring face. Yes, you've been the target for
the blasts of winter wind, and often...

Friends, too, were attacked, but without knowing the full context we cannot
tell how seriously. Some of these fragments could come from poems of fairly
light-hearted banter, like fr. 124 to Pericles, who is berated for coming to a
party 'like a man from Mykonos', uninvited and without a present, but none
the less having plenty to drink: 'Your belly perverted your mind and your
wits into shameful behaviour.' Fr. 185, which announces to one Cerycides that
it will tell the story of the fox and the monkey, sounds more threatening, as
though the addressee might have to be identified with the vain and foolish ape.

It would be particularly interesting to know more about the poems in which
the speaker is someone other than 'Archilochus'; fr. 19 and fr. 122 are identified as such by Aristotle (see above, p. 77), but there could well be others.
As they stand these fragments are cryptic – we have to guess the dramatic
context – but in each the tone is clear enough. In fr. 122, a father's remarks
about his daughter on the theme of 'wonders will never cease', the hyperbole
is witty and striking:

Nothing can be surprising any more or impossible or miraculous, now that Zeus,
father of the Olympians, has made night out of noonday, hiding the bright
sunlight,[1] and...fear has come upon mankind. After this men can believe
anything, expect anything. Don't any of you be surprised in future if land beasts
change places with dolphins and go to live in their salty pastures, and get to like
the sounding waves of the sea more than the land, while the dolphins prefer
the mountains.

Fr. 19, which rejects the riches of the great Gyges of Lydia, presents a
perfectly traditional sentiment – on the lines of 'nothing too much' and
'think mortal thoughts' – but the use of a 'man in the street', Charon the
carpenter, as speaker suggests that Archilochus gave it an original twist:

'οὔ μοι τὰ Γύγεω τοῦ πολυχρύσου μέλει,
οὐδ' εἷλέ πώ με ζῆλος, οὐδ' ἀγαίομαι
θεῶν ἔργα, μεγάλης δ' οὐκ ἐρέω τυραννίδος·
ἀπόπροθεν γάρ ἐστιν ὀφθαλμῶν ἐμῶν.'

'I have no interest in the property of golden Gyges. Envy has never taken hold
of me, and I don't begrudge what is the work of the gods or have any longing
to be a mighty tyrant. For these things are far beyond my sights.'

[1] The reference is to the total eclipse of the sun in 648 B.C. (see above p. 76).

Most scholars believe that Archilochus was a literate composer; but whether he was or not, more significant is the fact that literacy was established in Greece by his time (though we have no evidence for actual book production so early) and there was therefore more chance that his work could be recorded and widely disseminated. This is not to suggest that the initial 'publication' and much subsequent reiteration of the poems would not be oral; but it is hard to imagine Archilochus' being so popular in fifth-century Athens without the existence of a written tradition at some stage in the intervening generations. It is disappointing (though no surprise) that there was no place for so fine and important a poet in the Byzantine school curriculum, but the fact that he was read by the Alexandrian scholars makes possible the discovery of new texts in the papyri. After what has happened in the last decade it would be too pessimistic to suggest that we know as much of Archilochus now as we ever shall.

2. EARLY GREEK ELEGY: CALLINUS, TYRTAEUS, MIMNERMUS

The contemporaries of Archilochus whose work has survived confined themselves to elegy. The elegiac metre at first glance appears a hybrid, and has been regarded as an adaptation of the epic in the direction of lyric. Misleadingly described as an alternation of dactylic hexameters and pentameters to form a couplet, the metrical unit in fact consists of hexameter followed by two hemiepes with word division between each of the three elements; and it was the Romans who abridged the freedom of the earlier Greek poets by insisting that the end of the unit should coincide with the end of the sentence (see Metrical Appendix). Distinctions of genre are often clearer musically than metrically. Elegy was normally accompanied on the pipe, and is therefore quite distinct from the epic, which was chanted to the deep-voiced *cithara*, and from lyric, sung to the *lyra* or *barbitos*: of these only the elegy necessarily required two performers. The use of the pipe on campaign or at a party is known from Homer (*Il.* 10.13, 18.495), and the earliest elegiac specialists whose work has survived – Callinus, Tyrtaeus, Mimnermus – composed for precisely such occasions. From our knowledge of its later development we tend to think of elegy as above all the vehicle of lamentation and of short commemorative epigrams, funerary, dedicatory and so on. There is no evidence that these were among its primary functions at an early date. Archilochus used the form so variously that it may be doubted whether his occasional use of it in the context of grief (cf. fr. 13) is of any great significance. For the elegiac epigram our evidence is clear: the earliest elegiac inscriptions are of the sixth century, and in the seventh both dedications and commemoration of the dead were, if metrical, most commonly expressed in continuous hexameters.

Ancient scholars argued fruitlessly over the inventor of elegy, Archilochus, Callinus and Tyrtaeus all having their champions.[1] All that it clear is that the ancients possessed no earlier elegy than we ourselves possess, for the simple reason, no doubt, that these were the first elegists whose verses were committed to writing.

Callinus the Ephesian was an exact contemporary of Archilochus, whose experience of the Cimmerians and their 'heavy deeds' he shared (fr. 5A). He spoke of Magnesia at war with Ephesus before the Cimmerian sack (fr. 3) – that sack which moved Archilochus less than did the troubles of Thasos (above, p. 81); and he knew the Cimmerian tribe of the Treres who killed Gyges and burned Sardis in 652 B.C. His only substantial fragment is of twenty-one lines. It is a military song which strikes a discordant note amid the feasting, an appeal to the youth of Ionia to raise themselves from idleness and face the enemy (fr. 1):

μέχρις τέο κατάκεισθε; κότ' ἄλκιμον ἕξετε θυμόν,
ὦ νέοι; οὐδ' αἰδεῖσθ' ἀμφιπερικτίονας
ὧδε λίην μεθιέντες; ἐν εἰρήνηι δὲ δοκεῖτε
ἧσθαι, ἀτὰρ πόλεμος γαῖαν ἅπασαν ἔχει...

How long will you go on lounging? When will you show a bold spirit, young men? Do you not fear the scorn of neighbours round about, in your excessive idleness? You think you are sitting at peace, when war grips the whole land...

There is a lacuna at this point. The text resumes,

...and let each man as he dies make one final javelin-cast. For it is honourable and glorious for a man to fight against the enemy for his land and children and wedded wife. Death will come whenever the Fates spin their decree. But each man must go forward with spear upraised and stout heart covered by his shield, the moment war begins. There is no way a man can escape the destiny of death, not even if he were a child of immortal ancestors. Often a man avoids the fighting and the thud of spears, and comes home to meet the death that is his fate. But the people do not regard him as their special friend or grieve over him. But the warrior, if anything happens to him, is mourned by great and small. For the whole people feels grief when a brave man dies, and while he lives he is reckoned the equal of heroes. For they see him as a tower before their eyes, since all alone he does the work of many.

It is a stirring piece, evoking the world of Homer in a more straightforward manner than Archilochus. The appeal is direct and unadorned. The one simile in the passage, the comparison of a brave man to a tower, was already traditional (cf. *Od.* 11.556, of Ajax). In the context of patriotism and self-sacrifice we think of Hector; and there is a reminiscence of Hector's words to Andromache in *Il.* 6.487ff., that Death awaits the brave man and the coward alike, and of Sarpedon's similar remarks to Glaucus in 12.322ff. The diction is as traditional

[1] Didymus *ap.* Orion, *Et.Mag.* p. 57, and schol. on Ar. *Birds* 217; cf. Horace, *A.P.* 77.

as the sentiments it conveys. The vocabulary is taken almost entirely from the epic, and the structure is formulaic, of phrases constructed in an Homeric mould or actually Homeric, some of them slightly adapted to fit the 'pentameter' line. The whole effect is to remind the Ionians of the heroes whose descendants they claimed to be, and to induce in them a spirit of emulation of their famous ancestors. What is remarkable and makes Callinus a poet of quality is his ability to strike an unmistakable note of freshness and directness through the use of such wholly traditional and formulaic material.

Across the Aegean, in rich Laconia, Tyrtaeus sang of political and military themes in elegies no less 'Homeric' than those of his contemporary Callinus – a measure of the extent to which the Ionian epics had by now created among the Greeks a cultural unity which transcended dialect and ethnic rivalry. The name of Tyrtaeus' father, Archembrotus, is preserved; everything else about the poet's life is at best deduction from his verses, at worst mere fiction. The supposed incongruity of Ionic dialect in Dorian Sparta prompted a rumour of Milesian origin, and Plato (echoed by many later writers) even claimed him for Athens. But the authoritative tone he adopts in teaching the Spartan warrior-class its business seems to tell against a foreign origin; and the occasional Dorisms of his diction – first declension accusatives in -ὄς, a future in -εῦμεν – perhaps betray the accents of one to whom Ionic was unaccustomed.

For a hundred years from the latter part of the seventh century Sparta was to enjoy a heyday of cultivated living which has left its traces in ivory and gold, in bronze vessels of surprising workmanship, in pottery of the finest quality, and in the odes of Alcman. This prosperity had been dearly purchased by Tyrtaeus' generation, who fought and died to suppress a revolt of the rich land of Messenia, which, first conquered by their grandfathers in the last third of the eighth century, had become the foundation of the Spartan economy. This military crisis about the middle of the seventh century, and the political discontent to which the loss of Messenian holdings gave rise, inspired the whole of Tyrtaeus' poetic production, so far as we can tell from what has survived. The political crisis took a form which was to become a regular feature of Greek history: the demand for redistribution of land. Those whose income had fallen or ceased with the loss of Messenia were driven to the verge of revolution; their demands were the more pressing among a people uneasily holding down a population of serfs; and they were, moreover, citizen-warriors of a state in which political rights were virtually confined to the soldiery. Tyrtaeus rallied their loyalty by appealing to the divine origin of the existing order, and at the same time castigated their defeatism and breathed into them the spirit to fight and recover what had seemed lost.

His poem *Eunomia*, 'Good order', which survives in only a few fragments, seems to have recapitulated the history of Sparta, emphasizing the part played by divine providence in the development of the Spartan constitution (frs. 1, 2, 4). Perhaps this religious propaganda sufficed, perhaps the successful outcome of the war and the economic recovery which followed victory removed the pressure for political change. At any rate, the Spartan constitution survived the test.

The Messenian revolt can hardly have come as a surprise. Tyrtaeus describes the bitter twenty-year war which the Spartan king Theopompus waged to win that rich territory (fr. 5) – no doubt as an example of endurance to be emulated – and there is no hint of pity in his description of the conditions to which its inhabitants were reduced (frs. 6–7):

> ὥσπερ ὄνοι μεγάλοις ἄχθεσι τειρόμενοι,
> δεσποσύνοισι φέροντες ἀναγκαίης ὕπο λυγρῆς
> ἥμισυ πάνθ᾽ ὅσσων καρπὸν ἄρουρα φέρει.

> δεσπότας οἰμώзοντες, ὁμῶς ἄλοχοί τε καὶ αὐτοί,
> εὖτέ τιν᾽ οὐλομένη μοῖρα κίχοι θανάτου.

...like asses weighed down by huge burdens, under bitter compulsion paying their lords half of all crops their soil produces...groaning at their masters – themselves and their wives alike – till the terrible fate of death claimed them.

The rising was inevitable, and Tyrtaeus' became the voice of repression.

We are fortunate in having three poems called forth by the war which may be complete, or virtually so, in twenty-two, nineteen and sixteen couplets respectively. Probably chanted on the march, to a flute accompaniment, they vividly express the Spartan military ethic, the limited concept of the 'good man' (ἀνὴρ ἀγαθός) and of 'virtue' (ἀρετή) which undervalues all but the steadfast soldier, a concept notorious from its revival in the fifth century. In Tyrtaeus' day the concept was new. In Homer men are 'good' (ἀγαθός), but *good at* some particular skill – the war-cry, perhaps, or boxing, or healing (e.g. *Iliad* 2.408, 3.237, 2.732) – not simply good in the abstract. Similarly *arete* in Homer, as in Hesiod, is the quality of being good at something, in fact a word generally denoting success. The transformation of a particular skill into the sole criterion of moral worth was the achievement of Tyrtaeus' propaganda. He develops the definition in fr. 12. The very reflective nature of this piece, which contains none of the poet's usual exhortation to battle, has led some to think it spurious. But the language and sentiments are entirely characteristic of Tyrtaeus, and it is absurd to suppose him incapable of composing anything but martial elegies. What makes a man manly? the poet asks. Not skill at athletics nor the strength of the Cyclopes, not if he were swifter than the North Wind, fairer than Tithonus, richer than Midas, more kingly than Pelops, more eloquent than Adrastus: no matter what, if he has not courage.

> No one is a 'good man' in war if he cannot stand the sight of blood and slaughter, or come up and reach out for the enemy. This is 'goodness' (*arete*), this is the best and fairest prize among mankind for a young man to win.

The theme is elaborated, the fruits of courage identified in terms of achievement and reputation – reputation which even makes immortality the recompense for death in action – together with the possibility of survival to enjoy the deference of young and old, in lines which recall in sharp contrast Callinus' descriptions of the man who avoids death in battle only to earn the contempt of all (fr. 1.14–17).

This concept of military virtue inspired the two other more or less complete poems which have come down to us, poems of exhortation. 'Be bold, for you are the race of Heracles the unconquered. Zeus has not yet turned his head away' (fr. 11). In this poem a general statement of the advantages of standing fast, the disadvantages of flight, the shame of a soldier dead from a wound in the back, leads to a demand for action, the first couplet of which (21–2) is repeated verbatim in the other poem (fr. 10. 31–2) and paraphrased elsewhere:

> One must take up a proper stance, feet apart and both firmly planted on the ground, and must wait, biting one's lip.

There follows a compelling picture of the battle, the clash of opposing hoplite lines (lines 29–34):

> Go close and get the enemy, hand to hand, with a wound of your great lance or your sword. Set foot to foot, push shield on shield, tangle crest in crest, helmet on helmet, breast on breast, and fight your man, gripping hilt of sword or long spear.

The other poem (fr. 10) has been regarded by some critics as a combination of two separate fragments, but it is cited by the fourth-century orator Lycurgus as a continuous text. It begins with the bleak doctrine that it is a fine thing for a 'good man' to fall and die in the front line, fighting for his country. Tyrtaeus goes on to contrast the result of failure to fight (lines 3–12):

> To abandon one's city and rich fields for the life of a beggar is the most miserable thing of all – wandering with dear mother and aged father, little children and wedded wife. Hateful will be his company to all when he approaches, giving in to need and wretched poverty: he shames his family, belies his good looks, and dishonour and disrepute of every kind attend him. So then a displaced person has no consideration, no respect – neither he nor his descendants to come.

The conclusion is inevitable. 'With spirit let us fight for this land and for our children: let us die and no longer hesitate to give our lives.' The poet then

turns to address specifically the young men, calling on them to fight stead-
fastly, and not to fly and desert their older comrades who can no longer run
so fast as they. Another vivid picture follows, the sight of an old soldier killed
in battle (lines 21–7):

αἰσχρὸν γὰρ δὴ τοῦτο, μετὰ προμάχοισι πεσόντα
κεῖσθαι πρόσθε νέων ἄνδρα παλαιότερον,
ἤδη λευκὸν ἔχοντα κάρη πολιόν τε γένειον,
θυμὸν ἀποπνείοντ' ἄλκιμον ἐν κονίηι,
αἱματόεντ' αἰδοῖα φίλαις ἐν χερσὶν ἔχοντα –   25
αἰσχρὰ τά γ' ὀφθαλμοῖς καὶ νεμεσητὸν ἰδεῖν –
καὶ χρόα γυμνωθέντα· νέοισι δὲ πάντ' ἐπέοικεν,
ὄφρ' ἐρατῆς ἥβης ἀγλαὸν ἄνθος ἔχηι,
ἀνδράσι μὲν θηητὸς ἰδεῖν, ἐρατὸς δὲ γυναιξὶ
ζωὸς ἐών, καλὸς δ' ἐν προμάχοισι πεσών.   30

This is indeed shameful, for an older man to lie fallen among the front rank,
out in front of the young men, his hair already white, his beard grey, breathing
out his brave spirit in the dust, clutching his blood-drenched genitals – a shameful sight for the eyes, a reproach – and naked flesh. To the young everything is
becoming as long as they have on them the bright bloom of lovely youth – they
attract the admiration of men and loving glances of women while they live, and
are a fine sight if they die in the front line.

The poem ends with the couplet already quoted from fr. 11 (21–2).

This poem employs the common archaic device of ring-composition;
within it, twice repeated, a general statement with which no one could disagree
– the horror of beggary, the shame of allowing an older man to be killed –
which is the cue for a call to action. The language is largely that of the epic
tradition. Indeed all of Tyrtaeus' poems show close knowledge of the vocabulary of the *Iliad* and *Odyssey*, with a sprinkling of words otherwise known
from the Homeric Hymns and from Hesiod. That the Ionian Callinus owed a
debt to Homer is not remarkable, though the contrary would have been. The
extent of Homeric influence as far afield as Sparta ought not to surprise, but
it is certainly very striking. For all that, there is one important difference.
There is no aristocratic celebration of battle in Tyrtaeus, only a stern devotion
to duty and an awareness of what misery awaits an individual if his community
is destroyed. His poems are the martial hymn-book of that discipline and
devotion to the state which held Spartan ranks steady in the face of certain
death at Thermopylae and became one of the enduring legends of western
history.

Tyrtaeus and (for all we know) Callinus were amateurs, prompted by
national crisis to use the only medium of propaganda they knew. That alone
is enough to rule them out as inventors of elegy, against the claims of Archilochus the lifelong poet. A generation later another professional of outstanding

skill was at work, Mimnermus of Colophon.[1] He lived in the latter part of the seventh century: the traditional date is confirmed by the knowledge of his works displayed by others (see below, pp. 95, 112). His *oeuvre* appears to have comprised at least two books (many, according to the Suda), containing a series of separate poems, evidently quite short, as well as a longer production later entitled *Nanno*, after a flute-girl whom the poet loved. Mimnermus was remembered primarily as a love poet (cf. Propertius 1.19.11); but the extant fragments of *Nanno* have little to say about love. This may be pure accident, and several of the fragments (4, 5, 12) could quite easily be associated with a larger erotic context. But it is more puzzling to find also attributed to *Nanno* the earliest surviving account of the Ionian migration, the settlement of Colophon and Smyrna from Pylos (frs. 9 and 10).

The opening of fr. 5 (a passage which also found its way into the *Theognidea*, see p. 96) recalls Sappho's account of her feelings at the sight of her beloved (fr. 31 LP) and could possibly have been known to her:

> αὐτίκα μοι κατὰ μὲν χροιὴν ῥέει ἄσπετος ἱδρώς,
> πτοιῶμαι δ' ἐσορῶν ἄνθος ὁμηλικίης
> τερπνὸν ὁμῶς καὶ καλόν· ἐπὶ πλέον ὤφελεν εἶναι·
> ἀλλ' ὀλιγοχρόνιον γίνεται ὥσπερ ὄναρ
> ἥβη τιμήεσσα· τὸ δ' ἀργαλέον καὶ ἄμορφον   5
> γῆρας ὑπὲρ κεφαλῆς αὐτίχ' ὑπερκρέμαται,
> ἐχθρὸν ὁμῶς καὶ ἄτιμον, ὅ τ' ἄγνωστον τιθεῖ ἄνδρα,
> βλάπτει δ' ὀφθαλμοὺς καὶ νόον ἀμφιχυθέν.

A river of sweat floods my flesh, and I tremble at the sight of the flower of youth, delightful and fair. I wish it would last longer. But precious youth is fleeting as a dream, and from the start painful and ugly old age hangs over its head, hateful and dishonoured. It makes a man unrecognizable, and shed over his eyes and his wits it does them harm.

These lines have an engaging immediacy, but they are not as artless as they appear at first glance. The rhetorical antithesis of τερπνὸν ὁμῶς καὶ καλόν (3) and ἐχθρὸν ὁμῶς καὶ ἄτιμον (7) and the vigorous use of words and images make this much more than a reworking of Homeric material.

In frs. 11 and 11a Mimnermus gives a version of the story of the Golden Fleece in which Aeetes' palace lies on the banks of Ocean, where Helios stores his rays in a golden chamber. And fr. 12, the lavish and imaginative description of the golden 'bed' in which the Sun travels from west to east, could also be part of his account of the story of Jason and Medea. All this could have been told to adorn or diversify the theme of a contemporary love affair, but we have no certain clues, and a quite different case can be plausibly argued.[2] Fr. 8,

---

[1] Or Smyrna; see Appendix.
[2] West (1974) 74–6.

which is also ascribed to *Nanno*, tempts the guess that part at least of the poem dealt directly with a relationship between two people: 'May there be truth between you and me, of all things the most just.'

Of the other poems the two best known (frs. 1 and 2) are on identical themes (and could even be part of a single work). Fr. 1 speaks of the 'desirable flowers of youth', asking 'What is life, what is joy without golden Aphrodite? May I die when these things no longer mean anything to me.' The poet goes on to lament the indignity and deprivation of old age. Fr. 2 is rather more elaborate:

ἡμεῖς δ', οἷά τε φύλλα φύει πολυάνθεμος ὥρη
ἔαρος, ὅτ' αἶψ' αὐγῆις αὔξεται ἠελίου,
τοῖς ἴκελοι πήχυιον ἐπὶ χρόνον ἄνθεσιν ἥβης
τερπόμεθα, πρὸς θεῶν εἰδότες οὔτε κακὸν
οὔτ' ἀγαθόν· Κῆρες δὲ παρεστήκασι μέλαιναι,   5
ἡ μὲν ἔχουσα τέλος γήραος ἀργαλέου,
ἡ δ' ἑτέρη θανάτοιο· μίνυνθα δὲ γίνεται ἥβης
καρπός, ὅσον τ' ἐπὶ γῆν κίδναται ἠέλιος.
αὐτὰρ ἐπὴν δὴ τοῦτο τέλος παραμείψεται ὥρης,
αὐτίκα δὴ τεθνάναι βέλτιον ἢ βίοτος.   10

Like the leaves which the flowery season of spring puts forth, when stirred to sudden growth by the sun's rays, so we enjoy the flowers of youth for a span, learning neither good nor ill at the hands of the gods. But the black Fates are at hand, the one with grievous old age as the end, the other with death. The fruiting of youth is brief, only as long as the sun shines over the earth. But when this season is ended, then it is better to be dead than to go on living.

And then he enumerates the miseries of old age, the common lot of all mankind, poverty, childlessness, disease. This poem indicates a mind not only stored richly with the inheritance of epic formulas (cf. also 6.2 and Tyrtaeus 7.2, 13a.2 and Tyrtaeus 19.7) but inclined also to dwell upon Homeric contexts. The use of the simile of the leaves, from *Iliad* 6.146, contributes much to the effect of the first four lines. Equally Homeric is the ensuing reference to the two Fates, *keres*, founded upon *Iliad* 9.411ff., in which Achilles discusses his own alternative *keres*, to die gloriously in battle or to survive in obscurity to a ripe old age. Mimnermus has been criticized for posing false alternatives, in that old age is not an alternative to death. But the Homeric context, and indeed Mimnermus' own, shows that it is death in one's prime that is meant. More starkly than Homer, Mimnermus declares that beyond youth nothing good awaits. Yet the tone is not always gloomy: in fr. 7 the poet's voice is jauntier. 'Please yourself: your fellow citizens have no mercy, and one will blame you while another praises.'

If the *Nanno* contained an account of the founding of Colophon and Smyrna, the poem entitled *Smyrneis* recalled events within living memory, the defence of Smyrna against Gyges of Lydia, c. 680. The elegy began with an invocation of the Muses, which distinguished the Muses as daughters of Zeus from their predecessors the children of Earth and Heaven. Little is preserved of the narrative, but enough to gauge its temper. A Smyrnaean warrior's charge is described (fr. 14): 'Pallas Athena found no fault with the keen strength of his spirit when he rushed forward with the front line in the bloody battle, forcing his way against the enemy's bitter shafts. For never was there among the foe a better man than he at doing the work of mighty war, as he ran forward, carried[1] by the rays of the swift sun.' No prosaic history, this, such as Tyrtaeus or Solon would have composed, however vividly; for Mimnermus, the life of battle is still heroic, the gods still watch upon the side-lines.

Mimnermus' poetry quickly won a wide circulation, as we can tell from allusions in other writers. The deep pessimism with which he repeated Homer's comparison of the life of man to that of leaves whose brief sprouting is soon ended (fr. 2) perhaps stung a later poet to the more bracing reflection that, since the comparison holds, one must be unstinting in enjoyment of the good things of life for as long as possible ('Simonides', see p. 116). Mimnermus' hope for survival in good health to the age of sixty (fr. 6), already perhaps ambitious in terms of the expectations of his time, seemed unduly modest to Solon, who would add a further score of years to the term (Solon, fr. 20). One of his rare and idiosyncratic pieces of mythology, the slaughter of Ismene by Tydeus (fr. 21, mentioned by no other writer), was illustrated on an early Corinthian amphora of c. 625–600. Nor does his fame seem to have faded in later centuries: there must be some significance in the fact that Callimachus singles him out in the famous programmatic prologue to the *Aetia* as a practitioner of the kind of poetry most admired by the *avant-garde*.[2] It is easy to understand Callimachus' enthusiasm: here was poetry that was brilliantly vivid and in its own way elegant and sophisticated.

3. THEOGNIS

Theognis is one of the few Greek poets (and the only poet of the archaic age) whose work has come down to us not as a small selection made by some anthologist, not in fragments quoted by late authors or on scraps of papyrus, but as a complete corpus preserved through late antiquity and the Byzantine period. Unfortunately the corpus is more than complete: we have too much. The text preserved in the medieval manuscripts consists of some 600 elegiac couplets;

---

[1] The text of this line is uncertain.

[2] The interpretation of *Aetia* fr. 1.10–12 is uncertain, but Callimachus seems either to be praising all of Mimnermus' poetry as 'small-scale' (*kata lepton* – a key phrase in Callimachus' critical vocabulary) or contrasting his more pleasing 'small-scale' poems with a long composition (the *Nanno?* the *Smyrneis?*). See *CHCL* I, Part 4, 13ff.

one manuscript, the oldest and the best, adds another hundred or so under the superscription 'Book 2'. The verses are written in unbroken sequence but there is no overall structure, no logical continuity which holds for very long. On the contrary, abrupt changes of subject, theme and even person addressed meet us at every turn; repetition – verbal (e.g. 853–4 = 1038ab, 571–2 = 1104ab, etc.) and thematic (cf. 527–8 with 1131–2, 585–6 with 1075–6, etc.) – incoherence (e.g. 1128ff.) and outright contradiction (813–14 ≠ 1181–2, etc.) are far from uncommon. The conclusion is hard to avoid that we are faced with a miscellaneous collection of elegiac poems, most of them very short, some of them incomplete; that they are not all from the same hand is clear from the fact that many short runs of verse found in 'Theognis' are elsewhere securely assigned to Solon, Mimnermus and Tyrtaeus. How much more of the work of these poets lies still unrecognized in the Theognidean corpus we do not know since we have only fragments of their work; we shall never know, either, how many other poets, now anonymous, have been drawn on to swell the muster.

The so-called second book harps on the same theme throughout – boy-love; it consists of a series of short units (one or two couplets for the most part) many of which begin ὦ παῖ ... 'Boy ...'. But the rest of the miscellany contains such diverse items as short addresses to divinities (Apollo, Artemis and the Muses, 1–18), poems addressed by Theognis (named only once, l. 22) to Cyrnus, son of Polypas (a fairly solid block, 19–254, with others strung out through the remainder, including Book 2), poems addressed to other men (Simonides and Onomacritus, for example, who may be the well-known figures mentioned elsewhere, but who equally well may not), gnomic moral exhortations of a general not to say banal character and drinking songs of the type in favour among the revellers at aristocratic symposia. It looks as if an original collection of poems by Theognis, addressed to Cyrnus, a much younger man, has grown over the course of many years of transmission, to its present shape and size by the addition of parallel (and contrasting) material, perhaps by the process of excerpting (ἐκλέγειν, cf. CHCL I, Part 4, 166f.).

Exactly when the anthology was fixed in its present form we do not know. The poets whose work we can identify (Solon, Mimnermus, Tyrtaeus) all predate the fifth century and (as far as we can tell) fifth-century poets who did use the elegiac couplet (Ion of Chios, for example, Simonides, Critias) are not represented.[1] The latest historical event referred to is the Persian invasion of

[1] Lines 467–96, 667–82 and 1341–50 are often assigned, in modern editions, to Euenus of Paros (active in the latter half of the fifth century). The basis for this attribution is the fact that Aristotle (*Metaph.* 1015a28) cites 472 (with one word changed) as a line of Euenus; Camerarius assigned the whole sequence 467–96 to Euenus and since these lines are addressed to one Simonides, gave Euenus the other two passages which contain that name. This structure is obviously shaky; everything depends on Aristotle's attribution of one line. But that line is not a very original observation

Greece in 480 B.C.; lines 773–82, an eloquent appeal to Apollo to save Megara, clearly refer to a present, not a far-off, danger and also deplore Greek disunity in the face of the invader.

> Lord Phoebus, it was you in person who built the towers on our city's high place, as a favour to Pelops' son Alkathoos. Now in person keep the savage army of the Medes away from this city, so that in gladness, when spring comes on, the people may bring you glorious animal sacrifices in procession, rejoicing in the sound of the harp and the lovely banquet, the cries and dance-steps of the hymns in your honour performed at your altar. Save us, I beseech you – for I am terrified when I see the mad folly and the destructive disunion of the Greek people. Be gracious to us, Phoebus, and watch over this our city.

These powerful lines are clearly the work of a Megarian poet, but most critics today agree that they cannot be the work of Theognis, who was probably a younger contemporary of Solon; their inclusion in a collection which seems otherwise to have confined itself strictly to poets of the archaic age can be easily explained: an anthology which went under the name of Theognis of Megara was the obvious place to put them.

The lines which are addressed to Cyrnus all bear the stamp of a particular strong personality. We know nothing about him except what we are told in the poems: that his name was Theognis, his city Megara. His voice is that of an embittered aristocrat, a loser in the social upheavals of archaic Greece, warning his beloved Cyrnus against the violence and vulgarity of the lower orders and later, perhaps in exile, lamenting his poverty and calling for revenge.

A suitable historical context for this poet could be found in almost any Greek city of the archaic age – in mainland Megara as well as Megara Hyblaea, its colony in Sicily, to which Plato (*Laws* 630a) assigns him. But there is fairly general agreement today that the mother-city is the more likely candidate. It suffered in the late seventh century under the regime of a particularly vicious tyrant, Theagenes, whose overthrow was followed by many decades of political turbulence; a democracy which seems to have been notorious for its extreme measures against the wealthy was brought to an end, we are told by Aristotle (*Pol.* 1304b34), when its confiscations had driven so many into exile that they were numerous enough to come back in force and establish an oligarchy.[1]

Theognis is the first poet in Greek literature to voice concern over the eventual fate of his productions; in fact he announces that he has taken measures to protect them.

> Cyrnus, as I compose my poems for you, let a seal be placed on the verses; if stolen they will never pass undetected nor will anyone exchange their present

---

– 'For everything forced on one by necessity is painful' – and even if the lines depend on each other, Euenus may be quoting Theognis, just as in fr. 1 (West) he quotes a 'παλαιὸς λόγος'.

[1] West (1978*b*) collects the ancient evidence for archaic Megara: 'Testimonia historica' pp. 4–6.

good content for worse – but everyone will say: 'They are the verses of Theognis of Megara, a name known to all mankind.' (19–23)

Unfortunately, we do not know what this 'seal' was; the single occurrence of the poet's own name could hardly serve to protect the integrity of his text and even the frequently recurring mention of Cyrnus would not be a barrier against interpolation. Perhaps a copy of the poem was entrusted under seal to a temple; we are told that Heraclitus of Ephesus deposited a copy of his book in the temple of Artemis there. Whatever the 'seal' may have been, it was obviously ineffective; disputes about how much of our present text should be attributed to Theognis have continued ever since Welcker made the first systematic attempt to separate the grain from the chaff in 1826. A recent editor, confining himself to those sequences which contain the name Cyrnus and those which are quoted as the work of Theognis by fourth-century authors (Plato and Aristotle), prints 306 lines, and although, as he says, the collection may contain still more genuine verses, this selection constitutes an acceptable core.[1] The traditional text opens with four invocations of divine beings, two addressed to Apollo, one to Artemis, and one to the Muses and Graces (Χάριτες). The lines addressed to Artemis are identified by Aristotle as the work of Theognis (*Eth. Eud.* 1243a18); they may well be the prologue of the original book, for they have a conciseness and a touch of wit – characteristics of Theognis at his best.

> Ἄρτεμι θηροφόνη, θύγατερ Διός, ἣν Ἀγαμέμνων
> εἴσαθ', ὅτ' ἐς Τροίην ἔπλεε νηυσὶ θοῇς,
> εὐχομένωι μοι κλῦθι, κακὰς δ' ἀπὸ κῆρας ἄλαλκε·
> σοὶ μὲν τοῦτο, θεά, σμικρόν, ἐμοὶ δὲ μέγα. (11–14)

Artemis, killer of wild beasts, daughter of Zeus, you whose sanctuary Agamemnon founded when he was about to sail for Troy in his swift ships, listen to my prayer and protect me from the evil death-spirits. Goddess, this means little to you, but much to me.

The form Theognis' original book may have assumed can be surmised from a phrase in the Suda entry: Θέογνις... ἔγραψεν... πρὸς Κύρνον... γνωμολογίαν δι' ἐλεγείων καὶ ἑτέρας ὑποθήκας παραινετικάς...'Theognis... wrote... addressed to Cyrnus ... a collection of maxims in elegiac verse, and other ethical prescriptions.' This word ὑποθῆκαι occurs in a didactic poem ascribed to Hesiod, the 'prescriptions of Chiron' Χίρωνος ὑποθῆκαι – Chiron the centaur gives ethical advice to his pupil Achilles. And the cognate verb ὑποθήσομαι 'I shall prescribe' occurs in Theognis' first announcement that he will take young Cyrnus' education in hand.

[1] West (1978*b*).

THEOGNIS

With your interest at heart, Cyrnus, I shall pass on the precepts (ὑποθήσομαι) which, still a child, I learned from good men and true. Be prudent; and do not try to win honour, prestige or wealth by actions which are shameful and unjust... Do not associate with bad men, but hold fast always to the good – with *them* drink and eat, sit with *them*... (27–34)

The end of the sentence makes it crystal-clear what Theognis means by 'good' men: '... try to please those whose power is great'.

Many of the 'prescriptions' are neatly phrased couplets which encapsulate traditional Greek morality: respect for the gods (1179–80), parents (131–2, 821–2), and strangers (143–4). It was lines like these which earned Theognis his reputation as a moralist – Isocrates, for example, (*Ad Nicoclem* 43) lists him among 'the best advisers for the conduct of human life' (ἀρίστους ... συμβούλους τῶι βίωι τῶι τῶν ἀνθρώπων...). But the teacher also urges on his young pupil the old aristocratic code which enjoined full requital for benefits and injuries received.

May Zeus grant me this, Cyrnus: to repay my friends who love me and to have greater power than my enemies. If this were so I would seem like a god among men – if the destined day of death found me fully paid up. (337–40)

Another version clarifies the veiled menace in the words 'have greater power than my enemies'.

May the thing feared by all men who walk the earth happen to me, may the great, wide, brazen sky fall on my head – if I do not give aid and comfort to those who love me, and become a torment and great affliction to my enemies. (869–72)

Though he assumes the role of tutor, he does not blithely assume that education is always effective. 'It is easier to beget and raise a human being than to put a sound mind in it ... If understanding could be made and implanted in a man, a son of a good father would never turn out bad – he would be ruled by his father's words of wisdom. But by teaching, you will never turn a bad man to good' (429–33, 435–8). This pessimistic estimate was apparently just; Theognis has cause later, at the end of the famous lines which claim that he has made Cyrnus' name immortal, to reproach the young pupil whom he loved for deceit and ingratitude.

σοὶ μὲν ἐγὼ πτέρ' ἔδωκα, σὺν οἷσ' ἐπ' ἀπείρονα πόντον
πωτήσηι, κατὰ γῆν πᾶσαν ἀειρόμενος
ῥηϊδίως· θοίνηις δὲ καὶ εἰλαπίνηισι παρέσσηι
ἐν πάσαις πολλῶν κείμενος ἐν στόμασιν,   240
καί σε σὺν αὐλίσκοισι λιγυφθόγγοις νέοι ἄνδρες
εὐκόσμως ἐρατοὶ καλά τε καὶ λιγέα
ᾄσονται. καὶ ὅταν δνοφερῆς ὑπὸ κεύθεσι γαίης
βῆις πολυκωκύτους εἰς Ἀΐδαο δόμους,

99

οὐδέποτ' οὐδὲ θανὼν ἀπολεῖς κλέος, ἀλλὰ μελήσεις   245
ἄφθιτον ἀνθρώποισ' αἰὲν ἔχων ὄνομα,
Κύρνε, καθ' Ἑλλάδα γῆν στρωφώμενος, ἠδ' ἀνὰ νήσους...

. . .

πᾶσι δ', ὅσοισι μέμηλε, καὶ ἐσσομένοισιν ἀοιδή   251
ἔσσηι ὁμῶς, ὄφρ' ἂν γῆ τε καὶ ἥλιος.
αὐτὰρ ἐγὼν ὀλίγης παρὰ σεῦ οὐ τυγχάνω αἰδοῦς,
ἀλλ' ὥσπερ μικρὸν παῖδα λόγοις μ' ἀπατᾶις.   (237–47, 251–4)

I have given you wings with which to fly aloft over the boundless sea and the
whole earth effortlessly; at banquets and festivals you will be there, at all of
them, your name on the lips of many, as, to the sound of high-pitched pipes,
handsome lads sing your praises loud and clear in lovely harmony. And when
you go down under the depths of the gloomy earth to the mournful house of
Hades, not even then, not even in death, will you lose your glory; you will be a
theme of men's song, Cyrnus, your name immortal forever as you range the
mainland of Hellas and the islands... For all those now and in time to come who
love to sing you will be there as long as earth and sun shall last. But as for me, you
have not the least consideration for me; you cheat me with words as if I were
a little child.

In style and vocabulary, as this specimen shows, Theognis differs little
from other archaic poets who wrote in elegiac couplets; like them, he is heavily
indebted to Ionian epic. This address to Cyrnus is hardly Homeric in tone and
content; yet, except for the Theognidean coinage πολυκωκύτους, the vocabulary
is entirely Homeric. The passage, in fact, is a mosaic of Homeric phrases and
formulas, some unchanged, some subtly varied. The ending of the first line,
for example, ἐπ' ἀπείρονα πόντον comes from Il. 1.350; the end of 243 ὑπὸ
κεύθεσι γαίης is a recurrent Homeric formula, like εἰς Ἀΐδαο δόμους (244)
γῆ τε καὶ ἥλιος (252) and ῥηϊδίως as a line opening (239). The rest of line 239
echoes Il. 10.217 with θοίνηις substituted for δαίτηισι and the striking phrase
ἐσσομένοισιν ἀοιδή in 251 comes from Od. 8.850. Tyrtaeus could use the
epic language for a situation and in a tone Homer (at least the Homer of the
Iliad) would have recognized; but Theognis adapts it for a new world of thought
and feeling – the celebration of a young man's fame and beauty, the reactions
of an aristocrat to social innovation and turbulence.

Cyrnus is to be a theme for song in feasts and festivals but especially in
those aristocratic, male drinking parties we know so well from the vase paint-
ings. Many of the poems of the collection develop themes appropriate for such
gatherings: the joys of wine, of male companionship, the exquisite short season
of youth.

As for us, let us devote our hearts to feast and celebration, while they can still
feel the joy of pleasure's motions. For glorious youth passes by swift as a thought,

swifter than the burst of speed shown by horses as they take a chieftain and his spear to the battle line, galloping furiously as they take their joy in the flatness of the wheatfields. (983-8)

The love poems which were at some point concentrated in the second book[1] (though a few remain in the first) are of course typical of this masculine world and in the last couplet of Theognis' claim to have made Cyrnus' name immortal there is a clear hint that Theognis sees himself in that love relationship between older and younger man which was characteristic of such milieux. 'You cheat me with words, as if I were a little child.' Elsewhere, using an image common in Greek erotic poetry, he even begs Cyrnus not to make him fall too deeply in love: 'Do not with your violent goading drive me, against my will, under the yoke, drawing me into excessive love' (371-2). And a recurrent theme is the complaint, familiar from other Greek sympotic song, that love and friendship are unstable, the protest against infidelity and, above all, deceit. 'Don't give me words of love as you turn your mind and heart elsewhere .. either wipe your mind clean and love me, or reject and hate me, picking a quarrel openly. The man whose one tongue conceals two minds is a dangerous comrade, Cyrnus, better your enemy than your friend' (87-92).

Perfidy, of course, is not confined to love relationships; in the wider world of commerce and politics it is just as prevalent, and Cyrnus is warned against it. He must choose the good, not the bad, as friends and these two words, ἀγαθός and κακός, as so often in archaic Greek literature, denote social as well as moral categories.

Let no man persuade you to love a bad man, Cyrnus; what use to have a base man as your friend? He will not rescue you from toil and trouble or from ruin and if he has anything good he will not be willing to share it. (101-4)

The social import of these words comes out clearly in the aristocrat's protest against marriages made for money; he views unions between well-born and *nouveaux riches* as tantamount to miscegenation.

When it comes to rams, donkeys and horses, Cyrnus, we search for thorough-breds (εὐγενέας) and we get mates of good stock (ἀγαθῶν) for them to mount. But a fine man (ἐσθλός) does not refuse to marry the lowest of the low (κακὴν κακοῦ) if she brings him lots of money. And a woman doesn't spurn the bed of a low born man (κακοῦ) if he's rich; she'd rather have a wealthy man than a good one (ἀγαθοῦ). Money is what they care about; noble (ἐσθλός) marries a base man's (κακοῦ) daughter, the base man (κακός) the noble's (ἀγαθοῦ). Wealth crosses the breeds. So don't be surprised, son of Polypas, that the purity of our citizens' stock is blurred; for good is being mixed with bad. (183-92)

[1] It seems fairly certain that the contents of Book 2 were once distributed throughout the collection, and were extracted to form a separate unit during the Byzantine period.

One of the most potent solvents of the old aristocratic order was the introduction of coinage, which made possible depths of indebtedness and rapid
accumulations of wealth unknown in the earlier economy; it also brought
into existence a class of newly-rich men who pressed for admission, by marriage,
bribery or political agitation into the hereditary ruling circles. Theognis sees
money as the destructive agent which has shattered the whole heroic mythic
tradition, the sacred book of aristocratic ethics. This trenchant assessment
is made in a poem which deliberately imitates the structure of Tyrtaeus'
celebration of martial courage as the only form of excellence (ἀρετή) – more
to be admired than the strength of the Cyclopes, the speed of Boreas, the
beauty of Tithonus, the wealth of Midas and Cinyras, the kingly power of
Pelops or the honey-sweet tongue of Adrastus (cf. pp. 90f.). Tyrtaeus' poem
uses the device known as priamel – a series building up towards the climactic
component, martial valour, which far outshines its predecessors. Theognis,
however, begins with a stark declaration of his bitter thesis and names his
highest virtue at once.

> In the eyes of most men (πλήθει) there is only one form of excellence (ἀρετή):
> this one, to be rich. Nothing else, it turns out, is any good (τῶν δ'ἄλλων οὐδὲν ἄρ'
> ἦν ὄφελος) not even if you had the sober wisdom (σωφροσύνην) of Rhadamanthys,
> not even if you were cleverer than Sisyphus son of Aeolus, who won over Perse-
> phone with lying speeches and came back up from Hades by his cunning...
> not if you could make false things sound true, had, in fact, the skilful tongue of
> god-like Nestor, not even if you were faster on your feet than the swift Harpies
> or the fast-running sons of Boreas. No, everyone must get this firmly in mind:
> money has most power for all men. (699–704, 713–18)

Another bitter poem defines more clearly the upstarts whose wealth prevails
over noble birth in the marriage market; it also gives a vivid impression
of the tense atmosphere of the period, the frustration of the propertied class
in a time of revolution.

> Cyrnus, the city is still a city, but the people are changed. Once they knew
> nothing of rights or laws; they wore out their goatskins against their flanks
> and grazed, like deer, outside the city. And now, Cyrnus, *they* are the good men
> and true (ἀγαθοί)! And those who once were noble (ἐσθλοί) are now low. Who
> can bear to see it? (53–8)

The situation is so fluid and confusing that old standards are no sure guide; a
man does not know how to avoid censure.

> I cannot read the mind of my fellow citizens, know what is in their thoughts.
> Whether I do them good or harm, no matter – I cannot please them. (367–8)

It is a world in which the poet has lost his bearings; he even comes to doubt
the justice of Zeus and the Olympian gods.

Dear Zeus, I wonder at you. For you rule all, you alone have the great power and the glory, you know the mind and heart of every man, and your strength, O Lord, is highest of all. How then... can you be so hard of heart, to treat the wicked and the just man alike? (373–8)

This despairing mood reached its ultimate expression in some lines which became the classic formulation of Greek pessimism, echoed in Bacchylides (5.160) and a famous Sophoclean ode (*O.C.* 1225ff.):

> πάντων μὲν μὴ φῦναι ἐπιχθονίοισιν ἄριστον
> μηδ' ἐσιδεῖν αὐγὰς ὀξέος ἠελίου,
> φύντα δ' ὅπως ὤκιστα πύλας 'Αΐδαο περῆσαι
> καὶ κεῖσθαι πολλὴν γῆν ἐπαμησάμενον. (425–28)

Not to be born is best of all for men, never to see the dazzling rays of the sun. Once born, to go as fast as may be through the gates of death, and lie under a heap of earth.

In the unpredictable world of political and social change one can no longer afford the traditional aristocratic virtue of loyalty.

> θυμέ, φίλους κατὰ πάντας ἐπίστρεφε ποικίλον ἦθος,
> ὀργὴν συμμίσγων ἥντιν' ἕκαστος ἔχει·
> πουλύπου ὀργὴν ἴσχε πολυπλόκου, ὃς ποτὶ πέτρηι,
> τῆι προσομιλήσηι, τοῖος ἰδεῖν ἐφάνη. (213–16)

My heart, in your dealings with all your friends, be versatile of character, vary according to the mood each one may have. Adopt the temper of the subtly-coiling octopus, who takes on the appearance of the rock to which he intends to cling.

But even this pliant attitude will hardly ensure survival in the catastrophe which Theognis foresees – the tyranny which was all too often the end result of Greek civil strife.

> Κύρνε, κύει πόλις ἥδε, δέδοικα δὲ μὴ τέκηι ἄνδρα
> εὐθυντῆρα κακῆς ὕβριος ἡμετέρης. (39–40)

Cyrnus, this city is big with child and I fear it may give birth to a man who will chastize our wicked pride.

This admission of general responsibility – '*our* wicked pride' – is an unusually objective formula for Theognis but it is soon abandoned; the fault lies not with the citizens or the 'good' but with the 'leaders', who are of course *kakoi*.

For our citizens are still of sound mind, but their leaders are set on a course towards much mischief – and a fall. No city, Cyrnus, was ever yet ruined by good men (ἀγαθοί), but when the bad men (κακοῖσιν) take to insolence (ὑβρίζειν), corrupt the masses (δῆμον) and give judgement in favour of the lawless in order to win power and private gain, then, you may be sure that the city, though it lies deep in tranquillity now, will not enjoy peace for very long – when this is what the bad men find dear to their heart: profit at the expense of the public good. For it is from things like this that factions are born and civil murders and a dictatorship. May this city never choose that way. (41–52)

In another couplet Theognis seems to be issuing a call to action rather than voicing the usual impotent complaint.[1]

Cyrnus, with those friends we have, let us scotch the evil at its source, seek remedy for this sore before it comes to a head. (1133–4)

But a lament for his lost estates suggests that whether or not he took any action, Theognis became one of the many casualties of Greek political life, one of those 'who told their lies too late | caught in the eternal factions and reactions | of the city-state'.[2] The voice of the migratory crane, on its way to Africa, was the signal, Hesiod tells us (W.D. 448ff.), to begin the late autumn ploughing. But for Theognis it is bitter reminder of his losses.

I heard the voice, son of Polypas, the high-pitched cry of the bird which comes to tell men: 'Plough in season'. And my heart was struck dark with anger, to think that other men possess my fertile acres now; it is not for me that the mules pull at the curved yoke...(1197–1201)

These lines sound the nostalgic note characteristic of the exile and some other lines (which contain no mention of Cyrnus) speak of travels to foreign cities.

For I have been in my time to the land of Sicily, and to the plains of Euboea with their vines, I have been to Sparta, the glorious town on the reedy Eurotas river – and everywhere I went I found hearty welcome and friendship. But from all of it no joy came to my heart; it is true, after all, that there is no place like one's homeland. (783–8)

Whether he was in fact exiled or suffered only confiscation we do not know (though if he went overseas late in life to settle in Sicilian Megara, Plato's description of him as a Sicilian becomes more intelligible) but we can be sure that like most losers in Greek faction fights, he was reduced to poverty. He is eloquent in his diatribes against it.

Poverty, Cyrnus, brings a good man (ἀγαθόν) to his knees more than anything else, more than grey old age or fever; to get away from it, throw yourself into the ocean's hollow deeps or down from precipitous rocks. (173–6)

The loss of his estates and the pain of exile must have been the fuel which fired a savage prayer for vengeance, a reformulation, in grim terms, of one aspect of the heroic code he had taught Cyrnus.

[1] See the note to no. 49 in West (1978b).
[2] Louis MacNeice, Autumn Journal, London 1939, IX.

Olympian Zeus, fulfil at least my prayer in season; grant me some experience of good to balance the evil. I would wish to die, unless I can find some relief from sad cares and give back pain for pain. For here stands my fate: I see no vengeance coming on those men who stripped me of my property and hold it still – I am the dog that crossed the flooding river in the gorge – he shook everything off. May it be mine to drink their dark blood...(341–9)

As far as we know he never lived to see the day of restoration and revenge. His enemies were no doubt as unforgiving and unforgetting as he was. And for all his calls to moderation in the gnomic passages of his poems, he reveals his true feelings in four lines which sum up the bitter contempt for the common people which brought him and his fellow aristocrats, in Megara, and elsewhere to disaster.

Drive the empty-headed vulgar herd with kicks, jab them with sharp goads and put a galling yoke on their neck; you will not find, among all the men the sun looks down on, a people that loves a master more than this one. (847–50)

4. SOLON

In Athens, Megara's next-door neighbour and her rival for the possession of Salamis, the same social and economic problems faced the old aristocracy, but Athens was more fortunate in the political outcome. She was saved from the worst excesses of *stasis* by a statesman whose reforms prevented civil war and who was regarded by the later democracy as one of its forerunners. But Solon was also a poet and his poems present us with an extraordinary phenomenon: a political leader using poetry as his principal means of communication, to agitate, to warn, to announce and defend his policies.

As usual, most of his work is lost. Diogenes Laertius tells us that his elegiac verses totalled 5,000 and that he wrote iambics and epodes as well. No trace of the epodes remains, but we have some 20 lines of trochaic tetrameter, 47 or so of iambic trimeter, and 219 of the 5,000 elegiac lines. This is a pitifully small remnant; yet it is enough to conjure up an unforgettable personality: a statesman and poet who is not only the first of an illustrious line of Athenian writers but also the first Athenian to emerge from the historical obscurity of illiterate ages. Plutarch's Athenian *Lives* begin with Theseus, the mythical founder of Attic unity; the next in time is Solon – the only historical figure before the fifth century for whom oral tradition and written documents had preserved material enough for a biography. Cylon, who made the first attempt to found an Athenian tyranny, and Draco, who wrote the laws in blood, are historical figures, but for us they are little more than names; the Solonian fragments give us glimpses of a many-sided individual and also of the context in which he lived – that sixth century which in literature, the arts and social experimentation laid the foundations for Athens' golden age.

He was known to later ages as ὁ νομοθέτης 'the Lawgiver', and Athenian orators of the fourth century never tire of invoking his name as the criterion of traditional legality. But his career began with a defiance of the spirit, if not the letter, of the law. An indecisive war with Megara (late seventh century) over the possession of the strategically vital island of Salamis had so disgusted the Athenians that they ceased fighting and decreed the death penalty for anyone who should speak or write in favour of renewing hostilities. Solon (pretending insanity and wearing the cap of an invalid on his head) came into the agora and declaimed his hundred-line elegiac poem, *Salamis*, a call for winning the island at all costs. 'I have come in person, a herald from lovely Salamis,' it began, 'delivering a song, a pattern of verse, instead of a speech' (ἀντ' ἀγορῆς, fr. 1). The burden of his song was reproof, a forcible expression of the ignominy that would follow the abandonment of Salamis. If we do not win it, one of the extant fragments goes on to say, 'in that case, I would rather change my homeland, instead of an Athenian be a man from Pholegandros or Sikinnos. For all too soon this word would be on all mens' lips: "He is from Attica, this man, one of the Salamis-losers"' (fr. 2):

εἴην δὴ τότ' ἐγὼ Φολεγάνδριος ἢ Σικινήτης
ἀντί γ' Ἀθηναίου πατρίδ' ἀμειψάμενος·
αἶψα γὰρ ἂν φάτις ἥδε μετ' ἀνθρώποισι γένοιτο·
"Ἀττικὸς οὗτος ἀνήρ, τῶν Σαλαμιναφετέων.'

He turns from reproach to exhortation. 'Let us go to Salamis, to fight for the lovely island and cast off the burden of disgrace' (fr. 3). They did go to Salamis and, though it was not done overnight, Salamis was won for Athens in the end; the threat to Eleusis and the harbours of Athens was removed.

This episode (which does not rest on Plutarch's authority alone, for a passage in Demosthenes (19.252, 255) shows that it was accepted history in the fourth century B.C.) is a vivid reminder of the fact that in the archaic age poetry was not a written text to be read but a performance to be watched and heard; *Salamis* is poetry in action. Tyrtaeus' elegies were, in later times, sung to Spartan troops to raise their morale (and perhaps were composed for this purpose) but Solon's performance is not only unofficial, indeed subversive propaganda, it is also, with its assumed identity (a herald) and disguise (the cap of the invalid), a fully dramatic performance.

The lines are remarkable also in that they present us with the first reference to Athens and Attica by an Athenian poet; they are informed by a fierce pride in the city's greatness and an assumption that Athenian citizenship imposes great obligations – the salient features of Pericles' ideal vision of Athenian democracy, the Funeral Speech of some two hundred years later.

Not all of Solon's poetry was addressed to the immediate political situation, in fact the longest poem we possess (fr. 13: 76 lines of elegiacs) is a leisurely reflection on moral issues and the vicissitudes of human life and the iustice of Zeus. In its rather rambling discursiveness it is often reminiscent of Hesiod's *Works and days* and there are correspondences in thought as well as in structure and style. It is, in form, a prayer to the Muses: the poet asks for prosperity (ὄλβον) and good reputation (δόξαν...ἀγαθήν) in the eyes of all men. This last phrase seems to be defined by the couplet which follows: 'let them say that I am honey to him that loves me, bitter gall to him that hates me, respected by the one, feared by the other.'

εἶναι δὲ γλυκὺν ὧδε φίλοις, ἐχθροῖσι δὲ πικρόν,
τοῖσι μὲν αἰδοῖον, τοῖσι δὲ δεινὸν ἰδεῖν.   (5–6)

Solon then returns to his first theme, prosperity, which is developed as the real subject of the poem as a whole. He wants prosperity but not to win it by injustice (ἀδίκως). The wealth given to a man by the gods stands on a firm foundation and will last, but wealth won by violence and wickedness will be destroyed by Zeus whose wrath is described in an impressive simile drawn from the storm winds (of which Zeus is the dispenser). His wrath, however, is not swift, like ours; punishment may come late, and it may fall on the next generation of the wrongdoer's family, or even on their children's children. There follows a long and detailed catalogue of the vanity of human wishes, the vain hopes (κούφαις ἐλπίσι, 36) of mankind, their different ways to wealth – as sailor, farmer, craftsman, poet, seer, doctor – all beset with uncertainty; only the seer, if the gods are with him, knows what the future will bring. For it is Fate (Μοῖρα, 63) which brings good or evil to mankind; the gifts of the immortal gods cannot be avoided. The poem returns to its earlier theme – wealth, and here the focus seems to move from the individual to the social level: 'There's no limit set to wealth for men to see. For those of us who now hold the greatest resources, struggle to double their possessions; and who could satisfy them all?'

Not only is the structure loose and the sequence of thought muddy; the style is careless – ἰδεῖν used as a line ending three times (6, 22, 24), the colourless adjective ἀργαλέος three times (37, 45, 61). But, outside of the long simile (18–25) and the catalogue of professions (43–62), the language is less dependent on Homer than anything seen in elegiac poetry so far and many individual linguistic traits appear – the use of the adverb πάντως in line 8 (a favourite word of Solon's), the first use of an adjective very common in later Attic, φλαῦρος (15).

There is nothing particularly new in the moral formulation, indeed lines 5–6 (see above) remind us forcibly that Solon, descended from the mythical King Codrus, was of aristocratic stock, for this attitude towards friends and enemies is the standard heroic ethic. But Solon, unlike Theognis, realized that this same personal code of martial honour, elevated to the level of political programme and blindly followed in the factions of the body politic, was a recipe for disaster. In a fragmentary elegy (quoted by Demosthenes in a fourth-century oration) Solon warns his fellow citizens against Δυσνομίη 'anarchy', for so, he tells us, 'my heart tells me to instruct the Athenians' (4.30).

> ἡμετέρη δὲ πόλις κατὰ μὲν Διὸς οὔποτ' ὀλεῖται
> αἶσαν καὶ μακάρων θεῶν φρένας ἀθανάτων·
> τοίη γὰρ μεγάθυμος ἐπίσκοπος ὀβριμοπάτρη
> Παλλὰς 'Αθηναίη χεῖρας ὕπερθεν ἔχει·
> αὐτοὶ δὲ φθείρειν μεγάλην πόλιν ἀφραδίηισιν
> ἀστοὶ βούλονται χρήμασι πειθόμενοι... (4.1–6)

Our city shall never perish by the destiny of Zeus and the will of the blessed immortal gods – such is the power of our protector, great-hearted Pallas Athena, daughter of mighty father, who holds her arm over us. But the citizens themselves, in their madness, want to bring to ruin our great city – and all for money's sake...

The poem gives a graphic description of the evils brought on by the unrestrained pursuit of riches, the plundering of the city's wealth by her leaders, the disregard of justice, the conspiracies of warring factions, with, as the crowning calamity, the lot of the poor – sold into slavery abroad. This is Δυσνομίη, bad government; its consequences no man, rich or poor, can escape.

So the communal evil comes home to every man alike, the gates of his house-court will no longer keep it out; it leaps high over the enclosure wall and finds its man no matter where – even hidden in the recesses of the bedroom. (4.26–9)

The greed of the rulers and the violence of partisans release forces of destruction which cannot be controlled; this is what had happened in Megara and was to happen again, much later, in Corcyra.

Solon's praise of the opposite state of affairs, Εὐνομίη 'good government', rises, in a highly skilled rhetorical arrangement, to lyrical heights.

> Εὐνομίη δ' εὔκοσμα καὶ ἄρτια πάντ' ἀποφαίνει,
> καὶ θαμὰ τοῖς ἀδίκοις ἀμφιτίθησι πέδας·
> τραχέα λειαίνει, παύει κόρον, ὕβριν ἀμαυροῖ,
> αὐαίνει δ' ἄτης ἄνθεα φυόμενα,
> εὐθύνει δὲ δίκας σκολιάς, ὑπερήφανά τ' ἔργα
> πραΰνει· παύει δ' ἔργα διχοστασίης,
> παύει δ' ἀργαλέης ἔριδος χόλον, ἔστι δ' ὑπ' αὐτῆς
> πάντα κατ' ἀνθρώπους ἄρτια καὶ πινυτά. (4.32–9)

The goddess Good Rule makes everything well-ordered and sound; and often she puts the wrongdoers in irons. She makes the rough smooth, checks excess, dims violence; she withers the flowers of ruinous madness on the stalk, straightens crooked judgements, tames the works of insolence, stops the working of faction. She checks the anger of deadly dissension; under her governance everything in the human world is sound and sensible.

But Solon's warnings went unheeded and affairs came to the critical stage which in so many other Greek cities resulted in civil war or tyranny. The Athenians managed to avoid civil war and, for the moment, tyranny as well; they appointed Solon archon with full power for one year, to act as διαλλάκτης 'conciliator' – an office which under various titles had been created in more than one faction-riven Greek city (Mytilene, for example, see p. 168) as a last resort. Solon, once in office, told both sides to curb their demands and inaugurated a series of reforms (known as the Seisachtheia – 'shaking off of burdens') which included remission of debts, prohibition of debt-slavery, the return to Athens of men who had fled abroad because of debt, a code of laws to replace the fierce punitive code of Draco and many other measures besides. But they were all compromises; none of them a complete victory for either side.

> To the people I gave the portion that was theirs; I took nothing from them in the way of honour, offered nothing more. As for those who already had power and were respected for their wealth, I took measures to protect them from outrage. I took my stand with my strong shield thrown over both sides; I would not allow either side an unjust victory. (fr. 5)

To the rich, his own class, he counselled moderation: 'You who have driven on to overabundance of all good things, quiet your strong hearts in your breasts, set your proud mind on moderate aims.' (fr. 4c). Aristotle, who quotes these lines, tells us that Solon blamed the rich for the civil discord. But he had no illusions about the other side; in an account of his actions written after his year of office he is just as hard on the leaders of the popular party, who had raised the classic revolutionary cry for a redistribution of the land.

> They came to plunder, with high hopes of riches; each one thought he would find great wealth and that I was coaxing with smooth speech but would reveal a ruthless mind. Their hopes were liars and now they are angry with me, give me black looks as if I were an enemy...(fr. 34)

He is proud to boast that he disappointed both sides, above all that he disregarded demands from both sides for the punishment of their adversaries.

> If someone else had taken the goad in hand, some man of evil intent and grasping hand, he would not have held the people back. If I had agreed to do what the people's opponents wanted or on the other hand to what the people had in mind for them, this city would have been full of widows...(36.20–5)

His loyalty was not to either side but to Athens. Aristotle tells us that the poem which induced the two factions to give him the supreme authority began with the lines: 'I know, and pain builds up in my heart, as I see the oldest land of

Ionia in decline...' (4a). He went on, Aristotle tells us, 'to champion each side against the other, argue their case, and then recommend an end to the continuing faction-fighting'.

Solon's love for Athens embraces not only the people but the land itself; there is a tender note in his famous boast that he removed the mortgage stones from Attic soil.

συμμαρτυροίη ταῦτ' ἂν ἐν δίκηι Χρόνου
μήτηρ μεγίστη δαιμόνων 'Ολυμπίων
ἄριστα, Γῆ μέλαινα, τῆς ἐγώ ποτε
ὅρους ἀνεῖλον πολλαχῆι πεπηγότας,
πρόσθεν δὲ δουλεύουσα, νῦν ἐλευθέρη.   (36.3–7)

Let my witness in the court of Time be the great mother of the gods on Olympus, black Earth; I pulled up the mortgage markers that were fixed in her far and wide – she was enslaved and now is free.

He loved the language too, the dialect which stamped a man as Athenian; his remission of debts brought home men who had been sold abroad or had left 'by sheer necessity, to escape debt' and now 'no longer spoke the Attic tongue, since they had wandered far and wide':

γλῶσσαν οὐκέτ' 'Αττικὴν
ἱέντας, ὡς δὴ πολλαχῆι πλανωμένους.   (36.10–12)

This is the first mention of that Attic dialect which, because of the unrivalled greatness of those who later wrote in it, was to become the literary language of Greece, relegating all other dialects to provincial status and exerting its powerful influence on writers of Greek all through antiquity and even beyond.

The dialect in which Solon writes is not Attic, however; his language is the modified Ionic of the elegiac and epic tradition, though he is less closely tied to Homeric diction than some of his predecessors and he introduced into the elegiac vocabulary words which later became common in Attic writing (φλαύρη 13.15 for example, λατρεύει 13.48). But it is in his iambic poems, trimeter and tetrameter, that his real originality as a poet stands revealed. The iambic trimeter had been employed for violent personal abuse by Archilochus and Hipponax, for satiric abuse of the whole female sex by Semonides; in all these cases the identity of the speaker was not necessarily, sometimes not possibly, that of the poet. But Solon speaks in his own name about his own actions, the voice of a statesman offering a defence of the measures taken during his year as ruler of Athens. The long passage preserved by Aristotle (fr. 36) which contains the lines cited above – the claim to have removed the mortgage stones and the reference to the Attic dialect – is couched in the metre which later will be used by the speakers in Attic tragedy; the style and pace of these lines, as a modern scholar has pointed out, make them an entirely new phenomenon in archaic

literature. 'The flow of the verses...rolls on like a great speech in classical
tragedy...Even the grammatical structure is different; the sentences are long
and carry one subject after another to completion...Surely and steadily, the
discourse presses forward without pause in a consistent and solid stream.'[1]
Another scholar has claimed that it was Solon who in iambic poems like these
created the model which enabled the epic hero, when he later became the tragic
hero, to speak 'a language to which the men of the sixth century could respond
in living terms'.[2]

Solon could vary the tone, however; the solemn dignity of the statesman
could be leavened by sardonic humour, as when, in a tetrameter passage, he
writes a speech for a critic who despised him for not holding on to office at the
end of the year, to establish that tyranny which was the usual solution of the
political dilemma.

> Solon was no deep thinker, it seems, but a man lacking in sense, for the gods
> offered him blessings and he simply refused. He had the catch inside his big net
> but just stood there agape, unable to pull it tight – a failure of spirit as well as
> lack of wits. Now I would have been willing – just to hold power, to get wealth
> without limit, and be despot of Athens for one single day – I'd have been willing
> to be flayed alive to make a wineskin, my whole line wiped out. (fr. 33)

The temptation to retain power, and the advice of his friends that he should do
so may have been hard to resist, but his refusal was uncompromising. 'I spared
the land of my fathers, held my hand back from tyranny and harsh violence...'
(fr. 32). Yet he was intelligent enough to know that others would be more ambitious than he; the strains in the body politic were relieved, not removed, and
Solon warned his fellow citizens to beware.

> From a cloud comes the force of hail and snow,
> From the lightning flash the rolling thunder
> And from great men comes the city's destruction.
> And the poor, in their ignorance,
> Stumble into slavery, under the rule of a despot. (fr. 9)

His warnings were dismissed by the Pisistratid faction as madness and he
replied: 'Time will show the Athenians whether I am mad or no; it will not be
long, as the truth comes to plain view' (fr. 10). And later, with Pisistratus in
the saddle, he reproaches his fellow citizens for not seeing through the classic
manoeuvre of the would-be tyrant, the request for a bodyguard: 'Do not
attribute any share of these things to the gods; you yourselves built these men
up by assigning them protection...' (fr. 11).

[1] Fränkel (1975) 226f.
[2] Else (1965) 45.

These and other bitter comments may have been addressed to his fellow citizens from abroad, for we are told that after his year as archon he left Athens, so that he would not be the object of pressure to repeal his laws. He seems to have travelled to Egypt; one line (fr. 28) mentions the Canopic mouth of the Nile, and Plato, much later, has Critias claim that Solon brought back from his Egyptian travels the story of Atlantis (*Ti.* 21c). A stay in Cyprus is attested by six elegiac lines addressed to a king on that island (fr. 19) but there is nothing in the fragments to support Herodotus' famous story of his visit to Croesus of Lydia.

Some of the smaller fragments show us a Solon who was not always obsessed by affairs of state. Plato quotes a couplet which sounds like a short aristocratic credo: 'Happy the man who has loving sons, horses with uncloven hoof, hunting dogs and a guest from abroad' (23). Another (25) celebrates the joys of boy-love and a surprising group of iambic fragments (38–40) deals in considerable detail with food. A rather dull elegiac poem (27) divides the life of man up into ten seven-year periods, with remarks on the virtues of each phase: the fourth (age 22–8) is the height of physical strength and the seventh and eighth (age 43–56) the best for 'mind and tongue'. 'And if anyone duly reaches the end of the tenth, it would not be untimely if he came to the end of his days.' Later, presumably, he saw fit to revise this estimate. In a poem addressed to Mimnermus of Colophon (see pp. 93ff.) he takes issue with that poet's wish to die at sixty. 'If you will still take my advice now, erase that line. Don't take it ill that I have a better idea than you, revise the line, Mimnermus, and sing this: when I am eighty let death come for me' (fr. 20). We do not know whether he reached that age himself but the insecure dates we are given for his life suggest that he went most of the way. And of his old age he said, in a line that has been quoted with admiration ever since: 'I grow old learning many things'

γηράσκω δ' αἰεὶ πολλὰ διδασκόμενος.   (fr. 18)

5. SEMONIDES

Semonides of Amorgos is one of our earliest representatives of a perennial literary mode – informal, humorous, down-to-earth – which manifests itself now in lampoon or parody, now in comedy, now in satire. As a writer of iambics he belongs to the same tradition as Archilochus and Hipponax, but in later antiquity he was often confused with his distinguished near-namesake, the lyric poet Simonides of Ceos (see pp. 182ff.).[1] Modern scholars have been able to disentangle what remains of the two poets' work with reasonable confidence, but a few pieces are likely to remain in doubt, particularly since they shared

---

[1] Only Choeroboscus (*Et.Magn.* 713, 17c) preserves the correct spelling of his name; in all our other sources he is called Simonides.

at least one metre, elegiacs, and many of the fragments are too short to yield much decisive evidence.

Semonides was probably a Samian who settled in Amorgos and may indeed have been a leader of colonists on the island, as one of the sources claims;[1] otherwise we know nothing about his family or personal circumstances. Even his date is uncertain, though the latter half of the seventh century seems plausible. The attitude he strikes in the poems is that of the 'ordinary man' (e.g. in fr. 7, his account of the mare-woman, quoted below), but no doubt that is a tone of voice dictated by the choice of genre. He is said to have written poems of invective: Lucian (*Pseudolog*. 2) mentions the name of his alleged *bête noire*, one Orodoecidas,[2] but the surviving fragments (which may be quite unrepresentative) give very few clues. Most of the scraps that have come down to us were quoted by grammarians to illustrate points of usage, not to characterize Semonides. Some of these snippets may possibly come from lampoons on individuals, like fr. 13 on a dung-beetle ('there flew up to us the creature with the worst life-style of all beasts'), which could easily be part of an attack on some offensive enemy, but there is no means of telling. All we can say for certain is that he frequently wrote in iambics, the appropriate metre for light-hearted, informal or abusive poetry, and that his style and subject matter are correspondingly 'low', though there is little obvious obscenity in what happens to survive, and at least one fragment (1) is quite serious and dignified. Food seems to be a favourite topic (fr. 15 mentions tunny, squid and gudgeon, fr. 23 a 'wonderful cheese'); so too are animals (heron, buzzard and eel, fr. 9; kite, fr. 12; pig, fr. 28). In fr. 24 the speaker is a cook, another sure sign of comic intent in an ancient poet.

His longest and most celebrated piece, fr. 7, clearly belongs to the same mode. It is a 118-line fragment on women, preserved for us in the anthology of Stobaeus (fifth century A.D.). The poem was undoubtedly meant to be funny (though Stobaeus may not have thought so), and it must be seen as an early example of a favourite theme in western literature, the attack on women written by men for men in a male-dominated society.[3] It is close to Hesiod in its general attitude to women (as in the story of Pandora, *Theog*. 570ff., where women are said to be a 'great bane for mortal men, companions not of poverty but of excess', cf. *W.D*. 54ff., 702ff.), but Semonides' purpose is more obviously to entertain. He purports to account for women's natures by telling of their creation from ten different sources, seven animals, two elements and one insect, in the order sow, vixen, bitch, earth, sea, donkey, ferret, mare, monkey, bee. All but the bee are highly unflattering images: the animal associations suggest women who

---

[1] Suda IV 363.1 and 360.7, discussed by Lloyd-Jones (1975) 15–18.

[2] Or Orodoecides. West (*IEG* II) 97, thinks the name is corrupt, but see Lloyd-Jones (1975) 14 n. 13.

[3] Cf. Hodgart (1969) ch. 3; Hipponax 68.

are lazy, dirty, greedy (sow), unscrupulous and too clever (vixen), inquisitive, nagging (bitch), inert and stupid (earth), fickle (sea), stubborn, promiscuous (donkey), lecherous, dishonest (ferret), extravagant and luxurious (mare), ugly, malevolent (monkey), but there is a good deal of overlapping in the detail given to the different types, and some of the satirical effect depends precisely on the vehement and 'unfair' exaggeration. The cumulative impression given by the insistent list – the technique is the same as Juvenal's – is that *almost all* feminine traits are inherently bad: both the dirty sow and her opposite, the elegant mare, and both the clod-like earth-woman and the mercurial sea-woman, are equally objectionable.

The description of the mare-woman exemplifies Semonides' vivid use of everyday detail, his outspokenness and wit – and his straightforwardness by comparison with writers of more decadent times:

> τὴν δ' ἵππος ἁβρὴ χαιτέεσσ' ἐγείνατο,
> ἣ δούλι' ἔργα καὶ δύην περιτρέπει,
> κοὔτ' ἂν μύλης ψαύσειεν, οὔτε κόσκινον
> ἄρειεν, οὔτε κόπρον ἐξ οἴκου βάλοι,
> οὔτε πρὸς ἰπνὸν ἀσβόλην ἀλεομένη
> ἵζοιτ'. ἀνάγκηι δ' ἄνδρα ποιεῖται φίλον·
> λοῦται δὲ πάσης ἡμέρης ἄπο ῥύπον
> δίς, ἄλλοτε τρίς, καὶ μύροις ἀλείφεται,
> αἰεὶ δὲ χαίτην ἐκτενισμένην φορεῖ
> βαθεῖαν, ἀνθέμοισιν ἐσκιασμένην.
> κᾱλὸν μὲν ὦν θέημα τοιαύτη γυνὴ
> ἄλλοισι, τῶι δ' ἔχοντι γίνεται κακόν,
> ἢν μή τις ἢ τύραννος ἢ σκηπτοῦχος ἦι.   (57–69)

Another was produced by a dainty mare with a flowing mane. She shirks menial tasks and anything painful: she wouldn't put her hand to a mill or lift up a sieve or throw dung out of the house or sit by the stove dodging the soot. She makes her husband a friend of Necessity; and she washes the dirt off herself twice, sometimes three times, every day, and rubs on scents, and always wears her thick hair well combed and garlanded with flowers. A woman like this is very nice for other people to look at, but a terrible bane to her husband – unless he's a tyrant or a king.

If the mare-woman has a certain charm, the ferret and the monkey conjure up more repulsive pictures, the woman who is 'crazy for sex but makes the man she has with her sick' (53–4), and one who is 'short in the neck and moves awkwardly, and has no bottom but is all legs' – and is a nasty character into the bargain (75–9). But unlike most of his successors in the genre, Semonides allows the possibility of good in womankind and ends his list with a picture of the virtuous bee-woman, devoted wife and mother, beautiful, chaste and sensible. This interesting if unromantic picture recalls Hesiod, who also thought good

SEMONIDES

women could exist and saw the practical advantages of marriage as well as its drawbacks (*Theog.* 603ff.; *W.D.* 695ff.), though he too emphasizes the bad side and in fact uses the bee image to bring out the laziness of women: they are the drones for whom the men work all day long (*Theog.* 596ff.). Semonides moves on from the picture of the bee-woman to some generally condemnatory sentiments on women as the greatest evil given to men by Zeus (l.96 is closely echoed by l.115, the familiar device of ring-composition used to mark off a section). This passage seems to have been designed as a bridge to a part of the poem now lost, on disastrous women in legend: the last two lines of our extant fragment run 'some have gone to Hades fighting for a woman' (117–18), and it seems best to suppose that a series of *exempla* followed. Helen is the notorious case, but the myths could supply many more *femmes fatales*.

Even in its incomplete state this is a lively and arresting poem. Semonides has a sharp eye for detail and a suitably knowing and cynical tone, but there is a lack of density in the writing that makes it intellectually undemanding; Archilochus, working in a similar medium, achieved altogether more brilliant effects.

Semonides' poetry feels close to popular life, though our evidence for that life is of course very slight. As well as using homely detail he may have incorporated beast fables into his verses (e.g. perhaps frs. 9 and 12), and there may be some link between his notion of women created from animals and a fable by Aesop about men with the souls of beasts. Perhaps, too, he knew and drew upon folk-tale;[1] but it would be quite wrong to set him apart from the mainstream of archaic literature with its shared values and its all-pervading use of epic language. Commentators have noted that his pictures of the donkey and the mare, for example, have links with famous Homeric similes (*Iliad* 11.557ff.; 6.506ff.) as well as with 'real life', and his language consistently reveals its debt to Homer and Hesiod. His tone, salty and unheroic, is particularly reminiscent of Hesiod; like Alcaeus (fr. 347), he seems to have made a point of reworking a Hesiodic passage in his own metre:

γυναικὸς οὐδὲν χρῆμ' ἀνὴρ ληίζεται
ἐσθλῆς ἄμεινον οὐδὲ ρίγιον κακῆς.   (fr. 6)

a man carries off no prize better than a good woman or more horrid than a bad one.

(Cf. Hesiod, *W.D.* 702f. οὐ μὲν γάρ τι γυναικὸς ἀνὴρ ληίζετ' ἄμεινον | τῆς ἀγαθῆς, τῆς δ' αὖτε κακῆς οὐ ρίγιον ἄλλο 'for a man carries off no prize better than the good woman, nor any more horrid than the bad'.)

When he chooses, Semonides can write quite seriously, as in fr. 1 on man's helplessness and vulnerability. Here the poet uses themes familiar in Mimnermus,

[1] Lloyd-Jones (1975) 20–2.

115

Solon and the lyric poets – the way man clings to hope, and the many disasters he is heir to – but there is a characteristic touch of wit in the expression of these 'great commonplaces':

Some people wait for another day to come, others for a whole year to pass; but there's not a single mortal who doesn't think that next year he will make friends with wealth and prosperity. (7–10)

The poem seems to be leading up to an exhortation to enjoy the present moment, but it has been cut short by the anthologist who quotes it, and breaks off before the climax.

There is no certainty that any of Semonides' elegiac work has been preserved, though he is said to have composed an 'elegy in two books'. We know nothing of his alleged history of Samos (ἀρχαιολογία τῶν Σαμίων); conceivably this was in elegiacs. One fine poem in this metre has often been attributed to him because of its closeness in sentiment to fr. 1, although others have preferred on stylistic grounds to assign it to Simonides. The most recent editor, M. L. West, cautiously treats it as a 'doubtful' fragment (= Simonides fr. 8), typical of the younger poet's period, but not certainly identifiable as his. Whoever its author was, it deserves to be quoted as a felicitous expression of archaic Greek feeling; its elegance perhaps tells against Semonides, though he would surely have endorsed its tone and message:

ἓν δὲ τὸ κάλλιστον Χῖος ἔειπεν ἀνήρ·
'οἵη περ φύλλων γενεή, τοίη δὲ καὶ ἀνδρῶν'·
παῦροί μιν θνητῶν οὔασι δεξάμενοι
στέρνοις ἐγκατέθεντο· πάρεστι γὰρ ἐλπὶς ἑκάστωι
ἀνδρῶν, ἥ τε νέων στήθεσιν ἐμφύεται.
θνητῶν δ' ὄφρά τις ἄνθος ἔχηι πολυήρατον ἥβης,
κοῦφον ἔχων θυμὸν πόλλ' ἀτέλεστα νοεῖ·
οὔτε γὰρ ἐλπίδ' ἔχει γηρασέμεν οὔτε θανεῖσθαι,
οὐδ', ὑγιὴς ὅταν ἦι, φροντίδ' ἔχει καμάτου.
νήπιοι, οἷς ταύτηι κεῖται νόος, οὐδὲ ἴσασιν
ὡς χρόνος ἔσθ' ἥβης καὶ βιότου ὀλίγος
θνητοῖς. ἀλλὰ σὺ ταῦτα μαθὼν βιότου ποτὶ τέρμα
ψυχῆι τῶν ἀγαθῶν τλῆθι χαριζόμενος.

The finest thing the man of Chios [Homer] said was this: 'Like the generation of leaves, so is that of men.' Few mortals taking this in with their ears have stored it in their hearts; for each man is attended by hope, which grows in young people's breasts. And while he has the lovely bloom of youth a mortal man is light-hearted and full of impossible ideas: he doesn't expect to grow old or die, and while he is healthy he has no thought of being ill. They are fools who think this way and don't understand that for mortals the time of youth – and life – is short. So be aware of this and bear up as you near life's end, indulging yourself with good things.

It was presumably the approving references in Plato and Aristotle to Theognis as a moralist which guaranteed the survival of his book through the Byzantine era. No such protective label was or possibly could be attached to the work of Hipponax of Ephesus; even though he was a favourite of the Alexandrian poets and scholars (who seem to have neglected Theognis entirely) he survives only in fragments. His abusive tone and unedifying subject matter could hardly have been expected to win the approval of the Christian fathers, but they were also displeasing to the last aggressive representative of paganism, the emperor Julian. He wanted his priests to 'abstain not only from impure and lascivious acts but also from speech and reading of the same character... No initiate shall read Archilochus or Hipponax or any of the authors who write the same kind of thing...' (*Ep.* 48). The fact that the poet's Ionic dialect and polyglot vocabulary were unsuitable for an educational system which emphasized Attic purity is one more reason why our text of Hipponax, apart from recent papyrus discoveries, is a miserable collection of fragments, none containing more than six complete consecutive lines and many only a short phrase or a single word.

Our sources mention two 'books'; these are probably the books of the Alexandrian edition. If they were anything like the *Iamboi* of Callimachus, who in his introductory poem brings Hipponax back from Hades to give the Alexandrian *literati* a piece of his mind, the contents were separate poems on a variety of subjects and in a wide range of metres. Our fragments contain iambic trimeters, trochaic tetrameters, hexameters and a combination of iambic trimeter with a shorter dactylic line.

Most poets of the archaic period, no matter what their provenance or the genre in which they worked, were strongly influenced by the Ionian epic tradition and particularly by its main representative, Homer. The dependence is most clearly marked in the poems of Hesiod the Boeotian, who composed in the same hexameter metre as Homer, and in the closely related elegiac couplets of poets whose origins are as diverse as Ionia (Mimnermus and Callinus), the Aegean islands (Semonides of Amorgos and Archilochus of Paros) and the Greek mainland (Tyrtaeus of Sparta, Theognis of Megara and Solon of Athens). The Lesbian poets, too, though they write in unhomeric metres and dialect, adapt his themes and techniques, while Archilochus, in his iambic as well as in his elegiac verse is, as Denys Page put it, 'seldom for long free from the influence of the traditional language of the epic'.[1] Hipponax, however, who came from one Ionian city, Ephesus, and went to another, Clazomenae, writes for the most part, to judge from the pathetically few fragments we have left, as though Homer had never existed. There is one significant exception: a

[1] Page (1964) 159.

hexameter passage satirizing a glutton which is a ludicrous travesty of Homeric style:

> Μοῦσά μοι Εὐρυμεδοντιάδεα τὴν ποντοχάρυβδιν, ·
> τὴν ἐν γαστρὶ μάχαιραν, ὃς ἐσθίει οὐ κατὰ κόσμον,
> ἔννεφ', ὅπως ψηφῖδι 〈   〉 κακὸν οἶτον ὀλεῖται
> βουλῆι δημοσίηι παρὰ θῖν' ἁλὸς ἀτρυγέτοιο.   (fr. 128)

Muse, sing of Eurymedontiades, sea-swilling Charybdis,
his belly a sharp-slicing knife, his table manners atrocious;
sing how, condemned by public decree, he will perish obscenely
under a rain of stones, on the beach of the barren salt ocean.

This is the only intelligible hexameter fragment we possess; we have also some trochaic tetrameters, but the bulk of Hipponax' extant work is couched in the metre he may have invented but which in any case he made his trademark: the 'limping' (*skazon*) or 'lame' (*choliambos*) iambic. It is the iambic trimeter we know from Archilochus, except that it ends with a spondee; the three long final syllables produce a dragging, breaking effect.

> ἐμοὶ δὲ Πλοῦτος – ἔστι γὰρ λίην τυφλός –
> ἐς τὦικί' ἐλθὼν οὐδάμ' εἶπεν "Ἱππῶναξ,
> δίδωμί τοι μνέας ἀργύρου τριήκοντα
> καὶ πόλλ' ἔτ' ἄλλα'· δείλαιος γὰρ τὰς φρένας.   (fr. 36)

It never happened to me. The god of wealth's stone blind.
He never came into my house and said to me: 'Hipponax,
Here's money for you, thirty minae of pure silver
And a lot more besides.' No, he's too hard-hearted.

The tone of that fragment is characteristic; with Hipponax we are in an unheroic, in fact, a very sordid world.

There is a remarkable (and rather suspect) parallel between the biographies and poetic activity of the two most famous writers of iambics, Hipponax and Archilochus. Archilochus, spurned by Lycambes, turned his satiric rage against father and daughters, who, we are told, hanged themselves for shame: Hipponax, insulted by two sculptors, Bupalus and Athenis of Chios, who made caricatures of his ugly features, drove them to suicide with his iambic onslaughts. We know nothing more about Lycambes and his daughters than what Archilochus tells us, but Bupalus and Athenis are known from other sources; they were active on the Aegean islands in the middle and late years of the sixth century B.C. Pliny dismisses the story that they hanged themselves – *quod falsum est* – and mentions a statue signed by them on Delos (*N.H.* 36.5.11–13); Pausanias tells us there was a statue of the Graces by Bupalus in the art collection of the Hellenistic kings of Pergamon (9.35.6). Athenis is rarely mentioned in our fragments (fr. 70.11 and possibly fr. 1); but Bupalus' name recurs again and again (three times in fr. 95, for example). It appears in what was probably the first line of Hipponax' book (fr. 1); elsewhere Bupalus is accused of sleeping with his mother (ὁ μητροκοίτης, fr. 12) and in another fragment Hipponax imagines a confrontation with him: 'Hold my coat; I'll knock Bupalus' eye out' λάβετέ μεο ταἰμάτια, κόψω Βουπάλωι τὸν ὀφθαλμόν (fr. 120), a line which possibly connects with another; 'For I can swing with left and with right and I land them on target' ἀμφιδέξιος γάρ εἰμι κοὐκ ἀμαρτάνω κόπτων (fr. 121).

In addition to the two sculptors, a painter, one Mimnes, also figures among the victims of Hipponactean invective. He is reproved for painting a serpent on a war ship wrong way round – facing back towards the pilot at the stern instead of forward towards the enemy.

> Mimnes, you lousy pervert, when you paint the serpent on the trireme's full-oared side, quit making it run back from the prow-ram to the pilot. What a disaster it will be and what a sensation – you low-born slave, you scum – if the snake should bite the pilot on the shin. (fr. 28)

Another figure in this low-life saga (whether it has any basis in fact we do not know) is a woman whose Homeric and programmatic name is singularly at odds with her conduct and surroundings. She is associated with some deceitful scheme of Bupalus in fr. 12 but elsewhere appears in intimate association with Hipponax. 'Bending down to me over the lamp Arete...' κύψασα γάρ μοι πρὸς τὸ λύχνον 'Αρήτη (fr. 17) clearly comes from an erotic context and may be from the same poem in which Hipponax says:

> ἐγὼ δὲ δεξιῶι παρ' 'Αρήτην
> κνεφαῖος ἐλθὼν ῥωδιῶι κατηυλίσθην.   (fr. 16)

At dark I came to Arete's place, with a heron – lucky sign – on the right hand, and there I settled in.

A drinking party seems to have ensued, of a vulgarity which reminds one irresistibly of François Villon and his *grosse Margot – en ce bordeau ou tenons nostre estat.*

> ἐκ πελλίδος πίνοντες· οὐ γὰρ ἦν αὐτῆι
> κύλιξ, ὁ παῖς γὰρ ἐμπεσὼν κατήραξε,
>
>   ἐκ δὲ τῆς πέλλης
> ἔπινον· ἄλλοτ' αὐτός, ἄλλοτ' 'Αρήτη
> προύπινεν.   (frs. 13, 14)

...drinking from a milk pail since she didn't have a goblet, a slave had fallen on it, smashed it...now I would take a drink and then Arete would drain it dry.

There is another line of dialogue which may fit into this context: 'Why did you go to bed with that rogue Bupalus?' τί τῶι τάλαντι Βουπάλωι συνοίκησας; (fr. 15).

Other fragments give us more glimpses of life in the *bas-fonds* of Clazomenae. A papyrus fills out two already known fragments to produce an enigmatic but fascinating description of a quarrel which is interrupted by the appearance of the god Hermes and followed by what sounds like a legal manoeuvre of some kind.

> ...beaten up...this madness...the jaw...crapped on...with gold-blazing wand...near the foot of the bed...Hermes followed to Hipponax' house... the dog stealer...hisses like a viper...He went right away, with three witnesses to where the blackguard peddles vino and found his man sweeping out the shop – no broom, though, he was using the stock of a thorn bush. (fr. 79)

It is not a very comfortable world, this; someone 'never stops warming his chilblains by the coal fire' (fr. 59) and Hipponax prays to Hermes for some warm clothing:

'Ερμῆ, φίλ' 'Ερμῆ, Μαιαδεῦ, Κυλλήνιε,
ἐπεύχομαί τοι, κάρτα γὰρ κακῶς ῥιγῶ
καὶ βαμβαλύζω...
δὸς χλαῖναν 'Ιππώνακτι καὶ κυπασσίσκον
καὶ σαμβαλίσκα κἀσκερίσκα καὶ χρυσοῦ...   (fr. 32)

> Hermes, dear Hermes, Maia's son, born on Cyllene, I beseech thee, for I am damnably cold, my teeth are chattering...Grant Hipponax a cloak and a dolman and alpergatas, fur-lined boots and gold...

The foreign words in this translation are an attempt to represent a conspicuous feature of Hipponax' style: his use of words drawn from the non-Greek languages of the Ionian hinterland and the orient in general. The 'vino' the blackguard is peddling in the first fragment quoted above is in Hipponax an Egyptian word ἔρπιν and in the prayer to Hermes the names of the items of clothing and footgear are all from Anatolian languages. One fragment (125) uses a word for 'bread' – *bekos* – which we know from a famous story in Herodotus (2.2) was Phrygian.

Hipponax can even address Zeus with a foreign title, *palmys*: 'Oh Zeus, father Zeus, shah of the Olympian gods, why haven't you given me any money...?' (fr. 38). So Hermes is addressed with a title – Kandaules – which Hipponax specifies as 'Maeonian' (fr. 3a) and we hear also of Zeus's daughter Kubebe (fr. 127). Such linguistic borrowings were almost certainly typical of the Greek spoken in the Ionian cities; their appearance in the poems reinforces the vivid local colour which is one of the charms of these somewhat disreputable fragments – the glimpses (the only ones we are given) into the everyday life of the Eastern Greek cities. A very corrupt fragment (42) seems to be giving directions to a traveller going west through Lydia towards Smyrna; he will pass the tombs, monuments and columns of Lydian kings (Gyges is the only one we can be sure of). Another fragment (50) speaks of someone 'who lives by the back of the

city, in Smyrna, between Roughroad and Cape Decay' μεταξὺ Τρηχέης τε καὶ
Λεπρῆς ἀκτῆς. (Smyrna, we are told by Strabo, who cites these lines, is not the
great city of that name but a part of Ephesus.) One line reminds us that the
prosperity of these cities was based on sea-borne commerce: 'caulking the
keel with pitch and wax' ἔπειτα μάλθηι τὴν τρόπιν παραχρίσας (51), and another
passage that the Asia Minor littoral was one of the reservoirs of supplies for the
slave market:

> καὶ τοὺς σολοίκους ἢν λάβωσι περνᾶσι,
> Φρύγας μὲν ἐς Μίλητον ἀλφιτεύσοντας.   (fr. 27)

...and if they catch any barbarians, they put them up for sale: the Phrygians to
work the grain mills in Miletus...

The presence of many such slaves in the Ionian cities may account for the
frequent references in the poems to non-Greek people: a woman dressed in a
Koraxian robe (fr. 2), an obscure (and obscene) mention of the Sindoi on the
Black Sea – 'Sindic slit' Σινδικὸν διάσφαγμα (fr. 2a), a woman speaking Lydian
(fr. 92).

Not all of the characters of these low-life sketches live in the city; we have
one fragment which seems to be the voice of a man reduced to peasant fare by
the profligacy of one of his sons:

> For one of them spent whole days at ease at table
> swilling down tunafish and cheese in a steady stream
> for all the world like a eunuch from Lampsacus
> and so ate up the family fortune. I have to dig
> rocks on the mountainside, munch medium-sized figs
> and barley-wheat loaves – slave fodder. (fr. 26)

Another fragment may be a partial list of what this disgruntled speaker no
longer gets to eat:

> ...not chewing on partridges and hares,
> not seasoning the pancakes with sesame,
> not dipping the fritters in honey...(fr. 26a)

But if eating plays a large role in the Hipponactean world, so does the opposite
process, evacuation; not until Aristophanes do we encounter so varied a
scatological vocabulary again. Fully worthy of Aristophanes is the compound
μεσσηγυδορποχέστης (fr. 114c) which is quoted with the explanation: 'a man
who goes to the toilet often during the meal so that he can fill up again'.
Elsewhere somebody is 'croaking like a raven in a privy' (fr. 61) and in fr. 155
somebody is doing something almost indecipherable (but certainly repre-
hensible) 'like a lizard in a privy'. The Aristophanic verb τιλάω and its compounds turn up frequently (frs. 73.4, 79.6, 86.2).

It is only to be expected that such a poet would be equally uninhibited in matters sexual but it is only in recent years that papyrus fragments have confirmed what the few book fragments with erotic content (mostly lexicographical entries) seemed to suggest – that Hipponax is a grand master of obscene fiction. One damaged papyrus gives us a tantalizing but lacunose portrayal of what seems to be a love encounter rudely interrupted.

> ...on the floor...undressing...we were biting and kissing...looking out through the door...so they wouldn't catch us...naked...she was hurrying things up...and I was doing my part...

An obscure (and certainly obscene) passage about a sausage is followed by 'telling Bupalus to go to hell...' and two lines later 'and just when we were on the job...' καὶ δὴ 'πὶ τοῖς ἔργοισιν εἴχομεν...(84). Another fragment (92) manages to combine two of Hipponax' themes, sex and evacuation, in one wild scene which may well have been the model for the Oenothea episode in Petronius' *Satyricon* (138). The papyrus, once again, is fragmentary; the right-hand end of the lines is missing, and interpretation is difficult. But clearly a woman, who is introduced as 'speaking Lydian' λυδίζουσα, carries out some magical and obscene rite on the narrator (it includes, besides some obscure anal operation, beating his genitals with a fig branch); the object, presumably, is, as in the *Satyricon*, to restore his lost virility. In Hipponax, however, all this takes place in a privy (its smell is singled out for mention); the protagonist gets spattered with excrement and this provokes an invasion of dung-beetles – they come 'whirring, more than fifty of them' – to provide a Rabelaisian finale.

The fig branch (κράδη) with which the narrator is stimulated in this passage turns up in another context, the religious rite of expelling the scapegoat, the *pharmakos*. The late Byzantine scholar Tzetzes, who quotes the passages in question (they amount to ten lines = frs. 5–10) tells us that in time of famine or plague the 'ancients' chose 'the ugliest man of all' and after various ceremonies mentioned by Hipponax, burned him and scattered his ashes in the sea. These last two details, however, are not derived from Hipponax and in fact the fate of the *pharmakos* in such ceremonies is still a controversial matter – it may have been merely a ceremonial expulsion. In any case the Hipponax passages are not descriptions of the rites but allusions to them, often for purpose of comparison. 'Beating in winter and thrashing with fig branches and squill-stalks, like a *pharmakos*...figs and cereal and cheese, the sort of things the *pharmakos* eats...' One passage – 'And on the genitals let the *pharmakos*, led away, be seven times thrashed' – recalls the Lydian lady's formula for restoring virility in the obscene fragment. What all this has to do with the lives of Hipponax' characters we do not know; perhaps they are parts of imprecations against Bupalus and Athenis, perhaps Hipponax sees himself in the role of victim; in one fragment (fr. 37) someone 'was giving orders to beat and stone Hipponax' ἐκέλευε βάλλειν καὶ λεύειν Ἱππώνακτα.

The tone of the fragments is not always abusive or obscene, nor is its background always sordid. One beautiful line, as clear, melodious and spare as a line of Sappho, tells of yearning for a girl: 'If only I had a maiden, fair and soft of skin' εἴ μοι γένοιτο παρθένος καλή τε καὶ τέρεινα (fr. 119); another (a Homeric reminiscence for once) has an epic quality:

> ἐπ' ἁρμάτων τε καὶ Θρεϊκίων πώλων
> λευκῶν †ὀείους κατεγγύς† 'Ιλίου πύργων
> ἀπηναρίσθη 'Ρῆσος, Αἰνειῶν πάλμυς... (fr. 72. 5–7)

He came on his chariot and white Thracian horses; but in his sleep, near the towers of Troy, he was slain, Rhesus, the shah (*palmys*) of the Aeneans...

But of course we do not know the context, which may have been decisive for the effect of these lines. One papyrus fragment (fr. 102), for example, contains elements which suggest a similar epic tone but soon belies it by adding incongruous details. The phrases '...hydra at Lerna...he crushed the crab...' obviously celebrate one of the labours of Heracles but a few lines later we read the name Kikon, a character known to us from other fragments (4,78,102,118) as one of the cast of disreputable characters who haunt not the heroic but the Hipponactean world.

Hipponax remains a mystery. We have lost the matrix of these fascinating but puzzling fragments; ripped from their frame they leave us in doubt whether to take them seriously as autobiographical material (unlikely, but it has been done), as complete fiction (but there is no doubt that Bupalus and Athenis were real people), as part of a literary adaptation of some ritual of abuse (a *komos* or something similar), or as dramatic scripts for some abusive proto-comic performance. Whatever they were, they are a pungent reminder of the variety and vitality of archaic Greek literature and of how much we have lost.

5

ARCHAIC CHORAL LYRIC

I. THE NATURE OF EARLY CHORAL POETRY

From Alcman in the seventh century to Timotheus at the beginning of the fourth, choral lyric remains an important literary form. Performed by citizen choruses – men, boys, women, or girls – as well as by guilds of professionals,[1] these poems were sung by a dancing chorus at public religious festivals or at important family events like weddings or funerals. Because the festivals in honour of the gods also celebrated the civic life of the polis, choral song played a major role in affirming the values and solidarity of the community. The connexion between music and ethical values, in fact, remains strong through the archaic and classical periods. Like much of early Greek poetry, choral lyric is public rather than personal in outlook, expression and orientation. In this respect it differs from monodic lyric, which is much more an expression of personal emotion.

The basic forms and sub-genres of choral lyric are already attested in Homer and doubtless reach back long before the literary evidence.[2] The Shield of Achilles in the *Iliad* describes a marriage song (*hymenaios*, *Il.* 18.491–6), a harvest song accompanied by dancing (18.569–72), and an elaborate performance of dance and song by youths and maidens at Cnossus (18.590–606). In the *Odyssey* the bard Demodocus sings the famous song about the illicit love of Ares and Aphrodite while all around him the young Phaeacians dance to its rhythm (8.262ff.). These passages imply a close interconnexion of music, dance and poetry in choral lyric. The lament for Hector in *Iliad* 24.720–76 illustrates the *threnos* or dirge and also reflects its formal structure: a 'singer' (*aoidos*) 'leads off' (ἐξάρχει, ἔξαρχος); he or she is followed by the collective voice of the chorus joining in some kind of refrain (*Il.* 24.720, 723, 747, 761, 776; cf. also *Il.* 18.51 and 314). The formulaic phrase ἀμειβόμεναι ὀπὶ καλῆι 'answering with lovely voice' (*Il.* 1.604, *Od.* 24.60, *Hymn to Apollo* 1.189) may also indicate the division of such songs into strophes, that is, stanzas whose set

---

[1] E.g. the Onitadai in Miletus and the Euneidai at Athens: see Schmid–Stählin I 1.452.
[2] Webster (1970) 46–55.

metrical and probably choreographic form is repeated to different words. Only later, possibly with Stesichorus in the early sixth century, does triadic composition develop. This is a more complex stanzaic arrangement, consisting of a strophe, corresponding antistrophe, and an epode, the last in a related but slightly varied metre.

Besides the marriage-song, dancing song, dirge and paean (*Il.* 1.472–4, a song in honour of Apollo), choral lyric also includes the maiden-song (partheneion), processional song (prosodion), hymn, dithyramb (in honour of Dionysus). Slightly later and of more secular character arise the enkomion (song in praise of men, not gods) and skolion (popular song sung at banquets and symposia).[1]

The division between choral and monodic lyric is convenient, but artificial, for many poets composed songs of both types. Alcman, chiefly a choral poet, composed love songs, some of which may have been monodic. The monodists Sappho, Alcaeus and Anacreon composed choral works: marriage-songs, hymns and partheneia. The elegist and iambist Archilochus may have composed dithyrambs (120 *IEG*) and paeans (121 *IEG*).[2]

The numerous local and religious festivals – the Carneia and Hyacinthia at Sparta, the Adrasteia at Sicyon, the Iolaia at Thebes, the Adonidia on Lesbos – provided the public occasions for choral song. Choral lyric also played an important part at the great cosmopolitan celebrations, like those at Delphi and Olympia or the Delian festival in honour of Apollo vividly described in the *Homeric Hymn to Apollo* (146–73). With the Greeks' typical love of competition, poets and choruses often competed against one another for prizes.

The poet (*aoidos*) composed both music and words. He also directed a chorus, led by a chorus-leader (*choregos*) and varying from seven to fifty members, which sang and danced the words to an instrumental accompaniment of lyre and flute. As surviving fragments attest, the richness of festal attire – robes, jewellery, hair-style, elaborately adorned musical instruments – was an important feature of the performance (cf. Alcman 1.64ff. *PMG*; *Hymn to Apollo* 182–5). Alcman's poetry makes frequent allusion to the dance-movements of the singer-performers (e.g. 3.9, 3.70 *PMG*).

Because archaic choral lyric developed especially in the Dorian-speaking areas of the Peloponnese and west Greece, its dialect remained Doric, unlike monody, which followed the poet's local dialect. There are a few exceptions: Alcman, our earliest preserved choral poet, composed in his local Laconian dialect; and some sixth- or early fifth-century Boeotian poets composed in their own dialects also (*PMG* 692–4). From Stesichorus on, however, and even in some poems of Alcman, choral poetry tends to be written in a more or less

---

[1] For more detailed discussion of the individual genres see *GLP* 4–9; Smyth (1900) Intro. xxiii–cxxxiv.

[2] Cf. Ibycus 296 *PMG*; Anacreon 500, 501, 502b *PMG*. In general *GLP* 6f.; Webster (1970) 63–5, 79.

conventional literary Doric, which admits many borrowings from the old Ionic language of Homeric epic and a certain mixture of Aeolic forms, the latter more frequent in Boeotian Pindar than elsewhere. The dialect, in other words, was an artificial literary language, a 'Kunstsprache'. Its conventional nature enabled the genre to transcend local or regional boundaries and stress the Panhellenic aspect of the festivals at Olympia or Delphi.

Despite changes over time and the different spirit and conventions of different types of cult songs, much in choral lyric remains constant: mythical narrations of gods or heroes; gnomic reflections on moral behaviour, the limitations of mortality, the nature of the human condition; comments on the art of song, predecessors, the poet's skill; a certain religious aura, even in the secularized forms of the sixth and fifth centuries.[1] Expressions of personal feelings, though not uncommon, tend to be more stylized and less emotional than in monody. Recent research has shown how misleading it may be to take first-person statements, even when not in the *persona* of the chorus, as reflections of the poet's sentiments.

Mythical narration forms a particularly important part of these poems, not only as ornament, but also as illustration of moral norms and precepts, often reinforced by a concluding ethical maxim. The poet could exploit a rich mythic tradition, confident that an audience brought up on Homer, Hesiod, the Cyclic epics would grasp and appreciate his allusions to or departures from earlier versions. Rapidity, selectivity of detail, elaborate compound adjectives, decorative richness, epithets borrowed or adapted from Homer are the most constant features of the style. There is also a tendency toward density of syntax, the isolation of vivid moments of action, powerful and often audacious metaphors, tightly phrased and weighty gnomic pronouncements.

The demands of cult and worship did not severely constrain the exuberance of choral lyric. Here, as elsewhere in Greek art, aesthetic brilliance counted for more than pious solemnity. Human emotions, pathos, the physical beauty of men and nature, the city and its legends are generally in the foreground. Celebration of the gods is a joyous affair; the more movement, colour, sensuous detail the better. Even in Pindar, the most religious in spirit of those poets, the religious element is personal and meditative rather than cultic.

The extant poetical fragments and the depiction of choral celebration on vases and sculpture attest to the concern with the beauty of the singers, the grace of their dance, the importance of both the vocal and instrumental music, incense, the altar, the crowd (cf. *Hymn to Apollo* 152ff.; Sappho 2, 44.24ff., 141, 154 *PLF*). For us only the bare words survive, and we must make an effort of imagination to supply the other elements, which were at least of equal importance for the ancient audience.

---

[1] See *GLP* 12f.; Schmid–Stählin 1 1, 452–7; Fränkel (1975) 159f.

The poets of early choral lyric are shadowy figures. They are more closely associated with the history of music than with literature. Much of our information about them, in fact, comes from the treatise *On music* attributed to Plutarch. Corinth and Sparta are particularly important. Of Eumelus of Corinth, a contemporary of Archias who founded Syracuse in 734 B.C., we have two lines in dactylic metre, part of a prosodion (processional song) written for the Messenians at the Delian festival (fr. 13 *EGF*, 696 *PMG*). The practice of commissioning foreign poets at the great international festivals clearly has a long history. Figures like Olympus of Phrygia, inventor of the musical scale, Pamphos and Olen of Lycia, early writers of hymns (cf. Hdt. 4.35) possibly in hexameter rather than lyric metres, are scarcely more than names.

Terpander of Lesbos is a little more substantial. A few fragments survive, of doubtful authenticity (697–8 *PMG*). He is celebrated for converting the older four-stringed instrument into the seven-stringed cithara or lyre, capable of a wider and subtler range of melodies. He established the 'first school of music' at Sparta, won a victory at the first festival of the Carneia in 676 B.C., and supposedly invented the skolion (see below, pp. 179f.; Ps.-Plut. *De musica* 28). Still partly in the realm of myth too is another Lesbian poet, Arion of Methymna, whose miraculous rescue by a dolphin is recounted by Herodotus (1.23f.). The Suda and Eusebius agree in placing his *floruit* in the last quarter of the seventh century. In Corinth, under the tyrant Periander, he seems to have raised dithyrambic choral song to the level of artistic composition. These early choral songs, involving satyrs with speaking parts and probably some mythical narration, are sometimes considered to have been one of the early influences on the development of tragedy (see *CHCL* I, Part 2, 1ff.).[1] The fragments attributed to him (Diehl vol. 1.5f.) are of doubtful authenticity.

2. ALCMAN

Only with Alcman does early choral lyric have a literary reality. He is the first choral poet of whom anything substantial is preserved. Both dates and origins are controversial. Traditional dates vary between early and late seventh century; recent evidence suggests the end rather than the beginning of the seventh century (see Appendix). Whether he was a native Laconian or a Lydian has also been disputed from antiquity on (13a, *PMG*). Fragment 16, *PMG*, 'He was no rustic fellow nor gauche…nor a Thessalian by race nor a shepherd from Erysiche [in Acarnania], but from lofty Sardis', was interpreted autobiographically, probably wrongly (see Appendix). The bias against believing that Sparta could have produced a native poet like Alcman may also have contributed to the notion of Lydian birth (cf. Aelian, *Var. Hist.* 12.50). Alcman's

[1] See Else (1965) 14–17; Webster (1970) 68f.; Lesky 225; *DTC* 10–13, 97–101.

use of the local dialect, intense familiarity with local customs, and his burial near the shrine of Helen in Sparta (Pausanias 3.15.3) favour Spartan or at least Laconian birth. It is, of course, possible that he was born in Sardis of parents who were Laconian or emigrated in his early years to Sparta. The question remains unsolved.

The Sparta of Alcman was a very different place from the austere militaristic society that it became in later times. In the late seventh and early sixth century Sparta and Corinth, not Athens, were the cultural centres of mainland Greece. The British School excavations at the sanctuary of Artemis Orthia near Sparta have amply documented the vigorous flourishing of the arts there, particularly between 650 and 550.[1] The success of the Second Messenian War, whose martial spirit Tyrtaeus sang, brought a period of prosperity, expansiveness, enjoyment of life. Alcman's Sparta was adorned with large temples and statuary in marble, ivory, bronze and terracotta. The shrine of Artemis Orthia contained numerous votive offerings of elegant design, elaborate jewellery in gold and silver, and imports from Egypt and the Near East. The pottery, sculpture and ivory plaques show the imaginative figures of Orientalizing art: vivid mythical scenes, inventive geometric designs, and fabulous creatures of all sorts. The simple elegance, gaiety, bold energy, vigour, and originality of the Laconian pottery of this time parallel in spirit the poetry of Alcman.

In the later seventh and early sixth century Sparta continued to attract poets and musicians: besides Alcman we hear of Terpander, Thaletas of Gortyn, Clonas of Thebes or Tegea, Xenocritus of Locri, Polymnastus of Colophon and Sacadas of Argos. They sang at festivals like the Carneia, Hyacinthia, Gymnopaidiai, and others. Even in its more austere period later, Sparta retained the reputation for brilliant choruses (see Pindar, fr. 199 Snell = 189 Bowra). Near the end of the fifth century Aristophanes reproduced a Laconian choral song in *Lysistrata* of 411 B.C. (1306ff.).

Like the early monodists, Sappho and Alcaeus, but unlike most later choral poets, Alcman composed in his local dialect; he also borrowed freely from the common storehouse of epic diction. He probably composed a few poems in Ionic, possibly as preludes (*prooimia*) to longer works, a practice vaguely attested for Terpander and other early lyricists (Ps.-Plut. *De mus.* 3 and see below, p. 141). His works were collected into six books of Lyrics (Μέλη), and a puzzling work, Κολυμβῶσαι 'The women diving', now confirmed as a separate poem by the discovery of the end of Book 6 on *P.Oxy.* 3209. Its character remains a problem: guesses range from a poem about Leda to some kind of marriage-song.

Alcman was especially celebrated for his love-poetry, not all of which was

---

[1] See Dawkins (1929) *passim*; Huxley (1962) 61–3; Forrest (1968) 71–3; Tigerstedt (1965) 39–44; Calame (1977) II 33ff.; Janni (1965) 25ff.

necessarily personal. Erotic themes were doubtless prominent in his marriage-songs or hymenaia, for which he was also famous (see 159 *PMG*), and in his partheneia or maiden-songs, as we can see from the extant fragments. Of these last we have two major examples: his most important surviving work, the Louvre Partheneion so called from the present location of the papyrus, discovered at Sakkara in 1855 and published at Paris in 1863, and substantial portions of a second Partheneion from Oxyrhynchus, published in 1957 (fr. 3 *PMG*). The Oxyrhynchus papyri have also enriched our knowledge of Alcman with a cosmogonic poem, important scholia on the Louvre Partheneion, and other fragments. Many short fragments, sometimes only a word or a phrase, quoted by lexicographers or metricians for their formal anomalies, are tantalizing, but mysterious.

The grace, liveliness, and range of Alcman's choral style are best seen in the Louvre Partheneion (fr. 1 *PMG*). This work was composed for a chorus of Spartan girls, to be sung at a local religious festival whose exact nature is uncertain.[1] The goddess to whom the girls offer the song and a *pharos* (generally a sacred tapestry or robe, but here glossed by the scholia as a plough) is called Aotis and, as her name suggests, may have some connexion with the dawn and possibly with marriage and fertility. (Attempts to elicit a reference to Artemis Orthia from ὀρθρίαι in line 61 are, for metrical and linguistic reasons, invalid.) Our ignorance of the cult, the obscurity of many of the allusions, and the lacunose state of the text leave many problems unsolved. Even so, we have a good overall picture of the whole work and can appreciate the general limpidity and richness of Alcman's style.

The scale of the poem was ample. There were probably ten stanzas of fourteen lines each, probably not in triadic composition. Thirty-five lines, or two-and-a-half stanzas have been lost from the beginning. These contained the invocation and part of a myth. A diacritical sign (a coronis) preserved on the papyrus and marking the end of the poem indicates the loss of the last four lines. We are also fortunate to have a number of scholia from Hellenistic commentaries, some in the margins of the Louvre papyrus, some found later on papyri from Oxyrhynchus.

Our text begins near the end of a myth about the defeat of the sons of Hippocoon. In other versions of this Laconian legend Heracles has an important role, restoring the exiled Tyndareus and thus helping to establish the line of Spartan kingship. There is no trace of Heracles in the preserved fragments, so that the exact version which Alcman is following is still a matter for speculation.[2]

[1] See Calame (1977) II 103ff.; Burnett (1964) 30–4; Garvie (1965) 185–7; Gentili (1976) *passim*; Griffiths (1972) 24ff.; Page (1951a) 72–4; Treu (1968a) 28.

[2] The presence of Heracles here rests on the indirect evidence of Sosibius *ap.* Clement Alex., *Protrept.* 36 with schol. *ad loc.* Other versions which include Heracles: Apollod. 2.7.3, Diod. 4.33.5f.; Paus. 3.15.4f. See Page (1951a) 30ff.; *GLP* 40ff.; Davison (1968) 148–53; Garvie (1965) 186; Griffiths (1972) 14.

The mention of 'Destiny and Resource, Aisa and Poros, eldest of the gods', at this point (13f.) suggests that the victory illustrated the triumph of the moral order, a function of myth familiar from Pindar. The warning against trying to wed Aphrodite (μηδὲ πηρήτω γαμῆν τὰν Ἀφροδίταν, 17) suggests that the myth had something to do with marriage, possibly the Tyndarids' defence of Helen, their sister, or possibly the Hippocoontids' rival suit for the future brides of the Tyndarids. The listing of the fallen Hippocoontids by name shows a fondness for local detail that we find elsewhere in choral lyric. A second myth, more briefly told and also extremely fragmentary (22–35), seems to have recounted the punishment of a crime against the gods, also of an amorous nature, perhaps committed by the Giants or the Aloadae, Otus and Ephialtes.[1]

Both myths were rounded off by gnomic statements about respecting the due limits of the mortal condition:

> μή τις ἀνθ]ρώπων ἐς ὡρανὸν ποτήσθω
> μηδὲ πη]ρήτω γαμῆν τὰν Ἀφροδίταν
> ϝάνασσαν...
>
> (16–18)

Let no mortal fly to the heavens nor attempt to marry goddess Aphrodite...

> ἄλαστα δὲ
> ϝέργα πάσον κακὰ μησαμένοι·
> ἔστι τις σιῶν τίσις.
>
> (34–6)

Devising evil deeds they suffered unforgettably; there is some requital from the gods.

As in Pindar and Bacchylides such 'gnomic bridge-passages' serve as a transition to a new subject, in this case the chorus' playful dispute about the beauty of two of their members, Agido and Hagesichora, the latter called the chorus-leader (36–43):

> ἔστι τις σιῶν τίσις·
> ὁ δ' ὄλβιος, ὅστις εὔφρων
> ἁμέραν [δι]απλέκει
> ἄκλαυτος· ἐγὼν δ' ἀείδω
> Ἀγιδῶς τὸ φῶς· ὁρῶ   40
> ϝ' ὥτ' ἄλιον, ὄνπερ ἄμιν
> Ἀγιδὼ μαρτύρεται
> φαίνην...

There is some requital from the gods. But he is happy who in joy of mind weaves a day through to its end without lamentation. But my song is Agido's radiance. I see her shine as the sun whom Agido summons to shine for us [or, to whose shining for us Agido bears witness]...

[1] See Page (1951a) 42f.; Janni (1965) 68–71.

The changefulness of mortal life defines man as *ephemeros*: even his precarious happiness must be measured within the limits of the 'single day' (cf. Pind. *Ol.* 2. 33–8). The poet's song both describes and exemplifies the necessity of staying within the norms of mortal life. Here implicitly, as far more explicitly and programmatically in Pindar, the poet places his art in a large moral framework and makes poetry itself part of the struggle for order and beauty against what is aesthetically and morally formless and chaotic. Not only the evil-doing in the preceding stanza, but also the recognition that mortal life is rarely without grief form the foil to this sun-like beauty in the festal joy of celebration.

As in choral lyric generally, the structure of the poem tends to be discontinuous, but the imagery of light is prominent throughout. If, as seems highly probable, the song was part of a *pannychis*, or 'all night festival', performed shortly before dawn, the movement from darkness to light underlined by the imagery would also have symbolic value, particularly in a cult concerned with fertility, marriage, growth and passage to maturity. The comparison of Agido to the sun may have religious or cultic significance too, but that does not exclude the note of playful exaggeration which dominates the next section of the poem, in sharp contrast to the more serious regal and martial themes of the first two strophes.

The chorus goes on (43–72):

ἐμὲ δ' οὔτ' ἐπαινῆν
οὔτε μωμήσθαι νιν ἁ κλεννὰ χοραγὸς
οὐδ' ἁμῶς ἐῆι· δοκεῖ γὰρ ἤμεν αὐτα   45
ἐκπρεπὴς τὼς ὥπερ αἴτις
ἐν βοτοῖς στάσειεν ἵππον
παγὸν ἀεθλοφόρον καναχάποδα
τῶν ὑποπετριδίων ὀνείρων·

ἦ οὐχ ὁρῆις; ὁ μὲν κέλης   50
Ἐνετικός· ἁ δὲ χαίτα
τᾶς ἐμᾶς ἀνεψιᾶς
Ἁγησιχόρας ἐπανθεῖ
χρυσὸς [ὡ]ς ἀκήρατος·
τό τ' ἀργύριον πρόσωπον,   55
διαφάδαν τί τοι λέγω;
Ἁγησιχόρα μὲν αὐτα·
ἁ δὲ δευτέρα πεδ' Ἀγιδὼ τὸ ϝεῖδος
ἵππος Ἰβηνῶι Κολαξαῖος δραμήται·
ταὶ Πεληάδες γὰρ ἇμιν   60
ὀρθρίαι φᾶρος φεροίσαις
νύκτα δι' ἀμβροσίαν ἅτε σήριον
ἄστρον ἀυηρομέναι μάχονται·

οὔτε γάρ τι πορφύρας
τόσσος κόρος ὥστ' ἀμύναι,   65

οὔτε ποικίλος δράκων
παγχρύσιος, οὐδὲ μίτρα
Λυδία, νεανίδων
ἰανογ[λ]εφάρων ἄγαλμα,
οὐδὲ ταὶ Ναννῶς κόμαι,   70
ἀλλ' οὐ[δ'] 'Αρέτα σιειδής,
οὐδὲ Σύλακίς τε καὶ Κλεησισήρα...

But the glorious chorus-leader in no way allows me either to praise or to blame her (Agido). For she herself (Hagesichora) seems outstanding, just as if one should set among cattle a well compacted horse, winner of prizes, of ringing hooves, a horse of winged dreams [or, a horse of dreams which lie beneath rocks].[1]

Do you not see her? The one is a Venetic pony; but the hair of my cousin, Hagesichora, blooms like gold unalloyed. Silver her face. Is my speech clear? Here she is, Hagesichora herself. But she who is second after Agido in beauty will run as a Colaxaean horse against an Ibenian. For the Pleiades early in the morning, rising like the star Sirius through the ambrosial night, fight against us as we bear the plough [robe?].

Nor is there such an abundance of purple to defend us, nor the dappled snake, all-gold, nor the Lydian cap, joy of soft-eyed girls, nor Nanno's tresses, no, nor Areta the godlike, nor Sylacis nor Cleësisera (can defend us)...

Agido's beauty is now balanced by Hagesichora's. The rivalry has a stylized, mock-serious character. The agonistic mood may be related to the cult setting. Some scholars have suggested rival choruses or a bridal serenade like Catullus 61, but there is no clear evidence for either. Cultic function, in any case, does not preclude playfulness. The repetition of 'see' (ὁρῶ, 40; ὁρῆις, 50), the language of brightness and clarity (54–6, 60–3), the comparison to horses, the playful military imagery (63, 65) and the comparison to precious metals (54f., cf. 67) maintain a certain formal unity; but the dominant tone is one of banter, rapid colloquial interchange, familiarity. The chorus' reference to Hagesichora as 'my cousin' (52) may indicate a relationship of a cultic as well as a familial nature. The listing of the girls' names in 70ff. is part of this atmosphere of friendly intimacy. The concreteness of detail, characteristic both of Alcman and choral lyric generally, both presupposes and celebrates the solidarity of this society. The girls named by Alcman in other poems are of high social standing: Timasimbrota, a king's daughter (5, fr. 2, col. i *PMG*) and Astymeloisa in 3.73f.; we may assume that these girls too are of good family or noble birth.

The lines on the Pleiades (60–3) are the poem's most notorious crux.[2] The

---

[1] 'Winged dreams' favoured by Page (1951a) 87; see also Calame (1977) II 67, with n. 40; 'dreams under (shady) rocks': West (1965) 195 and Marzullo (1964) 193f. The ancient lexicographers attest the meaning 'winged' (e.g. *Et.Gen.* s.v.; *Et.Magn.* 783.20ff. The linguistic objections to this meaning, though serious, are not perhaps decisive.

[2] See Page (1951a) 52ff., 75ff. Recent discussion and bibliographical surveys in Gerber (1967/8) 325–7 and (1975/6) 95–7; Puelma (1977) 53f.; Calame (1977) II 179–86; Gianotti (1978) 257–71.

scholiast says that the Pleiades ('doves') are Agido and Hagesichora, and it is probably safest to follow that view. An alternative, that 'Pleiades' is the name of a rival chorus, is widely assumed, but has no evidence to support it. The comparison to Sirius confirms that, whatever else the Pleiades may refer to, they are also the constellation and form part of the imagery of light in the poem. The two outstanding members of the chorus are now said to 'rise like Sirius through the ambrosial night' (the last phrase is a Homeric formula), possibly to contrast their joint beauty with that of the rank and file, the eight girls listed in the next stanza. In that case the comparison to the bright and generally baleful light of Sirius would be part of the tone of playful exaggeration and mock-combat between chorus and its two leading members. Other interpretations stress local connexions (one of the Pleiades is the Laconian nymph, Taygeta) or reference to the season or to the approach of daylight (the girls are racing to beat the dawn).[1] Scholarly consensus on the passage is still remote.

The list of the girls' charms in 64ff. makes clear the erotic colouring of the playful banter. This is implicit also in the comparison to horses (cf. Anacreon 346, 360, 417 *PMG* and Ibycus 287 *PMG*) and in the language of combat. The references to the chorus-members' hair, jewellery, and robes also serve to call attention to the festive brilliance of the present celebration. These erotic overtones may have some relation to the cult as well, particularly if Aotis is a goddess of fertility and marriage, like the Spartan Helen, or, if, as some have suggested, the song formed part of a marriage-celebration or an initiatory ritual of girls approaching marriageable age.

The erotic elements become stronger as the chorus concludes the listing of its own members and turns back to Hagesichora (73–7):

> οὐδ' ἐς Αἰνησιμβρ[ό]τας ἐνθοῖσα φασεῖς·
> 'Ασταφίς [τ]έ μοι γένοιτο
> καὶ ποτιγλέποι Φίλυλλα   75
> Δαμαρ[έ]τα τ' ἐρατά τε Ϝιανθεμίς·
> ἀλλ' 'Αγησιχόρα με τείρει.

Nor if you go to the house of Aenesimbrota will you say, 'May Astaphis be mine; may Philylla cast her glances at me and Damareta and the lovely Vianthemis'; but rather will you say, 'Hagesichora wears me down'.

Most recent interpreters have welcomed M. L. West's excellent suggestion that Aenesimbrota is a dealer in love-charms, a *pharmakeutria* like the old woman of Theocritus' second *Idyll*.[2] Vianthemis' epithet, ἐρατά 'lovely', is obviously erotic, as are Philylla's 'glances'; we may recall the Graces, ἐρογλεφάροι 'with

---

[1] Erotic associations of 'Pleiades': Calame (1977) II 75ff. and also 86–97; Gentili (1976) 63; cf. also Puelma (1977) 34f., n. 65. A 'race with the dawn' in a night festival or *pannychis*: Griffiths (1972) 17ff.; Burnett (1964) 30–4; Gianotti (1978) 268–71.
[2] West (1965) 199; see Puelma (1977) 40f.

love in their eyes', earlier (20f.) and the related epithet, ἰανογλεφάρων 'soft-eyed', in 69. The erotic sense of τείρει, 'wears me down', is now confirmed by a new papyrus fragment of a scholium (schol. B), as well as usage elsewhere in early Greek poetry (Hesiod fr. 298 M–W; cf. Telestes 805 *PMG*).

The poet now skilfully brings the ode back to its unifying figures, Hagesichora (77) and soon Agido (78–101):

οὐ γὰρ ἁ κ[α]λλίσφυρος
Ἀγησιχ[ό]ρ[α] πάρ' αὐτεῖ,
Ἀγιδοῖ .... ἀρμένει   80
θωστήρ[ιά τ'] ἄμ' ἐπαινεῖ.
ἀλλὰ τᾶν [..]... σιοὶ
δέξασθε· [σι]ῶν γὰρ ἄνα
καὶ τέλος· [χο]ροστάτις,
ϝείποιμί κ', [ἐ]γὼν μὲν αὐτὰ   85
παρσένος μάταν ἀπὸ θράνω λέλακα
γλαύξ· ἐγὼ[ν] δὲ τᾶι μὲν Ἀώτι μάλιστα
ϝανδάνην ἐρῶ· πόνων γὰρ
ἇμιν ἰάτωρ ἔγεντο·
ἐξ Ἀγησιχόρ[ας] δὲ νεάνιδες   90
ἰρ]ήνας ἐρατ[ᾶ]ς ἐπέβαν·
τῶ]ι τε γὰρ σηραφόρωι
..]τῶς εδ..........
τ[ῶι] κυβερνάται δὲ χρὴ
κ[ῆ]ν νᾶϊ μάλιστ' ἀκούην·   95
ἁ δὲ τᾶν Σηρην[ί]δων
ἀοιδοτέρα μ[ὲν οὐχί,
σιαὶ γάρ, ἀντ[ὶ δ' ἕνδεκα
παίδων δεκ[ὰς ἅδ' ἀείδ]ει·
φθέγγεται δ' [ἄρ'] ὢ[τ' ἐπὶ] Ξάνθω ῥοαῖσι   100
κύκνος· ἁ δ' ἐπιμέρωι ξανθᾶι κομίσκαι...

For is not the lovely-ankled Hagesichora present here? She remains beside Agido and praises our festival: Do you receive their [prayers], O gods; for in gods lies accomplishment and fulfilment.
Leader of the chorus, I would speak; yet I myself, a girl, cry in vain, like an owl from the rafters. Yet it is my desire to be pleasing to Aotis most of all. For to us she has been the healer of toils, and from Hagesichora have the girls entered upon (the paths of) lovely peace.
For...the trace-horse...and in a ship one must especially heed the steersman. She [Hagesichora], to be sure, is not more songful than the Sirens, for they are goddesses; but we, ten instead of eleven girls, sing as the swan at the stream of Xanthus, while she with her desirable yellow hair...

The appeal to present vision earlier in the comparison of Agido and Hagesichora ('Do you not see', 50) is now echoed in the appeal to Hagesichora's visible presence as Agido returns (78–80). Instead of mock-rivalry for praise between girls (cf. 43f.), the praise is now for the festival itself. The gnomic statement about the gods (83f.) recalls the generalization about the gods' 'requital' that led into the rivalry of the two girls at the end of the mythic section (36–40). 'Singing' is now re-established as a main theme, and the emphasis falls on Hagesichora's superiority in art rather than in beauty. The humour remains, however, in the self-deprecating simile of the owl, the foil to Hagesichora's swan in 100f. Possibly the bird-similes have some connexion with the Pleiades, 'doves', in 60ff. The homely comparison to the 'owl from the roof beam' contrasts with the highly poetical language of divine grace (87–9) and the Sirens. The 'lovely peace' that girls have from Hagesichora (90f.) may be part of the erotic colouring or the competitive setting; it may also be an allusion to the *topos*, common in lyric, of the joyful calm that comes from song.[1] In any case it forms a strong ending to the strophe. Despite the fragmentary condition of 92ff. we can still recognize the rhetorical figure known as the priamel in the lines about obeying a knowledgeable leader, the transition to another implicit praise of Hagesichora's artistry. Physical beauty and choral skill, however, are still being interwoven as our poem breaks off: Hagesichora has the voice of a swan and the golden hair of a desirable woman.

The shifting between Hagesichora and the chorus in these lines is confusing, and the reference to 'ten girls instead of eleven' is not entirely clear. The scholiast says that the chorus was sometimes of ten, sometimes of eleven, and ten girls have here been named. The rapid colloquial style, the plethora of connectives, and the companionable acknowledgement of Hagesichora's superiority continue the mood of gaiety, familiarity and girlish admiration. The style moves easily from proverb to mythical allusion, from local detail to Homeric reminiscence (the swan at the Xanthus, cf. *Iliad* 2.459ff. and 2.877).

Choral lyric, even at this early date, is still far from primitive. Despite the incompleteness of the text and the difficulties caused by our ignorance of the goddess, the cult and the context of the song, we can still recognize sophisticated structural devices like gnomic transitions, verbal echoes and parallelism.[2] There are also rhetorical figures: the developed simile, *praeteritio*, priamel, *adynaton*. Mythical narration is carried to some length, imagery is sustained, and diction is rich with compound adjectives in such phrases as 'prize-winning ringing-hoofed horses' (47f.), 'soft-eyed girls' (69), 'love-glancing Graces' (20f.). Alcman also enhances the atmosphere of playful exaggeration and mock-rivalry by using Homeric formulas in new contexts (e.g. the horses in 47–9, the 'ambrosial night' in 62, the swan in 100f.). Both song and singers must manifest the presence of beauty, symbolized, as in Pindar, by the superlative radiance of gold and the

---

[1] See Pavese (1967) 127. The epinician parallels to rest after toil in athletic contests in *GLP* 62 are not entirely apt. See also Puelma (1977) 21f. with n. 50.

[2] Puelma (1977) *passim*; Pavese (1967) *passim*; Rosenmeyer (1966) 353.

sun. Alcman achieves a wide and rapid variation of tones, from narratives of heroes and gods to proverbial commonplaces, from gnomic moralizing to lively personal exchanges in direct address (e.g. 50, 'Do you not see?'). There is also a trace of the 'kenning' that one finds in Pindar in a phrase like ποικίλος δράκων παγχρύσιος 'the dappled all-gold snake' (66f.), used to describe a bracelet.

The language itself, however, is clear and straightforward. Sentences tend to be brief and paratactic. The leaps and abrupt transitions characteristic of the genre, like the unintroduced proper names, include the audience in an assumed intimacy and communal spirit. Phrasing is sometimes conventional, like 'lovely-ankled Hagesichora' (78f.), but Alcman is also capable of bold expressions, like the girls 'walking upon the paths of lovely peace' (ἰρήνας ἐρατᾶς ἐπέβαν, 91) or the happy mortal 'weaving the day through to the end' (ἀμέραν διαπλέκει, 38), framed by two familiar but emphatic and contrasting adjectives, one positive, one negative (εὔφρων and ἄκλαυτος, 37 and 39). He can use striking contrasts too, like that between the 'solid horse' and the horse 'of dreams' (whether 'winged' or not) in 47–9. As in Pindar, figures of speech and comparisons tend to accumulate in progressions, like that from metals to horses to stars in 54–63 or that from owl to Siren to swan in 86–101. This figurative language sometimes creates sharp juxtapositions of prosaic reality and remoter mythical elements, as in the horses of 47–9 or the priamel of 92ff. which builds up from horsemanship to seamanship to the Sirens.

The poet's concern with his art and the nature of his song has moral as well as aesthetic significance. Proud of his expertise, he takes himself and his song as a microcosm of the world-order (cf. 13–23, 35–40), a nascent form of one of Pindar's most important themes (cf. *Pyth.* 1 and below, pp. 187–9). The mood of levity, perhaps characteristic of partheneia generally, is dominant; but beneath the lightness and play appears the deep moral seriousness which characterizes most of Greek choral poetry.

The recently published second partheneion (3 *PMG*) provides valuable perspective on the Louvre poem. Here the proem, lost in Partheneion 1, is partially preserved. The chorus calls on the Olympian Muses who have filled their hearts with desire for song. The inspiration for the new song takes the form of an awakening from sleep; it 'will scatter sweet sleep from the lids' ὕπνον ἀπὸ γλεφάρων σκεδασεῖ γλυκύν..., 3. 7); we may recall the awakening of song in the proem of Pindar's seventh *Isthmian*. The chorus then calls attention to their movements 'as the song [?] leads me to come to the dancing place where most of all I shall toss my yellow hair...and my soft feet [may dance]....'.

>]ς δέ μ' ἄγει πεδ' ἀγῶν' ἴμεν
> ἄχι μά]λιστα κόμ[αν ξ]ανθὰν τινάξω·
> ...ἁπαλοὶ πόδες...   (3.8–10 *PMG*)

After a gap of some fifty lines (which, on the analogy of Partheneion 1, may have held a myth), the text resumes with the theme of sleep again, but now with a mixture of erotic colouring and ritual action that closely parallels the Louvre Partheneion:

λυσιμελεῖ τε πόσωι, τακερώτερα
δ' ὕπνω καὶ σανάτω ποτιδέρκεται·
οὐδέ τι μαψιδίως γλυκ.. ῆνα·
'A[σ]τυμέλοισα δέ μ' οὐδὲν ἀμείβεται
ἀλλὰ τὸ]ν πυλεῶν' ἔχοισα   65
[ὤ] τις αἰγλά[ε]ντος ἀστήρ
ὡρανῶ διαιπετής
ἢ χρύσιον ἔρνος ἢ ἀπαλὸ[ν ψίλ]ον
..ᵔ]ν
]. διέβα ταναοῖς πο[σί·]   70
-κ]ομος νοτία Κινύρα χ[άρ]ις
ἐπὶ π]αρσενικᾶν χαίταισιν ἴσδει·
'Α]στυμέλοισα κατὰ στρατόν
] μέλημα δάμωι...

              . . .

]α ἴδοιμ' αἴ πως με.. ον φίλοι
ἆσ]σον [ἱο]ῖσ' ἀπαλᾶς χηρὸς λάβοι,   80
αἶψά κ' [ἐγὼν ἱ]κέτις κήνας γενοίμαν·

νῦν δ' [   ]δα παῖδα βα[.]ύφρονα...
                                          (3.61–74, 79–82 PMG)

...and with desire that looses the limbs, but she looks glances more melting than sleep and death; nor in vain she...sweet.
But Astymeloisa makes me no answer; but, like a star that falls through the radiant sky or a branch of gold or soft plume, holding the garland...she passed on slender feet; and on the tresses of the girls sits the lovely-haired dewy grace of Cinyras. Astymeloisa (moves) among the gathering, an object of care to the people...
If she should come near and take me by the soft hand, at once would I become her suppliant.
But now...a girl of deep [?] thought...

As in the Louvre Partheneion, the chorus of girls are lost in admiration for an outstanding member of their group. Astymeloisa, like Hagesichora, may be the chorus-leader, a position suggested also by the pun on her name in 74, μέλημα δάμωι, 'a concern to the people', a double pun, perhaps, if the first word, *melema* also alludes to *melos* 'song', which in fact occurs in the proem, καλὸν ὑμνιοισᾶν μέλος 'girls hymning lovely song'.

The erotic overtones of this admiration are even more overt than in the Louvre Partheneion. The helplessness of the girl if the object of her love should take her hand (79f.) recalls the chorus of the longer poem 'worn down' with love for Hagesichora (1.77). The celestial brightness of Astymeloisa's beauty

(3.66–8) reminds us also of the sun- and star-imagery of that poem (cf. 1.40–3, 60–3). Here too that beauty slips briefly into mythical allusion, the charm of Cinyras, darling of Aphrodite (3.71f.; cf. 1.96ff.). The love-motif is also treated with a certain playfulness and perhaps deliberate exaggeration. Lines 61–8 and 79–81 offer a glimpse of the same kind of personal exchange as in the Louvre Partheneion: the chorus casts itself in the role of a helplessly smitten lover before an overpoweringly beautiful beloved whom they praise with rather conventional details of physical grace and images of light and gold. Taken together, the two poems show a lively freshness, set in a rather stylized frame. That stylized character may be due to the ritual occasion of the song, possibly initiatory, possibly involving a goddess of sex, marriage, or fertility, like Helen or Aphrodite (cf. Cinyras in 3.71).

A very different area of Alcman's poetry has been revealed by another new papyrus, also published in 1957, a fragment of a commentary on a cosmogonic poem (*P.Oxy.* 2390 = 5, fr. 2, col. ii *PMG*). Only a few of Alcman's own words are quoted, but the commentary enables us to restore the general outline. Alcman seems to have posited the original condition of the world as an un-differentiated mass, akin to what later philosophers termed ὕλη, unformed matter. The goddess Thetis came into being and gave form to this matter as a craftsman forms metal (cf. 17–19). With this act appear the two ordering principles, Poros and Tekmor, 'Path' ('Resource') and 'Limit', or, as H. Fränkel suggests, 'Open Possibility' or 'Accessibility' and 'Binding Definition'.[1] With them the primal matter is differentiated into day and night, light and darkness (cf. 25f.). The process of differentiation has some affinity with the cosmogonic process in Hesiod (cf. *Theogony* 123–5); but the non-anthropomorphic agents, Poros and Tekmor, are quite unhesiodic and resemble the non-personal, non-sexualized elements, water, air, fire, in the Milesians Thales and Anaximander. Thetis' role is striking. Sea-goddesses elsewhere in early Greek literature, as Vernant has shown, serve as cosmogonic deities,[2] but Alcman may also owe something to Near-Eastern notions of a 'waste of waters' ruled by a female deity of the deep, like Tiamat in the Babylonian *Enuma Elish*.[3] In any event, the fragment is a precious piece of evidence for a far more advanced intellectual atmosphere in seventh-century Sparta than had ever been suspected and a valuable indication that philosophical speculation and Near-Eastern influences were not confined to Ionia in the early archaic period. It suggests too the artificiality of the sharp break sometimes assumed between poets and philosophers or between 'mythic' and 'philosophical' thought in this formative period in the intellectual history of early Greece.

The new fragment also enables us to put a number of hitherto unrelated scraps

[1] West (1967) 2f; Fränkel (1975) 164. See also Penwill (1974) 13–39; West (1963) 154–6.
[2] Vernant–Detienne (1974) 136–9. See also Hdt. 4.180.5.   [3] West (1967) 3–7.

of Alcman's work into perspective. First, we can recognize the same cosmogonic concerns in the gnomic generalization at the end of the myth in the Louvre Partheneion (1.13f.), for here Aisa and Poros, 'Destiny' and 'Path', called 'the oldest of the gods', have an important role as embodiments of the moral order. We can now make better sense of the scholiast's comment on this passage, 'By Poros (Alcman) means the same being as that represented by Chaos in Hesiod's mythology', for he is doubtless referring to the cosmogonic function of Poros in the poem of fragment 5. We can also better appreciate Alcman's interest elsewhere in connecting his poetry with the mythical beginnings of the world-order. In one fragment, for instance, he calls the Muses the daughters of Ouranos and Ge, Sky and Earth (67 *PMG*) not Zeus and Mnemosyne as in Hesiod. In another Erse, Dew, a fertilizing principle, appears as daughter of Zeus and Selene (57 *PMG*). He calls Akmon the son of Ouranos because of the sky's 'untiring' (*a-kamatos*) movement (61 *PMG*). Tyche, Chance, is the sister of Eunomia and Peitho, 'Lawfulness' and 'Persuasion', and the daughter of Prometheia 'Forethought' (64).[1]

From the sparse quotations by late grammarians and metricians it has long been clear that Alcman treated epic themes, often drawing upon Homeric language and showing a predilection for dactylic metres. His subjects, mostly mentioned only by name, include the fall of Troy (68-71 *PMG*), Heracles (72), Niobe (75), Tantalus (79) and Odysseus. On the last we have an interesting line and a half in dactyls telling how 'Circe once smeared (with wax) the ears of the companions of Odysseus, enduring in spirit' (80 *PMG*):

καί ποκ' 'Οδυσσῆος ταλασίφρονος ὦατ' ἑταίρων
Κίρκα ἐπαλείψασα.

Alcman has modified the Homeric narrative by having Circe actually perform what she only advises the hero to do in Homer.

That modification of Homeric detail is now substantiated at greater length by an important new papyrus fragment (*P.Oxy.* 2443, fr. 1, +3213).[2] Where the papyrus becomes intelligible there is a brief reference to Poseidon and a description of someone coming to 'a shrine of the Nereids':

]εφ.[....]ουδεις.[
]φρασάμαν μονός [
]ε Ποσειδᾶνος χα[.].
].ος   10
μα.λ̣ευκοθεᾶν ἐρατὸν τέμενος
ἐκ Τρυγεᾶν ἀνιών, ἔχον
δὲ σίδας δύω γλυκήας.

---

[1] Lloyd-Jones, in West (1963) 156, suggests that fr. 65 *PMG*, on the prerogatives of the gods, may come from the same cosmogonic poem as the Poros-Tekmor fragment. Still, we must recognize the rather light and humorous tone of this fragment; see Campbell (1967) *ad loc.* and Perrotta–Gentili (1965) *ad loc.*   [2] See West (1977) 38f.; Brown (1978) 36–8.

ταὶ δ' ὅτε δὴ ποταμῶι καλλιρρόωι
ἀράσαντ' ἐρατὸν τελέσαι γάμον   15
καὶ τὰ παθῆν ἃ γυναιξὶ καὶ ἀνδρά[σιν
φίλτ]ατα κωριδίας τ' εὐνᾶς [τυ]χῆν[,

...No one... (?)
...I took thought alone (?)...
Poseidon...Coming from Trygeai to the lovely grove of the Leucotheai
(= Nereids); and they held two sweet pomegranates.
And, when they prayed to the river of beautiful streams to accomplish lovely
marriage and to have experience of the endearments between men and women
and to enjoy the bed of wedlock...

The passage is possibly to be associated with fr. 81 *PMG*, Ζεῦ πάτερ, αἰ γὰρ
ἐμὸς πόσις εἴη 'O father Zeus, may he be my husband'. The scholiast on *Odyssey*
6.244, who cites this passage, notes that Alcman has substituted several girls
for the single maiden, Nausicaa, who speaks a similar prayer in the Homeric
passage. This situation would suit the new fragment, although the transition
from Odysseus and the sea (if such it is) to the girls' prayer for marriage is abrupt.
In Homer too, though a single Leucothea helps Odysseus to escape from the
sea, we hear nothing of a 'grove of Leucotheai' (glossed by Hesychius and the
Etymologium Magnum as 'Nereids'). Difficult too is the long dependent 'when-'
clause, uncharacteristic of Alcman's style. Still, the coincidences seem too great
to be fortuitous. Some of these difficulties would be resolved by supposing the
fragment to be a first-person narrative (cf. φρασάμην, 8) by Odysseus of his
landing on the Phaeacians' island. It is interesting to see Alcman's addition of
the characteristically concrete detail of the 'sweet pomegranates'. The passage
is further evidence for the knowledge of the Homeric poems on mainland
Greece in the late seventh century. This elaboration of and variation upon
Homeric myth in dactylic metres will be carried farther, as we shall see, in
Stesichorus.

In dactyls too, this time in hexameter, is one of Alcman's most celebrated
passages (26 *PMG*):

οὔ μ' ἔτι, παρσενικαὶ μελιγάρυες ἱαρόφωνοι,
γυῖα φέρην δύναται· βάλε δὴ βάλε κηρύλος εἴην,
ὅς τ' ἐπὶ κύματος ἄνθος ἀμ' ἀλκυόνεσσι ποτήται
νηδεὲς ἦτορ ἔχων, ἀλιπόρφυρος ἱαρὸς ὄρνις.

No longer, O maidens, honey-songed, holy-voiced, can my limbs bear me up.
Ah, would that I were the *kerylos* (male halcyon bird) who skims above the
wave's bloom (of foam) with the halcyons, fearless of heart, sea-purple sacred
bird.

The passage is an early expression of the nostalgia for 'escape' that recurs in
the lyrics of Greek tragedy, especially in Euripides. The note of romantic

longing and wistfulness, actually rather rare in early Greek poetry, shows us another side of Alcman, one that easily matches his interest in the passions of love. The accumulation of compound adjectives in the first line and the bird imagery are both familiar from the Partheneia. The poet is presumably addressing the girls who perform his choral songs, perhaps in a half-playful way, as he contrasts his age and feebleness with their vigour and beauty. If this is the situation, it may be compared with that of the maidens in the Delian *Hymn to Apollo* 166–73. Other early choral poets, like Terpander and Arion, are said to have written 'preludes' for the cithara in dactylic hexameter, and a similar context is probably to be imagined for Alcman's fine lines as well.[1]

The expressive use of natural phenomena characterizes another famous fragment (89 *PMG*):

> εὕδουσι δ' ὀρέων κορυφαί τε καὶ φάραγγες
> πρώονές τε καὶ χαράδραι
> φῦλά τ' ἑρπέτ' ὅσα τρέφει μέλαινα γαῖα
> θῆρές τ' ὀρεσκώιοι καὶ γένος μελισσᾶν
> καὶ κνώδαλ' ἐν βένθεσσι πορφυρέας ἁλός·
> εὕδουσι δ' οἰωνῶν φῦλα τανυπτερύγων.

Asleep are the mountains' peaks and the gulleys and the headlands and the torrent-beds and the creeping tribes, all that the black earth nurtures, and the mountain-dwelling beasts and the race of bees and the beasts in the depths of the darkling sea. Asleep are the tribes of the long-winged birds.

This cosmic sleep may have been the foil to the turmoil in the speaker's breast, as in later poets from Theocritus to Goethe.[2] Alcman's lines are remarkable both for the haunting beauty of sound and for the impression of objective clarity and inclusiveness. The accumulation of five strong nouns in the first two lines sets forth the massive, rocky face of nature, softened by the appearance of the first living creatures and the 'black earth' in line 3, and then in rapid sequence the other living beings, increasingly individualized as the austere phrasing of the opening changes to a more ornate, though still solemn, grandeur ('depths of the darkling sea', 'tribes of long-winged birds'). The poet makes a step-by-step visual survey of all of nature as he traverses the distance from the peaks of the mountains to the bottom of the sea and then looks back upward again to the birds.[3] The polysyndeton and the bareness of adjectives (until the general and Homeric 'black earth', 3) reinforce the impression of largeness and grandeur. There are more adjectives in the second group of three lines, but they are all generic, and the generalizing effect is reinforced by the repetition of φῦλα, 'tribes' and γένος, 'race' in 3, 6 and 4. For all the apparent simplicity and natural-

---

[1] See Plut. *De mus.* 3; Suda, s.v. 'Arion'; *GLP* 23; Gerber (1970) 99.
[2] Ancient and modern parallels in Perrotta–Gentili (1965) *ad loc.*
[3] Dawson (1966) 59f.

ness of movement, there is a studied repetition of word and sound in 1 and 6, εὕδουσι δ' ὀρέων...εὕδουσι δ' οἰωνῶν and in φῦλα τ' ἑρπέτ'...φῦλα τανυπτερύγων in 3 and 6.

We can trace this feeling for the mysterious beauty of nature in the star similes of the two Partheneia (cf. 1.62f. and 3.66ff.). It is present too, though in a different setting, in a fragment presumably addressed to a nymph or a bacchant, possibly in a dithyrambic chorus (56 *PMG*):

> πολλάκι δ' ἐν κορυφαῖς ὀρέων, ὅκα
> σιοῖσι ϝάδηι πολύφανος ἑορτά,
> χρύσιον ἄγγος ἔχοισα, μέγαν σκύφον,
> οἷά τε ποιμένες ἄνδρες ἔχοισιν,
> χερσὶ λεόντεον ἐν γάλα θεῖσα
> τυρὸν ἐτύρησας μέγαν ἄτρυφον 'Αργειφόνται.

Often on the peaks of mountains when the festival of many torches is pleasing to the gods, you, holding in your hands a golden vessel, a great tankard, such as shepherd men have, put into it lioness's milk and for Hermes Argus-Slayer made a great whole cheese.

The last line of this fragment illustrates another, quite different quality of Alcman: a hearty interest in food, often enumerated in loving detail (frs. 19, 20, 56, 95, 96, 98 *PMG*). 'All-devouring Alcman' (ὁ παμφάγος 'Αλκμάν, 17.4 *PMG*), the poet calls himself playfully in a poem where, as in Catullus 13, the dinner guest is expected to supply the more substantial part of the meal. Although on the one hand Alcman can follow conventional epic phraseology ('black earth', 'ambrosial night', 'yellow hair', etc.), he can also write with a keen, all-embracing sense of concrete particulars. In almost Aristophanic vein he can move from delicate, flower-like jewellery (91 *PMG*) to porridges and partridges, from sleeping mountains to tables and cheeses (cf. 17, 19, 39, 56, 96 *PMG*).

Alcman's wide range and diverse sources of poetic inspiration appear also from a series of fragments dealing with distant, semi-mythical peoples and places (frs. 131, 148–57 *PMG*), somewhat after the manner of Aristeas of Proconnesos, whose *Arimaspeia* could conceivably have influenced him.[1] Two lines are especially noteworthy for their imaginative and suggestive poetry (90 *PMG*):

> 'Ρίπας, ὄρος ἀνθέον ὕλαι,
> νυκτὸς μελαίνας στέρνον.

Rhipean range, mountain blooming with forest, breast of black night.

We may recall the evocative descriptions of mountains in fragments 89 and 56 cited above. Closer to home, Alcman also wrote about the local customs, history and myths of Sparta. One of his poems included a genealogy of legendary

---

[1] See *GLP* 27; West (1965) 193f.

ALCMAN

Spartan kings (5, fr. 2, col. i *PMG*), and the Louvre Partheneion gave a leisurely enumeration of the slain sons of Hippocoon (1.2–12). Other poems, all lost, described minor Laconian divinities (62 *PMG*), localities in Sparta (52, 92 *PMG*) and the Spartan *syssitia* or men's eating-club (98 *PMG*).

Alcman took a self-conscious pleasure in language. We have noted his puns on the names of Hagesichora and Astymeloisa (1.84, 3.73f.) and his etymology of Akmon-*akamatos* (61). This interest also appears in the curious hexameter line (107) Πολλαλέγων ὄνυμ' ἀνδρί, γυναικὶ δὲ Πασιχάρηα 'Say-much the man's name, Rejoicing-in-all the woman's'. The line may be a wry erotic joke about excessive compliance.[1] Equally well, it might be a condensed version of the traditional contrast between the hard-working man, 'Much-caring' (πόλλ' ἀλέγων), and the beautiful, but idle woman, 'Pleasing-to-all', but useless, like Hesiod's Pandora: χάρις δ' ἐπὶ πᾶσιν ἄητο 'and upon all was breathed grace' *Theog.* 583; cf. 590ff. and *W.D.* 373f. Beside the occasional 'kenning' (cf. 1.66f. above), Alcman also enjoys pithy proverbial statements, like the 'owl screeching from the roofbeam' (1.86f.), 'neighbour for neighbour is a big thing' (123), 'trial the beginning of learning' (125), 'narrow the path, pitiless Necessity' (102).

This interest in words has a possibly deeper significance in two short but important fragments (39 and 40 *PMG*):

> ϝέπη τάδε καὶ μέλος 'Αλκμὰν
> εὗρε γεγλωσσαμέναν
> κακκαβίδων ὄπα συνθέμενος.

These words and this song Alcman invented, understanding the tongued speech of partridges.

> ϝοῖδα δ' ὀρνίχων νόμως
> παντῶν.

Of all birds I know the tunes (ways).

Elsewhere keenly interested in birds, Alcman may be serious when he speaks of deriving his song from them. The first fragment looks like the poet's *sphragis* or personal 'seal' and reflects his pride in his art as intellectual discovery, not a gift of the Muses.[2] The fragment also, as Gentili suggests, may reflect the importance of imitation and mimicking in the oral context of early Greek poetry.[3] In many passages Alcman calls upon the Muses for divine inspiration (14, 27, 30, 67; cf. also 28, 43, 59b *PMG*). He also associates the power of song with the divine power of love and desire (e.g. 3.1ff.; fr. 27 *PMG*). The awareness of the intellectual side of his craft in fr. 39, however, is a small intimation of the self-

---

[1] See *GLP* 24f.; McKay (1974) 413f.
[2] For the implications see Gianotti (1975) 43–7.
[3] See Gentili (1971) 59–67.

conscious artistry which becomes important later in Pindar's pride in his *sophia* or poetic skill.

There is another trace of this poetic self-consciousness in an important new fragment (4, fr. 1.4–6 *PMG* = *P.Oxy.* 2388) in which Alcman seems to be commenting on his predecessors, who 'showed to men wondrous new songs, delicate, full of delight':

σαυμαστὰ δ' ἀνθ[ρώποισι
γαρύματα μαλσακὰ
νεόχμ' ἔδειξαν τερπ[

These lines are among the earliest indications in Greek lyric of a poet directly criticizing what has gone before. The generosity of Alcman's judgement is particularly interesting. The recent Oxyrhynchus fragment that confirms the existence of the sixth book of poems may also contain a reference to the *topos* of the poet's immortality of fame or κλέος (*P.Oxy.* 3209, fr. 1; cf. Sappho fr. 55 and 147 *PLF;* Ibycus fr. 282.47f. *PMG*).

In antiquity Alcman was famous for his treatment of love. Later writers characteristically construed as autobiographical professions of desire statements which were in fact part of the conventions of choral poetry. Thus Athenaeus (13.600f) interpreted the following fragment to mean that Alcman was madly in love with the poetess Megalostrata (59b *PMG*):

τοῦτο ϝαδειᾶν ἔδειξε Μωσᾶν
δῶρον μάκαιρα παρσένων
ἁ ξανθὰ Μεγαλοστράτα.

This gift of the sweet Muses did yellow-haired Megalostrata, happy among maidens, show forth.

Indeed, playfulness rather than passion seems to characterize Alcman's love-poetry, whether of heterosexual or of homosexual love. Two other verses which Athenaeus cites in the same context show the gentler rather than the impassioned side of love (59a):

Ἔρως με δηῦτε Κύπριδος ϝέκατι
γλυκὺς κατείβων καρδίαν ἰαίνει.

Sweet Eros, then, for the Cyprian's sake, drips down and warms my heart.

Another brief fragment on Eros suggests the playful inventiveness with which Alcman may have treated male homosexual love (58).[1]

Although we have lost much of the poetry that would justify Athenaeus' title, 'leader in the songs of love' (13.600f, 59 *PMG*), fortune has been kinder in preserving enough to document another epithet conferred on him by a later poet, 'graceful Alcman', τὸν χαρίεντ' Ἀλκμᾶνα (*Anth. Pal.* 7.19, 159 *PMG*).

[1] See Easterling (1974) 37–41.

3. STESICHORUS

Stesichorus of Himera, regarded in antiquity as the successor to Alcman in lyric, is best known for his retelling of epic themes in lyric metres. In this extended lyric narration Stesichorus seems not to have been unique. Sacadas of Argos, active in Sparta at the end of the seventh century, composed a *Sack of Troy* with even more detail than Stesichorus (Athenaeus 13.610c). Xanthus of Lydia, another rather shadowy predecessor of Stesichorus, composed an *Oresteia* which may have influenced Stesichorus (Athenaeus 12.512f; Aelian, *V.H.* 4.26; 699–700 *PMG*). The popularity of mythic subjects on contemporary vases parallels this interest in casting myths into new and vivid forms.

The sands of Egypt and the patient skill of papyrologists have spectacularly enhanced our knowledge of Stesichorus' poetry. Recently published papyri have added to our knowledge of the *Nostoi* (209 *PMG*), the *Palinode* for Helen (193), the *Oresteia* (217), and the *Hunt for the Calydonian Boar* (222); and the last ten years have brought to light major fragments of the *Geryoneis* (S7–87 *SLG*), *The Sack of Troy* (S88–132), the *Eriphyle* (S148–50), and, perhaps most important, a hitherto unknown poem on the fortunes of the house of Oedipus and the quarrel of Polynices and Eteocles (*P.Lille* 73 and 76). These new discoveries have substantiated the high value which ancient critics placed on Stesichorus' work, confirmed his role as a link between epic and lyric narrative, and demonstrated his importance for the representation of myths in sixth-century art.[1] A word of caution, however, is necessary. There is not total unanimity that all the new Trojan and Theban fragments belong to Stesichorus. In particular, some metrical features of the Lille Papyrus (below, pp. 156ff.) diverge from attested Stesichorean practice.[2] Subject matter and style afford a high degree of probability, but not absolute certainty.

The biographical tradition gives Stesichorus' dates as 632/29–556/53 B.C. (Suda), making him roughly contemporary with Sappho and Alcaeus (see Suda s.v. 'Sappho') and a generation later than Alcman.[3] He is associated both with Locrian Matauros in southern Italy and Himera in Sicily and is said to have been buried at Catane where his tomb was celebrated for its architecture. Most ancient writers connect him with Himera, but in Matauros too he would have encountered that mixture of Doric and Ionic in both language and literature that stamps his poetry. The synchronization of his death with Simonides' birth

---

[1] See *GLP* 119ff.; Robertson (1969) *passim*; Vallet (1958) 281ff. (on the metopes from the Heraion at the Foce del Sele now in the Paestum museum).

[2] Parsons (1977) 12. Parsons's point about the repetitiveness and slackness of the style (p. 7), however, tends to support rather than weaken the case for Stesichorean authorship.

[3] There seems to have been a later 'Stesichorus', perhaps even two poets of that name, with predictable confusion in biography and the attribution of certain works. For the chronology see Vallet (1958) 257–63; West (1971a) 302–14, esp. 302–7.

(556/53) may be taken as signifying a major division between older and newer styles. Simonides himself cites Stesichorus as an established authority, ranked with Homer (564 *PMG*). Eupolis in the *Helots* of *c.* 424 B.C. joins Stesichorus' songs with those of Alcman and Simonides as 'old-fashioned' (ἀρχαῖος, fr. 139 *CAF* = Stesich. 276b *PMG*).

The new fragments demonstrate Stesichorus' importance for the development of extended lyrical narrative in Bacchylides and odes of Pindar like *Pythian* 4. His poems, it appears, were probably more leisurely in their movement and closer to the flow of epic than to the highly selective techniques of late sixth- and early fifth-century lyric.

The new texts also raise a major problem. How were these poems sung and performed? Were they choral? The *Geryoneis*, for example, appears to have contained at least 1,500 lines, which would make it three and a half times as long as Pindar's fourth *Pythian*, our longest extant choral ode. This work, on a rough estimate, would require some four hours to perform, longer than a chorus could reasonably dance.[1] The freedom and flexibility of metre suggest that Stesichorus sang such poems to his own lyre, without choral accompaniment.[2] Such poetry, a spin-off of epic or rhapsodic recitation, is called 'citharodic'.[3] Unlike the rhapsode's work, it is original composition; unlike the monodist's, it is narrative and lengthy, not personal and relatively brief. Sacadas' *Sack of Troy* and Xanthus' *Oresteia*, mentioned above, would seem to fall into this same category.

At this point, however, a second problem arises. Stesichorus' name indicates some connexion with the chorus; it should mean 'he who sets up the chorus'. The Suda, in fact, says that the poet's real name was Teisias, and 'he was called Stesichorus because he first established a chorus of song to the lyre' (κιθαρωιδίας χορὸν ἔστησεν). It is possible that 'Stesichorus' was a title like 'choirmaster', an assumption made the more plausible by the reference to 'Stesichorus' in the *Marmor Parium* at two later dates.[4] There is, of course, no necessary contradiction between a Stesichorus/Teisias who composed choral poetry similar (say) to Alcman's and a Stesichorus/Teisias who also, possibly at a later point of his career, developed or perfected the long citharodic narrative poems, blending lyric metre with epic themes, for which he is celebrated. Still, the fact remains that the name suggests strong connexions with choral poetry, whereas the new texts point to poems which, on the face of it, do not look as if they were choral.

Be this as it may, Stesichorus' work wins high praise from the ancient critics, mainly for epic rather than strictly lyrical virtues. Horace places his

---

[1] Pavese (1972) 243f.; West (1971a) 307–9.

[2] See Haslam (1974) 33 with n. 53; West (1969 and 1971a) *passim*.

[3] See Pavese (1972) 239, 266f.; West (1971a) 313f. *Od.* 8.256–67 suggests that dances might be performed in accompaniment to rhapsodic narrative poetry. Cf. also *DTC* 11.

[4] See West (1970a) 206; Pavese (1972) 245.

'severe Muses' (*graues Camenae*) close behind Homer (*Odes* 4.9.8–11). Dionysius of Halicarnassus agrees (*De comp. verb.* 24) and commends his 'grandeur of subject matter' (*megaloprepeia*) and his attention to the 'character and rank of his personages' (*Vet. cens.* 2.7), qualities which we can now see amply attested in the new fragments. To 'Longinus' he is 'most Homeric' (*Subl.* 13.3). Quintilian places him second to Pindar for his 'strength of genius' (*ingenio ualidus*). He singles out his lofty epic themes of battles and heroes (*maxima bella et clarissimos canentem duces et epici carminis onera lyra sustinentem*) 'singing vast wars and glorious leaders and lifting on his lyre the full weight of epic song' (10.1.62), but criticizes his diffuseness:

> For he gives his characters their appropriate dignity in action and in speech; and, if he had exercised restraint, he could have been a close rival to Homer. But he is too abundant and spreads out (*redundat atque effunditur*), a flaw which, though worthy of blame, is yet a fault of his very fluency and copiousness.

The leisurely pace of the *Geryoneis* and the poem on the sons of Oedipus confirm Quintilian's judgement. Hermogenes found his abundant use of adjectives 'very pleasing' (σφόδρα ἡδύς, *Id.* 3.322 Walz).

This descriptive fullness characterizes most of Stesichorus' poetry. In the *Geryoneis* the Centaur Pholus offers Heracles a cup of wine (181 *PMG*):

σκύφιον δὲ λαβὼν δέπας ἔμμετρον ὡς τριλάγυνον
πί' ἐπισχόμενος, τό ῥά οἱ παρέθηκε Φόλος κεράσας.

Taking a cup-like tankard of three-bottles' measure, he held it up and drank, the cup which Pholus mixed and set beside him.

Nearly everything is said twice. Yet the accumulation of modifiers is not without structure. There are four nouns or adjectives and one verbal form in the first line and just the reverse proportion in the second. The profuseness seems to serve the narrative better in the account of the remote west where Geryon's herdsman, Eurytion, was born (184 *PMG*):

σχεδὸν ἀντιπέρας κλεινᾶς 'Ερυθείας
Ταρτησσοῦ ποταμοῦ παρὰ παγὰς ἀπείρονας ἀργυρορίζους
ἐν κευθμῶνι πέτρας.

. . .nearly across from famed Erytheia, by the limitless, silver-rooted streams of the river Tartessus in the hollow of the rock.

The richness of compound adjectives, a stylistic trait developed even further in the lyric narrative of Bacchylides, is not only decorative. The continuous narration in the new fragments, as we shall see, illustrates how this fullness of detail can also serve to awaken pathos.

In diction Stesichorus is indeed 'most Homeric'. His language is a literary Doric, with a strong predilection for Homeric formulas. His heavily dactylic metres facilitate the Homeric borrowings. He adapts Homeric phraseology, however, with considerable freedom and flexibility, as this fragment of the *Nostoi* shows (209 *PMG*):

θε[ῑ]ον ἐ[ξ]αίφνας τέρας ἰδοῖσα νύμφα
ὣδε δε[..]. Ἑλένα φωνᾶι ποτ[ὶ] παίδ᾽ ᾽Οδύσειο[ν·
῾Τηλέμαχ[..]τις ὃδ᾽ ἁμὶν ἄγγελ[ο]ς ὡρανόθεν
δι᾽ αἰθέρο[ς ἀτ]ρυγέτας κατέπαλτο βαδ[
          ].ε φοιναι κεκλαγγω[
]...ς ὑμετέρους δόμους προφα.[.......]υς
          ].....αν.υς ἀνὴρ
βο]υλαῖς ᾽Αθάνας
          ].ηις αυτα λακέρυζα κορώνα
          ].μ᾽ οὐδ᾽ ἐγώ σ᾽ ἐρύ[ξ]ω
Παν]ελόπα σ᾽ ἰδοῖσα φίλου πατ[ρ]ὸς υἱὸν...᾽

> ...Helen the bride, suddenly seeing the divine omen, and thus did she speak to the son of Odysseus: 'Telemachus, whatever messenger this is that has come to us hurtling down through the unharvested aether...shrieking...(Odysseus?) appearing in your halls...by the counsels of Athena...a screeching crow. Nor will I keep you back; but Penelope, on seeing you, the son of your dear father...'

Stesichorus is closely following the Homeric scene of Telemachus' departure from Sparta in *Odyssey* 15.113ff. In Homer the gifts come first and in much more detail (*Od.* 15.113–29); then, as Telemachus makes a parting speech, the omen appears (*Od.* 15.160–3):

> ὣς ἄρα οἱ εἰπόντι ἐπέπτατο δεξιὸς ὄρνις,
> αἰετὸς ἀργὴν χῆνα φέρων ὀνύχεσσι πέλωρον,
> ἣμερον ἐξ αὐλῆς· οἱ δ᾽ ἰύζοντες ἔποντο
> ἀνέρες ἠδὲ γυναῖκες.

> Thus as he spoke a bird flew by on the right, an eagle bearing in its claws a huge white goose, tame, from the yard; and they all followed shouting, the men and the women.

As all cry out with rejoicing, young Pisistratus asks Menelaus to interpret, but Helen anticipates him (171–8). Telemachus briefly prays for the fulfilment of the prophecy and departs (180–4). Stesichorus has obviously greatly condensed the scene while following the main outline as given in Homer. He puts the omen earlier and from the first makes Helen the one who sees, describes and expounds its meaning. The omen itself is different: to the Homeric eagle Stesichorus has added a lowly crow, borrowing a phrase which occurs in Hesiod (*W.D.* 747) but not in Homer. We should note especially the dramatic use of direct discourse, a feature of lyric style prominent in Pindar and Bacchylides. An additional small fragment (col. ii) shows that Stesichorus has changed Menelaus' gift of a silver and golden mixing bowl (*Od.* 15.115–19) to a vessel taken as booty from Priam's palace, again a colourful embroidering of Homeric detail.

An even more telling comparison emerges from this recently published fragment of the death of Geryon from the *Geryoneïs* (s15.14–17 *SLG*):

> ἀπέκλινε δ' ἄρ' αὐχένα Γαρ[υόνας
> ἐπικάρσιον, ὡς ὅκα μ[ά]κ̣ω̣[ν
> ἅτε καταισχύνοισ' ἁπαλὸν [δέμας
> αἶψ' ἀπὸ φύλλα βαλοῖσα...

And Geryon leaned his neck to one side, as when a poppy...befouling its soft body suddenly throwing off its petals...

The passage echoes the death of Gorgythion in *Iliad* 8.306–8:

> μήκων δ' ὡς ἑτέρωσε κάρη βάλεν, ἥ τ' ἐνὶ κήπωι
> καρπῶι βριθομένη νοτίηισί τε εἰαρινῆισιν·
> ὡς ἑτέρωσ' ἤμυσε κάρη πήληκι βαρυνθέν.

And as a poppy casts its head to one side, a poppy in a garden, weighed down with fruit and the rains of the spring, so did he droop to one side his head weighed down with his helmet.

Stesichorus, it seems, omits the spring rains (kept by a later imitator, Virgil, *Aen.* 9.436) and increases pathos by making his flower 'soft' and 'defiled' as it loses its petals. 'Blameless Gorgythion' in Homer is the son of King Priam and a beautiful mother, 'in form like the goddesses' (*Il.* 8.303–5); Stesichorus' Geryon has three bodies and wings to match, an improvement over the Hesiodic monster who has only three heads (*Theogony* 287).[1] The Homeric echo, if pressed, might seem bizarre; a poppy with 'soft body' (if δέμας is the right supplement) is a potentially grotesque point of comparison for a dying monster. Stesichorus presumably adopted this Homeric detail as part of his compassionate portrayal of Geryon. He seems unaware of the possible unsuitability of the comparison. In the high seriousness of the heroic style a monster exterminated by Heracles can also be a victim with whom we can sympathize.

The problem of the poppy simile is symptomatic of the dangers and limitations involved in perpetuating the Homeric style. Transferred to a different structure, the Homeric frame at a certain point seems strained, becomes overburdened and cracks. Other poets – Archilochus, Sappho, Alcaeus – turned Homeric language to new, entirely non-epic situations. At the same time we must not underestimate the sheer delight which the Greeks of the seventh and sixth centuries took in these stories for their own sake, as vase-painting and a monumental representation like the François Vase (*c.* 570 B.C.) indicate. Stesichorus may well have shared his contemporaries' growing malaise about the

---

[1] See *GLP* 91f.; Robertson (1969) 209.

epic as the norm for measuring human experience. His recasting not only of the form, but also of the substance of epic material is an indication of his awareness that the epic mould was not entirely satisfying.

His boldest innovations appear in his *Palinode* for Helen. 'This tale is not true', he recanted, 'nor did you go in the well-benched ships nor reach the citadels of Troy' (192 *PMG*). He developed the motif, possibly already in Hesiod's *Catalogue of women*, that not Helen herself, but a wraith or *eidolon* went to Troy.[1] As there is now evidence for not one but two *Palinodes*, it is probable that Stesichorus told two different versions of the *eidolon* story, one in which the real Helen never went anywhere (Dio Chrys. 11.40) and another in which she was protected by Proteus, as in Euripides' *Helen* (193.15ff. *PMG*).[2] The heroine of his original *Helen* seems to have resembled the figure of Aeschylus' *Agamemnon*, a dangerous, immoral, licentious woman (190 *PMG*). To this poem may also belong a fragment about Aphrodite's curse on the daughters of Tyndareus (223 *PMG*), a story already in Hesiod's *Catalogue* (176 M–W = 93 Rz). In this version, prior to Helen's marriage with Menelaus she is abducted by Theseus and bears him a child; the child is none other than Iphigenia (191 *PMG*). In his *Iliou persis* too Stesichorus may have given Helen a bad character, but the exiguous fragments do not admit of certainty (s104 *SLG*). Such a view of Helen was certainly widespread among his Lesbian contemporaries (cf. Sappho 16.6–10 and Alcaeus в 10 *PLF*).[3] The *Palinodes*, it has been suggested, made the poet's amends in Sparta or one of the Dorian colonies in Magna Graecia where Helen was an important cult-figure. The revision of the myth may be compared with Pindar's reworking of the story of Neoptolemus in *Paean 6* and *Nemean 7* (see below, p. 191 n. 1).

Stesichorus went blind, the story goes, as a result of Helen's wrath (presumably at the version of her character in the *Helen*); but he regained his sight when he sang the *Palinode*. This tale, already well established in the fourth century B.C. (cf. Plato, *Phdr.* 243a; Isocrates, *Helen* 64), may have arisen from a metaphorical statement about darkness and illumination, misunderstood as literal fact. The Oxyrhynchus commentary which cites the beginnings of the two *Palinodes* reports that Stesichorus criticizes Homer in the one and Hesiod in the other (193 *PMG*). This detail receives some support from Plato, who contrasts Homer's blindness with Stesichorus' restored vision (*Phdr.* 243a = 192 *PMG*):

For those who err in telling myths there is an ancient purification which *Homer* did not perceive, *but Stesichorus did*. Deprived of his sight because of his

[1] Hesiod 358 M–W = 266 Rzach; but the evidence for this motif as Hesiodic rests only on a late scholium to Lycophron (*Alex.* 822), of dubious value: see Sisti (1965) 307f.
[2] Scholars have remained reluctant to accept the notion of two separate palinodes, but the new evidence makes this conclusion almost inescapable: see Vallet (1958) 273–7; Sisti (1965) 301–13; Woodbury (1967), 157–76; Davison (1968), 196–225; Treu (1968b) 1254f.; Podlecki (1971) 313–27.
[3] See Page (1955) 280f.; Kirkwood (1974) 267 n. 75.

vilification of Helen, he did not fail to learn this, *as Homer did*, but, being musical, discovered the cause and at once wrote, 'This tale is not true...'

Not only is the relation of the two *Palinodes* to one another obscure, but there is also a question whether either was entirely separate from the *Helen*.[1] The way in which the ancients refer to these works, however, suggests separate poems.

Stesichorus' narratives are full of colourful detail, and it is not surprising that vase-painting in the sixth century drew heavily on them. His Cycnus, for instance, builds a grisly temple from the skulls of his victims (207 *PMG*).[2] He is probably the first poet to represent Athena leaping 'shining with arms' from the head of Zeus (223 *PMG*).[3] He graphically depicted Artemis' punishment of Actaeon by having her throw a stag's skin over him (236 *PMG*).[4] Sympathy for the defeated, grotesque monster though he be, appears not only in the *Geryoneis*; there is probably a touch of compassion in his picture of the Calydonian boar, 'hiding the tip of its snout beneath the ground', presumably in terror (221 *PMG*).

Innovation in genre as well as theme is suggested by the tradition that Stesichorus sang bucolic songs, like those of the neatherd Daphnis (280, 281 *PMG*), possibly drawing on the folklore of his native Sicily, but there is a question of authenticity.[5] Popular currents may appear too in a number of Aesop-like animal fables with a strongly moralizing point. Two on politics are attested by Aristotle; another, cited at length by Aelian, is more doubtful (281 *PMG*).[6] Two poems dealing with unhappy love, the *Calyce* and *Rhadine* (277, 278 *PMG*), are also attributed to him; but these stories have the look of a later age and may well be the work of the fourth-century Stesichorus mentioned by the *Marmor Parium*.[7] The same suspicion attaches to the above-mentioned *Daphnis*. On the other hand Stesichorus was celebrated as a poet of erotic themes (276 *PMG*). Evidence for these now appears in some of the new fragments, particularly a longish poem, erotically coloured, to a handsome youth, attributed by Page to Ibycus, but very possibly the work of Stesichorus (s166–219 *SLG*).

The list of Stesichorus' known works reveals a strong interest in the myth of Heracles, a favourite subject in Magna Graecia, as that hero's far-flung adventures included those distant colonies in the cycles of famous myths.[8] The *Cerberus*,

[1] See *GLP* 112; Davison (1968) 219.   [2] See *GLP* 81; Dawe (1972) 28–30.
[3] See *GLP* 123–6; Vallet (1958) 279 with n. 2 points out, however, that the motif occurs on a shield band at Olympia at the end of the seventh century.
[4] See *GLP* 99f.; Nagy (1973) 179f.   [5] See West (1970a) 206; Vürtheim (1919) 73–6.
[6] On the Aelian passage Vürtheim (1919) 79 remarks, 'Dass Stesichoros solch albernes Zeug geschrieben habe, ist kaum denkbar': Vallet (1958) 284–6 is more sanguine.
[7] See West (1970a) 206; *GLP* 87; Rose (1932) 88–92; Vallet (1958) 285 is more positive.
[8] See Vallet (1958) 263ff., who also suggests possible western connexions for the *Oresteia* (266ff.) if Stesichorus' Apollo sent Orestes to the west for purification.

Cycnus, *Geryoneis*, possibly the *Scylla*, all involve Heracles. The Trojan cycle is represented by his *Nostoi*, *Sack of Troy* and *Helen*; the Theban cycle in the *Eriphyle* and the new poem about Thebes (*P.Lille* 73, 76). His *Oresteia*, *Calydonian Boar hunt* and *Funeral games of Pelias* show his interest in other traditions, both Peloponnesian and north Greek.

Thanks to the recent discoveries, we can see Stesichorus' imagination at work over the large part of a whole poem, the *Geryoneis*.[1] An already existing fragment, quoted by Athenaeus, told of the Sun's journey in a golden cup across Ocean 'to the depths of dark sacred night to his mother and wedded wife and dear children', while Heracles proceeded 'on foot to a grove shadowy with laurel trees' (185 *PMG*). It is not certain whether Heracles is here entering or leaving the western lands of his encounter with Geryon. The former view, maintained by Barrett and Gentili against Page, is somewhat more probable.[2] The fantasy-geography, reminiscent of *Odyssey* 10–12, in any case pervades the mood of this work. This mythical geography and the ample scope of the poem are clear from the details about Geryon's herdsman, Eurytion (184 *PMG*, cited above). Eurytion's mother, one of the Hesperids, took him in infancy 'over the waves of the deep sea... to the most lovely island of the gods, where the Hesperids have their homes, all-golden' (s8 *SLG*). This geographical expansiveness and insistence on the genealogy of even secondary characters indicate the poem's broad scale. A stichometric sign in the papyrus marks line 1300, and this is not the end.

The most important new fragments depict the death of Geryon. Instead of describing a rousing victory over a terrible monster, Stesichorus shows a remarkable sympathy for Heracles' doomed enemy. Geryon delivers a long speech, possibly to Heracles, which is closely modelled on Sarpedon's speech to Glaucus in *Iliad* 12.310–28.[3] The epithets introducing the speech (of which 'immortal' is fairly certain) serve the function both of ennobling him and of stressing the contrast with his approaching mortal end (s11.1–12, 16–26 *SLG*):

τὸν

δ' ἀπαμ[ειβόμενος
ποτέφα [κρατερὸς Χρυσάορος ἀ-
θανάτοιο [γόνος καὶ Καλλιρόας·

'μή μοι θά[νατον προφέρων κρυόεν-   5
τα δεδίσκ[ε' ἀγάνορα θυμόν,
μηδεμελ[

---

[1] See especially Page (1973a) 138–54; Robertson (1969) 207–21; Webster (1968) 1–9. For an interesting interpretation of the myth, connecting Geryon with the herdsman of the dead, see Burkert (1977) 273–83; also Adrados (1978) 266.

[2] Gentili (1976) 745f., on the basis of Apollod. 2.5.10.

[3] Page favours Menoites as the interlocutor (s11 *SLG*); Gentili (1976) 747 argues for Heracles on the analogy of Achilles' speech to Lycaon in *Il.* 22.

αἱ μὲν γὰ[ρ γένος ἀθάνατος πέλο-
μαι καὶ ἀγή[ραος ὥστε βίου πεδέχειν
ἐν Ὀλύμπ[ωι,   10
κρέσσον[ἐ-
λέγχεα δ[12
. . .

αἱ δ᾿ ὦ φί[λε χρὴ στυγερόν μ᾿ ἐπὶ γή-   16
ρας [ἱκ]έσθαι,
ʒώ[ει]ν τ᾿ ἐν ἐ[φαμερίοις ἀπάνευ-
θε θ[ε]ῶν μακάρω[ν,
νῦν μοι πολὺ κά[λλιόν ἐστι παθῆν   20
ὅ τι μόρσιμ[ον

καὶ ὀνείδε[
καὶ παντὶ γέ[νει
ὀπίσω Χρυσ[άο]ρο[ς υ]ἱόν·
μ]ὴ τοῦτο φ[ί]λον μακά[ρε]σσι θε[ο]ῖ-   25
σι γ]ένοιτο᾿

Answering him so spoke the mighty son of immortal Chrysaor and Callirhoe:
'Do not hold chill death before me and try to frighten my manly spirit. . .
But if I am ageless and immortal in race (and partake of?) life on Olympus,
better (to fight than leave behind) shameful reproaches. . . But if, dear friend,
I must come to hateful old age and live among men creatures of a day far from
the blessed gods, better by far is it for me now to suffer whatever is my fated
portion; (not endurable) that the son of Chrysaor should leave behind reproaches for his whole race in aftertime. Let this not be pleasing to the blessed
gods. . .'

The Homeric situation and language is adapted with a poignant clarity. Against
the formulaic diction of the heroic ethos Stesichorus sounds a more vibrant
note of pathos in the repetition of 'blessed gods' (19, 25), in contrast with the
'chill death' facing the speaker.

That pathetic contrast between the concern of loved ones and the firmness of
the doomed warrior is even stronger in the scene between Geryon and his
mother, Callirhoe. This scene of warrior and *mater dolorosa* draws heavily on
the exchanges between Thetis and Achilles in *Iliad* 18 and Hector and Hecuba
in *Iliad* 22. Unfortunately we have only a few lines of Callirhoe's entreaty
(s13.1–5 *SLG*):

ἐγὼν [μελέ]α καὶ ἀλασ-
τοτόκος κ]αὶ ἄλ[ασ]τα παθοῖσα
Γ]αρυόνα γωνάʒομα[ι,
αἱ ποκ᾿ ἐμ]όν τιν μαʒ[ὸν] ἐ[πέσχεθον. . .

I who am unforgettably wretched, in my motherhood, in my suffering, Geryon, I
supplicate you, if ever I held out my breast to you. . .

These scenes prepared the way for the pathos of Geryon's end. Grotesque monster though he is, Geryon's situation and suffering are thoroughly humanized. We have already noted the poppy-simile of his death (s15. col. ii. 14–17 *SLG*). The earlier part of this fragment describes how Heracles poisons his arrows with the Hydra's venom (ὀλεσάνορος αἰολοδείρου ὀδύναισιν Ὕδρας 'with the agonies of the Hydra, man-destroying, of glittering neck', col. ii.5f.). Heracles takes advantage of tricks and guile to kill his foe (λάθραι, col. i.8; σιγᾶι...ἐπικλοπάδαν, col. ii.6f.). The death itself is painful:

> διὰ δ' ἔσχισε σάρκα [καὶ] ὀ[στ]έα δαί-
> μονος αἴσαι·
> διὰ δ' ἀντικρὺ σχέθεν οἱ[σ]τὸς ἐπ' ἀ-
> κροτάταν κορυφάν,
> ἐμίαινε δ' ἄρ' αἵματι πορφ[υρέωι
> θώρακά τε καὶ βροτόεντ[α μέλεα.   (col. ii.8–13)

The arrow split through the flesh and bones, in accordance with the destiny of the god; and it drove through to the topmost part of the skull and fouled with dark-red blood the breast-plate and the bloody limbs...

The addition, 'in accordance with the destiny of the god', keeps pity within the larger perspective of the divine plan and divine justice. Shortly before the battle, in fact, the gods met in council to discuss the outcome, and Athena and Poseidon somehow resolved their conflicting sympathies, possibly with the help of Zeus (s14 *SLG*). Unfortunately there is not enough left to determine whether the issue at stake was just a choice between favourites or some principle of order and justice. On the analogy of the deaths of Patroclus and Hector in the *Iliad*, the latter is the more likely.

Geryon's death formed the climax, but not the end of the poem. After his victory Heracles returns with Geryon's stolen cattle and on his journey meets the Centaur Pholus (181 *PMG*), possibly the encounter where he wounds Chiron with the incurable Hydra's venom. Pausanias mentions Pallanteum in Arcadia (181 *PMG*), the probable site of this adventure.

The other numerous papyrus fragments are too small to do more than offer tantalizing hints. Even with this small fraction of the work, we can still glimpse its richness of style set off against familiar motifs of heroic poetry, its blend of vivid action and evocative geographical fantasy, its imaginative plot, its mixture of traditional phraseology and 'occasional strokes of almost Pindaric boldness' (Page), as in the description of the Hydra's poison cited above.[1] The new fragments justify Dionysius of Halicarnassus' admiration for Stesichorus' 'grandeur' of subject and attention to 'the character and rank of his personages' (*Cens. vet.* 2.7).

---

[1] Page (1973a) 152.

Similar in scope, episodic character, and epic borrowings is the *Iliou persis* or *Sack of Troy* (s88–132 *SLG*) of which some fragments have recently been recovered. To judge by the remains, this poem must have had a leisurely tempo not unlike that of the *Geryoneis*. Unity seems not to have been among its virtues: it related the invention and deployment of the Trojan horse, the prophecy of Cassandra and her rape by Ajax, the death of Astyanax, Menelaus' pardon of Helen, and so on.[1] The existing quotations show us Stesichorus' innovating spirit. He has Hecuba carried off to Lycia by Apollo (198 *PMG*) and presents Athena pitying Epeius, inventor of the wooden horse, as he performs his lowly task of carrying water for the Atreids (200 *PMG*):

ὤικτιρε γὰρ αὐτὸν ὕδωρ
αἰεὶ φορέοντα Διὸς κούρα βασιλεῦσιν.

For the daughter of Zeus pitied him as he was always carrying water for the kings.

Stesichorus may have drawn this rather unheroic detail from folklore motifs (divine aid to the clever underdog); we may contrast the very different setting of Athena's help to Bellerophon in Pindar's thirteenth *Olympian* (66–86).

The new fragments of the *Iliou persis* show us Stesichorus 'lifting on his lyre the full weight of epic song', as in Quintilian's phrase. We have a bit of an energetic debate among the Trojans about bringing the horse within the citadel and the dramatic appearance of omens from the sky at a crucial moment (s88 *SLG*). As the Greeks attack from the horse, the city seems helpless and its gods of no avail (s105*b SLG*). This and a number of other fragments about a battle for Troy (s133–47 *SLG*), however, come from a different papyrus (*P.Oxy.* 2803), and Page assigns them to a separate poem specifically on the Trojan Horse.[2]

The *Oresteia*, in two books, must also have been of considerable length. Surely we must think here of citharodic recitation rather than choral performance. The extent of this poem's influence on the iconography of the myth in sixth- and fifth-century vase-painting is controversial, but there is little doubt of its influence on Attic tragedy.[3] Agamemnon's appearance to Clytemnestra in the form of a snake with bloodied head (219 *PMG*) may have suggested the Aeschylean Clytemnestra's vision of Orestes as a snake drawing blood from the breast. Stesichorus' version already contained the nurse and, according to a

---

[1] If the late relief sculpture known as the *Tabula Iliaca* owes its iconography to Stesichorus, as many believe (cf. 205 *PMG*), Stesichorus may have been the first to depict Aeneas leaving Troy with Anchises on his shoulders, but suspicion on this point, given the later celebrity of the tale, is justified. Vallet (1958) 270–3, however, believes that this story of Aeneas was included in the *Iliou persis*. See also Galinsky (1969) 106–13.

[2] Page (1973*b*) 47–65; *contra*, West (1971*b*) 262–4.

[3] See Davies (1969) *passim*, esp. 248–51; *GLP* 116f.; Vallet (1958) 266–70. On Clytemnestra's dream in Stesichorus see Devereux (1976) 171–9.

recent papyrus fragment of a commentary (217 *PMG*), also the recognition by the lock of hair and Apollo's support of Orestes against the Furies, though in a more purely martial form than in Aeschylus' *Eumenides*. As Stesichorus, following Hesiod, identified Iphigenia with 'the figure now called Hecate' (215 *PMG*), his version presumably included the death and transformation of Iphigenia (cf. also Paus. 1.43.1).

The most sensational find so far is the new fragment about Thebes (*P.Lille* 73 and 76). The papyrus begins a little after line 200 and ends shortly after line 300 (a stichometric mark for the latter is preserved); the middle portion is scrappy, but a good deal is preserved, particularly a virtually complete text of a speech by the Theban queen, perhaps Jocasta. Where the text becomes intelligible, she is desperately trying to find a solution to Tiresias' prophecy that Oedipus' two sons will kill one another (lines 26–56). The brothers seem to agree to divide Oedipus' kingdom and the property (60–76). Then, in a more legible portion of the papyrus, Tiresias is foretelling how Polynices will go to Argos and marry King Adrastus' daughter; the result will be 'grief' (πένθος, 112) for himself and the city. Polynices departs to Argos via Cithaeron, Athens, Corinth and Lerna. As in the *Geryoneis* Stesichorus does not stint on geographical detail.

The best preserved section of the text is, fortunately, the queen's speech. It may be compared with the speech of Geryon to Menoites and the exchange between Geryon and his mother in the *Geryoneis* (above, p. 153). The full characterization, the pathos, the situation of strong emotions in a mother's love for her children are all similar (26–59 = 201–34):[1]

'ἐπ' ἄλγεσι μὴ χαλεπὰς ποίει μερίμνας,   26 = 201
μηδέ μοι ἐξοπίσω
πρόφαινε ἐλπίδας βαρείας.

οὔτε γὰρ αἰὲν ὁμῶς
θεοὶ θέσαν ἀθάνατοι κατ' αἶαν ἱρὰν   30 = 205
νεῖκος ἔμπεδον βροτοῖσιν
οὐδέ γα μὰν φιλότατ', ἐπὶ δ' ἀμέραι ἐν νόον ἄλλον
θεοὶ τιθεῖσι.
μαντοσύνας δὲ τεὰς ἄναξ ἑκάεργος Ἀπόλλων
μὴ πάσας τελέσσαι.   35 = 210

αἰ δέ με παῖδας ἰδέσθαι ὑπ' ἀλλάλοισι δαμέντας
μόρσιμόν ἐστιν, ἐπεκλώσαν δὲ Μοῖρα[ι],
αὐτίκα μοι θανάτου τέλος στυγερο[ῖο] γέν[οιτο,
πρίν ποκα ταῦτ' ἐσιδεῖν
ἄλγεσ⟨σ⟩ι πολύστονα δακρυόεντα[– –,   40 = 215
παῖδας ἐνὶ μεγάροις
θανόντας ἢ πόλιν ἀλοίσαν.

---

[1] The text is that of Haslam (1978) 32f., which is a slightly modified version of Parsons's (1977). See also Bollack, Judet de la Combe, and Wismann (1977) *passim*. Adrados (1978) 274–5 assigns the Lille fragments to the first book of *Eriphyle*.

ἀλλ' ἄγε παῖδες ἐμοῖς μύθοις, φίλα [τέκνα, πίθεσθε·
τᾶιδε γὰρ ὑμὶν ἐγὼν τέλος προφα[ίνω·
τὸν μὲν ἔχοντα δόμους ναίειν πα[ρὰ νάμασι Δίρκας,   45 = 220
τὸν δ' ἀπίμεν κτεάνη
καὶ χρυσὸν ἔχοντα φίλου σύμπαντα [πατρός,
κλαροπαληδὸν ὃς ἂν
πρᾶτος λάχηι ἕκατι Μοιρᾶν.

τοῦτο γὰρ ἂν δοκέω   50 = 225
λυτήριον ὔμμι κακοῦ γένοιτο πότμο[υ,
μάντιος φραδαῖσι θείου,
αἴ γε νέον Κρονίδας γένος τε καὶ ἄστυ [σαώσει
Κάδμου ἄνακτος,
ἀμβάλλων κακότατα πολὺν χρόνον [ἃ βασιλείαι   55 = 230
πέπρωται γενέ[θ]λαι.'

ὡς φάτ[ο] δῖα γυνὰ μύθοις ἀγ[α]νοῖς ἐνεποίσα,
νείκεος ἐν μεγάροις π[αύο]ισα παίδας,
σὺν δ' ἅμα Τειρ[ε]σίας τ[ερασπό]λος· οἱ δ' [ἐ]πίθο[ντο...   59 = 234

P. Lille 73 and 76, *ZPE* 26 (1977) 7–36

'...Upon (existing) griefs do not set harsh cares nor show forth hard expectations for me in aftertime.

For not always have the immortal gods established equally for mortals strife firm-fixed upon the holy earth, no nor love either, but a mind changing to other moods do the gods set upon men; and do not, O lord far-shooter Apollo, accomplish all your prophecies.

But if it is my fated portion to see my children slaughtered by one another and the Fates have spun that out, let me have at once the fulfilment of chill death before seeing these things, amid griefs full of lamentation, full of tears, my children dead in the halls or the city taken.

But come, my sons, dear (children), (be persuaded) by my words, for I am showing you an end (of hostility) in this way: one of you keep the house and dwell in Thebes, and the other go away possessing the chattels and all the gold of his dear father, making the choice by lot, whoever first through the Fates draws the winning lot.

This, I think, would be a release for you from evil destiny in accordance with the thoughts of the divine prophet, if perchance Zeus (may save) the race afresh and the city of lord Cadmus, postponing for a long time the evil (which) is fated for the (royal family).'

So she spoke, regal lady, addressing them with gentle words to stop her sons from strife in the halls. And at the same time Tiresias..., and they obeyed...

The context of the narrative is rather obscure. The absence of Oedipus is particularly striking, and we do not know whether he is dead, exiled, or still alive but without power in Thebes. (The distribution of his property in 45–9 suggests that he is dead, but this is not certain.) We cannot even be sure that the speaker is Jocasta. In one early tradition the incestuous wife, Jocasta or

Epikaste, ostensibly childless, commits suicide when she learns that Oedipus is her son; a second wife, Euryganeia, then bears the children of Oedipus (*Odyssey* 11.271–80, *Oedipodeia*, fr. 1 Allen).[1] Stesichorus' emphasis on the family curse makes it likely that the sons are born from an incestuous union and that the speaker is therefore Oedipus' mother-wife, Jocasta or Epikaste. If so, the situation resembles that of the *Phoenissae* of Euripides, who also followed a Stesichorean variant of a myth in the case of Helen. The queen's intervention between the quarrelling brothers also resembles the *Phoenissae*. Her prayer at lines 38ff. may be a foreshadowing of her suicide, another detail which would strengthen the resemblance with Euripides and also square with the tradition of Jocasta's suicide elsewhere in epic and tragedy. For the sake of convenience we shall call the queen Jocasta, with the reservation that the identification is unproven. Here, as with Helen, Stesichorus may be following an unfamiliar early variant of the story of Oedipus. It may also be that some or all of the narrative details are his own innovation: making Jocasta the mother of Oedipus' children, postponing or omitting her suicide, and having her mediate between the rival brothers.

Jocasta speaks partly in gnomic utterances that recall Homeric situations like the speech of Priam in *Iliad* 24.211ff. The gnomic generality adds weight and dignity to a mother's intense concern for her children. The passage is heavy with a brooding sense of the ill-omened destiny of the house which Jocasta understands all too well but still hopes to avert. Her apostrophe to Apollo not to fulfil 'all his prophecies' (34f.), her direct address eight lines later to her sons with the simple παῖδες (43), her reference to Zeus in 53 all express her anguish and her hopes somehow to fit the oracles to a 'release from evil destiny' (51). Yet this Jocasta is not just a mother distraught by love and fear, like Hecuba in *Iliad* 22, or one bitterly resigned, like Hecuba in *Iliad* 24.209–12. She has practical proposals to offer, in lucid detail and in sharp antithetical clauses, τὸν μέν. . . τὸν δέ (45f.), and she is emphatic about the mechanism of the lottery to implement her solution (48f.). This is a strong woman, who well deserves the heroic epithet δῖα γυνά in 57. Her 'gentle words' take effect and end the quarrel, but there must have been an even greater pathos in the sequel as the respite proves only temporary and the house falls to its terrible doom after all.

The fullness of detail for which Quintilian criticizes Stesichorus is here not without its literary effectiveness. The repetitions of the theme of fate and prophecy (34, 37, 52, 56) and of the references to 'children' (παῖδας. . .παῖδας. . . παῖδες, 36, 41, 43) hammer home both the mother's concern and its ultimate futility. The repetition of the idea of prophecy in 37, 'If it is fated and the Fates have spun it out', and of the words for 'grief' in 40 all contribute to the intensity of her suffering. Stesichorus takes her through a complex emotional movement

---

[1] See Gostoli (1978) 23–7.

as she wishes for death at the idea of 'seeing' (ἰδέσθαι, ἐσιδεῖν, 36, 39) her sons dead, but comes back with practical and energetic measures as she addresses the living sons in a more positive mood (ἀλλ' ἄγε παῖδες, 43), to forestall that image of those 'sons dead in the halls' (παῖδας ἐνὶ μεγάροις | θανόντας, 41f.). Likewise to her prayer to Apollo not to 'fulfil' the doom (τελέσσαι, 35) and to her impulsive wish for a 'fulfilment of chill death' (θανάτου τέλος στυγεροῖο, 38) she opposes a realistic and immediate 'end' or 'fulfilment' (τᾶιδε γὰρ ὑμὶν ἐγὼν τέλος προφαίνω, 44) that may bring release from this 'evil' (cf. also πρόφαινε, 28 and προφαίνω, 44). Passion calms to a quieter and more hopeful closure; and yet her 'belief' (δοκέω, 50) that the 'release from evil destiny' may be in accordance with 'the thoughts of the divine prophet' (52) leaves open the possibility of tragic self-delusion.

Taken as a whole the passage is remarkable for its combination of great emotional power and the dignity of traditional epic diction. There is an emotional vibrancy that goes beyond epic forms. Even better than the speeches of Geryon in the *Geryoneis*, this text reveals Stesichorus' full mastery of his technique, handling epic situations and characters with the flexibility and poignancy of lyric.

The new fragments are particularly interesting for their documentation of the diverse interests of early sixth-century poets. The epic form of leisurely heroic narrative continues side-by-side with the monodists' personal and occasional short poems on contemporary politics or love-affairs. Stesichorus' mythical narratives remind us that the 'Lyric Age' of Greece was not all bent on self-expression and the discovery of the individual. Heroic values and epic themes remain a constant concern. It would probably be wrong to view this continuity as the conservatism of the provincial west or as a self-conscious opposition to new developments.[1] Rather, Stesichorus' citharodic narrative points to the simultaneous coexistence of different literary genres and currents in an age of great artistic energy and experimentation. It is one of the exciting qualities of early Greek culture that forms continue to evolve, but the old traditions still remain strong as points of stability and proud community, unifying but not suffocating.

Looking ahead from Stesichorus to Simonides, Bacchylides and Pindar, we can discern many changes: greater departures from epic language, freer and more complex metrical structures, bolder metaphors, even more emotional expressiveness, and, so far as the fragmentary state of the evidence allows, greater artistic self-consciousness on the part of the poet. Yet this distance between Stesichorus and Bacchylides is, in some ways, less than that between Homer and Archilochus or between Hesiod and Sappho. The generic similarities within large-scale choral lyric between 600 and 450 are perhaps greater than

[1] For these questions see Treu (1968*b*) 1256.

the differences. Stesichorus, however, as 'Longinus' perceived, is far more 'Homeric' than any of his three great successors in choral lyric. In this delight in objective narrative for its own sake and (so far, at least) the absence or relative unimportance of reflectiveness on his art, his true successor is Bacchylides.

6

MONODY

Monody or solo song was the product of sixth-century poets living in the Aegean islands. The most remarkable were Sappho and Alcaeus of Lesbos and Anacreon and Ibycus at the court of Polycrates in Samos. The poetry was distinguished by its metre, dialect and subject matter and by the conditions of its performance from elegiac and iambic verse on the one hand and choral lyric on the other. The poets used short stanzas in a variety of metres, and sang the songs to their own accompaniment on the lyre, presumably repeating the melody for each stanza. They composed for the most part in their own dialects, Sappho and Alcaeus in Aeolic,[1] Anacreon in Ionic, whereas the writers of choral lyric used an artificial language distinguished by some characteristic features of the western dialect group. The audience was presumably a small circle of friends who shared the poet's literary or political interests or lived at the court of his patron.

The poetry of Sappho and Alcaeus is the oldest monody to survive, but it had its antecedents in the earlier music and poetry of Lesbos and in the compositions of Archilochus. Seventh-century Lesbos was famous for its musicians Terpander and Arion (see above, p. 127), and although they wrote poetry of different types from Sappho and Alcaeus and gained their fame in other parts of the Greek world, they bear witness to the musical and literary prowess of the island. Archilochus mentions the Lesbian paean (fr. 121 *IEG*), and Sappho calls Lesbian singers superior to those of other lands (fr. 106).[2] Archilochus was influential in a different way: his themes were often amatory, sympotic or political, and his poetry has the intensity and direct forcefulness that mark the work of Sappho and Alcaeus. It is only his metres and musical accompaniment that exclude him from the genre of lyric poetry. Whether it was Sappho or some other who first sang songs in repeated stanzas we cannot say: perhaps earlier examples failed to survive because writing was not yet in common use or because they were inferior to the later poetry.

[1] For the dialect of the Lesbian poets see Lobel's introductions (1925, 1927), Page (1955), Gomme (1957), Hamm (1958).

[2] The poems and fragments of Sappho and Alcaeus are numbered by the marginal numeration of *PLF*, which is used as far as possible by Voigt (1971). The text is not invariably that of *PLF*.

I. SAPPHO

Sappho was probably born about 630 in the town of Eresus on the western shore of Lesbos, but seems to have spent most of her life in Mytilene, the principal city of the island. She went to Sicily in exile at some time in the period from 604/3 to 596/5, and so it is likely that her family or her husband's family was involved in the political life of Lesbos; in fr. 71 she appears to speak with hostility of the noble family of Penthilus into which the statesman Pittacus married. She may refer to her own old age in fr. 58, and Rhodopis, the courtesan with whom her brother Charaxus became entangled, was said to have flourished in the reign of Amasis of Egypt, who came to the throne in 568. The Suda says that her husband, Cercylas, was a wealthy trader from Andros, but it has been thought that his odd name and his provenance are due to some comic writer.[1] She certainly had a daughter, of whom she speaks with affection in her poetry.

Love was her main theme, and she often expressed strong homosexual feelings. Her audience must usually have been her circle of women and girls: in fr. 160, where she says, 'I shall now sing these songs beautifully to delight my companions', the term for 'companions' indicates that they are female. She may have taught her poetic and musical skills to members of her group: the Suda lists three 'pupils', all from overseas, and a commentator on her poetry (S261A SLG) says that she educated the best of the local girls and also of those from Ionia; her reference to 'the house of those who serve the Muses' (fr. 150) suggests some kind of literary association, however informal. Her friends were singers, and we hear of rival groups. Only a small amount of her work seems to have been intended for a wider audience: her epithalamia (frs. 27, 30, 103–17, perhaps 44) must have been written for actual weddings and fr. 140a for the worship of Adonis. Some Alexandrian scholar allocated her collected poems to nine books on metrical principles, Book 9 containing epithalamia which were excluded by their metre from other books. Book 1 alone had 1,320 lines, i.e. 330 Sapphic stanzas, perhaps 60–70 poems, but Book 8 was only one-tenth as long. Only one complete poem, her prayer to Aphrodite, survives, but we have substantial parts of a dozen others.

The complete poem (1) is preserved in the text of Dionysius of Halicarnassus (*De comp. verb.* 173–9) as an example of the 'polished and exuberant' style:

ποικιλόθρον' ἀθανάτ'Ἀφρόδιτα,
παῖ Δίος δολόπλοκε, λίσσομαί σε,
μή μ' ἄσαισι μηδ' ὀνίαισι δάμνα,
πότνια, θῦμον,

---

[1] Six comedies called *Sappho* are known, the earliest by Ameipsias, the latest by Diphilus; two plays called *Phaon* and five *The Leucadian* may also have dealt with her.

SAPPHO

ἀλλὰ τυίδ' ἔλθ', αἴ ποτα κἀτέρωτα   5
τὰς ἔμας αὔδας ἀίοισα πήλοι
ἔκλυες, πάτρος δὲ δόμον λίποισα
χρύσιον ἦλθες
ἄρμ' ὐπασδεύξαισα· κάλοι δέ σ' ἆγον
ὦκεες στροῦθοι περὶ γᾶς μελαίνας   10
πύκνα δίννεντες πτέρ' ἀπ' ὠράνω αἴθε-
ρος διὰ μέσσω,
αἶψα δ' ἐξίκοντο· σὺ δ', ὦ μάκαιρα,
μειδιαίσαισ' ἀθανάτωι προσώπωι
ἦρε' ὄττι δηὖτε πέπονθα κὤττι   15
δηὖτε κάλημμι,
κὤττι μοι μάλιστα θέλω γένεσθαι
μαινόλαι θύμωι· 'τίνα δηὖτε πείθω
ἄψ σ' ἄγην ἐς ϝὰν φιλότατα; τίς σ', ὦ
Ψάπφ', ἀδίκησι;   20
καὶ γὰρ αἰ φεύγει, ταχέως διώξει·
αἰ δὲ δῶρα μὴ δέκετ', ἀλλὰ δώσει·
αἰ δὲ μὴ φίλει, ταχέως φιλήσει
κωὐκ ἐθέλοισα.'
ἔλθε μοι καὶ νῦν, χαλέπαν δὲ λῦσον   25
ἐκ μερίμναν, ὄσσα δέ μοι τέλεσσαι
θῦμος ἰμέρρει, τέλεσον· σὺ δ' αὔτα
σύμμαχος ἔσσο.

Ornate-throned immortal Aphrodite, wile-weaving daughter of Zeus, I entreat you: do not overpower my heart, mistress, with ache and anguish, but come here, if ever in the past you heard my voice from afar and acquiesced and came, leaving your father's golden house, with chariot yoked: beautiful swift sparrows whirring fast-beating wings brought you above the dark earth down from heaven through the mid-air, and soon they arrived; and you, blessed one, with a smile on your immortal face asked what was the matter with me this time and why I was calling this time and what in my maddened heart I most wished to happen for myself: 'Whom am I to persuade this time to lead you back to her love? Who wrongs you, Sappho? If she runs away, soon she shall pursue; if she does not accept gifts, why, she shall give them instead; if she does not love, soon she shall love even against her will.' Come to me now again and deliver me from oppressive anxieties; fulfil all that my heart longs to fulfil, and you yourself be my fellow-fighter.

Dionysius commended the smoothness of the composition: 'Word follows word inwoven according to certain natural affinities and groupings of the letters'. He gave no examples, but we can see that Sappho showed a strong preference for the liquids, *l*, *m* and *n*, and avoided the hard consonant *b* completely, and that she devoted equal care to the vowel sounds, e.g. *a* and *o* in the first stanza. Alliteration is frequent, but obtrusive only in l. 22, where it underlines the antithesis of refusing and giving gifts and emphasizes the finality of Aphrodite's answer, as does the rhyming effect of ll. 21–3.

Sappho's poetic skill can be seen also in her handling of the Sapphic stanza, which seems to have been her favourite. In the sixth stanza, the climax of the poem, Aphrodite's promises are emphasized by the strong stops, by the fact that the stanza is the first to be self-contained, and by the short final line with its crushing κωὐκ ἐθέλοισα 'even against her will'. She exploits the structure of the stanza also at ll. 11–12 to illustrate the swoop of the chariot.

The prayer-form gives a tight structure to the poem: the framework, similar to that of a Homeric prayer, begins, 'I beseech you, come to me, if ever you came before': Sappho describes the previous coming, and finishes in l. 25 with 'Come again now', a clear example of ring-composition. The verbs ἔλθ' (5), ἦλθες (8) and ἔλθε (25) hold the poem together. Sappho's prayer, however, takes some interesting turns: the mention of the previous epiphany of the goddess leads into a leisurely narrative which occupies almost all of the five central stanzas, finishing with the words of Aphrodite, which move from indirect to direct question at l. 18 and to bluntly direct statement at l. 21.

Recent criticism has been concentrated on the tone of Sappho's poem. Page saw it as an expression of 'the vanity and impermanence of her passion', composed in a spirit of self-mockery; in his view, Aphrodite teased Sappho with the inconsistency of her passion and indicated that her suffering would soon pass. But this is not the most obvious interpretation of the poem, and it does not explain the emphasis which is laid throughout on the divinity and power of Aphrodite: everything leads up to her final words, 'even against her will'; Aphrodite is a goddess, child of Zeus, and she will have her way. She did not come to laugh and preach on the mutability of love, but smilingly gave proof of her divinity by helping Sappho.

It is just possible that a second poem (31) is complete: the author of Περὶ ὕψους, *On the sublime*, quotes four stanzas which form a satisfactory whole; but they are followed by six puzzling words which are almost certainly the beginning of a fifth stanza:

> φαίνεταί μοι κῆνος ἴσος θέοισιν
> ἔμμεν' ὤνηρ, ὄττις ἐνάντιός τοι
> ἰσδάνει καὶ πλάσιον ἆδυ φωνεί-
> σας ὐπακούει
>
> καὶ γελαίσας ἰμέροεν, τό μ' ἦ μὰν   5
> καρδίαν ἐν στήθεσιν ἐπτόαισεν·
> ὡς γὰρ ἔς σ' ἴδω βρόχε', ὤς με φώναι-
> σ' οὐδὲν ἔτ' εἴκει,
>
> ἀλλὰ †κὰμ† μὲν γλῶσσα †ἔαγε†, λέπτον
> δ' αὔτικα χρῶι πῦρ ὐπαδεδρόμηκεν,   10

ὀππάτεσσι δ' οὐδ' ἒν ὄρημμ', ἐπιβρό-
μεισι δ' ἄκουαι,
†έκαδε† μ' ἴδρως κακχέεται, τρόμος δὲ
παῖσαν ἄγρει, χλωροτέρα δὲ ποίας
ἔμμι, τεθνάκην δ' ὀλίγω 'πιδεύης   15
φαίνομ' ἔμ' αὔται.
ἀλλὰ πὰν τόλματον, ἐπεὶ † καὶ πένητα †

That man seems to me to be the equal of the gods who sits opposite you and
close by hears your sweet words and lovely laughter: this, I swear, makes my
heart pound in my breast; for when I glance at you for a moment, I can no
longer speak, my tongue (is fixed in silence?), a thin flame at once runs under my
skin, I see nothing with my eyes, my ears hum, sweat flows down me, trembling
seizes me all over, I am paler than grass, and I seem to be not far short of death.
But all can be endured, since. . .

The poem depends for its effect on the list of physical reactions which occupies
ll. 9–16: the directness of these two stanzas is in contrast with the greater
syntactical complexity of the first two. Sappho uses enjambment freely, and
there are scarcely any strong stops in the poem, so that everything leads up to
the climax of ll. 15–16, climactic whether or not the poem ended there. She
makes little use of imagery, although the expression 'thin fire' and the comparison 'paler than grass' are striking. Again it is Sappho's emotional state
that occupies critical attention: Page identified it as jealousy, caused by the
sight of a man, 'fortunate as the gods', enjoying the company of a girl she
loves; according to others, Sappho is contrasting the reactions of the man,
'strong as the gods', with her own lack of self-control.

Two stanzas of an incomplete poem (16) found on papyrus are among the
finest examples of Sappho's composition. She begins with a priamel, in which
she lists the views of others only to reject them for her own:

οἰ μὲν ἰππήων στρότον, οἰ δὲ πέσδων,
οἰ δὲ νάων φαῖσ' ἐπὶ γᾶν μέλαιναν
ἔμμεναι κάλλιστον, ἔγω δὲ κῆν' ὄτ-
τω τις ἔραται.

Some say that a host of cavalrymen is the fairest thing on the black earth, some
a host of infantry, others of ships: I say it is what one loves.

In the space of one stanza she sets out the contrast between three other views
and her own, and she unerringly positions the word ἔραται 'loves' at the
end. After the bravado of this opening she reduces the intensity with the
leisurely introduction of her proof: Helen, she says, was the most beautiful
of women, but she left husband, daughter and parents for Paris. The intensity
returns when she speaks of the absent Anactoria, of whom she has been reminded
by the story of Helen:

τᾶ]ς κε βολλοίμαν ἐρατόν τε βᾶμα
κἀμάρυχμα λάμπρον ἴδην προσώπω
ἢ τὰ Λύδων ἅρματα κἀν ὅπλοισι
πεσδομ]άχεντας.   20

Her lovely walk and the bright sparkle of her face I would rather see than those
chariots of the Lydians and infantry in armour.

The chariots and infantry clearly recall the soldiery of the opening stanza,
and the description of the girl is remarkable for the adjective ἔρατον applied
to her walk – the word has stronger erotic connotations than the English
'lovely' – and for the noun ἀμάρυχμα, a rare, melodious word used of flashing
eyes.

Two poems are concerned with absent friends. In one (94) Sappho reminds
the departed girl of their happy times together, and recalls garlands of violets
and roses, perfume, shrines, groves, and soft couches. In the other (96) she
uses the Homeric technique of expanded simile:

...(she thought) you like a goddess manifest, and in your song she took most
pleasure. Now she shines among Lydian women, as the rose-fingered moon
surpassing all the stars when the sun has set: it extends its light over salt sea and
flowery fields alike, dew is spread in beauty, roses flourish and delicate chervil
and blossoming clover. Often as she goes to and fro, remembering gentle Atthis
with longing, her tender heart is consumed...

Loneliness is the theme of four famous lines (976 *PMG*), the authorship of
which has been called in question by Lobel and Page among others:

δέδυκε μὲν ἀ σελάννα
καὶ Πληΐαδες· μέσαι δὲ
νύκτες, παρὰ δ' ἔρχετ' ὤρα,
ἔγω δὲ μόνα κατεύδω.

The moon has set and the Pleiads; it is midnight; time passes by; and I sleep
alone.

The lines are effective for the graceful rhythm, the simple paratactic structure,
similar to that of the first stanza of fr. 16, the enjambment at the end of the
second line, and above all the directness of the statement.

Writers like Pausanias and Himerius who knew all her work confirm the
impression created by the fragments that most of it was love poetry. Sometimes no more than a brief image survives in the debris: 'Love shook my heart,
like the wind falling on oaks on a mountain' (47), or 'Once again Love, the
loosener of limbs, shakes me, that sweet-bitter, irresistible creature' (130).
There are traditional elements here, for example, the epithet λυσιμέλης 'loosener
of limbs', but γλυκύπικρον 'sweet-bitter' is astonishing, particularly when

applied to ὅρπετον, a 'creature' or even a 'monster'. A substantial fragment (2) takes the form of an invitation to Aphrodite to visit a shrine:

...Come hither, I pray, from Crete to this holy temple, where your lovely apple orchard is, and altars smoking with frankincense. In it cold water gurgles through the apple branches, the place is all shadowy with roses, and from the quivering leaves sleep comes down. In it a meadow where horses graze blossoms with spring flowers, and the breezes blow sweetly...There, Cyprian goddess, take...and in gold cups gracefully pour nectar that mingles with our festivity...

In this poem as in others Sappho lingers over detail and in some of her most melodious lines creates a dream-like picture of an earthly paradise. The imagery of apples, flowers, gardens and horses is strongly erotic, and all the senses are involved, sight, smell, touch, hearing, even taste in the mention of nectar.

Domestic themes of various kinds are found in the fragments. She says of her daughter in 132, 'I have a beautiful child who looks like golden flowers, my darling Cleis, for whom I would not (take) all Lydia or lovely ...' Her brother distressed her by paying a large sum of money to buy the freedom of a famous courtesan of Naucratis: Herodotus (2.134–5) says that Sappho ridiculed him in one of her poems, but we also have parts of a poem (5) in which she prays for his safety and well-being.

The scraps of epithalamia which have survived vary greatly in tone. Some are strongly lyrical, for example, the address to Hesperus (104a), or the comparison of the bride to the hyacinth, trodden underfoot by shepherds (105c), or to an apple (105a):

> οἶον τὸ γλυκύμαλον ἐρεύθεται ἄκρωι ἐπ' ὔσδωι,
> ἄκρον ἐπ' ἀκροτάτωι, λελάθοντο δὲ μαλοδρόπηες·
> οὐ μὰν ἐκλελάθοντ', ἀλλ' οὐκ ἐδύναντ' ἐπίκεσθαι.

As the sweet-apple reddens on the bough-top, on the top of the topmost bough; the apple-gatherers have forgotten it – no, not forgotten it: they could not reach it.

The boisterous comedy and lyric metre of 110a are in sharp contrast: 'The door-keeper's feet are seven fathoms long, and his sandals are made from five ox-hides; ten cobblers worked hard to make them.' The humour of 111 is similar: 'On high raise up – Hymenaeus! — the roof, you carpenters – Hymenaeus! The bridegroom is coming, the equal of Ares, much larger than a large man.' Sappho may be mocking the convention that the bridegroom is of epic build: elsewhere she compares him to Achilles. At any rate the fondness for comparison is well attested: bridegrooms are likened to slender saplings or prize-winning horses, brides to roses. One long papyrus fragment (44) describes with lively detail Hector's return to Troy with his bride, Andromache, and it may well have been performed at a real wedding.

A few passages refer to her literary skill and to her confidence that it will bring her immortality, and in 55 she speaks harshly of a woman who has no such skill:

κατθάνοισα δὲ κείσηι οὐδέ ποτα μναμοσύνα σέθεν
ἔσσετ' οὐδὲ πόθα εἰς ὕστερον· οὐ γὰρ πεδέχηις βρόδων
τὼν ἐκ Πιερίας, ἀλλ' ἀφάνης κἀν 'Αίδα δόμωι
φοιτάσηις πεδ' ἀμαύρων νεκύων ἐκπεποταμένα.

But when you die you will lie there, and afterwards there will never be any recollection of you or any longing for you, since you have no share in the roses of Pieria; unseen in the house of Hades also, flown from our midst, you will go to and fro among the shadowy corpses.

2. ALCAEUS

Dionysius of Halicarnassus, commenting on the style of Alcaeus, says that often if one removed the metre one would find political rhetoric (*Imit.* 422), and Horace, looking for a single epithet for Alcaeus' songs, called them *minaces* 'threatening' (*Odes* 4.9.7). The turbulent politics of Lesbos were the immediate source of inspiration for perhaps half of his surviving poetry. A full generation before his birth the ruling aristocratic family, the Penthilidae, who traced their ancestry through Penthilus to Orestes and Agamemnon, were overthrown, and the tyrants who succeeded them, Melanchrus, Myrsilus and Pittacus, are all mentioned in the fragments of Alcaeus' poems.[1] He himself belonged to a noble family which competed unsuccessfully for political power in Mytilene; he was exiled three times, and was finally forgiven by Pittacus. The date of his birth was *c*. 620 B.C., perhaps as early as 630, and his reference to his 'grey chest' (50) suggests that he did not die young.

One of the longest surviving passages of his poetry (129) gives an idea of the forceful style attested by ancient critics: Alcaeus, in exile somewhere on Lesbos, appeals to Zeus, Hera and Dionysus for help:

ἄγιτ' εὔνοον
θῦμον σκέθοντες ἀμμετέρας ἄρας   10
ἀκούσατ', ἐκ δὲ τῶνδε μόχθων
ἀργαλέας τε φύγας ῥ[ύεσθε·
τὸν Ὕρραον δὲ παῖδα πεδελθέτω
κήνων 'Ε[ρίννυ]ς ὥς ποτ' ἀπώμνυμεν
τόμοντες[15
μηδάμα μηδ' ἔνα τὼν ἐταίρων
ἀλλ' ἢ θάνοντες γᾶν ἐπιέμμενοι
κείσεσθ' ὐπ' ἄνδρων οἳ τότ' ἐπικ[άν]ην

[1] For the politics of Lesbos see Page (1955) 149–243, Andrewes (1956) 92–9.

ἤπειτα κακκτάνοντες αὔτοις
δᾶμον ὑπὲξ ἀχέων ῥύεσθαι.   20
κήνων ὁ φύσγων οὐ διελέξατο
πρὸς θῦμον ἀλλὰ βραϊδίως πόσιν
ἔμβαις ἐπ' ὀρκίοισι δάπτει
τὰν πόλιν ἄμμι. . .

Come, with gracious spirit hear our prayer, and rescue us from these hardships
and from grievous exile; and let their Avenger pursue the son of Hyrrhas, since
once we swore, cutting (a lamb's throat?), never (to abandon?) any of our
comrades, but either to die at the hands of men who came against us then and to
lie clothed in earth, or else to kill them and rescue the people from their woes. But
Pot-belly did not talk to their hearts; he recklessly trampled the oaths
underfoot and devours our city. . .

Not all of the detail is clear, but it seems that Pittacus, 'son of Hyrrhas', had
conspired with Alcaeus and others against Myrsilus and had defected from
the alliance. Alcaeus' abuse of him is written with a sure touch: the alternatives
of death and victory are neatly set out, two lines to each, in ll. 17–20, and the
expressions 'clothed in earth', 'trampled the oaths underfoot', and 'devours
our city', are effective. 'Pot-belly' is only one of several opprobrious epithets
he applied to Pittacus: Diogenes Laertius lists also σαράπους and σάραπος
'splay-footed', χειροπόδης 'with chapped feet', γαύρηξ 'boaster', γάστρων
'big-belly', ζοφοδορπίδας 'diner in the dark' and ἀγάσυρτος 'filthy'.

The allegory of the storm-tossed ship of state is found in two fragments:
in one (6) Alcaeus speaks of waves pouring into the ship, and appeals to his
fellows to shore up the ship's sides and race for a secure harbour. Then,
moving from allegory to reality, he tells them to avoid soft fear, remember
previous hardship, show steadfastness and not disgrace their ancestors by
cowardice. Three stanzas later the word μοναρχίαν 'monarchy' appears in the
text and a marginal comment refers to Myrsilus. There is little doubt that
Heraclitus, the Homeric scholar who quotes the opening lines as an example of
allegory, was correct in his interpretation.

Heraclitus quotes the other piece (326) for the same purpose, declaring
that in spite of appearances the poem is about Myrsilus and his tyrannical
conspiracy against the Mytileneans:

ἀσυννέτημμι τὼν ἀνέμων στάσιν·
τὸ μὲν γὰρ ἔνθεν κῦμα κυλίνδεται,
τὸ δ' ἔνθεν, ἄμμες δ' ὂν τὸ μέσσον
νᾶϊ φορήμμεθα σὺν μελαίναι
χείμωνι μόχθεντες μεγάλωι μάλα·   5
πὲρ μὲν γὰρ ἄντλος ἰστοπέδαν ἔχει,
λαῖφος δὲ πὰν ζάδηλον ἤδη,
καὶ λάκιδες μέγαλαι κὰτ αὖτο,
χόλαισι δ' ἄγκυρραι. . .

I fail to understand the direction of the winds: one wave rolls in from this side, another from that, and we in the middle are carried along in company with our black ship, much distressed in the great storm. The bilge-water covers the masthold; all the sail lets the light through now, and there are great rents in it; the anchors are slackening...

The lines show Alcaeus' craftsmanship at its finest: he begins the poem, as often, with a verb, an unfamiliar one here and impressively long; the word στάσις fits both the storm description and the political allegory, since it can denote either the set of the winds or civil strife. Alcaeus makes cunning use use of the Alcaic stanza in ll. 3–4, where the jerky rhythm of the third line is followed by the rapid movement of the fourth in illustration of the headlong rush of the ship. Assonance in l. 1 and alliteration in ll. 2 and 5 are effective, and the paratactic construction makes for great clarity.

In another long political poem (298 Voigt, s262 *SLG*) Alcaeus devotes several stanzas to the myth of Locrian Ajax, who raped Cassandra in Athena's temple when the Greeks captured Troy. Alcaeus appears to tie the myth to contemporary affairs in his introduction: '... we must put (a noose?) on their necks and (kill them) by stoning. It would have been far better for the Achaeans if they had killed the man who did violence to the gods.' After devoting some nine stanzas to his account of the crime of Ajax, Alcaeus reverts to the politics of his own day with a mention of Pittacus: presumably it was he and his associates who, like Ajax, ought to have been stoned for their crimes.

The symposium must have provided the occasion for these poems, and wine is the theme of many of the surviving fragments. Athenaeus, who quotes most of our convivial pieces, comments that Alcaeus is found drinking in all seasons and circumstances. One scrap (367) mentions springtime: 'I heard the flowery spring coming ... mix a bowl of the honey-sweet wine as fast as you can.' The heat of the dogdays is given as the excuse for drinking in several poems, in one of which (347) Alcaeus recasts lines of Hesiod (*W.D.* 582–8) in lyric metre and Lesbian dialect: the detail is Hesiod's except for the opening flourish, which may be a popular turn of phrase or a colourful invention:

τέγγε πλεύμονας οἴνωι, τὸ γὰρ ἄστρον περιτέλλεται,
ἀ δ' ὤρα χαλέπα, πάντα δὲ δίψαισ' ὐπὰ καύματος.

Wet your lungs with wine: the dogstar is coming round, the season is harsh, everything thirsts under the heat.

A winter poem (338) may have provided inspiration for Horace's Soracte od (1.9):

ὔει μὲν ὀ Ζεῦς, ἐκ δ' ὀράνω μέγας
χείμων, πεπάγαισιν δ' ὐδάτων ῥόαι...
κάββαλλε τὸν χείμων', ἐπὶ μὲν τίθεις

170

πῦρ, ἐν δὲ κέρναις οἶνον ἀφειδέως
μέλιχρον, αὐτὰρ ἀμφὶ κόρσαι
μόλθακον ἀμφιβάλων γνόφαλλον.　　　　　　　(3-8)

Zeus sends down the rain, a great storm comes from the heavens, flowing
streams are frozen solid... Down with the storm! Stoke up the fire, mix the sweet
wine without sparing it, and put a soft pillow about your head.

The short phrases, the placing of the verbs at the beginning of the clauses,
the paratactic structure and the skilful handling of the metre are all typical
features of Alcaeus. They may be seen also in the following vigorous exhortation (346):

πώνωμεν· τί τὰ λύχν' ὀμμένομεν; δάκτυλος ἀμέρα.
κὰδ δ᾽ἀερρε κυλίχναις μεγάλαις, ἄῖτα, ποικίλαις·
οἶνον γὰρ Σεμέλας καὶ Δίος υἶος λαθικάδεον
ἀνθρώποισιν ἔδωκ'. ἔγχεε κέρναις ἕνα καὶ δύο
πλήαις κὰκ κεφάλας, ἀ δ᾽ ἀτέρα τὰν ἀτέραν κύλιξ
ὠθήτω...

Let's drink! Why do we wait for the lamps? A finger's breadth of daylight is all
that remains. Take down the great decorated cups, my friend; for the son of
Zeus and Semele gave men wine to make them forget their worries. Pour it in
brim-full, mixing one part of water to two of wine, and let one cup elbow the
next...

The first line is remarkable for containing an exhortation, a rhetorical question
and a statement of justification. We cannot say whether the striking phrase
δάκτυλος ἀμέρα 'a finger's breadth of daylight' was a commonplace or an
invention of Alcaeus: it was certainly proverbial after his time. The jostling of
the cups is another happy idea, and Alcaeus exploits the Asclepiad rhythm for
an amusing effect in ἀ δ᾽ ἀτέρα τὰν ἀτέραν.

As in the political songs, myth can be pressed into service in a convivial
context: Alcaeus exhorts a companion, Melanippus, to drink on the grounds
that we have only one life to enjoy, and he makes his point by alluding to the
story of Sisyphus, who cheated Death into releasing him from the underworld
but had to return and undergo punishment; such exploits are not for us, he
says, and we must make the most of our youth (38A).

We have considerable knowledge of some of the hymns written by Alcaeus,
and it is clear that the loss of the originals is one of the saddest in the field of
Greek lyric poetry. The Homeric Hymns, at least some of which belong
roughly to the same period as Alcaeus, are similar in that they record the
attributes and exploits of individual gods and were intended as entertainment
for a secular audience rather than as religious cult-hymns. The longest Homeric
Hymns, however, run to several hundred lines and use epic metre and technique, whereas Alcaeus wrote short songs in the same metres and dialect as

his other poetry. We can gain some impression of their form and scale from a poem such as Horace's hymn to Mercury (*Odes* 1.10), based according to the commentator Porphyrio on Alcaeus' hymn to Hermes (308), and from a few references in ancient writers. The opening of the Hermes hymn survives:

χαῖρε, Κυλλάνας ὁ μέδεις, σὲ γάρ μοι
θῦμος ὕμνην, τὸν κορύφαισ' ἐν αὔταις
Μαῖα γέννατο Κρονίδαι μίγεισα
παμβασίληϊ.

> Greetings, ruler of Cyllene – for it is of you that I wish to sing, you whom Maia bore on the very mountain-tops, having lain with Cronos' son, the king of all.

There are resemblances here to the opening of the *Homeric Hymn to Hermes*, but these are probably due simply to the genre, and in any case we cannot say which poem is the earlier. Alcaeus uses the short fourth line of the Sapphic stanza to stress the majesty of Hermes' paternity. He seems to have continued with references to the midwifery of the Graces and the nursing of the Horae, material which is not in the Homeric hymn. Pausanias tells us that Alcaeus described Hermes' theft of the cattle of Apollo, and Porphyrio adds that in the poem Hermes capped this by stealing Apollo's quiver. The poem may have comprised no more than Horace's five stanzas.

The hymn to Apollo (307) was given pride of place by the Alexandrian editor, who made it the first poem of Book 1. Alcaeus used his favourite Alcaic stanza: ὦναξ Ἄπολλον, παῖ μεγάλω Δίος 'Lord Apollo, son of great Zeus'. Scarcely anything else survives of the text, but the sophist Himerius gives a paraphrase of the contents: Zeus equipped his son with golden headband, lyre and swan-drawn chariot and sent him to Delphi to declare justice to the Greeks; but Apollo went instead to the land of the Hyperboreans and spent a year there before going to Delphi. Himerius describes Alcaeus' account of the god's arrival as follows: 'what with the blaze of summer and the presence of Apollo the poet's lyre also adopts a summer wantonness . . .: nightingales sing for him the sort of song that one might expect birds to sing in Alcaeus, swallows too and cicadas, not proclaiming their own fortunes in the world but telling of the god in all their songs. Castalia flows in poetic fashion with waters of silver, and Cephisus rises in flood . . .' This hymn too, which need not have been longer than seven stanzas, differs fundamentally from the Homeric Hymn in its account of Apollo's coming to Delphi.

The love songs of Alcaeus are lost, but Horace tells us (*Odes* 1.32.9–12) that among the themes of his poetry were 'Venus and the boy who ever clings to her, and Lycus, handsome with his black eyes and black hair'. He was thus one of the first poets to sing of male homosexual love. A tantalizing fragment

(10B) formed the opening of a poem in which a girl speaks of her misery: ἔμε δείλαν, ἔμε παίσαν κακοτάτων πεδέχοισαν 'Wretched me, who share in all ills!' If Horace's poem in the same rare Ionic rhythm (*Odes* 3.12) was based on it, the girl's miseries were the tortures of love.

The political faction or *hetaireia* must have provided the audience for Alcaeus' poetry: it seems likely that he sang his verses to his friends and allies at the symposium at the end of the day. The political poems with their personal invective are obviously at home in these surroundings: a famous one, echoed by Horace, begins, 'Now we must get drunk and drink with all our strength, since Myrsilus has died' (332). Alcaeus' emphasis on friendship (71), broken promises (67, 129, 306 fr. 9) and deceit (68, 69) suggests a circle in which loyalty was all-important. The Ajax-fragment indicates that even poems with considerable mythological content may have been essentially political. The drinking itself was not only a means of forgetting military setbacks, betrayals or the hardships of exile (73, 335): it was seen as an opportunity to test a man's true feelings, and fragments such as 'wine, dear boy, and truth' (366) and 'wine is a peep-hole into a man' (333) should be seen in this context. The love-poetry also belongs here: 'if I am to enjoy the symposium, I request that charming Menon be invited' (368). We can add that his companions must have shared his enthusiasm for poetry, since the very existence of hundreds of elaborate short poems and hymns is evidence for a willing and informed audience.

3. IBYCUS[1]

Ibycus belonged like Stesichorus to Magna Graecia: he was born at Rhegium and was buried there, but he left the west for the court of Polycrates, tyrant of Samos from c. 533 to c. 522. It is not certain that he wrote monody. He is known to have composed narrative poems on the same themes and in the same manner as Stesichorus, and the long papyrus fragment which is ascribed to him (282a) has the triadic structure of choral poetry. But the strongly personal and erotic nature of the best-known fragments (286, 287) and the fact that Ibycus' colleague in Samos was Anacreon, most of whose work is monodic, leave room for the possibility that some of his work was for solo performance.

Fr. 286 may be regarded as an elaboration of Sappho's comparison of love to a gale-force wind:

ἦρι μὲν αἵ τε Κυδώνιαι
μαλίδες ἀρδόμεναι ῥοᾶν
ἐκ ποταμῶν, ἵνα Παρθένων
κᾶπος ἀκήρατος, αἵ τ' οἰνανθίδες
αὐξόμεναι σκιεροῖσιν ὑφ' ἔρνεσιν   5

---

[1] The poems and fragments of Ibycus and Anacreon are numbered by the marginal numeration of *PMG*, but the text sometimes differs.

οἰναρέοις θαλέθοισιν, ἐμοὶ δ' ἔρος
οὐδεμίαν κατάκοιτος ὥραν.
†τε† ὑπὸ στεροπᾶς φλέγων
Θρηίκιος βορέας ἀίσ-
σων παρὰ Κύπριδος ἀʒαλέαις μανί-
αισιν ἐρεμνὸς ἀθαμβὴς
ἐγκρατέως πεδόθεν τινάσσει
ἀμετέρας φρένας.

In the spring flourish Cydonian quince-trees, watered from flowing rivers, where stands the inviolate garden of the Maidens, and vine-blossoms growing under the shady vine-branches; but for me Love rests at no season: like the Thracian north wind blazing with lightning, rushing from the Cyprian with parching fits of madness, dark and shameless, he powerfully shakes my heart from the roots.

Ibycus contrasts the seasonal regularity of nature with his ever-present love which knows no seasons, and makes a further contrast between the tranquillity of nature, which he illustrates by the repeated vowel sounds of the first six lines, and the harshness of love's attack. The image of κατάκοιτος is apt: Love 'goes to bed' at no season. In describing the wind of love Ibycus interweaves his epithets: ἐρεμνός 'dark' suggests the clouds carried by the wind, whereas ἀθαμβής 'shameless' belongs rather to a personified Love.

The imagery of fr. 287 is equally striking:

Ἔρος αὖτέ με κυανέοισιν ὑπὸ
βλεφάροις τακέρ' ὄμμασι δερκόμενος
κηλήμασι παντοδαποῖς ἐς ἄπει-
ρα δίκτυα Κύπριδος ἐσβάλλει·
ἦ μὰν τρομέω νιν ἐπερχόμενον,
ὥστε φερέʒυγος ἵππος ἀεθλοφόρος ποτὶ γήραι
ἀέκων σὺν ὄχεσφι θοοῖς ἐς ἅμιλλαν ἔβα.

Again Love, looking at me meltingly from under his dark eyelids, hurls me with his manifold enchantments into the boundless nets of the Cyprian. How I fear his onset, as a prize-winning horse still bearing the yoke in his old age goes unwillingly with swift chariot to the race.

The metaphor of the hunt, in which Eros drives the prey into Aphrodite's nets, is smoothly succeeded by the imagery of the racecourse, and there is humour as well as pathos in the picture of the old horse, successful in earlier days but now reluctant to compete. In fr. 288 Ibycus addresses a youth in equally rich language, reminiscent of choral poetry rather than monody:

Εὐρύαλε γλαυκέων Χαρίτων θάλος, ⟨'Ωρᾶν⟩
καλλικόμων μελέδημα, σὲ μὲν Κύπρις
ἅ τ' ἀγανοβλέφαρος Πει-
θὼ ῥοδέοισιν ἐν ἄνθεσι θρέψαν.

Euryalus, offshoot of the blue-eyed Graces, darling of the lovely-haired Horae, the Cyprian and soft-lidded Persuasion nursed you among rose-blossoms.

No other early Greek poet expressed his love with this hymnal elaboration.

The choral poem written for Polycrates (282a) is insipid by comparison. The first 35 lines of the fragment tell of the fall of Troy and list Trojans and Greeks of whom the poet will not or cannot speak; one of the Greek warriors, we are told, rivalled the Trojan Troilus in beauty; and the poem ends in Pindaric manner with the assurance that Polycrates will have undying fame, thanks to the poetic ability and fame of the writer. This puzzling work has been seen as a sample of the poet's wares offered to his potential patron, as a *recusatio* in which he declares his intention of avoiding epic themes in favour of love-poetry, and as simple glorification of Polycrates' son of the same name. Ibycus may have made his purpose clear in the beginning of the poem, now lost.

4. ANACREON

Anacreon was born in the Ionian city of Teos in Asia Minor, and when Harpagus, Cyrus' general, attacked the Greek coastal cities, he sailed with the rest of the Teians to Thrace, where they founded Abdera *c.* 540 B.C. He is next heard of at the court of Polycrates of Samos, whose tyranny is dated *c.* 533–522, and after the murder of his patron he was taken to Athens by Hipparchus, son of Pisistratus, who during the tyranny of his brother Hippias was responsible for cultural affairs. Anacreon may have lived on in Athens after Hipparchus' assassination in 514, or he may have gone to Thessaly: epigrams written for the Thessalian ruler Echecratidas and his wife Dyseris are attributed to him (frs. 107, 108 Diehl). If he did visit Thessaly, he must have returned to Athens and may have spent much of his later life there: he is said to have sung the praises of Critias, grandfather of the Athenian politician of that name, and to have enjoyed the poetry of Aeschylus. He may have been born *c.* 570 and died *c.* 485: he was said to have lived 85 years.

Most of his poetry was concerned with love and wine: Maximus of Tyre (37.5) summed up its content as 'the hair of Smerdies and Cleobulus, the pipes of Bathyllus and Ionian song', but Cicero (*Tusc. Disp.* 4.71) exaggerates when he says it was all erotic. The symposium must have provided the occasion for its performance; Critias indeed called him συμποσίων ἐρέθισμα 'the excitement of the drinking-party' (Athen. 13.600d). Samian politics appear twice in the fragments, one satirical poem remains and more is attested, and we hear also of choral poetry, although nothing remains except a doubtful fragment of the Maiden-songs.

Anacreon does not write in the rich, sensuous style of Ibycus, but relies for his effect on careful craftsmanship, elegance and wit. These qualities may

be seen in his address to a young girl, written in a lilting trochaic rhythm
which contributes much to the gaiety (417):

πῶλε Θρηικίη, τί δή με λοξὸν ὄμμασι βλέπουσα
νηλέως φεύγεις, δοκεῖς δέ μ' οὐδὲν εἰδέναι σοφόν;
ἴσθι τοι, καλῶς μὲν ἄν τοι τὸν χαλινὸν ἐμβάλοιμι,
ἡνίας δ' ἔχων στρέφοιμί σ' ἀμφὶ τέρματα δρόμου·
νῦν δὲ λειμῶνάς τε βόσκεαι κοῦφά τε σκιρτῶσα παίζεις·
δεξιὸν γὰρ ἱπποπείρην οὐκ ἔχεις ἐπεμβάτην.

Thracian filly, why do you look at me out of the corner of your eye and run
pitilessly from me, and suppose that I have no skill? Let me tell you, I could
neatly put a bridle on you and holding the reins turn you round the limits of
the course; as it is, you graze the meadows and play, skipping lightly, for you
have no clever horseman to ride you.

The imagery is common in Greek poetry and is sometimes used coarsely, as
by Aristophanes, sometimes delicately, as here and in Alcman's Maiden-songs.
Thracian horses were famous, but if the poem was addressed to a Thracian
girl, there would be added point. There is a pleasant touch in the adverb νηλέως
'pitilessly', which belongs to the language of epic and is used with mock-
heroic effect.

Another encounter with a girl forms the material for one of Anacreon's
wittiest poems, in which much is stated and much suggested in very short
space (358):

σφαίρηι δηῦτέ με πορφυρῆι
βάλλων χρυσοκόμης ˝Ερως
νήνι ποικιλοσαμβάλωι
συμπαίζειν προκαλεῖται·
ἡ δ', ἐστὶν γὰρ ἀπ' εὐκτίτου
Λέσβου, τὴν μὲν ἐμὴν κόμην,
λευκὴ γάρ, καταμέμφεται,
πρὸς δ' ἄλλην τινὰ χάσκει.

Once again golden-haired Eros hits me with a purple ball and challenges me to
play with the girl with the fancy shoes; but she, coming as she does from Lesbos
with its proud cities, finds fault with my hair, since it is white, and gawps after
another girl.

Anacreon sets the scene of this miniature drama in his first stanza: he has fallen
in love, this time with a girl distinguished by her elaborate footwear; the
description, like 'the Thracian filly', no doubt served to identify her for the
audience. The pictorial quality of the stanza is remarkable, each noun being
accompanied by a colour-epithet, so that the whiteness of the poet's hair is in
contrast. In the second stanza Anacreon misleads his listeners more than once
before revealing the truth of the matter: Lesbos is distinguished by an epic
adjective εὐκτίτου which draws attention to its fine ancient cities, and the

suggestion is that a girl from such a background might consider Anacreon's social status too mean for her; but the reason she actually gives for her rejection is Anacreon's age. The sad truth is reserved for the last line of the poem: the proclivities of Sappho and her friends were not forgotten, and this girl like them comes from Lesbos. She has eyes only for some other girl, and she concentrates, open-mouthed in her single-mindedness, on her.[1] The poem, which began with bright colours and gay imagery, finishes with mutual fault-finding and the harsh hiss of the verb χάσκει.

Love, the ball-player in this poem, has other roles, as boxer (396), dice-player (398), blacksmith (413). In another poem it is not Love but the beloved boy himself who is a charioteer (360):

> ὦ παῖ παρθένιον βλέπων,
> δίζημαί σε, σὺ δ' οὐ κοεῖς,
> οὐκ εἰδὼς ὅτι τῆς ἐμῆς
> ψυχῆς ἡνιοχεύεις.

Boy with the virgin glance, I pursue you, but you pay no attention, not realizing that you hold the reins of my soul.

This short stanza is a fine example of Anacreon's technique: l. 1 is notable for the alliteration, ll. 2-4 for the rhyme and near-rhyme which tighten the structure of the stanza. He creates a neat antithesis in l. 2 by juxtaposing the pronouns σέ, σύ. The stanza moves surely to the impressive epic verb ἡνιοχεύεις with its unexpected metaphor.

One poem (357) takes the form of a prayer to Dionysus, who is asked to advise Cleobulus to accept the singer's love. Dionysus was not the obvious addressee for such a prayer, but Anacreon, like Alcaeus, probably sang his song with a wine-cup before him. There is no sharp distinction between the erotic and the convivial poetry. One imagines the typical setting as an all-male drinking-party given by Polycrates or Hipparchus: the content of Ibycus' poems suggests that Polycrates' court appreciated poems about homosexual love,[2] and Thucydides (6.54.3ff.) tells us that it was homosexual passion that led to the assassination of Hipparchus.

Anacreon and other poets from the second half of the sixth century onwards display two attitudes towards wine-drinking. There is still the straightforward exhortation to unrestrained revelry, but a small group of Anacreon's poems preaches moderation: Scythian-style carousal with clatter and shouting is forbidden in favour of moderate drinking and beautiful hymns (356b); and

---

[1] Most recent studies take ἄλλην τινά to refer to a κόμη other than the hair on Anacreon's head: see Woodbury (1979a) for full bibliography.

[2] Athenaeus, presumably arguing from the content of Anacreon's poems, says (12.540e) that Polycrates was 'passionately devoted to the company of males'; cf. Aelian, V.H. 9.4.

MONODY

in elegiac couplets, the usual medium for reflective poetry and prescriptive
writing, he says (fr. eleg. 2 West):

οὐ φιλέω ὃς κρητῆρι παρὰ πλέωι οἰνοποτάζων
νείκεα καὶ πόλεμον δακρυόεντα λέγει,
ἀλλ' ὅστις Μουσέων τε καὶ ἀγλαὰ δῶρ' 'Αφροδίτης
συμμίσγων ἐρατῆς μνήισκεται εὐφροσύνης.

I don't love the man who while drinking his wine beside the full mixing-bowl
talks of quarrels and tearful war, but the man who by mixing the splendid gifts
of the Muses and Aphrodite keeps lovely festivity in mind.

Love-song, the poetry for which Anacreon himself was most renowned, is
what the civilized drinker should sing, not poetry on epic themes or Alcaeus'
songs of violent politics.

When Anacreon does choose a political theme, he writes a hymn in his
customary lyric metre (348):

γουνοῦμαί σ', ἐλαφηβόλε,
ξανθὴ παῖ Διός, ἀγρίων
δέσποιν' Ἄρτεμι θηρῶν,
ἥ κου νῦν ἐπὶ Ληθαίου
δίνηισι θρασυκαρδίων   5
ἀνδρῶν ἐσκατορᾶις πόλιν
χαίρουσ', οὐ γὰρ ἀνημέρους
ποιμαίνεις πολιήτας.

I beseech you, deer-shooter, fair-haired child of Zeus, Artemis, queen of wild
beasts, who now somewhere by the eddies of the Lethaeus look down on a city
of bold-hearted men and rejoice, since the citizens whom you shepherd are
not untamed.

The poem must have continued with a request that Artemis preserve the
people of Magnesia, the city on the river Lethaeus, near which was a temple of
Artemis Leucophryene. Anacreon speaks of them as courageous and civilized
as a reminder that they are Greeks, citizens of a Greek city (πόλιν ... πολιήτας),
although they are at present under Persian rule and Magnesia is the headquarters of a Persian satrap. As always, Anacreon writes with a firm touch,
making his point by the alliteration of l. 8 and the metaphor of the shepherdess,
appropriate for Artemis.

Satirical themes are attested by an isolated line about an effeminate who 'did
not marry but got married' (424), and by the lines, possibly a complete poem,
on the social upstart Artemon (388), who once wore shabby clothes, had
wooden dice in his ears, kept low company and was often in trouble with the
law:

νῦν δ' ἐπιβαίνει σατινέων χρύσεα φορέων κατέρματα
παῖς ⟨ὁ⟩ Κύκης καὶ σκιαδίσκην ἐλεφαντίνην φορεῖ
γυναιξὶν αὔτως ⟨ἐμφερής⟩.   (10–12)

178

But nowadays the son of Cyce rides in a carriage wearing gold ear-rings, and he carries an ivory parasol exactly like the ladies.

It is not only Artemon's social advancement that is satirized but the effeminacy of his accoutrements.

Solemnity is rare in Anacreon, but in one poem (395) the theme is the finality of death:

πολιοὶ μὲν ἡμὶν ἤδη
κρόταφοι κάρη τε λευκόν,
χαρίεσσα δ' οὐκέτ' ἤβη
πάρα, γηραλέοι δ' ὀδόντες,
γλυκεροῦ δ' οὐκέτι πολλὸς   5
βιότου χρόνος λέλειπται·
διὰ ταῦτ' ἀνασταλύζω
θαμὰ Τάρταρον δεδοικώς·
Ἀίδεω γάρ ἐστι δεινὸς
μυχός, ἀργαλῆ δ' ἐς αὐτὸν   10
κάτοδος· καὶ γὰρ ἑτοῖμον
καταβάντι μὴ ἀναβῆναι.

My temples are already grey and my head is white; graceful youth is no more with me, my teeth are old, and no long span of sweet life remains now. So I often weep in fear of Tartarus: the recess of Hades is grim, and the road down to it grievous; and it is certain that he who goes down does not come up again.

The short clauses and paratactic structure are an effective medium for this catalogue of woes, and the chiasmus of ll. 1–2 and the frequent enjambment prevent any sense of monotony. Word-position is particularly striking in ll. 3 and 5, where the adjectives χαρίεσσα 'graceful' and γλυκεροῦ 'sweet' are immediately cancelled out by the negative οὐκέτι 'no more'. The rare verb ἀνασταλύζω 'I weep' stands impressively at the beginning of the second half of the poem, and the repetition of the prefix κατα- in the last two lines emphasizes the message. Although the thought is gloomy, Anacreon expresses it in his slight, frivolous anacreontic lines, giving what Kirkwood has called 'a somewhat macabre air' to the poem.[1] Here as elsewhere we find the grace in which Anacreon took pride: χαρίεντα μὲν γὰρ ἄιδω, χαρίεντα δ' οἶδα λέξαι 'for I sing graceful songs, and I know how to speak graceful words' (402c).

5. SKOLIA

Some of the drinking-songs of the monodists were current in fifth-century Athens under the title 'skolia'. A fragment from Aristophanes' *Banqueters* (223 K) runs, 'Take one of the skolia of Alcaeus or Anacreon and sing it for me', and in the *Wasps* the ability to sing skolia is represented as the mark of the civilized guest at a drinking-party.

[1] Kirkwood (1974) 173.

MONODY

Athenaeus preserves a collection of twenty-five 'Attic skolia', most of which must have been composed in Athens in the late sixth or early fifth century. The majority are in four-line stanzas in aeolic rhythm, and they were presumably sung to one or two standard tunes. The best-known have a political content:[1] the austere lament for comrades who died at Leipsydrion (907) clearly belongs to Alcmaeonid circles, whereas the Harmodius-song, known in several versions, may have belonged to factions which refused to give the Alcmaeonids credit for the establishment of democracy (893):

> ἐν μύρτου κλαδὶ τὸ ξίφος φορήσω
> ὥσπερ Ἁρμόδιος κ' Ἀριστογείτων
> ὅτε τὸν τύραννον κτανέτην
> ἰσονόμους τ' Ἀθήνας ἐποιησάτην.

I shall carry my sword in a myrtle-branch, as did Harmodius and Aristogeiton when they killed the tyrant and made Athens a city of equal rights.

Loyal friendship, a favourite topic of Alcaeus, is commended in four songs (889, 892, 903, 908), and there are prayers to Athens and to Demeter and Persephone to protect the city (884, 885). The two-line stanzas are more light-hearted in tone (900):

> εἴθε λύρα καλὴ γενοίμην ἐλεφαντίνη
> καί με καλοὶ παῖδες φέροιεν Διονύσιον ἐς χορόν.

Oh that I might become a handsome ivory lyre, and that handsome boys might carry me to the choir of Dionysus.

Athenaeus says that the skolia might be sung in chorus or in succession round the table or by the best singers present, and he derives the name σκόλια 'crooked songs' from their irregular course among the guests. In Aristophanes' *Wasps* (1222ff.) old Philocleon is asked to 'take up' skolia from his fellow-guests and does so by improvising the second line after being given the first. Whatever their origin, Athenaeus' collection had become traditional, by reason either of their political content or of their high quality as concise lyric utterance.

---

[1] The skolia are numbered by the marginal numeration of *PMG*.

7

CHORAL LYRIC IN THE FIFTH CENTURY

I. INTRODUCTION

The development of monodic lyric in the sixth century toward greater variety, expressiveness and flexibility in poets like Sappho, Alcaeus, Ibycus and Anacreon cannot be documented for choral lyric. Whether because of historical accident, the popularity of monody, or an actual decline in the genre, very little choral poetry is preserved between Stesichorus and Simonides. We have a few lines of Lasus of Hermione (702–6 *PMG*), who is said to have introduced dithyrambic competitions into Athens under Pisistratus and competed against Simonides (cf. Aristophanes, *Wasps* 1410f.).[1] He also wrote an asigmatic poem, *Centaurs* (704 *PMG*), and a poem on the death of the children of Niobe (706 *PMG*). A paean by one Tynnichus of Chalcis, perhaps in the sixth century, won the admiration of both Aeschylus and Plato (*Ion* 534d, 707 *PMG*), but only a small phrase survives.

Certainly the religious and social occasions for choral poetry did not diminish. On the contrary, musical performances and competitions continued to hold an important place in the cultural life of sixth- and fifth-century Greece, both at public festivals, whether local or Panhellenic, and at the courts and houses of individual tyrants and nobles, an important source of patronage for travelling poets. Hymns, paeans, dithyrambs and partheneia continued to be performed at religious celebrations, while enkomia, dirges, marriage-songs and victory-odes were commissioned by rulers or nobles for private festivities. Many of these latter, as we shall see in the case of Pindar, would be public in nature, a display of munificence affirming the donor's high standing in the community.

Helped by the expansion of the great public festivals like the Athenian Dionysia and Panathenaea in the sixth century and stimulated by the stirring historical events of the early fifth – the rise of the powerful Sicilian tyrant-states, the defeat of the Persians and Carthaginians, the resultant affirmation of the

[1] On Lasus of Hermione see *GLP* 318; Else (1965) 73f.; *DTC* 13–15; Privitera (1965) *passim*. For choral lyric generally between Alcman and Simonides see Schmid–Stählin I. 1, 468f.

Greek polis and its traditions – choral lyric reached a new flowering in the first half of the fifth century in the work of Simonides, Pindar and Bacchylides.

Beside the numerous local festivals for which choral poets like Alcman or Stesichorus composed their songs, the four great international festivals, Olympian, Pythian (at Delphi), Nemean and Isthmian become particularly important for choral lyric in the fifth century. Athletic victories here were celebrated with elaborate care, the glory preserved for all time in an imperishable monument of song. Most of Pindar's victory odes or epinikia, the largest single body of choral lyric extant, celebrate victories at these four festivals. Since Hellenistic times the poems have been divided into four books according to the festival in question (in the citations below *O.* = *Olympian Odes*, *P.* = *Pythian*, *N.* = *Nemean*, *I.* = *Isthmian*). Commissioned by the victor or his family, these odes were performed at the festival or, more commonly, at the celebration in the victor's home city on his triumphant return. If the victor was a ruler, like Hieron of Syracuse, Theron of Acragas, or Arcesilaus of Cyrene, the celebrations could have the status of major state festivals (this seems to have been the case for *Pythian* 1 and possibly *Pythian* 4), and the poet would aim at a grandeur and solemnity appropriate to the occasion. Though choral lyric in this period continues to reflect the religious themes and mood of its beginnings, i.e. song celebrating the gods, there is a more self-conscious interest in literary artistry, the moral seriousness of poetry, and intellectual, political or aesthetic concerns.

2. SIMONIDES

Simonides of Ceos is a good example of how the humanistic spirit of late sixth- and early fifth-century choral lyric operates within its religious frame. His long lifetime (557/6 to 468) witnessed both the flowering of late archaic art and the turbulence and change that led into the classical period. Widely travelled, at home in the courts of tyrants as well as in democratic Athens, commissioned to compose important dedicatory epigrams on the Persian Wars, celebrated for his wisdom in practical affairs as well as for his skill in his art, Simonides is not only a major influence on the poetry of Bacchylides (his nephew) and Pindar, but also has a fair claim to being considered a precursor of the sophistic enlightenment.

No complete poem survives. The most important fragment is part of an ode for Scopas of Thessaly (542).[1] Plato quotes large portions of the poem as a showpiece of Protagoras' interpretative skill (*Protag.* 339a–46d). Because of the nature of the citation and our ignorance of the genre to which it belongs (enkomion and dirge are the likeliest possibilities) there are many uncertainties. The most widely held view (largely supported by the new Oxyrhynchus frag-

---

[1] For further discussion see Appendix. The fragments of Simonides are numbered by the marginal numeration of *PMG*.

ment, 541) is that Simonides is criticizing the traditional definition of the 'good', 'noble', or 'successful' man (*agathos, esthlos*). Such 'goodness' or 'nobility' depends upon external achievements and possessions (wealth, honour, prowess in battle) which are too insecure to form a real basis for human excellence. Instead Simonides stresses intention, justice that benefits the city, acknowledgement of the fragility of life:

> I praise and embrace everyone who willingly does nothing base (*aischron*), but with necessity not even the gods fight. . . A man not too helpless (*apalamnos*) suffices for me, one who knows the justice that benefits the city, a sound and healthy man. I will not lay blame, for the generation of fools is limitless. Everything is noble (*kala*) with which base deeds (*ta aischra*) are not mingled.
>
> (542.27–40)

To the heroic absolutes of the aristocratic tradition Simonides opposes a tolerant, flexible ethic which takes fuller account of the tension between inner probity and the uncertainty of fortune. For this reason the poem may have appealed to Protagoras. Pindar too can challenge a patron's values, as in his admonitions to Hieron in *Pythians* 1 and 2. Yet Pindar still identifies with the heroic ethic, whereas Simonides adopts its vocabulary only to analyse and revalue it, as he does in the case of words like *agathos, kakos, aischros* ('goodly', 'mean', 'shameful'). His sharply antithetical style expresses this same tension between the new and the traditional. We may note the contrast between the Homeric phrasing of 'all of us who enjoy the fruit of the wide-seated earth' (. . . εὐρυεδέος ὅσοι καρπὸν αἰνύμεθα χθονός) and the almost breezy colloquialism of 'when I find him [*sc.* the faultless man], I'll send you back news' (ἐπὶ δ' ὑμὶν εὑρὼν ἀπαγγελέω, 24–6).

'Sadder than the tears of Simonides' (Catullus 38.8): this proverbial expression reflects the celebrity of Simonides' dirges (*threnoi*) and his power of pathos. Dionysius of Halicarnassus (*De comp. verb.* 26) quotes a twenty-seven line fragment describing Danae adrift with her infant son Perseus (543). Dionysius admires the fluency and unity of the rhythms, but the passage is equally remarkable for its fine contrasts between the wild, dark sea and the sleeping child and between the elaborately described setting (lines 1–12) and the simplicity of Danae's opening words (7–9):

> ὦ τέκος οἷον ἔχω πόνον·
> σὺ δ' ἀωτεῖς, γαλαθηνῶι
> δ' ἤθεϊ κνοώσσεις. . .

> O my child, what suffering I have. But you sleep and drowse like the tender infant you are. . .

We find a similar pathos in a two-line fragment (perhaps from a dirge) in which the followers of the mythical king Lycurgus of Nemea 'wept at the infant child of the violet-crowned (Eurydice) that breathed out its sweet life' (ἰοστεφάνου γλυκεῖαν ἐδάκρυσαν | ψυχὰν ἀποπνέοντα γαλαθηνὸν τέκος, 553). It is this ability to present basic human situations with affecting simplicity and yet with just the right admixture of poetic detail that earned Simonides his great acclaim as a writer of funeral epigrams.

With Simonides the epinician or victory ode comes into its own as a full-fledged literary form, coinciding with the increasing importance of athletic contests in the sixth century. Of Simonides' epinikia, however, only the tiniest scraps remain (including some recent papyrus finds, 511, 519). The pun on the 'shearing' of Krios, 'Ram' (507), and the claim that a victor surpasses even Polydeuces and Heracles suggest a less solemn and less reverent tone than Pindar's.[1] Simonides also composed choral poems on historical subjects relating to the Persian Wars, including the *Battle at Artemisium* (532–5), *Battle at Salamis* (536) and *Dirge for the fallen at Thermopylae* (531); nine lines of the last survive. Some recently published scraps of the Oxyrhynchus papyri provide small additions to our scanty evidence for the *Paeans*. One fragment seems to describe the birth of Artemis and Leto's 'shout as the august birth-pangs weighed her down' (519, fr. 32), a scene with which we can compare two passages in Pindar (*O*. 6.43 and *N*. 1.35).

The extant fragments reveal a rich repertory of mythical subjects, ranging from familiar heroic legends like those of the Argonauts, Theseus, perhaps the sacrifice of Iphigenia (544, 550–1, 608), to the fantastic: Talos guarding Crete (568) or the daughters of Anius who change whatever they touch into wine, olives, and grain (537). We have a few glimpses of what must have been brilliant and moving scenes. 'Longinus' compares Simonides' description of Achilles' ghost at Troy to the finale of the *Oedipus at Colonus* (557); Pindar's description of the Muses singing at Achilles' burial perhaps gives some idea of what such a scene might be (*I*. 8.62–6). There survive some splendid verses describing the birds and fish following the singing Orpheus (567) and a haunting dactylic passage spoken by a deserted woman like Danae (571): ἴσχει δέ με πορφυρέας ἁλὸς ἀμφιταρασσομένας ὀρυμαγδός 'the roar of the heaving sea dashing all around holds me'.

Though Simonides uses the compound adjectives and decorative, colourful epithets that characterize late archaic lyric poetry, he is equally remarkable for his restraint and balance. Ancient critics admired his 'sweetness and elegance' (Cicero, *Nat. deor.* 1.22) and his 'smooth and decorative composition' (Dion. Hal. *De comp. verb.* 230; cf. Quintilian 10.1.64). Beside the sensuous details of passages like 597, 'Dark-blue swallow, glorious messenger of sweet-smelling spring', or the description of the 'halcyon days' (508), there stands the austere gnomic style of the ode on the dead at Thermopylae (531), with its succession

---

[1] See Page (1951*b*) 140–2.

SIMONIDES

of short antithetical clauses and heavy nouns, its sparsity of adjectives and almost total absence of figurative language. Fragment 521 can illustrate Dionysius' praise of Simonides for his 'choice of words and his accuracy in combining them':

> ἄνθρωπος ἐὼν μή ποτε φάσῃς ὅ τι γίνεται αὔριον
> μηδ' ἄνδρα ἰδὼν ὄλβιον ὅσσον χρόνον ἔσσεται·
> ὠκεῖα γὰρ οὐδὲ τανυπτερύγου μυίας
> οὕτως ἁ μετάστασις.

Being human never say what will happen tomorrow nor how long a happy man will remain so. For not even of a long-winged fly is the change so swift.

The only decorative word in the passage is 'long-winged' (τανυπτέρυγος.) Standing out in the otherwise unadorned generalization, it forms a suggestive 'objective correlative' for the fragility of the human condition.

The fifth-century choral poets often reflected on their craft and its significance. Like Pindar, Simonides asserts the power of song over the violent forces of nature (595; cf. Pindar fr. 94b.11–20 Snell). Like Pindar too Simonides quotes and comments on the earlier poetic tradition (542, 564, 579), and he may have defended himself against his younger rival (602; cf. Pindar, O. 9.48–9). Two fragments relating to his art are especially interesting: 'Seeming does violence even to truth' (598) and 'Painting is silent poetry, poetry is painting that speaks' (Plut. De glor. Ath. 3.346f). Following a tradition which can be traced back to Homer, Hesiod and Solon (cf. Odyssey 19.203; Hes. Theog. 27–8, Solon fr. 29 West), Simonides stresses the power of poetic art to create illusion or even falsehood, unlike Pindar who solemnly emphasizes Truth (see below).[1] Simonides was notorious for charging high fees, but his apparently mercenary attitude also reflects a different conception of his art: it is the professional practice of a craft of words, not the inspired gift of the Muses or the gods. In this secularization of his art he may have helped pave the way for the sophistic movement.[2]

3. PINDAR

Pindar is the most brilliant of fifth-century choral poets. He was born near Thebes, probably in 518, received some training in Athens, and wrote an early ode (P. 7) for the Alcmaeonid Megacles in the year of the latter's ostracism (486).[3] The medizing of Thebes in the Persian Wars must have been a strain for one whose sympathies were so strongly with the Greek values of order, discipline

[1] See Detienne (1967) 109ff.; Thayer (1975) 13–19.
[2] See Detienne (1967) 105–19; Gentili (1972) 77f.
[3] P.Oxy. 2438 adds some new details on Pindar's life and helps confirm the date of his death. For a searching critique of the ancient Lives and the biographical data in the scholia see Lefkowitz (1975b) 71–93 and (1978) 460–2.

and valour in battle. According to an anecdote in the *Vita* Thebes fined him a thousand drachmas (ten thousand in Isocrates, *Antid.* 166) for composing a dithyramb for Athens (fr. 76 Snell). A number of passages express his uneasiness in these years (*I.* 5:48ff., *I.* 8.10–16, frs. 109–10 Snell). Possibly these tensions led to his sojourn in Sicily between 476 and 474, where he composed *Olympian* 1 for Hieron of Syracuse and *Olympians* 2 and 3 for Theron of Acragas.

Pindar's work spans a half-century. He wrote his earliest ode (*P.* 10) in 498, his last (*P.* 8) in 446. The most majestic odes date from the two decades 480–460: *O.* 1–3, *O.* 6, 7, 13, *P.* 1–5, *P.* 9, *N.* 1, 9, *I.* 3–5, *I.* 8. Among the later odes *N.* 7 and 8, *I.* 7 (which may not be late), and *P.* 8, are especially impressive. The dates of the epinikia, however, are often uncertain. The scholia leave many undated, and where they do propose a date it is not always reliable.[1]

Although there are many fragments of lost poems,[2] especially the *Paeans*, the epinikia are Pindar's most important work and constitute by far the largest single body of Greek choral poetry to have been read continuously from classical antiquity to the Byzantine era and from the Renaissance to the present day. From Horace to Hölderlin and on to Ezra Pound they have strongly influenced the modern conception of the 'ode' and the high style of poetic inspiration.

For the ancient critics Pindar represented the 'severe' or 'rough' style (αὐστηρὰ ἁρμονία), difficult because of his bold collocations, abrupt transitions, loftiness of thought and expression. Horace compares him to a soaring eagle and a rushing stream (*Odes* 4.2); 'Longinus' likens him to a vast fire (*Subl.* 33.5). Athenaeus speaks of 'the great-voiced Pindar' (13.564c).

Despite the conventional 'programme' which the epinician poet must follow (praise of the victor and his family, his generosity, ancestors, mention of previous victories, friendship and obligation between poet and victor),[3] he has still a wide range of flexibility. He can vary ornamental epithets, invocations, rhythm and metre; he can contract or expand images or myths.

For a hundred and fifty years the major issue of Pindaric scholarship has been the question of the unity of the ode.[4] Of those who believe that the ode has a unity there are essentially two camps: the one side finds unity in content, a unifying thought or idea (*Grundgedanke*) or a single pervasive image; the other finds it in external criteria. The latter approach has come to the fore recently in the work of Bundy and Thummer, who have concerned themselves with the formal conventions governing the movement of the ode.[5] But if unity of

[1] See Fränkel (1961) 385–97; Lefkowitz (1975a) 173–85.
[2] Fragments are cited from Snell and Maehler (1975). There is a useful discussion of the new papyrus fragments in Lesky 177–208 and in Griffith (1968) 65–82.
[3] This aspect of the Pindaric ode has been studied by Schadewaldt (1928); see also Hamilton (1974), esp. 3–25.
[4] See Young (1964) for an excellent survey of the question, also Köhnken (1971) 1–18, 227–32.
[5] Bundy (1962); Thummer (1968–9); Hamilton (1974).

'thought' or 'idea' is too abstract and conceptual, the formulaic approach of Bundy is too rigid. The Pindaric epinikion is more than a carefully structured sequence of encomiastic motifs. Although it clearly utilizes formulaic sequences and traditional themes and expressions, its unity is organic rather than mechanical. The progression of thought and meaning in an ode depends not merely on the 'horizontal' linear unfolding of certain programmatic topics, but also on a 'vertical' metaphorical association of images and symbols and a parallelism between metaphor and actuality, myth and historical present.

While Norwood's view that each ode is given its unity by a single symbol is too narrow and often rather arbitrary,[1] Pindar does seem to weave myth and imagery together more or less densely in different odes, developing resonances between parallel myths or clusters of related images within an ode. In *Olympian* 1, for example, the parallels and contrasts between Pelops and Tantalus and between Hieron and Pelops, the imagery of light and darkness, eating and starvation, festivity and isolation, upward and downward movement all interlock into a complex pattern which cannot be encompassed in a single 'idea' or 'image', but is nevertheless vital to the poem's structure and movement. The themes of water, gold, light out of darkness in the proem recur in the two mythical narratives of Pelops and Poseidon (26–7, 71–87). The 'brilliance' and 'far-shining glory' of the victor, Hieron, find resonances in Pelops' cult at Olympia (compare 14 and 22–4 with 90–5).

The first *Pythian* provides an especially clear and powerful instance of how parallelism and contrast interlock within a complex unified structure. The extended analysis which is offered here is meant to be exemplary rather than exhaustive.

Written as a kind of coronation hymn for Hieron's foundation of his new city Aetna, *Pythian* 1 moves through a series of ever-expanding analogies between the political order of well-ruled cities, the aesthetic and moral order of dance, music and poetry, the governance of the universe by Olympian Zeus and the physical order of nature. The hymnic invocation to the 'Golden Lyre, rightful and joint possession of Apollo and the violet-tressed Muses' (1–2), establishes a parallelism between the music and dance of the present moment, 'the step which begins the festive brilliance' (2), and the music of the gods on Olympus. Thus the Muses connected generally with the lyre in 1–2 recur in a more specifically Olympian setting at the end of the antistrophe (13). The lyre which leads the dance among men (1–4) also calms the violence of Zeus's thunder, of the eagle, and of harsh Ares on Olympus (5–13). This symbolical and emblematic statement of the triumph of order over chaos is then developed both in myth and in historical reality, both in local and remote settings. Aetna, mentioned three times in the ode, is simultaneously part of the present festal context, a manifestation of the divine order in the punishment of the monster Typhon (19b–28), and an expression of political order in Hieron's new foundation (60–6). As the 'heavenly pillar' (κίων οὐρανία, 19b) which confines the monster, the volcano is also the physical link between Tartarus below (cf. 15) and Olympus above. It is thus itself a visible sign of an ordered world: the spatial coherence parallels the moral coherence.

In the large temporal context of historical events this same order finds realization in the Greek victories over Persian, Carthaginian, and Etruscan foes (71–80b), the equivalents on the human and political plane to the monstrous Typhon. They have a closer and more human mythic analogue also in the Greek defeat of the Trojans, alluded to in the myth of the ailing Philoctetes, a paradigm for the unwell Hieron (50–7). Hieron's two great achievements, the founding of Aetna (60) and the defeat of the Etruscans at Cumae (72), assure the political order in complementary ways: the former action, in peace, creates a Greek polis with 'god-built freedom' (61); the latter, in war, preserves Greeks from 'heavy slavery' (75). Aetna and Cumae, therefore, embody the order created by Hieron as king. It is significant that on the mythic plane Aetna and Cumae are also combined in the cosmic order established by Zeus (17–19), the sceptred king of gods and men (cf. 6), in his repression of Typhon, symbol of cosmic disorder. The flaming lava which Aetna hurls into the sea (21–2, 24b) parallels Hieron's hurling the Etruscan youth into the sea at Cumae (74) to check hubris (72). The constraint (cf. συνέχει, 19b) of Typhon whom the volcano 'presses down' (πιέζει, 19), on the other hand, contrasts with the soft rise and fall of Zeus's eagle asleep on Olympus, lulled by the magic of Apollo's lyre (6, 8–9). The slumbering eagle 'raises his liquid back' (ὑγρὸν νῶτον αἰωρεῖ, 9), whereas the monster, 'bound' in the depths of Tartarus beneath Aetna's 'black-leaved summit and plain' has his 'whole back' (ἅπαν νῶτον, 28) scratched and torn by this harsher manifestation of Zeus's order.

The beautiful description of Aetna as 'all-year nurse of sharp snow, from whose depths there belch forth the most holy springs of unapproachable fire' (20–2), not only incorporates the fearful 'wonder' (26) of a volcanic eruption into the framework of Olympian order, but also makes explicit the almost Heraclitean tension of opposites which that order encompasses. Beneath the physical contrasts of earth and sky (cf. 19b), fire and water, heat and cold (20–2), darkness and light (23–4) lies a more complex polarity of force and gentleness. Aetna is the cold snow's 'nurse' (20b), as well as the source of the blazing and smoking lava (22–3). These fiery streams are 'most holy' (21) and are associated with the Olympian Hephaestus (25): that is, they are a manifestation of fire and force in the service of order, not the *uis consili expers* of the monster. Yet in the proem Zeus's fire is something to be 'quenched' by the peaceful harmony of the Golden Lyre (5–6). The Lyre also calms the violence of Zeus's eagle, with his dangerously hooked beak (cf. 8), and charms the heart of 'Ares the violent' (10–11). The Zeus who protects the mountain of Aetna, 'brow of the fair-fruited land' (30), and the Apollo who 'loves Parnassus' Castalian spring' (39b, in contrast to Aetna's 'springs' of fire in 22) exemplify the gentler side of this Olympian order, just as Hieron's foundation of Aetna is the gentler side of the regal and martial force exhibited at Cumàe.

The symbolical music of the lyre has these two aspects from the very beginning: its sound calms and enchants (1–13), but is also a 'shout' (*boa*) which can affright those 'whom Zeus holds not in his love' (13). On the plane of historical actuality, the 'harmonious calm' (σύμφωνος ἡσυχία, 70) which the poet invokes for Hieron's son, Deinomenes, ruler of Aetna, contrasts with the war cry and groans of the defeated Etruscans at Cumae (ἀλαλατός, ναυσίστονον, 72). More distantly, but still in history rather than myth, the allusion to the Sicilian tyrant Phalaris, notorious for roasting his victims in a bronze bull (95), may suggest the screams which cruelly simulated the animal's bellowing. In any case Phalaris' 'evil reputation' contrasts with the good name of King Croesus' 'kindly excellence' (93–6). The lyres at festal gatherings refuse honour to Phalaris (97–8). These lyres take us back to the symbolical Golden Lyre of the invocation (φόρμιγξ 1 and φόρμιγγες 97). Here too the present festal occasion becomes transparent to all those occasions for song whose task (*inter alia*) it is to distinguish virtue and evil, celebrate and perpetuate the fame of the noble and condemn the vicious; hence the close parallel between the 'lyres' which do not receive Phalaris and the 'Golden Lyre' which leads the 'festive brilliance' (2) of the present celebration of Hieron (cf. 1–4 and 97–8).

The fire with which the 'pitiless' Phalaris roasted his victims (95) also contrasts with the metaphorical fire which will flash forth from the anvil of Hieron's tongue (86–7) and thus resumes the antithesis between the violent and creative aspects of Zeus and Aetna's fire (5f., 21ff.). Likewise the evil fame which 'holds down' Phalaris (κατέχει, 96) echoes the effect of the Golden Lyre which 'holds down' the eagle in sleep (κατασχόμενος, 10) and the armed might of Hieron which forced the Etruscan war cry to stay at home (κατ' οἶκον...ἔχῃ, 72), or, with a different punctuation, 'to keep its violence at home'. In keeping with the importance of harmonious or discordant sound in the ode, 'war cry' is virtually personified.

The relation between Croesus and Phalaris, however, reverses the ode's consistent opposition of Greek and barbarian. Now the oriental monarch is the exemplar of 'kindly excellence', the Greek of cruel despotism. We have also moved, with Phalaris, from gold to bronze (1 and 95). The bronze anvil of Hieron in the metaphor of 86f., therefore, has an ominous resonance in the behaviour of his Sicilian predecessor (95). Pindar may be hinting at the destructive violence inherent in all absolute power, be it Zeus's thunder or Hieron's kingship.

Beginning and ending with music and the importance of a 'good name' (99b; cf. 96–8), Pindar also underlines the fact that poetry too has its power. Its 'enchantments' are also 'arrows' (κῆλα in 12 has both meanings), just as the Muses' song can both calm and terrify (6ff. and 13f.). In a certain sense all of Pindar's odes celebrate the power of poetry as well as the prowess of the victor. The poet who sings the 'due measure' (*kairos*, 81; cf. 57) and joins together the 'limits of many things in small compass' (81f.) holds the balance between potentially dangerous extremes, between destructive and ordering power. He teaches the *kairos* of this force which may be released for good or for ill.

Pythian 1 shows Pindar in his most expansive conception of his poetic role. He moves between present and past, myth and history, Olympus and Tartarus, Greek and barbarian, to reveal the universal paradigms in which the present achievement must take its place in order to be fully meaningful. His lyre, like the king's sceptre or Zeus's thunder, unlocks the hidden analogies between the cosmic, political, moral, and natural order. The poet fashions on earth the 'harmonious calm' (70) which the Golden Lyre creates on Olympus.

In praising the victor the poet is not merely glorifying a particular successful athlete. Through metaphor, gnomic generalization and mythic paradigm the epinikion seeks to link the present victory with the timeless world of myth and to place it within the common realm of values, the *Wertewelt* (to use H. Fränkel's term), of aristocratic society.[1] The 'purpose' of the ode, therefore, transcends its immediate encomiastic function, for it is the poet's task to relate the victory to the ultimate issues of life: change, suffering, the gods, the rhythms of nature, old age and death. The victor exemplifies the highest ideals of discipline, energy, generosity, beauty, grace. His *arete* or excellence is not merely a matter of the competitive virtues or technical skill, but involves the quieter 'cooperative virtues' (Adkins's term[2]) of 'justice', 'restraint', 'lawfulness', 'calm' (*dike, sophrosyne, eunomia, hesychia*). Through disciplined form and creative effort the ode, like the victory itself, enacts man's conquest of 'darkness', chaos and death (cf. *O.* 1.81–4, *N.* 7.11–16, *P.* 8.92–7).

Bundy's study of the formulaic elements in Pindar has had one important consequence. References to envy, danger, silence, and the gnomic formulas which frequently break off the myth and effect a transition to a new topic (*Abbruchsformel*) cannot be read as certain allusions to events in the lives of the victor or the poet. Hence the historical and biographical allegorization of Pindar, which reached its acme in Wilamowitz's *Pindaros* (1922), must be critically re-examined. Pindar often alludes openly to historical events (*P.* 1, *I.* 5, *I.* 8 are the clearest examples) and sometimes to personal experiences (*P.* 8.56–60; *N.* 7 is

---

[1] See Fränkel (1962) 559–67 (488–96 of Engl. tr. 1975).   [2] Adkins (1960).

still a matter of controversy).[1] But we must now be more cautious about finding covert allusions to the waning of Theban power and the advance of Athens in poems like *I*. 7, *N*. 8, *P*. 8.

Grandeur and sublimity are the hallmarks of Pindar's style. He states it almost as a principle of his art to make an impressive beginning (*O*. 6.1–4). Hence he opens his odes with monumental architectural or sculptural imagery (*O*. 6, *P*. 7, *N*. 5) or with a ponderous gnomic statement framed in dynamic antitheses (*O*. 1, *N*. 6) or with a ringing invocation to a place (*O*. 14, *P*. 2, *P*. 12) or a goddess ('Kindly Quietude, daughter of Justice, you who make cities of greatest might and hold the highest keys of councils and of war', *P*. 8).

Though Pindar excels in the rich decorative language and florid compound adjectives of his contemporaries, he is especially effective in his vivid flashes of detail or touches of pathos: the sons of Boreas 'their backs ashiver with purple wings' (*P*. 4.182f.); the tears falling from old Aeson's eyes as he looks upon his long-lost son, now 'handsomest of men' (*P*. 4.120–4); Alcmena leaping nude from her bed of childbirth to save her new-born children from Hera's serpents while Amphitryon brandishes his great sword (*N*. 1.50–2); Bellerophon on Pegasus shooting at the Amazons 'from the cold bosom of the empty aether' (*O*. 13.88). There are wide variations of mood, from the pathos of Polydeuces' grief over his dying brother in *N*. 10 to the sensuousness of Zeus's union with Aegina in *Paean* 6 where 'the mist's golden tresses covered in shadow the spine of the land', or the flamboyant brilliance of the advent of spring in a dithyramb, where, amid the mingling of roses, violets, flutes and dancing, 'at the opening of the chamber of the crimson-robed Seasons the nectarous flowers usher in sweet-smelling spring' (fr. 75 Snell).

Pindar's myths unfold through a few grand, majestic gestures which stand out against a backdrop of large, often symbolical elements: sea, sky, or mountain, darkness or fire. Thus Iamus, like Pelops in *O*. 1, calls to the god in the night from the river (*O*. 6.57–63); fire surrounds Apollo's rescue of the infant Asclepius from his mother's body on the flaming pyre (*P*. 3.36–46); Ajax drives the sword through his breast 'in the late night' (*I*. 4.38–40). Even the massive fourth *Pythian*, which contains Pindar's most expansive, 'Bacchylidean' narrative, jumps back and forth between the various stages of the myth, tells prophecy within prophecy, and emphasizes the vast sweep of time and the succession of generations (cf. 54–65) rather than the single strand of continuous event. Sometimes Pindar pulls back abruptly from a myth which he thinks unworthy of a god or hero, as in the story of the gods eating Pelops (*O*. 1.51f.) or the tale of Phocus' murder by his half-brothers Peleus and Telamon (*N*. 5.9–18). A

---

[1] See Lloyd-Jones (1973) 127–37; Köhnken (1971) 37–86. Woodbury's careful study (1979*b*) of the historical and geographical bases of the Neoptolemus myth tends to support the scholiasts' connexion of *Paean* 6 and *Nemean* 7.

number of odes lack a fully developed myth, and in some a weighty gnome or apophthegm serves as the chief poetical embellishment (e.g. *O.* 11, *N.* 6, *N.* 11). Pindar's boldness of metaphor rivals that of his contemporary, Aeschylus. Occasionally a violent metaphor is almost a kenning. 'The fruit of olive in fire-scorched earth' carried in 'all-adorned enclosures of vessels' describes the oil-filled amphora won in the Panathenaic games (*N.* 10.35–6); a cloak won as a prize is 'warm medicine against cold breezes' (*O.* 9.97). He does not use such expressions, as a Hellenistic poet might, to demonstrate erudition or to tease the reader with riddling obscurity. Such metaphors, rather, serve to transfigure and exalt everything connected with the victory. Pindar's mixed metaphors have a similar purpose: they intensify the effect of sensuous concreteness and exuberance by crossing between different realms of experience. Thus they heighten the festive joy of the occasion and even add a certain playfulness, as in the enkomion for Theoxenus (fr. 123 Snell).

Pindar is the most concrete of poets. Even what we would consider abstractions or psychological processes have a physical tangibility: 'the cloud of forgetfulness' (*O.* 7.45); 'the leaves of strife' (*I.* 8.47); 'the flowers of lawfulness' (*Paean* 1.10); 'hammer-welded necessities' (fr. 207 Snell). Excellence, *arete*, can 'blossom' like a flower and (within the same ode) 'scale a tower' (or, in another interpretation, 'fortify a tower' *I.* 5.17 and 44f.); honours are 'planted' (τιμαὶ φυτευθέν, *P.* 4.69).

Possibly attacking Simonides' secular conception of his art (see above, p. 185), Pindar protests strongly against the idea that he works for hire (*I.* 2). He is a 'prophet of the Muses' and the servant of Truth, Aletheia, herself the child of Zeus (*O.* 10.3–6, *Paean* 6.6, fr. 205 Snell).[1] Poetry teaches, confers fame and gives pleasure. But poetry for him is not all a matter of honey, garlands, sweet liquids. It has associations also with the mystery of the sea and the violence of wind (*N.* 7.79, fr. 94b.13ff. Snell), with arrows and the javelin (*O.* 2.83–5, *P.* 1.43–5, *N.* 7.71f.), with the eagle who seizes his bloody (or tawny) prey in his claws (*N.* 3.80–2; cf. *N.* 5.21). Song can be a healing, medicinal 'charm' or drug (*N.* 4.1–5), but it is also a dangerous siren luring men to their death (*Paean* 8.70–9). In *Pythian* 12 he traces the origin of flute music to the painful death-wail of Medusa.[2] The 'grace' or 'charm' (*charis*) of song fashions all that brings joy to mortals (*O.* 1.30; cf. *O.* 14.5ff.); yet the shifting play of crafted words can also obscure the truth with meretricious falsehood (*O.* 1.28–9; cf. *N.* 8.25, where we may contrast the 'variegated falsehood' that leads to Ajax' death with the positive significance of Pindar's 'varied art' or *poikilia* in *N.* 8.15). As a 'craft' or 'skill' (*sophia*, *mechane*), poetry, like any art, can be misused to distort the true worth of men and their achievements. The true poet will use his

---

[1] See Bowra (1964) ch. 1; Davison (1968) 289–311; Svoboda (1952) 108–20.
[2] See Schlesinger (1968) 275–86; Köhnken (1971) 117–53.

art for truth, not for gain or *kerdos*: the latter is a concept which Pindar frequently associates with the wily, dangerous aspects of 'craft' (cf. *N.* 7.14–24, *I.* 2.5–12, *P.* 3.54 and 113–14). The poet's *logos* serves the gods, life, rebirth; over against it stand the envy and calumny which cut off the 'life' or 'bloom' of great achievements or, in mythical terms, bring death to the great Ajax (*N.* 7.23–32, *N.* 8.25–34; contrast *I.* 4.36–46).

In Pindar the Olympian religion of the early classical period finds its full majesty of expression. He studiously portrays the gods as dignified and solemn, maintaining order and suppressing injustice (*O.* 1, *P.* 1–3, *P.* 8), compassionate (*N.* 10) and even forgiving (*O.* 7.45ff.), helpful guardians of civilization and morality. Pindar celebrates Apollo for his omniscience (*P.* 3.27–30, *P.* 9.44–9) and for the art of healing, music and prophecy (*P.* 5.63–9), Athena for inventing the flute (*P.* 12), Heracles for exploring the sea and land (*N.* 3.23–6) and planting trees to shade the Olympian games (*O.* 3). He suppresses or reinterprets myths which show the gods' violence, lust, or meanness (*O.* 1.46ff.; *O.* 9.35–9). The loves of Zeus and Apollo are orderly and lead to the foundation of great cities and families (*O.* 6, *O.* 9, *P.* 9, *Paean* 6).

Yet the gods retain an element of inscrutable force. As the proem of *Nemean* 6 puts it, sheer power, *dynamis*, sets the gods apart from mortals in their remote 'brazen sky'. Anthropomorphic features, like the gods' loves, remain, but are often given a new meaning. Zeus and Poseidon are conquered by lust for Ganymede and Pelops respectively (*O.* 1.40–5), but the passion of Poseidon plays a major role in the foundation of rites at Olympia (*O.* 1.75–96). 'Eros gripped' both Zeus and Poseidon, but they obey the prophecy of 'wise-counselling Themis' (*I.* 8.29–37). Apollo's wrath nearly destroys the innocent along with the guilty, until he reverses his decision and saves the unborn Asclepius (*P.* 3.34–42). 'Golden-throned Hera, queen of the gods' can implement her bitter anger against the infant Heracles (*N.* 1.37–40), but this too is part of Zeus's 'solemn law' (*N.* 1.72).

Though not a religious innovator, Pindar seems to have been impressed by the south Italian belief in the afterlife and the purgation and transmigration of souls. These ideas inspire some of his richest poetry (*O.* 2; frs. 129–34 Snell; cf. fr. 94a). Pindar, however, may here be reflecting the beliefs of his Sicilian patrons rather than his own.[1] The controversy about what Pindar really believed may never be settled, but it is clear that at the least he could respond to such conceptions with deep sympathy.

That sympathy is all the more likely as he seems to have been susceptible to visionary experiences (*Vita Ambrosiana* p. 2.1ff. Drachmann) and incorporated them into his poetry (*P.* 8.56–60, frs. 37 and 95 Snell). More important still is his conviction that the 'Zeus-given gleam' (*P.* 8.96–7) or the 'clear light of the

[1] Good discussion in Bowra (1964) 92ff.; Zuntz (1971) 83–9.

melodious Graces' (*P.* 9.89–90) can illuminate the brevity and darkness of mortal life. Like Plato, he is concerned with the moments when the present life becomes transparent to a more lasting reality, the eternal beauty of the gods. At such moments the Muses or Graces are present among men (*N.* 5.22ff., *P.* 3.88ff., *I.* 8.61ff.; cf. *O.* 1.30ff.; *O.* 14.5ff.). The famous passage at the end of his last ode comes as close as any single statement can to presenting this vision of his art (*P.* 8.95–7):

ἐπάμεροι· τί δέ τις; τί δ' οὔ τις; σκιᾶς ὄναρ
ἄνθρωπος. ἀλλ' ὅταν αἴγλα διόσδοτος ἔλθῃ,
λαμπρὸν φέγγος ἔπεστιν ἀνδρῶν καὶ μείλιχος αἰών.

Creatures of the passing day. What is any one? What is any one not? Shadow's dream is man. But when the radiance given of Zeus comes, there is a bright light upon men, and life is sweet.

4. BACCHYLIDES

Until 1897, when F. G. Kenyon published a papyrus containing substantial portions of fourteen epinikia and six dithyrambs, Bacchylides was little more than a name. Few discoveries have been more sensational in restoring to us a virtually unknown poet of high quality. The dates of Bacchylides' birth and death are uncertain. Younger than Pindar and nephew of Simonides, he was born on Ceos perhaps around 510 B.C.[1] Most of his works seem to fall between *c.* 485 and 452, the latest date we can establish (*Odes* 6 and 7).

Ever since 'Longinus' made his unflattering comparison between the flawless smoothness of Bacchylides and the all-encompassing blaze of Pindar (*Subl.* 33.5), Bacchylides has suffered by comparison with his great contemporary. But it is perhaps fairer to consider Bacchylides as the successor to Stesichorus' tradition of extended lyrical narrative than as the rival of Pindar. He is more concerned than Pindar with storytelling *per se*; and the characteristics of oral recitation are rather more evident in his poetry: his narrative is marked by a graceful leisureliness, a fullness and clarity of detail, and a heavy reliance on ring composition (verbal repetition which signals the resumption of a theme after a digression in a kind of *da capo* effect). The art of the rhapsode, we may recall, flourished vigorously in Bacchylides' lifetime.

Bacchylides' myths are distinguished not only for their fluidity and grace of movement, but also for their pathos, their high proportion of direct discourse, and especially for the richness and lushness of their epithets. There is no appreciable difference in style between his epinikia and dithyrambs, save that the latter have a higher proportion of narrative. His virtues appear at their best in *Odes* 3,

[1] For the evidence see Severyns (1933) 15–30, who argues unsuccessfully for an earlier birthdate of 518/17. Apollodorus' date is 507.

194

5 and 17, which relate respectively the stories of Croesus on the pyre, Heracles'
encounter with Meleager in Hades, and Minos' challenge to Theseus. Of special
interest also are *Odes* 11 (the madness of the daughters of Proetus), 13 (the
Trojan burning of the Greek ships), 15 (Odysseus and Menelaus in Troy to
plead for Helen's return) and 16 (Deianira's plan to anoint Heracles' robe with
the magical philtre of Nessus' blood). *Ode* 18 is interesting for its form:
a dialogue between Aegeus and the chorus relates the early deeds of young
Theseus as he approaches Athens.[1]

Bacchylides' epinikia share many of the conventions and motifs of Pindar's.
There are brilliant invocations (5.1ff.), a vivid sense of place (cf. 14B.4–8), rich
mythic narration. Both poets dwell on the dangers of envy offset by the value of
the lasting glory which the poet confers (cf. 13.199–225), the generosity of the
victor and his proper display and use of wealth (cf. 3.13f.), the poet's tie of
friendship or hospitality (*philia, xenia*) with the victor (3.16, 5.49), the limits of
human happiness. Both poets use similar imagery for the victor's success:
flowers, growth, bloom, brightness, sweetness.

The scholiasts to Pindar find allusions to a rivalry between him and Bacchylides. The most famous instance is *O.* 2.86–8: 'Wise is he who knows much by
nature; but those who learn, like a pair of raucous ravens, chatter in vain in their
fulness of tongue against Zeus's divine bird.'[2] The 'twin ravens' are explained
as Simonides and Bacchylides; but, of course, birds do chatter in pairs, and
Hellenistic scholars tend to interpret conventional motifs or metaphors in
biographical terms. In several passages, however, Bacchylides does seem to be
'imitating' Pindar, but this imitation is more like creative adaptation of the kind
frequent in ancient poetry, and one must also reckon on the possibility of a
conventional motif used by both poets independently. Pindar's collocation of
water, gold and sky in the proem to *O.* 1, for example, which Bacchylides is
thought to imitate in 3.86f., may be such a motif.[3] Like Pindar, Bacchylides
draws heavily on the earlier poetic tradition: Homer, Hesiod, the *Cypria*, the
epic *Capture of Oechalia* (for *Ode* 16), Sappho, Alcaeus, Solon, Theognis,
Stesichorus.

Bacchylides has little of Pindar's brilliant density of metaphor or abrupt
transitions. He generally gives more attention to details of the victory itself,
and he effects more obvious connexions between the mythical paradigm and the
victor. He is a master of the rich sensuous vignette, like 'young men, their hair
teeming with flowers' (6.8–9) or the 'brilliant moon of the mid-month night'
which outshines the 'lights of the stars' (9.27–9), a Sapphic reminiscence. At

[1] This use of dialogue is sometimes compared, rather inaccurately, with the dialogue between
chorus and chorus-leader in the early dithyramb from which, according to Aristotle, tragic dialogue
arose. For critical discussion see *DTC* 28f.
[2] For the quarrel see Gentili (1958) 24–9.
[3] Cf. Simonides 541; Wind (1971/2) 9–13.

his worst, he can be blandly conventional (cf. *Ode* 10). His open, limpid style favours simile over metaphor. Pindar offers no simile quite so extensive as the long Homeric simile of 5.6–30 or 13.124–32. His metaphors are milder than Pindar's too, but he can also experiment with the striking phrase: τόθεν γὰρ | πυθμένες θάλλουσιν ἐσθλῶν 'from song bloom the foundations of noble deeds' (5.198); δνόφεόν τε κάλυμμα τῶν | ὕστερον ἐρχομένων 'a dark veil of things later to come [destroyed Deianira]' (16.32–3), an expression which brilliantly foreshadows the poisoned robe.

Though Bacchylides prefers to trace out the whole line of the narrative rather than highlight details, as Pindar does, nevertheless his technique is far from naive or simplistic. *Ode* 5 exploits a striking collocation of the tales of Meleager and Heracles; *Ode* 11 sets the madness of the Proetides in a rich temporal and spatial framework which encompasses the dynastic quarrels of Argos, the founding of Tiryns, and the establishment of a cult of Artemis in Arcadia. *Ode* 13, the most Homeric of the poems, uses a striking simile of a storm at sea to effect a skilful transition between the two Aeacid heroes, Achilles and Ajax, and to strengthen the unifying effect of the marine setting (cf. 13.105, 125–32, 149–50). *Ode* 17 systematically exploits verbal and thematic repetitions to create a series of parallels and contrasts between its two mythical events, Minos' insult and Theseus' underwater quest.[1] In the case of this latter myth, as also in the case of the story of Croesus on the pyre in *Ode* 3, there are close parallels between Bacchylides' version and contemporaneous vase-painting, a fact which suggests not only that Bacchylides follows the traditional version of a legend, but also that he has an eye for its graphic aspects.[2]

Bacchylides uses direct speech in his myths more abundantly than Pindar; like Pindar he reserves it for moments of great emotional intensity (cf. 5.160–9, Heracles' weeping at Meleager's tale of woe). He can use brevity of quotation to effect. Croesus ends his speech with the clipped, 'Things once hateful are now dear; sweetest to die' (τὰ πρόσθεν ἐχθρὰ φίλα· θανεῖν γλύκιστον, 3.47). There are effective silences, too, like Daedalus' when Pasiphae reveals her love for the bull: 'When he learned her tale he held back in thought' (26.14–15).

Bacchylides shares with the other lyric poets a predilection for colour and light. Of the ninety-odd compound adjectives which occur only in Bacchylides, a large proportion are compounded of elements denoting these properties ('dark-', 'crimson-', 'shining-', κυανο-, φοινικο-, ἀγλαο-). Like earlier lyric poets, Bacchylides borrows a number of epithets directly from Homer, but he often gives them a new twist. 'Rose-fingered' describes not the Dawn, as always in Homer, but the daughter of Inachus, Io (ῥοδοδάκτυλος κόρα 'rose-fingered | maid', 19.18). His Dawn is not 'rose-fingered', like Homer's, but 'of golden arms' (χρυσόπαχυς Ἀώς, 5.40).

---

[1] See Stern (1967) 40–7; Segal (1977).   [2] See Smith (1898) 267–80.

These Homeric echoes can sometimes add an epic grandeur or reflective breadth to the narrative, as in the description of the sack of Sardis (cf. 3.31–2 and 44–6) or the quotation of Homer's famous comparison of men to leaves at the beginning of Heracles' encounter with Meleager in the Underworld (5.64–7). The frequent borrowings from the Homeric underworld of *Odyssey* 11 in this latter passage also evoke the melancholy shadowiness of the Homeric dead and point up a contrast between the active heroic quality in epithets like 'gate-wrecking', 'bold-enduring', 'spear-brandishing' and the futility and emptiness in the setting.[1]

Bacchylides' use of the noun–epithet combination, however, is totally different from Homer's. Whereas the Homeric epithet generally occurs in metrically fixed formulas and stresses the generic, universal quality of the object or person within an established literary tradition, Bacchylides' epithets highlight particular details and thereby enhance the emotional vibrancy and the pathetic contrasts sought by the lyric style. The mood of austerity produced by the functional repetition of the fixed noun–epithet combination in Homer becomes in Bacchylides a decorative, individualizing lushness. Yet Bacchylides' epithets have a thematic as well as a decorative function.[2] They sometimes effect contrasts and parallels between related sections of an ode or a myth. In *Ode* 3, for example, the 'bronze-walled court' and 'well-built halls' of Croesus (3.30–1, 46, reinforced also by the image of Hieron's 'towered wealth', 13) create a grandiose architectural foil to Croesus' near-death on the humbler 'wooden house' of his pyre (ξύλινον δόμον, 49).

Even where Bacchylides follows Homer closely, the tone is utterly different. *Ode* 13, for example, builds the Homeric materials of battle, cloud, sea, shore, into a rich figurative interplay of light and dark, nearness and distance, human valour and impersonal natural forces (cf. 62ff., 127, 153, 175ff.). And in the midst of the martial narrative the brief two-line description of 'the yellow-haired woman, Briseis of the lovely limbs' stands out with a sharpness of detail that is distinctively lyrical (ξανθᾶς γυναικός, | Βρισηΐδος ἱμερογυίου, 13.136–7). *Odes* 5 and 17 exploit a deliberate movement from heroic themes to a gentler, more wistful, more personal mood: compassion and marriage in 5, the sensuous richness of the Nereids after the scenes of heroic challenge in 17.

Though Bacchylides calls himself 'the divine prophet of the violet-eyed Muses' (9.3), he exhibits less of Pindar's deep commitment to his art as a god-given mission. Indeed, this less intense moral earnestness may have helped Bacchylides against his rival: Hieron commissioned Bacchylides alone for his Olympian victory of 468, possibly out of uneasiness with Pindar's sternness and insistent warnings on tyranny, violence, outrage in earlier odes (*O.* 1, *P.* 1–3). Bacchylides' narrative grace probed less deeply and was less threatening.

[1] See Lefkowitz (1968) 69f., 84f.   [2] See Segal (1976).

For Bacchylides poetry is a matter of brightness, joy, open exuberance. For Pindar it is also something dark and mysterious, in touch with strange forces and hidden powers. It is instructive to juxtapose two descriptions of the Muse: 'Like a skilful pilot, O Cleo, ruler of hymns, do you guide now my heart if ever before you have done so' (Bacch. 12.1–4). 'To weave garlands is easy. Strike up the tune. The Muse joins together gold and white ivory and the lily-flower which she lifts from beneath the sea's dew' (Pind. *N.* 7.77–9). Bacchylides' lines have a lucid confidence, Pindar's a poetic depth and a rich allusiveness of diction and symbol.

It would be mistaken, however, to exaggerate too much the differences between the two poets. They share a common repertory of motifs, images, conventions, diction; and they affirm and celebrate the heroic values of an ancient aristocracy. Both seek to bridge the gap between the fleeting present in its glorious display of beauty and energy and the eternal world of the gods. Pindar, however, grasps the contrast between the extremes of mortality and divinity with greater intensity than Bacchylides and for this reason seems the more philosophical and meditative, more concerned with ultimate questions of life and death, transience and permanence. Bacchylides prefers to observe the gentler play of shadow and sadness over the sensuous surface of his brilliant world. Pindar's bolder, more steadfast vision takes in the 'power set apart' that separates men from the gods in their 'brazen heaven' (*N.* 6). Bacchylides characteristically lingers over the freshness of youth and the charm and infatuation of 'golden Love' in the dark realm of the insubstantial dead (5.171–5):

ψυχὰ προσέφα Μελεά-
γρου· 'λίπον χλωραύχενα
ἐν δώμασι Δαϊάνειραν,
νῆϊν ἔτι χρυσέας
Κύπριδος θελξιμβρότου.'

The shade of...Meleager addressed him: 'I left in my halls Deianira, throat fresh with the green life of youth, still ignorant of golden Aphrodite, enchantress of mortals.'

5. WOMEN POETS: CORINNA, MYRTIS, TELESILLA, PRAXILLA

We possess fragments of four Boeotian or Peloponnesian poetesses: Corinna of Tanagra, Myrtis of Anthedon, Telesilla of Argos, Praxilla of Sicyon.[1] Of these the most important and the most puzzling is Corinna, whose work is represented by significant portions of three poems surviving in papyrus fragments (654–5). These poems, in Boeotian dialect, seem from their orthography to belong to the third century B.C., and there is no reference to Corinna in any writer earlier

---

[1] The fragments are numbered by the marginal numeration of *PMG*.

than the first century B.C. On the other hand a late tradition makes her a contemporary of Pindar. If the latter is correct she was presumably ignored by the Alexandrian scholars on account of the provincial character of her language and subject matter, but was rediscovered and copied for local reasons in Boeotia in the third century. The alternative is to believe that she actually wrote in the third century and was much later added as a tenth poet to the Hellenistic canon of nine.

Scholars are still divided between the early and the late date, although there is a tendency, especially in England, to place her late. Not only are the circumstances of the alleged transcription suspicious, but the reference to secret balloting (654.i.20ff.) suggests familiarity with an institution which, so far as we know, developed only in Athens around the middle of the fifth century.[1] Plutarch, however, reports a celebrated anecdote in which she appears as an older mentor of Pindar (*De glor. Ath.* 4.347f), and the Suda has her defeat Pindar five times. Pausanias saw a painting at Tanagra depicting her being crowned in victory over Pindar (Paus. 9.22.3). These legends, however, may have arisen when Boeotia experienced a new period of political and cultural self-consciousness in the third century. The question of Corinna's date remains open.

It is not absolutely certain that all of Corinna's poetry is choral, but references to choruses of girls in the most recently discovered poem suggests that it probably is (655.i.2–3 and 11; cf. 690.12).[2] In the first part of the so-called Berlin papyrus, the longest text, Corinna describes a singing contest between the mountains Helicon and Cithaeron. The latter sings the Hesiodic tale of the concealment of Zeus from Cronos. He wins, and Helicon, in childish frustration, hurls a boulder into the air, smashing it into a thousand pieces. On a recent reconstruction, however, the two contestants are mythical heroes, Helicon and Cithaeron; Helicon hurls himself, not a boulder, down the mountainside; and from his death Mount Helicon takes his name.[3] An aetiological myth of this sort has a Hellenistic rather than an archaic look.

After a long gap of badly mutilated text the papyrus resumes with a dialogue between the river god Asopus, grieving for his daughters, and the prophet Acraiphen, who reassures Asopus about his daughters' fate and tells the history of Apollo's oracular shrine on Mt Ptoon near Thebes. In the third and most recently discovered fragment (655) Corinna speaks in the first person and tells of the pleasure she gave her city with her legends of Boeotian heroes like Cephalus and Orion. She seems to have restricted herself to Boeotian myths. Even her *Orestas* (if the few lines remaining can be assigned to her, 690) seems to have had a Theban setting, probably Orestes' presence at a spring rite of Apollo at Thebes.

[1] See Boegehold (1963) 368 n. 6; Bolling (1956) 285f.; Segal (1975) 1–8.
[2] See West (1970*b*) 280, 283; Kirkwood (1974) 192.   [3] Ebert (1978) 5–12.

Despite the unfamiliar Boeotian vernacular, Corinna's style is lucid and simple. She uses short clauses and paratactic sentences. There are few metaphors and few tropes of any kind. The narrative has a certain vividness and fresh charm suggestive of folk poetry. There are touchès of humour: the elaborate voting procedures on Olympus (654.i.19ff.) or possibly the grotesque anthropomorphization of Mount Helicon 'held by harsh pains' as he hurled his rock, groaning 'piteously'. She uses a few compound epithets of the type familiar from Bacchylides; but apart from λιγουροκωτίλυς 'coaxing in high tones' (655.5), they are not especially recherché ('crafty-minded', 'gold-shining', 'white-robed'). Her metres are simple and regular, a fact which may suggest archaism or, conversely, the metrical simplification of the later period. Given the simplicity of Corinna's style and the restrictions of her material, it is interesting, not to say puzzling, that she could have won five victories (or, with Pausanias, one victory) over her brilliant fellow-Boeotian.

Of Myrtis we have almost nothing. She is best known from a fragment of Corinna who criticizes her, a woman, for venturing to compete with Pindar (664a):

> μέμφομη δὲ κὴ λιγουρὰν
> Μουρτίδ' ἰώνγ' ὅτι βανὰ φοῦ-
> σ' ἔβα Πινδάροι πὸτ ἔριν.

I blame too the clear-voiced Myrtis because born a woman she went to contest against Pindar.

Like Corinna she too seems to have related local legends like the love of Ochne for the Tanagran hero Eunostos, a variation on the Potiphar's wife motif.

Telesilla wrote poems, perhaps choral, for Apollo and Artemis. A lost poem told the story of Niobe (721). Of Praxilla a little more is preserved. She wrote a 'hymn' to Adonis of which three melodious lines survive and gave rise to the proverb, 'sillier than Adonis' (747). Asked in Hades what he most regretted, Adonis answered,

> κάλλιστον μὲν ἐγὼ λείπω φάος ἠελίοιο,
> δεύτερον ἄστρα φαεινὰ σεληναίης τε πρόσωπον
> ἠδὲ καὶ ὡραίους σικύους καὶ μῆλα καὶ ὄγχνας.

Loveliest of what I leave behind is the light of the sun
Next the bright stars and the moon's face
And the ripe cucumbers and apples and pears.

These lines, however, are in dactylic hexameters, not in any of the usual choral metres. Praxilla also wrote a dithyramb on Achilles, whose sole remaining line suggests close adherence to Homer: 'But never did they (I?) persuade the spirit within your breast' (ἀλλὰ τεὸν οὔποτε θυμὸν ἐνὶ στήθεσσιν ἔπειθον, 748). Some bits of proverbial wisdom have also survived (749–50); and, like Telesilla, she gave her name to a type of metre (717, 754).

6. CHORAL LYRIC TO THE END OF THE FIFTH CENTURY

Although the odes of Pindar and Bacchylides mark the end of the great period of Greek choral poetry as an independent form, it continues to be written to the end of the fifth century (fragments in *PMG*, pp. 359–447). The competition among dithyrambic choruses at the Dionysiac festivals in Athens assured a steady production of dithyrambs. Most of the scanty fragments that survive, therefore, are from dithyrambs. There are also scraps of a paean by Sophocles (737), an epinikion for Alcibiades by Euripides (755), and notices of hymns, prosodia, enkomia. Ion of Chios, Sophocles' contemporary, wrote a dithyramb narrating the death of Antigone (740) in a version quite different from Sophocles'. Among the earliest pieces are fifteen lines (708) by Pratinas (*fl.* 500), known chiefly for his satyr plays. This lively fragment (which may well be from a chorus in a satyr play)[1] uses outlandish compounds in a way that anticipates Timotheus at the very end of the century. It complains that the instrumental accompaniment of the flute players has begun to dominate the vocal part of the chorus. This predominance of music over words becomes more marked in the choral lyric of the fifth century, especially the dithyramb, perhaps under the influence of the tragic performances.

The period from 450 on saw a general loosening of the old forms, both of music and of verse, and an increasing tendency toward exaggerated diction. The strict strophic composition of the earlier period (strophe, antistrophe, epode) gives way to free or 'loosened' verse (ἀπολελυμένα). Philoxenus of Cythera (436/4–380/79) is said to have introduced monodies into the choral songs of the dithyramb (Plut. *De mus.* 1142a; Aristophanes, fr. 641 K). In the comic poet Pherecrates (145 K) Music appears on stage denouncing Melanippides (*fl. c.* 440) to Justice for taking the lead in making her 'looser' (χαλαρωτέραν); and she then goes on to list Cinesias, Phrynis and Timotheus, the worst of all with his trills and arpeggios like the twisting paths of ants (ἄιδων ἐκτραπέλους μυρμηκιάς, line 23). Aristophanes provides a delicious parody of Cinesias (*Birds* 1373ff.), suggesting that this etherial bard would find wings especially appropriate to his 'air-whirling and snow-driven' poems:

> κρέμαται μὲν οὖν ἐντεῦθεν ἡμῶν ἡ τέχνη.
> τῶν διθυράμβων γὰρ τὰ λαμπρὰ γίγνεται
> ἀέρια καὶ σκότιά γε καὶ κυαναυγέα
> καὶ πτεροδόνητα.

> Why our whole trade depends upon the clouds;
> What are our noblest dithyrambs but things
> Of air, and mist, and purple-gleaming depths,
> And feathery whirlwings? (*Birds* 1387–90, tr. Rogers)

[1] See Garrod (1920) 129–36, especially 134f.; *DTC* 17–20, with bibliography; Lloyd-Jones (1966) 11ff.

The choral lyrics of late Euripidean tragedy show parallel tendencies and also drew Aristophanes' fire in the brilliant parody of the *Frogs* (1301–63). On the other hand the new style had its admirers. Aristodemus in Xenophon's *Memorabilia* (1.4.3) puts Melanippides' excellence in the dithyramb on a par with the art of Sophocles, Polyclitus, Zeuxis. The comic poet Antiphanes has a character praise Philoxenus for his inventions of new words and his shifting rhythms and melodies (207 K). Philoxenus and Timotheus were still popular in the schools of Arcadia in Polybius' day (Polyb. 4.20).

Most of these poets seem to have carried on the literary dithyramb as we have seen it in Bacchylides, *Odes* 17–20; they relate mythical tales in a decorative style and with a certain amount of dialogue (e.g. Melanippides 758). Athena and Marsyas, Persephone, Peleus and Thetis, the Danaids, Asclepius' resurrection of Hippolytus, Endymion are some of the subjects. Licymnius of Chios wrote on a quasi-historical subject recalling Bacchylides 3, the betrayal of Sardis to Cyrus by Croesus' own daughter, Nanis (772).

The most extensive piece of later choral lyric to survive, once more thanks to· the luck of a papyrus discovery, is the *Persians* of Timotheus (*c.* 450–360). This work is a 'nome', an ancient form developed by Terpander in the seventh century, but in Timotheus' time a rather free composition without strophes and dominated by the music.[1] Its style and narrative technique closely resemble the 'literary' dithyramb of Bacchylides and later.[2] But Timotheus' pomposity and bombast are a far cry from either the grandeur of Pindar or the grace of Bacchylides. They look forward to the worst traits of Hellenistic poetry. Wine mixed with water is 'the blood of Dionysus mixed with the fresh-flowing tears of the nymphs' (from the *Cyclops*, 780). Teeth are 'the mouth's light-flashing children' (*Pers.* 91ff.). There are occasional touches of solemnity and pathos: the lament of the Persian women (100ff., 120ff.) and Xerxes' heroic decision (189ff.); but the pidgin Greek of the Persian women (150ff.) sinks to comical bathos that is hard to imagine in an earlier poet. Yet the abrupt break-off from the myth (202), the poet's defence of his own art and closing prayer for the city (206–28) illustrate the continuity of traditional motifs even in this late and florid style.

The work of Timotheus and his contemporary, Philoxenus of Cythera, who wrote a humorous version of the loves of Galatea and Polyphemus that anticipates Theocritus, reveals one of the reasons for the decline of choral lyric. The poet no longer regarded his art with the high seriousness of a Simonides or a Pindar. Rather than a 'prophet of the Muses' who seeks to interpret the ways of

---

[1] See Wilamowitz (1903) 79ff., 89ff.

[2] This 'literary' dithyramb is a lyrical narrative in honour of gods and heroes, not a poem in honour of Dionysus, as the term originally implied. All of Bacchylides' preserved dithyrambs are of the former, 'literary' type except 19, which ends with the birth of Dionysus.

the gods and to understand the limitations of mortality, the choral poet becomes merely an entertainer. Aesthetic novelty and ingenuity are demanded rather than moral depth or religious power; or, as Plato charges in the *Laws*, taste formed by aristocratic values has given way to taste formed by the mob and the 'theatocracy' (3.700c, 701a, cf. *Gorgias* 501e).

More than almost any other literary form, choral lyric is bound up with the values of city and clan in a world where things changed slowly. By 450 the tyrants and aristocratic families which had commissioned the odes of Pindar and Bacchylides were gone or endangered, their values threatened by the fast-rising power of Athenian democracy. By the last quarter of the century the festivals which provided the occasion for choral song were losing their religious basis. The power politics of the latter half of the fifth century, the scepticism and rationalism brought by the sophistic enlightenment, the disruptions of the Peloponnesian War, and the rapid social and cultural changes which these movements precipitated were all inimical to the old poetry. With the exception of Pindar's very last ode (*P.* 8), all the significant choral poetry that we have predates 450. Choral lyric implied a stable community founded on universally shared religious and moral beliefs, well established rituals and firm traditions. By the midpoint of the century these old values were no longer unquestioned. Tragic drama rather than the genre of lyric poetry *per se* expressed the forces and tensions of greatest concern to the thinking and feeling men of the day.

APPENDIX OF
AUTHORS AND WORKS

HOMER

LIFE

Worked probably in latter half of 8th c. B.C., but nothing plausible known about his life or background. His date depends mainly on refs. in *Il.* and *Od.* to 8th-c. practices and artefacts (e.g. hoplite-style fighting, gorgon-head brooch, tripod-cauldrons), on the probable posteriority of Hesiod, the decline of oral composition by the time of Archilochus, the appearance of epic scenes on vases etc. after 680, and on ancient opinions (esp. Herodotus (2.53) and Hesychius, citing a probably classical source on date of Arctinus (Suda s.v.)). His region is indicated by predominantly Ionic dialect of the poems, by local east-Aegean detail and colour (e.g. *Il.* 2.144–6, 459–63, 13.12–14) and by the unanimous ancient tradition, which associated him primarily with Chios and Smyrna (so e.g. Pindar according to *Vit. Thom.* 2); other *Lives* (in OCT v; mostly of Graeco-Roman date and feebly fictitious) add Cumae and Colophon, agreeing that he died on Ios. See G. S. Kirk, *The songs of Homer* (Cambridge 1962) 271–87.

WORKS

(All in hexameters except *Margites*.) (1) *Iliad* and *Odyssey*. On division of each into twenty-four books see Kirk, *Songs* 305f.; on possibility of two monumental composers, above pp. 8–10. *Odyssey* was considered by 'Longinus' (*Subl.* 9–13) to be the product of H.'s old age, a not impossible explanation for the minor stylistic and lexical differences between the two poems (excluding those caused by different subjects). (2) Erroneously attributed to H. in antiquity were: thirty-three *Hymns* (see pp. 210f.), esp. *Hymn to Apollo* (Thuc. 3.104; see l.172); *Thebais*; other parts of the Epic Cycle (see pp. 209f.) – though Herodotus thought that *Cypria* was not his (2.116f.) – and probably also *Epigoni* (4.32); even *Margites*, a trivial work in iambics and hexameters (Arist. *Poet.* 4.1486b) and *Batrachomyomachia* (see p. 69). Many of these are several centuries later than H.; see e.g. on *Hymns* p. 70 and D. B. Monro, *Homer's Odyssey* (Oxford 1901) 340–84.

HOMER

TRANSMISSION

The *Iliad* and *Odyssey* come from close to the end of the oral heroic tradition. Essentially oral in technique, their debt to writing (alphabet becoming known in Greece by mid-8th c.), either through the listing of topics or through dictation, is disputed. In any case, transmission through 7th c. must have been partly or mainly oral, primarily through rhapsodes (reciters not singers) prone to subjective choice and virtuoso embellishment (see Plato's *Ion*); their activity at Sicyon in early 6th c. is attested by Herodotus (5.67.1). The establishment of rhapsodic competitions at the Athenian Panathenaic festival necessitated both a rule that H.'s work should be recited fully and consecutively, and also, presumably, an official text to act as control (rule attributed to Hipparchus towards end of 6th c. (Ps.-Plat. *Hipparch.* 228b), less plausibly to Solon (Diog. Laert. 1.57)). Written texts seem to have proliferated from then on, esp. in Athens, although learning by heart was still widely practised; hence quotations are still inaccurate in 4th c. Systematic librarianship and scholarship in Alexandria and Pergamum from 3rd c. onwards intensified efforts to establish an accurate and agreed text. Greatest of Homeric scholars was Aristarchus of Samothrace (*c.* 215–*c.* 145 B.C.), head of the Alexandrian library. Basing his judgements both on conjecture and on the evaluation of earlier texts, he extruded certain obvious doublets and additions due to rhapsodic or learned elaboration, cast doubt on many other verses and passages, as well as discussing difficulties of grammar and sense. His text became standard to the extent of causing the disappearance of 'wild' versions, known from papyrus fragments, with many additional and palpably non-Homeric verses. H.'s popularity in the Roman period and the multiplication of copies of his work ensured his survival through the early Middle Ages; with the revival of classical studies in the 9th c. A.D. much of the best Homeric criticism was collected, excerpted and written as scholia in luxurious minuscule codices; these editions formed the basis of the first printed texts and, eventually, of the modern vulgate. See Kirk, *Songs* 301–15.

BIBLIOGRAPHY

TEXTS AND COMMENTARIES: TEXTS: *Il.*: D. B. Monro, T. W. Allen, 3rd ed. (OCT, 1920). *Od.*: T. W. Allen, 2nd ed. (OCT, 1917). LIVES: T. W. Allen (OCT, 1912: with *Hymns*, Epic Cycle etc.). COMMENTARIES: *Il.*: W. Leaf, 2 vols. (London 1899–1901). Bks 1–4: G. S. Kirk (Cambridge 1985); Bk 24: C. W. Macleod (Cambridge 1982). See also M. M. Willcock, *A companion to the Iliad* (Chicago 1976: brief comm. on R. Lattimore's tr.). *Od.*: W. B. Stanford, 2 vols., 2nd ed. (London 1959). Bks 1–4: S. West, 5–8: J. B. Hainsworth, 9–12: A. Heubeck, 13–16: A. Hoekstra, 17–20: J. Russo; 21–24: M. Fernández-Galiano and A. Heubeck (Rome 1981–6; in Italian, with tr.); Eng. tr. (Oxford 1988–). *Scholia. Il.*: H. Erbse (Berlin 1969–83). *Od.*: W. Dindorf (Oxford 1855: repr. Amsterdam 1962).

TRANSLATIONS. *Il.*: A. Lang, W. Leaf, E. Myers, rev. ed. (London 1892); R. Lattimore (Chicago 1951); R. Fitzgerald (Oxford 1984). *Od.*: S. H. Butcher and A. Lang (London 1921); R. Lattimore (Chicago 1965); W. Shewring (Oxford 1980).

STUDIES. (1) SURVEYS: H.-J. Mette, 'Homer 1930–56', *Lustrum* 1 (1956) 7ff., cont. in vols. 2, 4, 5, 11, 15; A. Heubeck, *Gymnasium* 58 (1951) 362ff., cont. in vols. 62, 63, 66, 71; A. Lesky, *A.A.H.G.* 6 (1953) 129ff., cont. in vols. 8, 12, 13, 17, 18; F. M. Combellack, *C.W.* 49 (1955) 17ff., 29ff., 45ff.; E. R. Dodds, L. R. Palmer, D. H. F. Gray in *FYAT* ch. 1; J. B. Hainsworth, *G.&R.* New surveys in the classics III (1969); J. Holoka, *C.W.* 66 (1973) 257–93; A. Heubeck, *Die homerische Frage* (Darmstadt 1974); D. W. Packard and T. Meyers, *A bibliography of Homeric scholarship 1930–1970*, preliminary ed. (Malibu, Calif. 1974). (2) GENERAL: C. H. Whitman, *Homer and the heroic tradition* (Cambridge, Mass. 1958); W. Schadewaldt, *Von Homers Welt und Werk* (Stuttgart 1959); G. S. Kirk, *The songs of Homer* (Cambridge 1962), abbrev. as *Homer and the epic* (Cambridge 1964); Lesky ch. III; idem, 'Homeros', *RE* suppl. XI (1968) 687ff.; C. R. Beye, *The Iliad, the Odyssey and the epic tradition* (London 1968); (ed.) F. Codino, *La questione omerica* (Rome 1976); M. I. Finley, *The world of Odysseus*, 2nd ed. (London 1977); J. Griffin, *Homer on life and death* (Oxford 1980). (3) *Iliad*: W. Schadewaldt, *Iliasstudien*, 2nd ed. (Leipzig 1943: repr. Darmstadt 1966); (ed.) P. Mazon, *Introduction à l'Iliade* (Paris 1948); H. T. Wade-Gery, *The poet of the Iliad* (Cambridge 1952); D. L. Page, *History and the Homeric Iliad* (Berkeley 1959); K. Reinhardt, *Die Ilias und ihr Dichter* (Göttingen 1961); J. M. Redfield, *Nature and culture in the Iliad* (Chicago 1975); H. van Thiel, *Iliaden und Ilias* (Basel & Stuttgart 1982). (4) *Odyssey*: W. B. Stanford, *The Ulysses theme* (Oxford 1954); D. L. Page, *The Homeric Odyssey* (Oxford 1955); B. Fenik, *Studies in the Odyssey* (Wiesbaden 1974); N. Austin, *Archery at the dark of the moon* (Berkeley 1975); E. Delebecque, *Construction de l'Odyssée* (Paris 1980). (5) LANGUAGE, FORMULAS, ORAL TRADITION: W. Arendt, *Die typischen Szenen bei Homer* (Berlin 1933); M. Leumann, *Homerische Wörter* (Basel 1950); P. Chantraine, *Grammaire homérique*, 2 vols. (Paris 1953–8); A. B. Lord, *The singer of tales* (Cambridge, Mass. 1960); B. Fenik, *Typical battle scenes in the Iliad* (Wiesbaden 1968); J. B. Hainsworth, *The flexibility of the Homeric formula* (Oxford 1968); A. Hoekstra, *Homeric modifications of formulaic prototypes* (Amsterdam 1969); D. Lohmann, *Die Komposition der Reden in der Ilias* (Berlin 1970); (ed.) A. Parry, *The making of Homeric verse* (Oxford 1971: contains all writings of Milman Parry, with introductory survey by ed.); G. P. Shipp, *Studies in the language of Homer*, 2nd ed. (Cambridge 1972); M. N. Nagler, *Spontaneity and tradition; a study in the oral art of Homer* (Berkeley 1974); G. S. Kirk, *Homer and the oral tradition* (Cambridge 1976); C. Moulton, *Similes in the Homeric poems*, Hypomnemata XLIX (Göttingen 1977); (ed.) J. Latacz, *Homer: Tradition und Neuerung*, Wege der Forschung CDLXIII (Darmstadt 1979); G. C. Horrocks, *Space and time in Homer* (New York 1981). (6) ARCHAEOLOGY, HISTORY: H. L. Lorimer, *Homer and the monuments* (London 1950); A. J. B. Wace and F. H. Stubbings, *A companion to Homer* (London 1962); E. T. Vermeule, *Greece in the bronze age* (Chicago 1965); (edd.) F. Matz and H.-G. Buchholz, *Archeologia Homerica* (Göttingen 1967–: series of monographs); G. S. Kirk, 'The Homeric poems as history', *CAH* II 2 (1975) 820–50. (7) TRANSMISSION: G. M. Bolling, *The external evidence for interpolation in Homer* (Oxford

HESIOD

1925: repr. 1968); H. Erbse, *Beiträge zur Überlieferung der Iliasscholien* (Munich 1960); R. A. Pack, *Greek and Latin literary texts from Graeco-Roman Egypt*, 2nd ed. (Ann Arbor 1965); S. West, *The Ptolemaic papyri of Homer* (Cologne 1967); M. J. Apthorp, *The manuscript evidence for interpolation in Homer* (Heidelberg 1980).

LEXICA: H. Ebeling, 2 vols. (Leipzig 1880–5: repr. Hildesheim 1963); (*Il.*) G. L. Prendergast, (*Od.*) H. Dunbar, both rev. B. Marzullo (Hildesheim 1962).

HESIOD

LIFE

Son of a native of Cyme in Asia Minor who emigrated to Ascra in Boeotia (*W.D.* 633–40). In conflict with his brother Perses over patrimony (if what he claims in *W.D.*, esp. at 34–9, is to be trusted). Won poetry contest at funeral games of Amphidamas at Chalcis in Euboea (*W.D.* 651–9). Scholars in antiquity disagreed over the relative chronology of Homer and H. (evidence in the *Lives*: see below). H.'s date is still disputed: Amphidamas died in the Lelantine War (Plut. *Mor.* 153f), which many scholars date to late 8th c. (see J. N. Coldstream, *Geometric Greece* (London 1977) 200–1), but others to 7th (see R. C. M. Janko, *Homer, Hesiod and the Hymns* (Cambridge 1982) 94–8). For full discussion see M. L. West, *Hesiod, Theogony* (Oxford 1966) 40–8; G. P. Edwards, *The language of Hesiod in its traditional context* (Oxford 1971) 199–206. According to legendary tales current in antiquity H. was related to Homer, was father of Stesichorus, competed with Homer and defeated him in the poetry contest, and was ultimately murdered in Locris. Later his remains were transferred to Orchomenus, where a tomb was built for him in the agora (recorded by Pausanias, 9.38.3). For *Lives* and testimonia and for text of Περὶ Ὁμήρου καὶ Ἡσιόδου καὶ τοῦ γένους καὶ ἀγῶνος αὐτῶν (= *Certamen Homeri et Hesiodi*) see U. von Wilamowitz-Moellendorff, *Vitae Homeri et Hesiodi*, Kleine Texte CXXXVII (Bonn 1916). (Texts of *Lives* also in F. Solmsen's OCT of Hesiod (1970), text and tr. of *Certamen* in H. G. Evelyn-White, *Hesiod* (Loeb, 1914).) On the legends see R. Scodel, *G.R.B.S.* 21 (1980) 301–20; M. Lefkowitz, *The lives of the Greek poets* (London 1981) ch. I. On *Certamen*: M. L. West, *C.Q.* n.s.17 (1967) 433–50; N. J. Richardson, *C.Q.* n.s.31 (1981) 1–10.

WORKS

(1) EXTANT: *Theogony, Works and days, Shield* (*Scutum*, Ἀσπίς). Only *Theog.* and *W.D.* are regarded as genuine. On *Shield* see R. M. Cook, *C.Q.* 31 (1937) 204–14. (2) FRAGMENTARY: *Catalogue of women* or *Ehoiai* (a later continuation of *Theog.* in five books), *Great Ehoiai, Marriage of Ceyx, Melampodia, Descent of Pirithous, Idaean dactyls, Precepts of Chiron, Great works, Astronomy, Aegimius* (also ascribed to Cercops of Miletus), *Caminus* or Κεραμεῖς. *Ornithomanteia* and Ἐπικήδειον εἰς

HESIOD

Βάτραχον (a lover's lament to one Batrachus) appear to be completely lost. None of these works is thought to be genuine; for other dubious or spurious fragments see R. Merkelbach and M. L. West, *Fragmenta Hesiodea* (Oxford 1967) 171–90.

BIBLIOGRAPHY

TEXTS AND COMMENTARIES: TEXTS: (1) Complete corpus. A. Rzach, ed. maior (Leipzig 1902), ed. minor, 3rd ed. (BT, 1913); F. Solmsen (*Theog.*, *W.D.*, *Shield*), R. Merkelbach and M. L. West (*Fragmenta selecta*) (OCT, 1970). (2) *Theog.*, *W.D.*, *Shield*. P. Mazon (Budé, 1928). (3) *Theogony*. F. Jacoby (Berlin 1930). (4) *Works and days*. A. Colonna (Milan 1959). (5) Fragments. R. Merkelbach, *Die Hesiodfragmente auf Papyrus* (Leipzig 1957: with notes); R. Merkelbach and M. L. West, *Fragmenta Hesiodea* (Oxford 1967); (edd.) P. J. Parsons, P. J. Sijpesteijn and K. A. Worp, *Papyri, Greek and Egyptian, in honour of E. G. Turner* (London 1981) = *P. Leiden* inv. 502–9 (*Catalogue*). COMMENTARIES: (1) *Theogony*. W. Aly (Heidelberg 1913); M. L. West (Oxford 1966). (2) *Works and days*. P. Waltz (Brussels 1909: with tr.); P. Mazon (Paris 1914); U. von Wilamowitz-Moellendorff (Berlin 1928: repr. 1962: *Works* only); T. A. Sinclair (London 1932: repr. Hildesheim 1966); M. L. West (Oxford 1978). (3) *Shield*. C. F. Russo, 2nd ed. (Florence 1965: with tr.). (4) *Catalogue*. A. Traversa (Naples 1951). *Scholia. Theog.*: L. di Gregorio (Milan 1975). *W.D.*: A. Pertusi (Milan 1955). Byzantine scholia: T. Gaisford, *Poetae minores Graeci* (Oxford 1814, Leipzig 1823).

TRANSLATIONS: (1) PROSE: A. W. Mair (Oxford 1908); H. G. Evelyn-White (Loeb, 1914: rev. 1920, 1936); W. Marg (Zurich & Stuttgart 1970: with notes); D. Wender (Harmondsworth, 1973; M. L. West (Oxford 1988). (2) VERSE: R. Lattimore (Ann Arbor 1959).

STUDIES: (1) GENERAL: P. Waltz, *Hésiode et son poème morale* (Paris 1906); A. R. Burn, *The world of Hesiod* (London 1936); F. Solmsen, *Hesiod and Aeschylus*, Cornell Stud. in Class. Phil. XXX (Ithaca, N.Y. 1949); H. Diller, 'Die dichterische Form von Hesiods Erga', *Abh. Akad. Mainz* 1962, 2; H. Fränkel, *Early Greek poetry and philosophy* (New York & London 1975) = *Dichtung und Philosophie des frühen Griechentums*, 2nd ed. (Munich 1962) ch. III; *Entretiens VII: Hésiode et son influence* (Fondation Hardt, Geneva 1962); M. Detienne, *Crise agraire et attitude religieuse chez Hésiode*, Coll. Latomus LXVIII (Brussels 1963); W. Nicolai, *Hesiods Erga: Beobachtungen zum Aufbau* (Heidelberg 1964); E. Will, 'Hésiode: crise agraire? Ou recul de l'aristocratie?', *R.E.G.* 78 (1965) 542–56; P. Walcot, *Hesiod and the Near East* (Cardiff 1966); (ed.) E. Heitsch, *Hesiod*, Wege der Forschung XLIV (Darmstadt 1967); J. Blusch, *Formen und Inhalt von Hesiods individuellem Denken* (Bonn 1970); L. Bona Quaglia, *Gli Erga di Esiodo* (Turin 1973); J.-P. Vernant, 'The myth of Prometheus in Hesiod', in *Myth and society in ancient Greece*, tr. J. Lloyd (Brighton 1980) = *Mythe et société en Grèce ancienne* (Paris 1974); P. Pucci, *Hesiod and the language of poetry* (Baltimore 1977);

M. Griffith, 'Personality in Hesiod', *Classical Antiquity* 2 (1983) 37–65. On the Hesiodic fragments: J. Schwartz, *Pseudo-Hesiodeia* (Leiden 1960); I. Löffler, *Die Melampodie* (Meisenheim am Glan 1963); M. L. West, *The Hesiodic Catalogue of Women* (Oxford 1985). (2) LANGUAGE AND STYLE: I. Sellschopp, *Stilistische Untersuchungen zu Hesiod* (Hamburg 1934: repr. Darmstadt 1967); H. Troxler, *Sprache und Wortschatz Hesiods* (Zurich 1964); G. P. Edwards, *The language of Hesiod in its traditional context*, Philol. Soc. Publ. XXII (Oxford 1971); B. Peabody, *The winged word* (Albany 1975), reviewed by J. B. Hainsworth, *C.R.* 28 (1978) 207–8; R. C. M. Janko, *Homer, Hesiod and the Hymns* (Cambridge 1982). (3) TEXT: N. A. Livadaras, 'Ιστορία τῆς παραδόσεως τοῦ κειμένου τοῦ 'Ησιόδου (Athens 1963), reviewed by M. L. West, *Gnomon* 37 (1965) 650–5; M. L. West, 'The medieval and Renaissance manuscripts of Hesiod's *Theogony*', *C.Q.* n.s.14 (1964) 165–89; idem, 'The medieval manuscripts of the *Works and Days*', *C.Q.* n.s.24 (1974) 161–85.

LEXICA: J. Paulson, *Index Hesiodeus* (Lund 1890: repr. Hildesheim 1962); M. Hofinger, *Lexicon Hesiodeum cum indice inverso* (Leiden 1973–8; with Supplement, 1985); W. W. Minton, *Concordance to the Hesiodic corpus* (Leiden 1976); J. R. Tebben, *Hesiod-Konkordanz: a computer concordance to Hesiod* (Hildesheim 1977).

THE CYCLIC EPICS

Many epic poems were composed in the archaic period besides the *Iliad* and *Odyssey* and the Hesiodic corpus; at an unknown date a large number were grouped into a 'cycle' in the following order (with names of poets to whom they were attributed): (1) *Theogony*. (2) *Battle of the Titans*: Arctinus of Miletus or Eumelus of Corinth. (3) Theban epics. *Oedipodeia*: Cinaethon of Lacedaemon; *Thebais*: Homer; *Epigoni*: Homer ('Antimachus' in schol. on Ar. *Peace* 1270). (4) Trojan cycle. *Cypria* (11 bks): Homer, Stasinus of Cyprus or Hegesinus of Salamis (in Cyprus); *Iliad*; *Aethiopis* (5 bks): Arctinus; *Little Iliad* (4 bks): Lesches of Mytilene or Pyrrha, Thestorides of Phocaea, Cinaethon, Diodorus of Erythrae, Homer; *Iliou persis* (2 bks): Arctinus or Lesches; *Nostoi* (5 bks): Agias or Hegias of Trozen, Eumelus(?); *Odyssey*; *Telegonia* (2 bks): Eugammon of Cyrene. Very few fragments survive; the Trojan Cycle is better attested than the rest because summaries of its contents are preserved in the *Chrestomathia* of Proclus.

Other epics not included in the Cycle: (1) *Corinthiaca* (incl. Argonautic legends): Eumelus of Corinth, 8th c. (2) Heracles epics. *Capture of Oechalia*: Homer or Creophylus of Samos; *Heraclea*: Panyassis of Halicarnassus, 5th c. Further discussion in Rzach under *Studies* below *ad init*. and Lesky 79–84.

Mock epic: only extant example of this genre is the pseudo-Homeric *Batrachomyomachia* (*Battle of frogs and mice*); for other titles see Suda s.v. 'Ομηρος 45, 103.

BIBLIOGRAPHY

TEXTS: *EGF*; T. W. Allen, *Homeri opera* v (OCT, 1912: rev. 1946); E. Bethe, *Homer, Dichtung und Saga* II (Leipzig 1922); A. Bernabé, *Poetae epici Graeci* I (BT, 1988). Proclus only: A. Severyns, *Recherches sur la Chrestomathie de Proclus* IV (Liège 1963). *Batrachomyomachia*: H. Ahlborn (Berlin 1968: with tr.). Panyassis: V. J. Matthews, *Mnemosyne* suppl. XXXIII (1974: with comm.).

TRANSLATIONS: H. G. Evelyn-White (Loeb, 1914: rev. 1920, 1936: with Hesiod).

STUDIES: A. Rzach, *RE* VIII (1913) 2146–82 ('Homeridai') and XI (1922) 2347–435 ('Kyklos'); E. Bethe, *Homer, Dichtung und Saga* II–III (Leipzig 1922–7); W. Kullmann, *Die Quellen der Ilias*, *Hermes* Einzelschriften XIV (1960); A. Severyns, *Le cycle épique dans l'école d'Aristarque* (Paris & Liège 1928); idem, *Recherches sur la Chrestomathie de Proclos* IV (Liège 1963); G. L. Huxley, *Greek epic poetry* (London 1969); M. L. West, 'Greek poetry 2000–700 B.C.', *C.Q.* n.s.23 (1973) 179–92; J. Griffin, 'The Epic Cycle and the uniqueness of Homer', *J.H.S.* 97 (1977) 39–53; W. Burkert, 'Seven against Thebes: an oral tradition between Babylonian magic and Greek literature', in (edd.) C. Brillante, M. Cantilena, C. O. Pavese, *I poemi epici rapsodici non omerici e la tradizione orale* (Padua 1981) 29–51; R. C. M. Janko, *Homer, Hesiod and the Hymns* (Cambridge 1982). *Batrachomyomachia*: H. Wölke, *Untersuchungen zur Batrachomyomachia* (Meisenheim am Glan 1978).

LEXICON: B. Snell *et al.*, *Lexicon des frühgriechischen Epos* (Göttingen 1955–).

THE HOMERIC HYMNS

At some stage in antiquity all the hexameter hymns not associated with other famous hymnodists were gathered with those specifically (but wrongly) attributed to Homer to form the corpus of thirty-three 'Homeric Hymns'. The four longest (to Demeter, Apollo, Hermes and Aphrodite; from 293 to 580 verses) probably date from between 650 and 400 B.C.; the rest (from three to fifty-nine verses) are likely to be later. Earliest allusion is Thuc. 3.104, quoting *Hymn to Apollo* 145–50.

BIBLIOGRAPHY

(See Richardson under *Commentaries* below, 86–92, and Janko (1982) under *Studies* below, 280–96.)

TEXTS AND COMMENTARIES: TEXTS: T. W. Allen, *Homeri opera* v (OCT, 1912); J. Humbert (Budé, 1936). COMMENTARIES: A. Gemoll (Leipzig 1895); T. W.

ARCHILOCHUS

Allen, W. R. Halliday, E. E. Sikes (Oxford 1936: earlier ed. of Allen and Sikes (London & New York 1904) still valuable, esp. for *Hymn to Apollo*); F. Càssola (Milan 1975: with Italian tr.); A. N. Athanassakis (Baltimore 1976: with tr.). *Hymn to Aphrodite*: P. Smith, *Nursling of mortality. A study of the Homeric Hymn to Aphrodite* (Frankfurt, Berne & Cirencester 1981). *Hymn to Demeter*: N. J. Richardson (Oxford 1974). *Hymn to Hermes*: L. Radermacher. *S.A.W.W.* 213 (1931) 1–264; L. Kahn (Paris 1978: French tr. and comm., no text).

TRANSLATIONS: H. G. Evelyn-White (Loeb, 1914: rev. 1920, 1936: with Hesiod).

STUDIES: O. Zumbach, *Neuerungen in der Sprache der homerischen Hymnen* (Zurich 1955); E. Heitsch, *Aphroditehymnos, Aeneas und Homer: sprachliche Untersuchungen zum Homerproblem*, Hypomnemata xv (Göttingen 1965); A. Hoekstra, *The sub-epic stage of the formulaic tradition* (Amsterdam 1969); L. H. Lenz, *Der homerische Aphroditehymnus und die Aristie des Aineias in der Ilias* (Bonn 1975); K. Förstel, *Untersuchungen zum homerischen Apollonhymnos* (Bochum 1979); (edd.) C. Brillante, M. Cantilena, C. O. Pavese, *I poemi rapsodici non omerici e la tradizione orale* (Padua 1981); R. C. M. Janko, *Homer, Hesiod and the Hymns* (Cambridge 1982).

ELEGY AND IAMBUS

GENERAL WORKS

Bowra, C. M., *Early Greek elegists* (London 1938: repr. Cambridge 1960)
Burn, A. R., *The lyric age of Greece* (London 1960)
Campbell, D. A., *The golden lyre: the themes of the Greek lyric poets* (London 1983)
Degani, E., *Poeti greci giambici ed elegiaci* (Milan 1977)
Fatouros, G., *Index verborum zur frühgriechischen Lyrik* (Heidelberg 1966)
Fränkel, H., *Early Greek poetry and philosophy*, tr. M. Hadas and J. Willis (New York & London 1975)
Pfohl, G., *Die griechische Elegie*, Wege der Forschung cxxix (Darmstadt 1972)
West, M. L., *Studies in Greek elegy and iambus* (Berlin & New York 1974)

ARCHILOCHUS

LIFE

(Testimonia are numbered as in Tarditi under *Texts* below.) b. in Paros, son of Telesicles (T 2), who is generally thought to have led a Parian colony to Thasos (T 116, but see A. J. Graham (*B.S.A.* 73 (1978) 72–86) who argues that Telesicles may have done no more than report the oracle that gave directions for the foundation; the colonization could have been as late as *c.* 650). According to Critias (T 46) A.'s mother was a slave woman, Enipo, but this has been doubted by many scholars. His grandfather(?) Tellis was probably associated with the taking of the cult of Demeter to Thasos (T 121). A.'s links with Thasos, frequently mentioned in his poetry, are borne out by T 1, a 7th-c. inscription commemorating his friend Glaucus son of Leptines (cf. e.g. frs. 96, 105, 131). He saw military action (whether as a mercenary soldier is not clear) and was killed in battle by a Naxian called Calondas (T 141). Most scholars place his date in the first half of the 7th c.: see F. Jacoby, *C.Q.* 35 (1941) 97–109. (Fr. 19 refers to Gyges, king of Lydia *c.* 687–652; in fr. 20 the 'troubles of the Magnesians' are usually associated with the destruction of Magnesia in the late 650s; the total eclipse of the sun mentioned in fr. 122 is most likely to be that of 648.) A. was famous in antiquity for his turbulent way of life and violent attacks on others. His most notorious quarrel was with Lycambes over his daughter Neobule (frs. 30–87, 172–81, 196A). A.'s poems allegedly drove Lycambes and his daughters to suicide (testimonia in *IEG* 1 15 and 63f.). See M. L. West, *Studies in Greek elegy and iambus* (Berlin & New York 1974) 25–8 for a sceptical view of the whole story. A. achieved an outstanding posthumous reputation (testimonia in Tarditi 232–8, discussion in H. D. Rankin, *Archilochus of Paros* (Park Ridge, N.J. 1978) ch. 1, M. Lefkowitz, *The lives of the Greek poets* (London 1981) 25–31) and was venerated as a hero on Paros; a shrine (the Archilocheion) was built in his honour by Mnesiepes in the 3rd c. B.C., with a long inscription recording legends about A. (T 4). In the 1st c. B.C. a further inscription was set up by Sosthenes giving details (based on the work of Demeas) of A.'s doings and writings (T 5).

WORKS

Short poems in a variety of metres: elegiacs, iambic trimeters, trochaic tetrameters, and 'epodes', strophic combinations of long and short lines, usually a hexameter or an iambic trimeter followed by shorter dactylic or iambic cola (see Metrical Appendix). The fragments have been augmented in recent years by papyrus finds, but must still represent a small proportion of A.'s total output.

BIBLIOGRAPHY

(See Treu under *Commentaries* below, 142–9; D. E. Gerber, *C.W.* 61 (1967/8) 274–8 and 70 (1976/7) 84–91.)

TEXTS AND COMMENTARIES: TEXTS: Diehl 1 3, 3rd ed. (1952); G. Tarditi (Rome 1968: with tr.); *IEG* 1 1–108. The Cologne fragment (*P.Col.* inv. 7511 = fr. 196A West): R. Merkelbach and M. L. West, *Z.P.E.* 14 (1974) 97–113; D. L. Page, *SLG* s478, with review by R. Führer, *G.G.A.* 229 (1977) 35–44. COMMENTARIES: T. Hudson-Williams, *Early Greek elegy* (Cardiff 1926); F. Lasserre, with tr. and notes by A. Bonnard (Budé, 1958); M. Treu (Munich 1959: with tr.). Select fragments: D. A. Campbell, *Greek lyric poetry* (London 1967: repr. Bristol 1982); D. E. Gerber, *Euterpe* (Amsterdam 1970); J. M. Bremer, et al., *Some recently found Greek poems* (Leiden 1987).

CALLINUS

TRANSLATIONS: (1) PROSE: J. M. Edmonds, *Elegy and iambus* II (Loeb, 1931).
(2) VERSE: R. Lattimore, *Greek lyrics*, 2nd ed. (Chicago 1960); M. Ayrton (London 1977); G. Davenport, *Archilochos Sappho Alkman* (Berkeley & Los Angeles 1980).
Iambics only: Z. Franyó, B. Snell, H. Maehler, *Frühgriechische Lyriker* II (Berlin 1972); fr. 196A: M. Robertson in H. Lloyd-Jones, *Females of the species* (London 1975) 101 (see pp. 84–5).

STUDIES: F. Lasserre, *Les épodes d'Archiloque* (Paris 1950); *Entretiens X: Archiloque* (Fondation Hardt, Geneva 1964); M. L. West, *Studies in Greek elegy and iambus* (Berlin & New York 1974); H. D. Rankin, *Archilochus of Paros* (Park Ridge, N.J. 1978) with review by M. L. West, *C.R.* n.s.29 (1979) 137; B. Seidensticker, 'Archilochus and Odysseus', *G.R.B.S.* 19 (1978) 5–22; A. P. Burnett, *Three archaic poets. Archilochus, Alcaeus, Sappho* (London 1983). On fr. 196A: R. Merkelbach, *Z.P.E.* 16 (1975) 220–2; M. L. West, *Z.P.E.* 16 (1975) 217–19 and 26 (1977) 44–8. Discussion in *Museum Criticum* 8/9 (1973/4) 1–106, ed. B. Marzullo; *Poetica* 6 (1974) 468–512 (H. Flashar, T. Gelzer, L. Koenen, K. Maurer, W. Theiler, M. L. West); *Arethusa* 9.2 (1976) (J. Van Sickle, D. A. Campbell, J. Henderson, M. R. Lefkowitz, G. Nagy, L. A. Rossi); *Rh.M.* 119 (1976) 97–126 (M. Treu), 242–66 (F. Stoessl), 289–310 (W. Rösler).

CALLINUS

LIFE

From Ephesus, active in mid-7th c. B.C.: according to Strabo (14.1.40, 13.4.8) he mentioned the war between Magnesia and Ephesus (fr. 3; Magnesia was destroyed in the late 650s) and the fall of Sardis in 652 (fr. 5).

WORKS

Of his elegies only one substantial fragment (fr. 1 = twenty-one verses) and a few scraps remain. For bibliography see pp. 214–15 under Mimnermus.

TYRTAEUS

LIFE

Son of Archembrotus, active at Sparta at the time of the second Messenian War (mid-7th c. B.C.). The Suda gives his *floruit* as 640–637. Probably Laconian despite the story first mentioned in Plato (*Laws* 1.629a) that he was of Athenian origin (testimonia in Gentili and Prato under *Texts* below, nos. 43–64). According to Strabo (8.4.10) T. described himself as leading the Spartans as a general (cf. Athen. 14.630f quoting Philochorus), but this may be based on a misinterpretation (see Schmid–Stählin I 1 358 n.2).

WORKS

According to the Suda he wrote 'a constitution [or 'on government'] for the Spartans, exhortations in elegiacs, and war songs, in five books'. The genuine surviving fragments are all in elegiacs: frs. 1–4 come from a poem entitled *Eunomia* 'Good order' on the Spartan constitution; the rest mainly deal with military virtue. There is no evidence that *PMG* 856 and 857 (popular songs on military subjects) were composed by T. For bibliography see below under Mimnermus.

MIMNERMUS

LIFE

From Colophon (Strabo 14.1.4); from Smyrna according to Pausanias (9.29.4), but this could be a mistaken inference from fr. 9.3–6. Active in latter half of 7th c. B.C. (the Suda gives 632–629 as his *floruit*). See M. L. West, *Studies in Greek elegy and iambus* (Berlin & New York 1974) 72–4. Testimonia in Gentili and Prato under *Texts* below.

WORKS

Wrote either two books (Porph. on Hor. *Epist.* 2.2.101) or 'many' (Suda): elegiac collections including a long poem called *Nanno* and a *Smyrneis* on the battle between Smyrna and the Lydians under Gyges. Testimonia on these poems in *IEG* II 81–2, Most of the surviving fragments are from quotations in later authors: M. was much admired in antiquity. Some fragments of iambics are dubiously attributed to him (frs. 24–6).

BIBLIOGRAPHY

(See D. E. Gerber, *C.W.* 61 (1967/8) 265–71 and 70 (1976/7) 72–8; Gentili and Prato under *Texts* below, xiv–xxxi.)

TEXTS AND COMMENTARIES: TEXTS: Diehl I 1, 3rd ed. (1949); *IEG* II 47–50, 81–90, 149–63; B. Gentili and C. Prato, *Poetarum elegiacorum testimonia et fragmenta* (BT, 1979) 1–61. COMMENTARIES: T. Hudson-Williams, *Early Greek elegy* (Cardiff 1926); J. Defradas, *Les élégiaques grecs* (Paris 1962). Select fragments: D. A. Campbell, *Greek lyric poetry* (London 1967: repr. Bristol 1982); D. E. Gerber, *Euterpe* (Amsterdam 1970). Tyrtaeus: C. Prato (Rome 1968).

TRANSLATIONS: (1) PROSE: J. M. Edmonds, *Elegy and iambus* I (Loeb, 1931). (2) VERSE: R. Lattimore, *Greek lyrics*, 2nd ed. (Chicago 1960). Text with German tr.: Z. Franyó, B. Snell, H. Maehler, *Frühgriechische Lyriker* I (Berlin 1971).

STUDIES: C. M. Bowra, *Early Greek elegists* (London 1938: repr. Cambridge 1960); K. J. Dover, 'The poetry of Archilochos', in *Entretiens X: Archiloque* (Fondation Hardt, Geneva 1964) 188–95; H. Fränkel, *Early Greek poetry and philosophy* (New York & London 1975) ch. IV; M. L. West, *Studies in Greek elegy and iambus* (Berlin & New York 1974); E. Degani, *Poeti greci giambici ed elegiaci* (Milan 1977). Mimnermus: S. Szádeczky-Kardoss, *RE* suppl. XI (1968) 935–51.

THEOGNIS

LIFE

Late authorities (Suda etc.) place his *floruit* at various times in the period 552–541 B.C. If he was a citizen of mainland Megara, the social upheavals reflected in his poems may have been those which followed the overthrow of the tyrant Theagenes in that city: this would locate his work in the first half of the late 6th c. But there is no certainty here: West, for example (under *Studies* (1974) below), makes a case for the turbulence preceding the establishment of Theagenes' tyranny, i.e. the second half of the 6th c. According to Plato (*Laws* 630a) he was a citizen of Sicilian Megara. A scholiast on this passage refers to the long-standing controversy and asks: 'Why should he not have been born of this (i.e. mainland) Megara and then have gone to Sicily...and become a citizen of Sicilian Megara?' Most modern scholars have thought this a reasonable suggestion.

WORKS

Some 700 elegiac couplets are attributed to T. in the MSS. These include, however, verses belonging to other poets (Solon, Mimnermus, Tyrtaeus, (?)Euenus), repetitions and near-repetitions, and one passage (773–82) referring to events later than the probable date of T. See pp. 95ff.

BIBLIOGRAPHY

(See D. E. Gerber, *C.W.* 61 (1967/8) 272–4 and 70 (1976/7) 80–4.)

TEXTS AND COMMENTARIES: TEXTS: Harrison (1902) under *Studies* below; D. Young, 2nd ed. (BT, 1771); M. L. West, *IEG* I, 172–241; idem, *Theognidis et Phocylidis fragmenta* (Berlin 1978). COMMENTARIES: T. Hudson-Williams (London 1910); J. Carrière, 2nd ed. (Budé, 1948). Bk I: B. A. van Groningen (Amsterdam 1966). Select fragments: D. A. Campbell, *Greek lyric poetry* (London 1967: repr. Bristol 1982); D. E. Gerber, *Euterpe* (Amsterdam 1970).

TRANSLATIONS: (1) PROSE: J. M. Edmonds, *Elegy and iambus* I (Loeb, 1931). (2) VERSE: R. Lattimore, *Greek lyrics*, 2nd ed. (Chicago 1960: brief selections).

SOLON

STUDIES: E. Harrison, *Studies in Theognis* (Cambridge 1902: incl. text); A. Peretti, *Teognide nella tradizione gnomologica* (Pisa 1953); A. Garzya, *Teognide: Elegie* (Florence 1958); A. R. Burn, *The lyric age of Greece* (London 1960) 247–64; M. L. West, *Studies in Greek elegy and iambus* (Berlin & New York 1974) 40–71, 149–67; H. Fränkel, *Early Greek poetry and philosophy* (New York & London 1975) 401–25; (edd.) T. J. Figueira and G. Nagy, *Theognis of Megara: poetry and the polis* (Baltimore & London 1985).

SOLON

LIFE

b. *c.* 640 B.C., son of Execestides. Prominent in Athens' war with Megara for possession of Salamis, and chief archon of Athens 594/593. Allegedly travelled overseas for ten years after his reforms, returned to Athens and d. sometime after Pisistratus' usurpation of 561. He had already become a semi-mythical figure by the 5th c. B.C. – his meeting with Croesus of Lydia, one of the showpieces of Herodotus' *Histories* (1.29–33), is generally agreed, on chronological grounds alone, to be unhistorical. Plutarch's *Life* preserves the anecdotal tradition and Aristotle's *Constitution of the Athenians* (5–12) gives a late-fourth-century view of S.'s political and economic reforms. (It is also the source of the most important fragments of the poems dealing with his archonship.) See I. M. Linforth, *Solon the Athenian* (Berkeley, Calif. 1919: with text, tr. and comm. of works); K. Freeman, *The life and work of Solon* (London 1926: with tr.); W. J. Woodhouse, *Solon the liberator* (Oxford 1938); A. Masaracchia, *Solone* (Florence 1958); A. Martino, *Solone. Testimonianze sulla vita e l'opera* (Rome 1968: complete collection of the ancient sources); Gentili and Prato under *Texts* below, 61–92 (selected sources).

WORKS

According to Diog. Laert. 1.61 S. wrote 5,000 elegiac verses and also iambics and epodes: there survive 219 lines of elegiacs, some 20 of trochaic tetrameter and some 47 of iambic trimeter. Longest extant poem is fr. 13 (75 lines of elegiacs).

BIBLIOGRAPHY

(See D. E. Gerber, *C.W.* 61 (1967/8) 269 and 70 (1976/7) 78–80; also the works under *Life* above and Gentili and Prato under *Texts* below, xxxi–xxxvii.)

TEXTS AND COMMENTARIES: TEXTS: *IEG* 119–45; B. Gentili and C. Prato, *Poetarum elegiacorum testimonia et fragmenta* (BT, 1979) 93–126. COMMENTARIES: W. Jaeger, *Solons Eunomie, Sitz. Preuss. Ak. Wiss. phil.-hist. Klasse,* 1926; L. Massa Positano, *L'elegia di Solone alle Muse* (Naples 1947). Select fragments: D. A. Campbell, *Greek lyric poetry* (London 1967: repr. Bristol 1982); D. E. Gerber, *Euterpe* (Amsterdam 1970).

SEMONIDES

TRANSLATIONS: (1) PROSE: J. M. Edmonds, *Greek elegy and iambus* I (Loeb, 1931). (2) VERSE: R. Lattimore, *Greek lyrics*, 2nd ed. (Chicago 1960).

STUDIES: R. Lattimore, 'The first elegy of Solon', *A.J.Ph.* 68 (1947) 161ff.; H. Fränkel, *Early Greek poetry and philosophy* (New York & London 1975) 217–37.

SEMONIDES

LIFE

From Samos; led colony to Amorgos (Suda IV 363.1 and IV 360.7 (latter ref. in entry on Simmias of Rhodes, which contains material relevant to S.)). Usually dated to mid- or late 7th c. B.C.; for discussion see Lloyd-Jones under *Commentaries* below, 15–16. His name is regularly spelled Simonides in the ancient sources, but Choeroboscus (*Et.Magn.* 713, 17C) gives the correct spelling.

WORKS

At least two books of iambics, also an 'archaeology [i.e. history] of the Samians' and an elegy in two books (Suda): the two latter may be identical. Some fragments attributed to Simonides of Ceos may belong to S. (see *IEG* II 112). Apart from frs. 1 and 7 very little remains of his work.

BIBLIOGRAPHY

(See D. E. Gerber, *C.W.* 61 (1967/8) 278 and 70 (1976/7) 91–3.)

TEXTS AND COMMENTARIES: TEXTS: Diehl I 3, 3rd ed. (1952); *IEG* II 96–102. COMMENTARIES: Select fragments: D. A. Campbell, *Greek lyric poetry* (London 1967: repr. Bristol 1982); D. E. Gerber, *Euterpe* (Amsterdam 1970); H. Lloyd-Jones, *Females of the species: Semonides on women* (London 1975: with tr.). Fr. 7: W. Marg, *Der Charakter in der Sprache der frühgriechischen Dichtung*, 2nd ed. (Würzburg 1967); W. J. Verdenius, *Mnemosyne* 21 (1968) 132–58.

TRANSLATIONS: (1) PROSE: J. M. Edmonds, *Elegy and iambus* II (Loeb, 1931); Lloyd-Jones under *Commentaries* above. (2) VERSE: R. Lattimore, *Greek lyrics*, 2nd ed. (Chicago 1960).

STUDIES: P. Maas, *RE* IIIA (1929) 184–6; H. Fränkel, *Early Greek poetry and philosophy* (New York & London 1975) 200–7; M. L. West, *Studies in Greek elegy and iambus* (Berlin & New York 1974); E. Degani, *Poeti greci giambici ed elegiaci* (Milan 1977); N. Loraux, *Les enfants d'Athéna* (Paris 1981) ch. 2.

HIPPONAX

LIFE

There is no really reliable information; ancient notices are clearly based on deductions from the texts. According to the Suda he came from Ephesus, but lived in Clazomenae after being expelled by the tyrants Athenagoras and Comas. For story of H. and sculptors Bupalus and Athenis see Pliny, *N.H.* 36.5.11–13; same source gives H.'s *floruit* as 540–537 B.C.

WORKS

Poems in two 'books' (probably the books of the Alexandrian edition): the few remaining fragments contain iambic trimeters (mostly in the choliambic form that H. may have invented), trochaic tetrameters, hexameters and a combination of iambic trimeter with a shorter dactylic line.

BIBLIOGRAPHY

(See D. E. Gerber, *C.W.* 61 (1967/8) 278–9 and 70 (1976/7) 93–4.)

TEXTS AND COMMENTARIES: TEXTS: *IEG* I 109–71; H. Degani (BT 1983). COMMENTARIES: W. de Sousa Madeiros, *Hipponax de Efeso, Fragmentos dos iambos* (Coimbra 1961); O. Masson (Paris 1962); A. Farina (Naples 1963: with Italian tr.); W. de Sousa Madeiros, *Hipponactea* (Coimbra 1969). Select fragments: D. A. Campbell, *Greek lyric poetry* (London 1967: repr. Bristol 1982); D. E. Gerber, *Euterpe* (Amsterdam 1970); E. Degani and G. Burzacchini, *Lirici Greci* (Florence 1977).

TRANSLATIONS: A. D. Knox in *Herodes, Cercidas and the Greek choliambic poets* (Loeb, 1929: with Theophrastus' *Characters* tr. J. M. Edmonds).

STUDIES: M. L. West, *Studies in Greek elegy and iambus* (Berlin & New York 1974) 28–31, 140–9; J. M. Bremer, et al., *Some recently found Greek poems* (Leiden 1987).

ARCHAIC CHORAL LYRIC

GENERAL WORKS

Bowra, C. M., *Greek lyric poetry*, 2nd ed. (Oxford 1961)
Campbell, D. A., *The golden lyre: the themes of the Greek lyric poets* (London 1983)
Färber, H., *Die Lyrik in der Kunsttheorie der Antike* (Munich 1936)
Fatouros, G., *Index verborum zur frühgriechischen Lyrik* (Heidelberg 1966)

Fränkel, H., *Early Greek poetry and philosophy*, tr. M. Hadas and J. Willis (New York & London 1975)

Gentili, B., 'Lirica greca arcaica e tardo-arcaica', in *Introduzione allo studio della cultura classica* (Milan 1972)

idem, 'Storicità della lirica greca', in *Storia e civiltà dei greci* I I (Milan 1978) 383ff.

Johnson, W. R., *The idea of lyric: Lyric modes in ancient and modern poetry* (Berkeley & Los Angeles 1982)

Wilamowitz-Moellendorff, U. von, *Textgeschichte der griechischen Lyriker* (Berlin & Göttingen 1900)

ALCMAN

LIFE

Active probably in late 7th c. B.C. at Sparta, but neither his dates nor birthplace are certain. *Chronology*: three dates for his *floruit*: (1) 631–628 (Suda), synchronized also with reign of Ardys of Lydia (probably *c*. 679–630); (2) 659/8 (Eusebius); (3) 611/10 (Eusebius). The list of Spartan kings in *P.Oxy.* 2390 = fr. 5.2 col. i *PMG* favours the later date: see F. D. Harvey, *J.H.S.* 87 (1967) 69; M. L. West, *C.Q.* n.s.15 (1965) 191f. Older than Stesichorus, b. *c*. 632–629 (Suda s.v. 'Stesichorus'). Activity in last quarter of 7th c. would probably fit most of evidence. See J. A. Davison, 'Notes on Alcman', *From Archilochus to Pindar* (London 1968) 176–9; M. L. West, *C.Q.* n.s.15 (1965) 188–94; P. Janni, *La cultura di Sparta arcaica. Ricerche* I (Rome 1965) 96–120. *Origins*: Laconian from village of Messoa (Suda); Lydian: Ael. *V.H.* 12.50. Lively debate in antiquity as to whether he was Lydian or Laconian by birth: *PMG* 10 and 13 ('Laconian Alcman' and Aristotle's support of Lydian origin, *PMG* 13a). Lydian birth based in part on interpreting fr. 16 *PMG* autobiographically; also *Anth.Pal.* 7.18 ('strife between two continents whether he was Lydian or Laconian'); Vell.Pat. 1.18.2. See also *P.Oxy.* 2802 = *SLG* 85. Said to be a slave of Agesidas, set free because of his extraordinary gifts: Heraclides Ponticus, *Politeiai* fr. 2 = Arist. fr. 611.9 Rose.

See Davison 173–87, West, Janni (cited above) and Page under *Commentaries* below, 164–70.

WORKS

Six books of lyric poems (Suda, confirmed by *P.Oxy.* 3209), plus Κολυμβῶσαι 'Diving women', of unknown contents: see G. L. Huxley, *G.R.B.S.* 5 (1964) 26–8. Placed first in Hellenistic canon of lyric poets. Famous for love-poems, of which only a few fragments survive in quotation. Extant works include substantial fragments of two partheneia or maiden-songs (*PMG* 1 and 3), summary of a cosmogonic poem (*PMG* 5), diverse fragments on mythical subjects, food, local Laconian cults and remote peoples; recently published poem on Odysseus(?) in dactylic metre (*P.Oxy.* 2443 fr. 1 + 3213). Language: local Laconian dialect, with free borrowings from epic diction;

ALCMAN

fondness for rare words, some possibly of Lydian origin. See Page under *Commentaries* below, 102–63; E. Risch, 'Die Sprache Alkmans', *M.H.* 11 (1954) 20–37. Metre: dactylic, trochaic, iambo-trochaic, Aeolic. Generally fairly simple metres. Probably did not use triadic structure in choral odes; see *PMG* 14.

BIBLIOGRAPHY

(See (1936–52) G. M. Kirkwood, *C.W.* 47 (1953) 49; (1952–67) D. E. Gerber, *C.W.* 61 (1967/8) 325–7; (1967–75) idem, *C.W.* 70 (1976) 94–100; also, under *Studies* below, Calame (1977) II 179–86 and Puelma (1977) 53f.)

TEXTS AND COMMENTARIES: TEXTS: D. L. Page, *PMG*; idem, *Lyrica Graeca selecta* (OCT, 1968). COMMENTARIES: D. L. Page, *Alcman, the Partheneion* (Oxford 1951); A. Garzya, *Alcmane, I frammenti* (Naples 1954); G. Perrotta and B. Gentili, *Polinnia* (Rose 1965: does not include *Parthen.* 1); D. A. Campbell, *Greek lyric poetry* (London 1967: rpr. Bristol 1982); D. E. Gerber, *Euterpe* (Amsterdam 1970). New 'Odyssey' fragment: M. L. West, *Z.P.E.* 26 (1977) 38f.; A. L. Brown, *Z.P.E.* 32 (1978) 36–8.

STUDIES: (ed.) R. M. Dawkins, *The sanctuary of Artemis Orthia at Sparta, J.H.S.* suppl. V (1929); B. A. van Groningen, 'The enigma of Alcman's Partheneion', *Mnemosyne* 3.3 (1935/6) 241–61; C. M. Bowra, *Greek lyric poetry*, 2nd ed. (Oxford 1961); M. L. West, 'Three Presocratic cosmogonies', *C.Q.* n.s.13 (1963) 154–76 (154–6 on Alcman); A. P. Burnett, 'The race with the Pleiades', *C.Ph.* 59 (1964) 30–4; B. Marzullo, 'Il primo Partenio di Alcmane', *Philologus* 108 (1964) 174–210; A. F. Garvie, 'A note on the deity of Alcman's Partheneion', *C.Q.* n.s.15 (1965) 185–7; P. Janni, *La cultura di Sparta arcaica. Ricerche*, 2 vols. (Rome 1965–70); M. L. West, 'Alcmanica', *C.Q.* n.s.15 (1965) 188–202; T. G. Rosenmeyer, 'Alcman's Partheneion 1 reconsidered', *G.R.B.S.* 7 (1966) 321–59; F. D. Harvey, 'Oxyrhynchus Papyrus 2390 and early Spartan history', *J.H.S.* 87 (1967) 62–73; C. O. Pavese, 'Alcmane, il Partenio del Louvre', *Q.U.C.C.* 4 (1967) 113–33; M. L. West, 'Alcman and Pythagoras', *C.Q.* n.s.17 (1967) 1–15; J. A. Davison, *From Archilochus to Pindar* (London 1968) 146–95; M. Treu, 'Alkman', *RE* suppl. XI (1968) 19–29; M. F. Galiano, 'Iris Murdoch, Alcman, Safo y la siesta', *E.Clás.* 13 (1969) 97–107; J.-P. Vernant, 'Thétis et le poème cosmogonique d'Alcman', in *Hommages à Marie Delcourt* (Brussels 1970) 38–69, repr. in Vernant and M. Detienne, *Les ruses de l'intelligence: la Métis des Grecs* (Paris 1974) 134–64 (Eng. tr. by Janet Lloyd, *Cunning intelligence in Greek culture and society* (Hassocks 1978)); T. B. L. Webster, *The Greek chorus* (London 1970); M. L. West, 'Melica', *C.Q.* n.s.20 (1970) 205–15; B. Gentili, 'I frr. 39 e 40 P di Alcmane e la poetica della mimesi nella cultura greca arcaica', in *Studi filologici e storici in onore di V. de Falco* (Naples 1971) 59–67; A. Griffiths, 'Alcman's Partheneion: the morning after the night before', *Q.U.C.C.* 14 (1972) 7–30; J. W. Halporn, 'Agido, Hagesichora, and the Chorus', *Antidosis, Festschrift W. Kraus, W.S.* suppl.

220

v (1972) 124–38; P. E. Easterling, 'Alcman 58 and Simonides 37', *P.C.Ph.S.* n.s.20 (1974) 37–43; J. L. Penwill, 'Alcman's cosmogony', *Apeiron* 9 (1974) 3–39; B. Gentili, 'Il Partenio di Alcmane e l'amore omoerotico femminile nei tiasi spartani', *Q.U.C.C.* 22 (1976) 59–67; C. Calame, *Les choeurs de jeunes filles en Grèce archaïque* II, *Alcman* (Rome 1977) 1–55; M. Puelma, 'Die Selbstbeschreibung des Chores in Alkmans grossem Partheneion-Fragment', *M.H.* 34 (1977) 1–55; G. F. Gianotti, 'Le Pleiadi di Alcmane', *R.F.I.C.* 106 (1978) 257–71.

STESICHORUS

LIFE

Dates 632/629–556/553 B.C. (Suda), his death synchronized with that of Simonides (Cic. *Rep.* 2.20, Suda s.v. 'Simonides'). Born or active either at Himera in Sicily (Plato, *Phaedr.* 244a, Arist. *Rhet.* 2.1393b, Glaucus of Rhegium *apud* Plut. *De mus.* 7, Suda) or in Matauros, a Locrian colony of s. Italy (Steph. Byz. s.v. 'Matauros'; cf. Arist. *Rhet.* 2.1395a). Original name Teisias; called Stesichorus because he 'first set up chorus for the lyre' (πρῶτος κιθαρωδίας χορὸν ἔστησεν, Suda); 'Stesichorus' may be a kind of professional name or title. Contemporary of Sappho, Alcaeus and Pittacus (Suda s.v. 'Sappho'). Son of Euphemus (Suda, Plato, *Phaedr.* 244a) (also Euphorbus, Hyetes, Hesiod: Suda). *Marmor Parium* 50 notices arrival of 'Stesichorus' in Greece in 485; idem 73 sets victory at Athens in 370/69; these notices presumably refer to later poets of the same name: cf. M. L. West, *C.Q.* n.s.20 (1970) 206; idem, *C.Q.* n.s.21 (1971) 302–7; J. Vürtheim, *Stesichoros' Fragmente und Biographie* (Leiden 1919) 103–5. Tomb at Himera (Pollux 9.100) or Catane (Pollux 9.7, Phot. s.v. πάντα ὀκτώ, *Anth. Pal.* 7.75, Suda), where 'Stesichorean Gate' was named after him (Suda). His exile from Pallantion in Arcadia to Catane (Suda) was possibly based on mention of Arcadian Pallantion in *Geryoneis* (Paus. 8.3.2 = fr. 182 *PMG*).

See West (1970), (1971) 302–14, Vürtheim 99–112, cited above.

WORKS

Twenty-six books, in Doric dialect (Suda), with ample borrowings from epic diction. Mainly on mythical subjects. Substantial papyrus fragments of *Geryoneis* and a poem of unknown title about the royal house of Thebes. Important fragments also of *Eriphyle, Iliou persis, Nostoi, Oresteia,* two *Palinodes.* Some works were of considerable length and unlikely to be choral: e.g. *Geryoneis* reached at least 1,500 lines. Celebrated as a love-poet (Athen. 13.601a); but the erotic works *Kalyke* and *Rhadine* are perhaps spurious, possibly the work of the 4th-c. Stesichorus. Bucolic themes in *Daphnis* (Ael. *V.H.* 10.18 = fr. 279 *PMG*), but this work too is suspect and may be the work of the 4th-c. Stesichorus: see West (1970) and Vürtheim 73–6, under *Life* above. Said to have written fables on political topics (Arist. *Rhet.* 2.1393b and 1395a)

STESICHORUS

and on popular wisdom (Ael. *N.A.* 17.37, frs. 280, 281 *PMG*), of which the latter is of highly dubious authenticity. Best known for lyrical narrative of epic themes and celebrated for dignity, grandeur and Homeric spirit (*Stesichori graves Camenae*, Hor. *Odes* 4.9.8); cf. Dion. Hal. *Cens. Vet.* 2.7, 'Longinus', *Subl.* 13.3, Quint. 10.1.62. Metre: early form of dactylo-epitrite; preponderance of dactylic metres. See M. Haslam, *Q.U.C.C.* 17 (1974) 9–57; idem, *G.R.B.S.* 19 (1978) 29–57. Said to have developed triadic structure of choral ode, 'the three of Stesichorus', i.e. strophe, antistrophe, epode: Suda s.v. τρία Στησιχόρου; see M. L. West, *C.Q.* n.s.21 (1971) 312f.

BIBLIOGRAPHY

(See (1952–67) D. E. Gerber, *C.W.* 61 (1967/8) 327f.; (1967–75) idem, *C.W.* 70 (1976) 100–5.)

TEXTS AND COMMENTARIES: J. Vürtheim, *Stesichoros' Fragmente und Biographie* (Leiden 1919); D. L. Page, *PMG*; idem, *Lyrica Graeca selecta* (OCT, 1968), with Addenda for *Geryoneis*; idem, *SLG* for *Geryoneis, Iliou persis*. New poem on Theban royal house: *P. Lille* 73, 76, in *Cahiers de recherches de l'institut de papyrologie et d'égyptologie de Lille 4, Études sur l'Égypte et le Soudan ancien:* Publications de l'Université de Lille III (Lille 1977) 287ff. (*P. Lille* 76); C. Meillier, *Z.P.E.* 26 (1977) 1–5 (*P. Lille* 73); P. Parsons, 'The Lille Stesichorus', *Z.P.E.* 26 (1977) 7–36; J. M. Bremer, et al., *Some recently found Greek poems* (Leiden 1987). Select fragments: D. A. Campbell, *Greek lyric poetry* (London 1967: rpr. Bristol 1982); D. E. Gerber, *Euterpe* (Amsterdam 1970).

STUDIES: J. Vürtheim, *Stesichoros' Fragmente und Biographie* (Leiden 1919); G. Vallet, *Rhégion et Zancle*, Bibl. d'Écoles françaises d'Athènes et de Rome CLXXXIX (Paris 1958) 255–86; C. M. Bowra, *Greek lyric poetry*, 2nd ed. (Oxford 1961) 74–129; L. Woodbury, 'Helen and the Palinode', *Phoenix* 21 (1967) 157–76; J. A. Davison, 'Stesichorus and Helen', *From Archilochus to Pindar* (London 1968) 196–225; M. Treu, 'Stesichorus', *RE* suppl. XI (1968) 1253–6; T. B. L. Webster, 'Stesichorus: *Geryoneis*', *Agon* 2 (1968) 1–9; M. I. Davies, 'Thoughts on the *Oresteia* before Aischylos', *B.C.H.* 93 (1969) 215–60; M. Robertson, '*Geryoneis*: Stesichorus and the vase-painters', *C.Q.* n.s.19 (1969) 207–21; M. L. West, 'Stesichorus redivivus', *Z.P.E.* 4 (1969) 135–49; A. Garzya, *La poesia lirica greca nella Magna Grecia*, Le Parole e le Idee XIII (Naples 1970) 9–14; M. L. West, 'Stesichorus', *C.Q.* n.s.21 (1971) 302–14; C. O. Pavese, *Tradizioni e generi poetici della Grecia arcaica* (Rome 1972) 239–46; D. L. Page, 'Stesichorus: the *Geryoneis*', *J.H.S.* 93 (1973) 136–54; B. Gentili, *Gnomon* 48 (1976) 745–8 (review of Page's edd., under *Texts* above); J. Bollack, P. Judet de la Combe, H. Wismann, *La réplique de Jocaste*, Cahiers de Philologie II, avec un supplément, Publications de l'Université de Lille III (Lille 1977); F. Bornmann, 'Zur *Geryoneis* des Stesichorus', *Z.P.E.* 31 (1978) 33–5.

SAPPHO

MONODY

GENERAL WORKS

Bowra, C. M., *Greek lyric poetry*, 2nd ed. (Oxford 1961)
Burn, A. R., *The lyric age of Greece* (London 1960)
Campbell, D. A., *The golden lyre: the themes of the Greek lyric poets* (London 1983)
Degani, E. and Burzacchini, G. *Lirici Greci* (Florence 1977).
Fatouros, G., *Index verborum zur frühgriechischen Lyrik* (Heidelberg 1966)
Fränkel, H., *Early Greek poetry and philosophy*, tr. M. Hadas and J. Willis (New York
   & London 1975 = *Dichtung und Philosophie des frühen Griechentums*, 2nd ed. 1962)
Kirkwood, G. M., *Early Greek monody* (Ithaca & London 1974)
Wilamowitz-Moellendorff, U. von, *Textgeschichte der griechischen Lyriker* (Berlin &
   Göttingen 1900)
idem, *Sappho und Simonides* (Berlin 1913)

SAPPHO

LIFE

b. probably *c.* 630 B.C. in Eresus in Lesbos; apparently lived mainly in Mytilene.
Parents Scamandronymus and Cleis, brothers Charaxus (for whose affair with the
courtesan Rhodopis see Hdt. 2.134), Eurygyus (or Erigyus) and Larichus, husband
Cercylas (?: see p. 203), daughter Cleis. Exiled to Sicily sometime between 604/3
and 596/5. Date of death unknown. Sources (see Campbell under *Texts* below, 2–29):
P. Oxy. 1800 fr. 1 and Suda (biographies; see also Ps.-Ovid, *Her.* 15, esp. for S.'s
legendary association with Phaon and her lover's leap); *Marm. Par.* 36, Euseb.
Chron. Ol. 45.1, Strabo 13.2.3, Athen. 13.598b–599d, Hdt. 2.134 (chronology); Suda,
Strabo *loc. cit.* (birthplace); Max. Tyr. 18.9 (literary rivals).

WORKS

(For testimonia see Campbell under *Texts* below, 28–51.) Suda records nine books of
lyric poems together with epigrams, elegiacs, iambics and monodies (surely another
title for her lyric poems); the elegiacs and iambics do not survive, and the three epigrams attributed to her in *Anth. Pal.* (6.269, 7.489, 505) are almost certainly Hellenistic. Bk 1 contained poems in Sapphic stanzas (schol. metr. on Pind. *Pyth.* 1), Bk 2
'Aeolic dactyls' (Heph. *Ench.* 7.7), and so on: see Page under *Commentaries* below,
318–20. Metres are almost exclusively aeolic, built round choriambs (–∪∪–).

BIBLIOGRAPHY

(See D. E. Gerber, *C.W.* 61 (1967/8) 317–20 and 70 (1976/7) 106–15.)

223

TEXTS AND COMMENTARIES: TEXTS: E. Lobel and D. L. Page, *PLF*; M. Treu, 4th ed. (Munich 1968); D. L. Page, *Lyrica Graeca selecta* (OCT, 1968); E.-M. Voigt, *Sappho et Alcaeus* (Amsterdam 1971); D. L. Page, *SLG* (Oxford 1974) 74–6, 87–102; D. A. Campbell, *Greek Lyric* I (Loeb, 1982). COMMENTARIES: Select fragments: D. L. Page, *Sappho and Alcaeus* (Oxford 1955); D. A. Campbell, *Greek lyric poetry* (London 1967: repr. Bristol 1982); D. E. Gerber, *Euterpe* (Amsterdam 1970).

TRANSLATIONS: Campbell under *Texts* above; selections in R. Lattimore, *Greek lyrics*, 2nd ed. (Chicago 1960); W. Barnstone (New York 1965); S. Q. Groden (Indianapolis 1966).

STUDIES: (1) GENERAL: E. Lobel, Σαπφοῦς μέλη (Oxford 1925); R. Merkelbach, 'Sappho und ihr Kreis', *Philologus* 101 (1957) 1–29; E.-M. Hamm, *Grammatik zu Sappho und Alkaios* (Berlin 1957); A. W. Gomme, 'Interpretations of some poems of Alkaios and Sappho', *J.H.S.* 77 (1957) 255–66, with 78 (1958) 84–6; C. M. Bowra, *Greek lyric poetry*, 2nd ed. (Oxford 1961) 176–240; R. Bagg, 'Love, ceremony and daydream in Sappho's lyrics', *Arion* 3 (1964) 44–82; J. A. Davison, *From Archilochus to Pindar* (London 1968) 226–41; M. Treu, *RE* suppl. XI (1968) 1222–40; M. L. West, 'Burning Sappho', *Maia* 22 (1970) 307–30; H. Saake, *Zur Kunst Sapphos* (Paderborn 1971); idem, *Sapphostudien* (Paderborn 1972); M. R. Lefkowitz, 'Critical stereotypes and the poetry of Sappho', *G.R.B.S.* 14 (1973) 113–23; G. Nagy, 'Phaethon, Sappho's Phaon, and the White Rocks of Leucas', *H.S.C.Ph.* 77 (1973) 137–77; G. M. Kirkwood, *Early Greek monody* (Ithaca & London 1974) 100–49; C. Segal, 'Eros and incantation: Sappho and oral poetry', *Arethusa* 7 (1974) 139–60; A. P. Burnett, *Three archaic poets. Archilochus, Alcaeus, Sappho* (London 1983). (2) INDIVIDUAL POEMS: Fr. 1: G. L. Koniaris, *Philologus* 109 (1965) 30–8; K. Stanley, *G.R.B.S.* 17 (1976) 305–21. Fr. 2: T. McEvilley, *Phoenix* 26 (1972) 323–33. Fr. 16: E. M. Stern, *Mnemosyne* 4.23 (1970) 348–61. Fr. 31 (and Catullus 51): G. Wills, *G.R.B.S.* 8 (1967) 167–97. Fr. 94: T. McEvilley, *Phoenix* 25 (1971) 1–11. Fr. 96: T. McEvilley, *Hermes* 101 (1973) 257–78; C. Carey, *C.Q.* n.s.28 (1978) 366–71. Fr. 976 *PMG*: see under *Studies* (1) above Gomme (1957 and 1958) and Kirkwood (1974) 128, 261.

ALCAEUS

LIFE

b. in Mytilene on Lesbos *c.* 620 B.C. (perhaps as early as 630), apparently of a noble family which unsuccessfully competed for power after the Penthelidae were overthrown. Was too young to help his brothers and Pittacus in deposing Melanchrus 612–609 (fr. 75.7ff.), but old enough to fight against Athenians for Sigeum before 600 (fr. 428: threw away his armour). Allied with Pittacus against Myrsilus, but a fierce critic of Pittacus when he was tyrant 590–580. Exiled on Lesbos more than once, and is known to have gone to Egypt. Date of death unknown (but see ref. to 'grey chest' in fr. 50). Sources (see Campbell under *Texts* below, 206–19): own works *passim*, Suda, *P. Oxy.* 2307, 2506 (biographical material); Euseb. *Chron. Ol.* 45.1 (chronology); Arist. *Pol.* 1285a 35ff., Strabo 13.2.3, Diog. Laert. 1.74–5 (relations with tyrants).

WORKS

(For testimonia see Campbell under *Texts* below, 218–33.) Poems arranged according to subject-matter in at least ten books. One book contained over 1,000 lines (*Ox. Pap.* XXIII 106), and the 800th line of a book is attested (*P. Oxy.* 2295 fr. 4). For editions of Aristophanes and Aristarchus see Hephaestion pp. 73f. Consbruch. Metres mostly aeolic, built round choriambs (–∪∪–).

BIBLIOGRAPHY

(See D. E. Gerber, *C. W.* 61 (1967/68) 317–18, 322–3 and 70 (1976/7) 115–17.)

TEXTS AND COMMENTARIES: TEXTS: E. Lobel and D. L. Page, *PLF*; M. Treu, 2nd ed. (Munich 1963); W. Barner, *Neuere Alkaios-Papyri aus Oxyrhynchos* (Hildesheim 1967); D. L. Page, *Lyrica Graeca selecta* (OCT, 1968); E.-M. Voigt, *Sappho et Alcaeus* (Amsterdam 1971); D. L. Page, *SLG* 77–102; D. A. Campbell, *Greek lyric* 1 (Loeb, 1982). COMMENTARIES: Select fragments: D. L. Page, *Sappho and Alcaeus* (Oxford 1955); D. A. Campbell, *Greek Lyric poetry* (London 1967: repr. Bristol 1982); D. E. Gerber, *Euterpe* (Amsterdam 1970); J. M. Bremer, et al., *Some recently found Greek poems* (Leiden 1987).

TRANSLATIONS: Campbell under *Texts* above; selections in R. Lattimore, *Greek lyrics*, 2nd ed. (Chicago 1960); W. Barnstone, *Greek lyric poetry* (Bloomington, Indiana 1961).

STUDIES: (1) GENERAL: E. Lobel, ʼΑλκαίου μέλη (Oxford 1927); E.-M. Hamm, *Grammatik zu Sappho und Alkaios* (Berlin 1957); A. W. Gomme, 'Interpretations of some poems of Alkaios and Sappho', *J.H.S.* 77 (1957) 255–66; C. M. Bowra, *Greek lyric poetry*, 2nd ed. (Oxford 1961) 130–75; M. Treu, *RE* suppl. XI (1968) 8–19; G. M. Kirkwood, *Early Greek monody* (Ithaca & London 1974) 53–99; A. P. Burnett, *Three archaic poets. Archilochus, Alcaeus, Sappho* (London 1983). (2) INDIVIDUAL POEMS: Fr. 129: A. J. Beattie, *C.R.* n.s.6 (1956) 189–91. Fr. 298: R. Merkelbach, *Z.P.E.* 1 (1967) 81–95; H. Lloyd-Jones, *G.R.B.S.* 9 (1968) 125–39; G. Tarditi, *Q.U.C.C.* 8 (1969) 86–96; R. L. Fowler, *Z.P.E.* 33 (1979) 17–28. Fr. 326: B. Marzullo, *Philologus* 119 (1975) 27–38.

IBYCUS

LIFE

b. at Rhegium, but left the West for the court of Polycrates, tyrant of Samos *c.* 533–
c. 522 (the Suda's dating of his arrival to 564–561 is normally discounted because of
discrepancies with Herodotus 3.39). Date of death unknown; buried at Rhegium.
Sources (see Edmonds under *Translations* below, 78–85): Suda (biography); Euseb.
Chron. Ol. 59.3 (chronology); Diogen. *Paroem.* 1.207 (story that I. might have been
tyrant in Rhegium, had he not left); *Anth. Pal.* 7.714 (burial).

WORKS

Seven books of poetry in the Alexandrian edition. His narrative poetry, almost
completely lost, dealt with such epic themes as the adventures of Heracles, Meleager
and the Argonauts, and the Trojan War and its sequel. For predominance of erotic
themes in his poems see Cic. *Tusc.* 4.71.

BIBLIOGRAPHY

(See D. E. Gerber, *C.W.* 61 (1967/8) 328 and 70 (1976/7) 117–19.)

TEXTS AND COMMENTARIES: TEXTS: D. L. Page, *PMG* 144–69; F.
Mosino (Reggio Calabria 1966); D. L. Page, *Lyrica Graeca selecta* (OCT, 1968) 134–
45; idem, *SLG* 44–73. COMMENTARIES: Select fragments: D. A. Campbell, *Greek lyric
poetry* (London 1967: repr. Bristol 1982); D. E. Gerber, *Euterpe* (Amsterdam 1970).

TRANSLATIONS: J. M. Edmonds, *Lyra Graeca* II (Loeb, 1924); selections in
R. Lattimore, *Greek lyrics*, 2nd ed. (Chicago 1960); W. Barnstone, *Greek lyric poetry*
(Bloomington, Indiana 1961).

STUDIES: D. L. Page, 'Ibycus' poem in honour of Polycrates', *Aegyptus* 31 (1951)
158–72; C. M. Bowra, *Greek lyric poetry*, 2nd ed. (Oxford 1961) 241–67; J. P. Barron,
'The sixth-century tyranny at Samos', *C.Q.* n.s.14 (1964) 210–29; F. Sisti, 'L'ode a
Policrate', *Q.U.C.C.* 4 (1967) 59–79; J. P. Barron, 'Ibycus: to Polycrates', *B.I.C.S.*
16 (1969) 119–49; M. L. West, 'Melica', *C.Q.* n.s.20 (1970) 206–9; M. Robertson,
'Ibycus: Polycrates, Troilus, Polyxena', *B.I.C.S.* 17 (1970) 11–15.

ANACREON

LIFE

b. *c.* 570 B.C. in Teos in Asia Minor. After Persian attack on Greek coastal cities sailed with Teians to Thrace, where they founded Abdera *c.* 540. Invited to court of Polycrates of Samos (ruled *c.* 533–*c.* 522), on whose murder he was brought to Athens by Pisistratus' son Hipparchus. After Hipparchus' assassination in 514 he either remained in Athens or went to Thessaly (cf. frs. 107, 108D). If he did go to Thessaly, he returned to Athens and may have spent much of later life there. d. *c.* 485 B.C. Sources (see Edmonds under *Translations* below, 120–37): Suda (biography); Eusebius, *Chron. Ol.* 61.1, Ps.-Lucian, *Macr.* 26, schol. on Aesch. *P.V.* 128 (chronology); Himerius, *Or.* 28.2, 29.24 Colonna, Strabo 14.1.16, Ael. *V.H.* 9.4, 12.25, Paus. 1.2.3, Hdt. 3.121 (connections with Polycrates); Ps.-Plato, *Hipparch.* 228b–c, Plato, *Charm.* 157e, Himerius, *Or.* 39.11 Colonna (activity at Athens).

WORKS

Only a few complete poems survive. A.'s work was edited by Aristarchus (Hephaestion p. 68.22, 74.11–14 Consbruch), possibly in five books arranged on metrical principles: see Crinagoras, *Anth. Pal.* 9.239. Most of the surviving poems and fragments are in lyric metres, especially anacreontics and glyconics linked with pherecrateans, but he also wrote elegiacs (some are preserved in *Anth. Pal.*) and iambics (388 is the most substantial extant example). He may have written maiden-songs (see Page, *PMG* 500–1).

BIBLIOGRAPHY

(See D. E. Gerber, *C.W.* 61 (1967/8) 323–4 and 70 (1976/7) 119–22.)

TEXTS AND COMMENTARIES: TEXTS: B. Gentili (Rome 1968); D. L. Page, *PMG* 172–235; idem, *Lyrica Graeca selecta* (OCT, 1968) 148–66; idem, *SLG* 103–4. COMMENTARIES: Select fragments: D. A. Campbell, *Greek lyric poetry* (London 1967: repr. Bristol 1982); D. E. Gerber, *Euterpe* (Amsterdam 1970).

TRANSLATIONS: J. M. Edmonds, *Lyra Graeca* II (Loeb, 1924); selections in R. Lattimore, *Greek lyrics*, 2nd ed. (Chicago 1960); W. Barnstone, *Greek lyric poetry* (Bloomington, Indiana 1961).

STUDIES: (1) GENERAL: K. Latte, *Gnomon* 27 (1955) 495–7 (review of *Ox. Pap.* XXII, edd. Lobel and Roberts); B. Gentili, 'I nuovi frammenti papiracei di Anacreonte', *Maia* n.s.8 (1956) 181–96; D. L. Page, *C.R.* n.s.9 (1959) 234–7 (review of Gentili's edition); C. M. Bowra, *Greek lyric poetry*, 2nd ed. (Oxford 1961) 268–307; M. H. da

SKOLIA

Rocha Pereira, 'Anakreon', *Das Altertum* 12 (1966) 84–96; M. Treu, *RE* suppl. XI (1968) 30–7; M. L. West, 'Melica', *C.Q.* n.s.20 (1970) 209–10; G. M. Kirkwood, *Early Greek monody* (Ithaca & London 1974) 150–77. (2) INDIVIDUAL POEMS: Fr. 348: D. Page, in *Studi in onore di L. Castiglioni* (Florence 1960) 661–7. Fr. 358: L. Woodbury, *T.A.Ph.A.* 109 (1979) 277–87 with bibliography. Fr. 388: W. J. Slater, *Phoenix* 32 (1978) 185–94.

SKOLIA

A collection of twenty-five 'Attic skolia' (drinking-songs) is preserved by Athenaeus 15.693f–695f. Majority were completed late 6th or early 5th century in four-line stanzas in Aeolic rhythm. Athenaeus mentions Alcaeus, Anacreon and Praxilla as writers of skolia. See also schol. on Ar. *Wasps* 1216ff.; schol. on Plato, *Gorg.* 451e; Plut. *Quaest. conv.* 1.1.5.

BIBLIOGRAPHY

TEXTS AND COMMENTARIES: TEXTS: D. L. Page, *PMG* 472–8; idem, *Lyrica Graeca selecta* (OCT, 1968) 238–45. COMMENTARIES: Selection in D. A. Campbell, *Greek lyric poetry* (London 1967: repr. Bristol 1982).

TRANSLATIONS: J. M. Edmonds, *Lyra Graeca*, 2nd ed., III (Loeb, 1940) 560–75; selection in R. Lattimore, *Greek lyrics*, 2nd ed. (Chicago 1960).

STUDIES: R. Reitzenstein, *Epigramm und Skolion* (Giessen 1893) 3–44; C. M. Bowra, *Greek lyric poetry*, 2nd ed. (Oxford 1961) 373–97; A. J. Podlecki, 'The political significance of the Athenian 'Tyrannicide'-Cult', *Historia* 15 (1966) 129–41.

CHORAL LYRIC IN THE FIFTH CENTURY
(for *General works* see pp. 218–19)

SIMONIDES

LIFE

b. 557/6 B.C. at Iulis in Ceos. Invited by Hipparchus to Athens before 514. Commissioned by Scopadae in Thessaly and survived collapse of their palace 514. Active in Athens in 490s; defeated Aeschylus in competition for epigram on the fallen at Marathon. Invited to Syracuse *c.* 476 and mediated between Hieron, his host, and

PINDAR

Theron of Acragas. d. in Sicily and buried in Acragas 468. Inventor of a mnemonic technique. Sources: fr. 77 D, Strabo 10.486, Suda (birth and background); fr. 88 D, Ps.-Plato, *Hipparch.* 228c, *Vit. Aesch.* 4, Plut. *Them.* 5, Cic. *Fin.* 2.32.104 (Athens); Call. fr. 71, Cic. *De or.* 2.86.353, schol. on Theocr. *Id.* 16.36f., Simon. fr. 510 P (Thessaly); Ps.-Plato, *Epist.* 2.311a, Athen. 14.656d, Ael. *V.H.* 9.1, Timaeus *apud* schol. on Pind. *Ol.* 2.29d (Sicily); Cic. *De or.* 2.87.357 (mnemonics); *Marm. Par.* 73 (death). See J. M. Edmonds, *Lyra Graeca* II (Loeb, 1924) 246–73.

WORKS

(1) LYRIC: Hymns, paeans, dithyrambs (fr. 79 D commemorates fifty-six victories), encomia, epinicia, dirges (especially famous; see Quint. 10.1.64, Cat. 38.8), skolia (drinking-songs). No complete work survives, and only two fragments exceed twenty-five lines (542–3 *PMG*). (2) ELEGIES AND EPIGRAMS, many of doubtful authenticity.

BIBLIOGRAPHY

(See (1949–68) P. A. Bernardini, *Q.U.C.C.* 8 (1969) 140–68; (1952–75) D. E. Gerber, *C.W.* 61 (1967/8) 328–9 and 70 (1976/7) 122–5.)

TEXTS AND COMMENTARIES: TEXTS: Diehl II (1925) 61–118; *PMG* 238–323 (lyrical frs. only). COMMENTARIES: D. A. Campbell, *Greek lyric poetry* (London 1967: repr. Bristol 1982: selection).

TRANSLATIONS: J. M. Edmonds, *Lyra Graeca* II (Loeb, 1924) 273–417.

STUDIES: U. von Wilamowitz-Moellendorff, *Sappho und Simonides* (Berlin 1913) 137–209; D. L. Page, 'Simonidea', *J.H.S.* 71 (1951) 133–42; A. W. H. Adkins, *Merit and responsibility: a study in Greek values* (Oxford 1960) 165–6, 196–7, 355–9; C. M. Bowra, *Greek lyric poetry*, 2nd ed. (Oxford 1961) 308–72; B. Gentili, 'Studi su Simonide', *Maia* n.s.16 (1964) 278–306; M. Detienne, *Les maîtres de vérité dans la Grèce archaïque* (Paris 1967) 105–23; P. E. Easterling, 'Alcman 58 and Simonides 37', *P.C.Ph.S.* n.s.20 (1974) 37–43; H. Fränkel, *Early Greek poetry and philosophy*, (New York & London 1975) 303–24; J. Svenbro, *La parole et le marbre* (Lund 1976) 141–72.

PINDAR

LIFE

b. 522 or 518 B.C. at Cynoscephalae in Boeotia; member of aristocratic clan of Aegeidae. Trained in Athens (tutor Lasos of Hermione); won dithyrambic victory there 497/6. Secured early commissions for aristocratic families of Thessaly (*Pyth.* 10, 498), Sicily

PINDAR

(*Pyth.* 6 and 12, 490) and Athens (*Pyth.* 7, 486). Fined by Thebes for composing dithyramb for Athens at time of Persian war. Visited courts of Hieron of Syracuse and Theron of Acragas 476. d. in Argos sometime after 446 (latest dated poem *Pyth.* 8), perhaps in 438. Sources: fr. 183 Bo = 193 Sn, *Pyth.* 5.75f. with schol. *ad loc.*, Suda (birth and background); *Vit. Amb.* p. 1.11ff. (training); *P. Oxy.* 2438.9f. (victory); fr. 64 Bo = 76 Sn, *Vit. Ambr.* p. 1.15ff., Isoc. *Antid.* 166, Paus. 1.8.4. (fine); *Ol.* 1–3 (Sicily); *Vit. Metr.* p. 9.21 (death; cf. *Vit. Thom.* p. 7.11f., *P. Oxy.* 2438.6ff.). Ancient *Lives* (*Ambrosiana, Thomana, Metrica*) in Drachmann's ed. of scholia (see below) 1 1–11; see M. Lefkowitz, *The lives of the Greek poets* (London 1981) ch. VI.

WORKS

(1) EXTANT: Four books of epinician *Odes*: *Olympian* (14), *Pythian* (12), *Nemean* (11), *Isthmian* (8: incomplete). *Pyth.* 3 and *Nem.* 11 are not epinicia. *Ol.* 5 may be spurious. (2) LOST OR FRAGMENTARY: One book each of encomia, hymns, paeans, dirges; two each of dithyrambs, hyporchemata (dance-songs), prosodia (processionals); three of partheneia (maiden-songs).

BIBLIOGRAPHY

(See D. E. Gerber, *A bibliography to Pindar, 1513–1966, A. Ph. A.* monographs XXVIII (1969); M. Rico, *Ensayo de bibliografía pindarica*, Manueles y anejos de *Emerita* XXIV (Madrid 1969); E. Thummer, *A.A.H.G.* 11 (1958) 65–88; 19 (1966) 289–322; 27 (1974) 1–34; (1967–75) D. E. Gerber, *C.W.* 70 (1976/7) 132–57).

TEXTS AND COMMENTARIES: TEXTS: C. M. Bowra, 2nd ed. (OCT, 1947); A. Turyn, 2nd ed. (Oxford 1952); B. Snell, 8th ed. rev. H. Maehler (BT, 1987–8). COMMENTARIES: (1) Complete. A. Boeckh (comm. on *Nem.* and *Isth.* by L. Dissen), 2 vols. in 4 (Leipzig 1811–21: with Latin tr.: vol. II 2 repr. Hildesheim 1963); L. R. Farnell, 3 vols. (London 1930–2: with tr.). (2) Individual works. *Ol.* and *Pyth.*: B. L. Gildersleeve, 2nd ed. (New York 1890: repr. Amsterdam 1965). *Nem.*: J. B. Bury (London & New York 1890). *Isth.*: E. Thummer, 2 vols. (Heidelberg 1968–9: with German tr.). (3) Selections. G. Kirkwood (Chico, Calif. 1982); C. Carey, *A commentary on five odes of Pindar* (New York 1981); W. J. Verdenius, 2 vols. (Leiden 1987–8). *Scholia.* A. B. Drachmann, 3 vols. (BT, 1903–27: repr. Amsterdam 1964).

TRANSLATIONS: C. M. Bowra (Harmondsworth, 1969); F. J. Nisetich, *Pindar's victory songs* (Baltimore & London 1980).

STUDIES: (1) GENERAL: U. von Wilamowitz-Moellendorff, *Pindaros* (Berlin 1922); W. Schadewaldt, *Der Aufbau des pindarischen Epinikion* (Halle 1928); G. Norwood, *Pindar* (Berkeley & Los Angeles 1945); F. Schwenn, 'Pindaros', *RE* XX.2 (1950) 1606–97; J. Duchemin, *Pindare, poète et prophète* (Paris 1955); E. L. Bundy, *Studia Pindarica* (Berkeley & Los Angeles 1962); C. M. Bowra, *Pindar* (Oxford 1964); A.

BACCHYLIDES

Köhnken, *Die Funktion des Mythos bei Pindar* (Berlin & New York 1971); J. Peron, *Les images maritimes de Pindare* (Paris 1974); H. Fränkel, *Early Greek poetry and philosophy*, tr. M. Hadas and J. Willis (New York & London 1975) 425–504; G. F. Gianotti, *Per una poetica pindarica* (Turin 1975); K. Crotty, *Song and action: the victory odes of Pindar* (Baltimore & London 1982). (2) INDIVIDUAL WORKS: R. W. B. Burton, *Pindar's Pythian Odes* (Oxford 1962); D. C. Young, *Three odes of Pindar*, *Mnemosyne* suppl. IX (1968: *Pyth.* 3, 11, *Ol.* 7); idem, *Pindar Isthmian 7, Myth and example*, *Mnemosyne* suppl. XV (1971); C. Carey, 'Three myths in Pindar: *Nem.* 4, *Ol.* 9, *Nem.* 3', *Eranos* 78 (1980) 143–62. (3) MISCELLANIES: (edd.) W. C. Calder and J. Stern, *Pindaros und Bakchylides*, Wege der Forschung CXXXIV (Darmstadt 1970). (4) MSS: A. Turyn, *De codicibus Pindaricis* (Cracow 1932); J. Irigoin, *Histoire du texte de Pindare* (Paris 1952).

LEXICON: W. J. Slater (Berlin 1969).

BACCHYLIDES

LIFE

b. *c.* 510 B.C. at Iulis in Ceos; nephew of Simonides, contemporary and rival of Pindar. Early activities unknown. Invited by Hieron to Syracuse mid-470s and celebrated his host's Olympian victory of 468 (*Ode* 3). Exiled from Ceos to Peloponnese, perhaps in 460s (possible date of *Ode* 9 and *Dith.* 20). Composed *Odes* 1 and 2 between 464 and 454, 6 and 7 (latest dated poems) in 452. d. *c.* 450 (despite Euseb. *Chron. Ol.* 87.2). Sources: Suda, *Et. Magn.* 582.20, Strabo 10.486, *Chron. Pasch.* 162b, Euseb. *Chron. Ol.* 78.2, 82.2 (dates and antecedents); Ael. *V.H.* 4.15 (Sicily); Plut. *De exil.* 14.605c–d (exile); schol. on Pind. *Ol.* 2.154ff., *Pyth.* 2.97, 131a, 132c, 163b, 166d, *Nem.* 3.143 (rivalry with Pindar; cf. 'Longinus', *Subl.* 33.5); IG^2 XII 5 608 = Dittenberger SIG^3 1057; *P. Oxy.* 222 (dated poems). See J. M. Edmonds, *Lyra Graeca* III (Loeb, 1927) 80–6; A. Severyns, *Bacchylide. Essai biographique* (Liège & Paris 1933).

WORKS

(1) EXTANT: Substantial papyrus fragments of *Epinicia* and *Dithyrambs*, several between 100 and 200 lines long and virtually complete; two dedicatory epigrams (*Anth. Pal.* 6.53 and 313). Three poems (13, 5, 4) celebrate same victories as odes of Pindar (*Nem.* 5, 485 or 483; *Ol.* 1, 476, *Pyth.* 1, 470). (2) LOST: Hymns, paeans, prosodia (processionals), partheneia (maiden-songs; Ps.-Plut. *De mus.* 17.1136f.), hyporchemata (dance-songs), encomia, erotica.

BIBLIOGRAPHY

(For 1952–75 see D. E. Gerber, *C.W.* 61 (1967/8) 384–6 and 70 (1976/7) 125–30.)

CORINNA

TEXTS AND COMMENTARIES: TEXTS: B. Snell, 10th ed. rev. H. Maehler (BT, 1970: with bibliography and *index verborum*). COMMENTARIES: F. G. Kenyon (London 1897); R. C. Jebb (Cambridge 1905); D. A. Campbell, *Greek lyric poetry* (London 1967: repr. Bristol 1982: selection); H. Maehler, with German tr. (Leiden 1982).

TRANSLATIONS: R. Fagles (New Haven 1961).

STUDIES: A. Körte, 'Bacchylidea', *Hermes* 53 (1918) 113–47; idem, 'Bakchylides', *RE* suppl. IV (1924) 58–67; B. Gentili, *Bacchilide. Studi* (Urbino 1958); A. Parry, 'Introduction' in Fagles under *Translations* above; G. M. Kirkwood, 'The narrative art of Bacchylides', in (ed.) L. Wallach, *The classical tradition: literary and historical studies in honor of Harry Caplan* (Ithaca, N.Y. 1966) 98–114; (edd.) W. M. Calder and J. Stern, *Pindaros und Bakchylides*, Wege der Forschung CXXXIV (Darmstadt 1970); M. Lefkowitz, *The victory ode* (Park Ridge, N.J. 1976); C. Segal, 'Bacchylides reconsidered: epithets and the dynamics of lyric narrative', *Q.U.C.C.* 22 (1976) 99–130; J. Peron, 'Les mythes de Crésus et Méléagre dans les Odes III et V de Bacchylide', *R.E.G.* 91 (1978) 307–39; C. Segal, 'The myth of Bacchylides 17: heroic quest and heroic identity', *Eranos* 77 (1979) 23–37.

CORINNA

LIFE

According to Suda a pupil of Myrtis and contemporary of Pindar, whom she defeated five times, b. in Thebes or Tanagra. Date in 5th c. much contested: not mentioned before second half of 1st c. B.C. (Antipater of Thessalonica, *Anth. Pal.* 9.26), nor in the Alexandrian canon of lyric poets; late authors and scholia add her as a tenth. To Propertius (2.3.19–21) she is *antiqua Corinna*, vaguely associated with Sappho; but Statius (*Silv.* 5.3.156–8) brackets her with Callimachus and Lycophron (though also Sophron): *tenuisque arcana Corinnae*. In fr. 664a *PMG* she criticizes Myrtis for vying with Pindar, but this need not mean she is contemporary with either. The orthography of the longest fragment, the Berlin Papyrus (654 *PMG*; see under *Works*) belongs to the latter part of the 3rd c. B.C. Either C. wrote then or else her poems, if she wrote in the 5th c., were transliterated then into the current spelling. Sources: brief biography in Suda; fr. 655.3 *PMG*, Paus. 9.22.3, Ael. *V.H.* 13.25, Plut. *Glor. Athen.* 4.347f., schol. on Ar. *Ach.* 720 (Tanagran citizenship, relationship to Pindar); schol. on Pind. *proem.* 1.11.20ff. Drachmann, Tzetzes, *Prol. ad Lycophron.* p. 2.3ff. Scheer, *CGF* 35.19.22 (added to canon of lyric poets).

CORINNA

WORKS

Five books (Suda), possibly called ϝεροῖα 'Tales' or 'Narratives' (cf. D. L. Clayman, *C.Q.* n.s.28 (1978) 396f.): frs. 655.ii, 656, 657 *PMG*. Titles of other works on mythical subjects, mainly Boeotian, including *Seven against Thebes*, *Iolaus*, perhaps *Orestes* (690 *PMG*). Main texts: 654 *PMG* (*P. Berol.* 284): two long narrative fragments, one on a singing contest between Helicon and Cithaeron, the other on the daughters of Asopus; 655 *PMG* (*P. Oxy.* 2370): some twenty lines, perhaps from the ϝεροῖα (line 2), a first-person description of her poetry. Dialect: the artificial literary language common to Greek lyric, but with an admixture of Boeotian vernacular. Metres: choriambic dimeter, glyconic, pherecratean, of rather simple type, rather more characteristic of Hellenistic than of archaic style: see Page under *Commentaries* below, 61f., 87f. For other indications of possible later date in prosody see E. Lobel, *Hermes* 65 (1930) 362f.

BIBLIOGRAPHY

(See D. E. Gerber, *C.W.* 61 (1967/8) 329–30 and 70 (1976/7) 130.)

TEXTS AND COMMENTARIES: TEXTS: *PMG*. COMMENTARIES: D. L. Page (London 1953: repr. 1963); D. A. Campbell, *Greek lyric poetry* (London 1967: repr. Bristol 1982) 103–6 and 408–13; D. E. Gerber, *Euterpe* (Amsterdam 1970) 391–400.

STUDIES: U. von Wilamowitz-Moellendorff, *Die Textgeschichte der griechischen Lyriker*, *Abh. Göttingen* phil.-hist. Klasse n.s.4.3 (1900) 21–3; P. Maas, *RE* XI.2 (1922) 1393–7; E. Lobel, 'Corinna', *Hermes* 65 (1930) 356–65; C. M. Bowra, 'The daughters of Asopus', *Problems in Greek poetry* (Oxford 1953) 54–65; D. L. Page, *Corinna* (London 1953: repr. 1963); A. E. Harvey, 'A note on the Berlin papyrus of Corinna', *C.Q.* n.s.5 (1955) 176–80; G. M. Bolling, 'Notes on Corinna', *A.J.Ph.* 77 (1956) 282–7; K. Latte, 'Die Lebenszeit der Korinna', *Eranos* 54 (1956) 57–67; P. Guillon, 'Corinne et les oracles béotiens: la consultation d'Asopus', *B.C.H.* 82 (1958) 47–60; idem, 'À propos de Corinne', *Annales de la Faculté de Lettres d'Aix* 33 (1959) 155–68; C. M. Bowra, *Pindar* (Oxford 1964) 279–81; Lesky 178–80; M. L. West, 'Corinna', *C.Q.* n.s.20 (1970) 277–87; A. Allen and J. Frel, 'A date for Corinna', *C.J.* 68 (1972) 26–30; G. M. Kirkwood, *Early Greek monody* (Ithaca, N.Y. & London 1974) 185–93, 278–80; C. P. Segal, 'Pebbles in golden urns: the date and style of Corinna', *Eranos* 73 (1975) 1–8; D. L. Clayman, 'The meaning of Corinna's ϝεροῖα', *C.Q.* n.s.28 (1978) 396–7; J. Ebert, 'Zu Korinnas Gedicht vom Wettstreit zwischen Helikon und Kithairon', *Z.P.E.* 30 (1978) 5–12.

METRICAL APPENDIX[1]

(1) BASIC PRINCIPLES

(A) STRESSED AND QUANTITATIVE VERSE

In metres familiar to speakers of English, rhythm is measured by the predictable alternation of one or more stressed syllables with one or more unstressed syllables (distinguished by the notation – and ◡, or ´ and ˣ). Consequently, it is word-accent that determines whether or not a word or sequence of words may stand in a certain part of the verse. Thus the word *Hellenic* may occupy the metrical unit represented by the notation ◡–◡ by virtue of the stress imparted to its second syllable in everyday pronunciation. In contrast, the rhythms of classical Greek metres are measured by the predictable alternation of one or more 'heavy' syllables with one or more 'light' syllables (defined below, and distinguished by the notation – and ◡), so that in the construction of Greek verse the factor of primary importance is not word-accent but syllabic 'weight'. Thus the word Ἑλλήνων, although accented in normal speech on the second syllable, consists for metrical purposes of three heavy syllables, and for this reason can only occupy the metrical sequence – – –. Verse constructed upon this principle is conventionally designated *quantitative*: it should be emphasized that this term refers to the quantity (or 'weight') of syllables, and that throughout this account such quantity is described by the term 'heavy' and 'light' to distinguish it from the intrinsic length of vowels; unfortunately, both syllabic weight and vowel-length are still generally denoted by the same symbols, – and ◡.

(B) SYLLABIFICATION

A syllable containing a long vowel or diphthong is heavy (e.g. the first syllables of δῶρον and δοῦλος).

A syllable containing a short vowel is light if it ends with that vowel (e.g. the first syllable of θέρος), but heavy if it ends with a consonant (e.g. the first syllable of θέρμος).

---

[1] References by name only are to bibliography under (4) below.

To decide whether or not a short-vowelled syllable ends with a consonant (and thus to establish its quantity), the following rules should be observed:[1] (i) word-division should be disregarded; (ii) a single consonant between two vowels or diphthongs belongs to the succeeding syllable (thus λέγω → *lĕ–go*; πάθεν ἄλγεα → *pă–thĕ–nal-ge–a*); (iii) of two or more successive consonants, at least one belongs to the pre-ceding syllable (thus λέμμα → *lēm–ma*; φίλτατε ξένων → *phĭl–ta–tēk–se–non*).

Note: the rough breathing does not count as a consonant (except in the case of ῥ, which normally makes the preceding syllable heavy; see West 15–16); 3, ξ and ψ count as two (*zd, ks* and *ps*).

To (iii) there is an important exception. In the case of the combination of a plosive and a liquid or nasal consonant (πβφ, τδθ, κγχ followed by λ or ρ, or by μ or ν), the syllabic division may be made either between the consonants (e.g. πατρός → *pāt–ros*) or before them (e.g. *pă–tros*), resulting in *either* a heavy *or* a light preceding syllable. However, when two such consonants belong to different parts of a compound or to two different words, the division is always made between them, giving a heavy preceding syllable e.g. ἐκλέγω → *ēk–le–go* not *ĕ–kle–go*; ἐκ λόγων → *ēk–lo–gon*, not *ĕ–klo–gon*). Lastly, when, after a short final vowel, these consonants begin the next word, the division is nearly always (except in epic) made before them, giving a light preceding syllable (e.g. ὁ κλεινός → *hŏ–klei–nos*).

See further West 15–18.

(C) ACCENT

The accent of ancient Greek was basically one of pitch (i.e. 'tonal'). It had a negligible influence on the construction of recited verse (though it clearly affected the melody of the spoken line), and in lyric verse was completely subordinate to the requirements of the musical accompaniment. Whether there was also an element of stress in the accentuation of classical Greek (either related to the tonal accent or independent of it), and, if there was, whether it had any significant effect on the construction of recited verse, are matters of debate: see Allen (1973) 274–334, (1974) 120–5, 161–7 (with bibliography 161; see also M. L. West, *Gnomon* 48 (1976) 5–6).

A fundamental change in accentuation took place by gradual stages in later an-tiquity. By the latter part of the 4th c. A.D. the tonal accent had been replaced by a 'dynamic' one: i.e. the accented syllable was no longer differentiated by variation of pitch but by stress. This change was reflected in the structure of verse, which ceased to be quantitative and came to be based on the opposition of stressed and unstressed syllables; see Allen (1974) 119–20, West 162–4.

[1] The resulting division is practical only; for the difficulties involved in an absolute definition of the syllabic unit see Allen (1973), esp. 27–40.

(2) TECHNICAL TERMS

Anceps ('unfixed'): term used to describe a metrical element which may be represented by either a heavy or a light syllable. The final element of many Greek metres is regularly of this nature, but not in certain lyric metres in which there is metrical continuity (*synaphea*) between as well as within lines. In this account the convention is followed of marking final anceps as heavy.

Antistrophe: see *Strophe*.

Aphaeresis: see *Synecphonesis*.

Arsis: see *Thesis*.

Caesura ('cutting') and *diaeresis*: division between words within a verse is traditionally termed *caesura* when occurring inside a foot or metron, and *diaeresis* when occurring at the end of a foot or metron (but cf. M. L. West, *C.Q.* n.s.32 (1982) 292–7). The varied distribution of these plays an important part in avoiding monotony in the construction of verse; in particular, the caesura prevents a succession of words co-extensive with the feet or metra of a line.

Catalexis: the truncation of the final syllable of one colon or metron in relation to another (e.g. the pherecratean is the catalectic form of the glyconic; see under (3b) below).

Contraction: the substitution of one heavy syllable for two light ones.

Correption: see *Elision*.

Crasis: see *Synecphonesis*.

Diaeresis: see *Caesura*.

Elision and *hiatus* ('cleft'): a short final vowel is generally suppressed or *elided* when immediately preceding another vowel. When it is not elided in these circumstances it is said to be in *hiatus*; by the process of *correption* (commonest in early epic and elegy) a long vowel or diphthong in hiatus (either within a word or at word-juncture) may be scanned short to make a light syllable. See further West 10–15.

Epode: (1) A two-line period in which a short line follows a longer line (e.g. Archilochus uses iambic trimeter plus dactylic hemiepes, hexameter plus iambic dimeter etc.). (2) See *Strophe*.

Prodelision: see *Synecphonesis*.

Responsion: see *Strophe*.

Resolution: the substitution of two light syllables for a heavy one.

Strophe: metrical structure used by the dramatists and lyric poets, made up of one or more periods and recurring in the same form either once (when the second strophe is called the *antistrophe*) or more often. *Triadic structure* denotes the scheme in which two strophes (strophe and antistrophe) are followed by a third of different metrical form (*epode*); the scheme may be repeated *ad lib*.

Synaphea: see *Anceps*.

Synecphonesis: the merging into one syllable either of two vowels within a word (e.g. θεός as a monosyllable) or of a final diphthong or long vowel (or ὁ, ἁ, τό, τά) and an initial vowel; when the second word begins with ε (generally ἐστι) this is known as *prodelision* or *aphaeresis* (e.g. ποῦ 'στιν). According to whether or not the synecphonesis is indicated in writing, it is sometimes termed *crasis* (e.g. καὶ ἐγώ→κἀγώ) or *synizesis* (e.g. ᾗ οὐ as a monosyllable).

Synezesis: see *Synecphonesis*.

Thesis and *arsis*: terms used originally to designate those parts of Greek verse accompanied by the setting down and raising of the foot (i.e. the down beat and up beat). Since the terms are now generally used in the opposite of their original meanings, West recommends abandoning them and using substitutes such as *ictus* for the down beat.

Triadic structure: see *Strophe*.

Units of analysis:

Period: metrical structure, sometimes extending over many written lines (e.g. the Sapphic strophe), (i) whose boundaries do not cut into a word, (ii) within which there is metrical continuity (synaphea), and (iii) whose final element is anceps.

Colon: single metrical phrase of not more than about twelve syllables (e.g. the glyconic); generally cola are subdivisions of periods, though some may be used as short periods in themselves.

Metron: the rhythm of some verse is regular enough to be divided into a series of identical or equivalent units known as metra, and the period may be described according to the number of metra it contains (dimeter, trimeter, tetrameter, pentameter, hexameter = metron × 2, 3 etc.).

Foot: metrical unit which is identical with the metron in some types of verse (e.g. dactylic), a division of it in others (e.g. in iambic, trochaic and anapaestic verse there are two feet in each metron).

(3) COMMON METRES

For the sake of simplicity only the most basic characteristics of each metre are given here. For the numerous divergencies regarding anceps, resolution, position of caesura etc., see Dale, Raven and West. The notation used below is basically that of West: – = heavy, or final anceps; ∪ = light; × = anceps; ≅ = usually heavy; ◡ = usually light; ∪∪ = resolvable heavy; ◠◡ = contractible pair of lights).

(a) Stichic verse (constructed by repetition of same metrical line; chiefly intended for recitation or recitative, though some stichic metres were sung)

Iambic tetrameter catalectic:

$$\times \ -\cup-|\ \times\ -\cup-|\times\ -\cup-|\cup--$$

(very common metre of comedy, used mainly for entries and exits of chorus and in contest scenes)

Iambic trimeter:

$$\times -\cup - | \times -\cup - | \times -\cup -$$

(principal metre of dramatic dialogue; used by iambographers as an 'informal' metre for satirical and abusive poetry; used by Archilochus in alternation with a shorter line (hemiepes, iambic dimeter etc.) to form an epode)

Choliambus or scazon:

$$\times -\cup - | \times -\cup - | \times ---$$

(= iambic trimeter with heavy in place of final light; used for satirical and scurrilous poetry (Hipponax, Callimachus, Herodas), for philosophical invèctive (Timon) and for fable (Babrius))

Trochaic tetrameter catalectic:

$$-\cup -\times | -\cup -\times | -\cup -\times | -\cup -$$

(apparently (Arist. *Poet.* 1449a21) the original metre of tragic dialogue, but in extant tragedy (where it is associated with scenes of heightened tension) far less common than the iambic trimeter; very common in comedy, particularly in the epirrhemes of the parabasis (see pp. 358ff.))

Dactylic hexameter:

$$-\cup\cup | -\cup\cup | -\cup\cup | -\cup\cup | -\cup\cup | --$$

(regular metre for epic, pastoral and didactic poetry; also used for oracles, riddles, hymns and laments; occasionally found in drama; used by Archilochus in alternation with a shorter line (hemiepes, iambic dimeter etc.) to form an epode)

Dactylic 'pentameter' (properly = hemiepes × 2):

$$-\cup\cup -\cup\cup - | -\cup\cup -\cup\cup -$$

(almost invariably following the hexameter to form the elegiac couplet, which is regarded as an entity and hence as stichic (or 'distichic'); used for a wide variety of themes (sympotic, military, historical, descriptive, erotic) and the standard metre for epigram)

Anapaestic tetrameter catalectic:

$$\cup\cup -\cup\cup - | \cup\cup -\cup\cup - | \cup\cup -\cup\cup - | \cup\cup --$$

(dignified metre, very common in comic dialogue)

(b) Non-stichic verse (constructed by combination and expansion of different metrical cola and metra; chiefly intended for singing, either solo (monody) or choral, to the accompaniment of music and/or dance)

The principal units may be classified as follows (though n.b. units from different categories are frequently found in combination):

Iambic: based on metron ×‒◡‒; commonest sequences are of dimeters and trimeters; often combined with other cola.

Trochaic: based on metron ‒◡‒×; commonest sequences are of dimeters and trimeters; often combined with other cola.

lekythion:	‒◡‒◡|‒◡‒	(= catalectic dimeter)
ithyphallic:	‒◡‒◡|‒‒	
scazon:	‒◡‒× |‒◡‒× |‒◡‒× |‒‒‒	

Dactylic: based on metron ‒◡◡; commonest sequences are of from two to six metra; often combined with iambics and trochaics.

hemiepes: ‒◡◡‒◡◡‒

Dactylo-epitrite: based on the hemiepes (‒◡◡‒◡◡‒) and cretic (‒◡‒), which may be preceded, separated or followed by an anceps which is normally heavy (epitrite = ‒◡‒‒; for the terminology see West 70); particularly common in Pindar and Bacchylides.

Anapaestic: based on metron ◡◡‒◡◡‒; traditionally a marching metre, and particularly associated with parts of drama where movement takes place on stage; commonest sequence is of dimeters, often ending in a paroemiac (◡◡‒◡◡‒\|◡◡‒‒ = catalectic dimeter).

Dochmiac: based on metron ◡‒‒◡‒; associated with scenes of great excitement; very common in tragedy, rare in comedy except in parodies; commonest sequences are of metra and dimeters; often combined with iambics, cretics and bacchii (= ◡‒‒).

Cretic: based on metron ‒◡‒ or ‒◡◡◡ ('first paeon') or ◡◡◡‒ ('fourth paeon'); common in comedy, rare in tragedy; commonest sequences are of dimeters, trimeters and tetrameters.

Ionic: based on metron ◡◡‒‒ (minor ionic) or ‒‒◡◡ (major ionic); associated with cult, and with the exotic and barbaric; commonest sequences are of dimeters and trimeters; often found in combination with the anacreontic = ◡◡‒◡‒◡‒‒.

Aeolic: term sometimes used to include other cola of asymmetrical length, but here restricted to those containing as a nucleus the choriamb (‒◡◡‒):

glyconic:	× × |‒◡◡‒|◡‒
pherecratean:	× × |‒◡◡‒|‒
telesillean:	× |‒◡◡‒|◡‒
reizianum:	× |‒◡◡‒|‒
hipponactean:	× × |‒◡◡‒|◡‒‒
hagesichorean (or enoplian):	× |‒◡◡‒|◡‒‒
aristophanean:	‒◡◡‒|◡‒‒
dodrans:	‒◡◡‒|◡‒
adonean:	‒◡◡‒|‒

Some Aeolic cola are used as periods in themselves; more often they are used to form longer periods, (i) by combination with other cola (Aeolic or otherwise), (ii) by the

addition of prefix or suffix (e.g. addition of bacchius to glyconic gives the phalaecian =
× × |–⏑⏑–|⏑–⏑––), or (iii) by dactylic or choriambic expansion from within (e.g.
choriambic expansion of glyconic gives the lesser asclepiad = × × |–⏑⏑––⏑⏑–|⏑–).
Two common Aeolic strophes based on Aeolic cola are the Sapphic (= –⏑–× |–⏑⏑–|
⏑–– (three times) plus –⏑⏑–|– = adonean) and the Alcaic (= × –⏑–× |–⏑⏑–|⏑–
(twice) plus × –⏑–× –⏑–– plus –⏑⏑–⏑⏑–|⏑––); for different analyses of these strophes
see West 32–3, Raven 77–9, *OCD* 683.

(4) BIBLIOGRAPHY

Allen, W. S., *Accent and rhythm* (Cambridge 1973)
idem, *Vox Graeca*, 2nd ed. (Cambridge 1974)
Dale, A. M., *The lyric metres of Greek drama*, 2nd ed. (Cambridge 1968)
eadem, *Metrical analyses of tragic choruses*, fasc. I, *B.I.C.S.* suppl. XXI.1 (1971); fasc.
    II, *B.I.C.S.* suppl. XXI.2 (1981)
Maas, P., *Greek metre*, tr. H. Lloyd-Jones (Oxford 1962)
Raven, D. S., *Greek metre*, 2nd ed. (London 1968)
Sommerstein, A. H., *The sound pattern of ancient Greek* (Oxford 1973)
West, M. L., *Greek metre* (Oxford 1982)
White, J. W., *The verse of Greek comedy* (London 1912)
Wilamowitz-Moellendorff, U. von, *Griechische Verskunst* (Berlin 1921)

WORKS CITED IN THE TEXT

Adkins, A. W. H. (1960). *Merit and responsibility*. Oxford.
Adrados, F. R. (1978). 'Propuestas para una nueva edición et interpretación de Estesícoro', *Emerita* 46: 251–99.
Allen, T. W. (1912). *Homeri opera* v. OCT.
Allen, T. W., Halliday, W. R. and Sikes, E. E. (1936). *The Homeric Hymns*. Oxford.
Andrewes, A. (1956). *The Greek tyrants*. London.
Boegehold, A. L. (1963). 'Toward a study of Greek voting procedure', *Hesperia* 32: 366–74.
Bollack, J., Judet de la Combe, P. and Wismann, H. (1977). *La réplique de Jocaste, Cahiers de Philologie*, II, *avec un supplément*, Publications de l'Université de Lille III. Lille.
Bolling, G. M. (1956). 'Notes on Corinna', *A.J.Ph.* 77: 282–7.
Bowra, C. M. (1964). *Pindar*. Oxford.
Brillante, C., Cantilena, M. and Pavese, C. O. (1981). (edd.). *I poemi epici rapsodici non omerici e la tradizione orale*. Padua.
Brown, A. L. (1978). 'Alkman, P. Oxy. 2443 Fr. 1 and 3213', *Z.P.E.* 32: 36–8.
Bundy, E. L. (1962). *Studia pindarica*. Univ. of Calif. Studies in Classical Philology XVIII.1 and 2. Berkeley & Los Angeles.
Burkert, W. (1977). 'Le mythe de Géryon: perspectives préhistoriques et tradition rituelle', in B. Gentili and G. Paioni (ed.), *Il Mito Greco, Atti del Convegno Internazionale* (Urbino 7–12 maggio 1973) 273–83. Rome.
Burnett, A. P. (1964). 'The race with the Pleiades', *C.Ph.* 59: 30–4.
Calame, C. (1977). *Les choeurs de jeunes filles en Grèce archaïque*, II, *Alcman*. Rome.
Campbell, D. A. (1967). *Greek lyric poetry*. London & New York.
Cook, R. M. (1937). 'The date of the Hesiodic *Shield*', *C.Q.* 31: 204–14.
Davies, M. I. (1969). 'Thoughts on the Oresteia before Aischylos', *B.C.H.* 93: 214–60.
Davison, J. A. (1968). *From Archilochus to Pindar*. London. (= *Phoenix* 16 (1962) 219–22)
Dawe, R. D. (1972). 'Stesichorus, frag. 207 P', *P.C.Ph.S.* n.s. 18: 28–30.
Dawkins, R. M. (1929). (ed.). 'The Sanctuary of Artemis Orthia at Sparta', *J.H.S.* suppl. v. London.
Dawson, C. M. (1966). '*Spoudaiogeloion*: random thoughts on occasional poems', *Y.Cl.S.* 19: 39–76.
Detienne, M. (1967). *Les maîtres de vérité dans la Grèce archaïque*. Paris.
Devereux, G. (1976). *Dreams in Greek tragedy*. Oxford.
Dickie, Matthew (1978). 'The argument and form of Simonides 542 *PMG*', *H.S.C.Ph.* 82: 21–33.

Dover, K. J. (1964). 'The poetry of Archilochos', in *Entretiens Hardt* 10: 181–212. Geneva.

Easterling, P. E. (1974). 'Alcman 58 and Simonides 37', *P.C.Ph.S.* n.s. 20: 37–43.

Ebert, J. (1978). 'Zu Corinnas Gedicht vom Wettstreit zwischen Helikon und Kithairon', *Z.P.E.* 30: 5–12.

Edwards, G. P. (1971). *The language of Hesiod.* Publications of the Philological Society XXII. Oxford.

Else, G. F. (1965). *The origin and early form of Greek tragedy.* Cambridge, Mass.

Fenik, B. C. (1968). *Typical battle scenes in the Iliad. Hermes* Einzelschriften XXI.

Finley, M. I. (1956). *The world of Odysseus.* London. (2nd ed. London 1977.)

Forrest, W. G. (1968). *A history of Sparta, 950–192 B.C.* London.

Fränkel, H. (1961). 'Schrullen in den Scholien zu Pindars Nemeen 7 und Olympien 3', *Hermes* 83: 385–97.

(1962). *Dichtung und Philosophie des frühen Griechentums.* 2nd ed. (Engl. tr. as Fränkel 1975.)

(1975). *Early Greek poetry and philosophy.* New York & London. (Tr. of Fränkel 1962.)

Galinsky, G. K. (1969). *Aeneas, Sicily, and Rome.* Princeton, N.J.

Garrod, H. W. (1920). 'The hyporcheme of Pratinas', *C.R.* 34: 129–36.

Garvie, A. F. (1965). 'A note on the deity of Alcman's Partheneion', *C.Q.* n.s. 15: 185–7.

Garzya, A. (1954). *Alcmane. I frammenti.* Naples.

Gentili, B. (1958). *Bacchilide. Studi.* Urbino.

(1971). 'I frr. 39 e 40 di Alcmane e la poetica della mimesi nella cultura greca arcaica', in *Studi filologici e storici in onore de V. de Falco,* 59–67. Naples.

(1972). 'Lirica greca arcaica e tardo-arcaica', in *Introduzione allo studio della cultura classica.* Milan.

(1976). Review of D. Page, *PMG, LGS, SLG,* in *Gnomon* 48: 740–51.

Gerber, D. E. (1967/8). 'A survey of publications on Greek lyric poetry since 1952, III', *C.W.* 61: 373–85.

(1970). *Euterpe, an anthology of early Greek lyric and iambic poetry.* Amsterdam.

(1975/6). 'Studies in Greek lyric poetry: 1967–75', *C.W.* 70: 66–154.

Gianotti, G. F. (1975). *Per una poetica pindarica.* Torino.

(1978). 'Le Pleiadi di Alcmane', *R.F.I.C.* 106: 257–71.

Gomme, A. W. (1957). 'Interpretations of some poems of Alkaios and Sappho', *J.H.S.* 77: 255–66.

Gostoli, A. (1978). 'Some aspects of the Theban myth in the Lille Stesichorus', *G.R.B.S.* 19: 23–7.

Griffin, J. (1977). 'The Epic Cycle and the uniqueness of Homer'. *J.H.S.* 97: 39–53.
(1980). *Homer on life and death.* Oxford.

Griffith, J. G. (1968). 'Early lyric poetry', in *FYAT,* ch. 2. Oxford.

Griffiths, A. (1972). 'Alcman's Partheneion: The morning after the night before', *Q.U.C.C.* 14: 7–30.

Guillon, P. (1958). 'Corinne et les oracles béotiens: la consultation d'Asopos', *B.C.H.* 82: 47–60.

Halporn, J. W. (1972). 'Agido, Hagesichora, and the chorus (Alcman 1.27ff. PMG)', *Antidosis, Festschrift für Walter Kraus, W.S.* Beiheft v 125–38.

Hamilton, R. (1974). *Epinikion.* The Hague.

Hamm, E.-M. (1958). *Grammatik zu Sappho und Alkaios.* Berlin.

Harvey, F. D. (1967). 'Oxyrhynchus Papyrus 2390 and early Spartan history', *J.H.S.* 93: 62–73.

Haslam, M. W. (1974). 'Stesichorean meter', *Q.U.C.C.* 17: 9–57.

(1978). 'The versification of the new Stesichorus (P. Lille 76 abc)', *G.R.B.S.* 19: 29–57.

Heubeck, A. (1979). *Schrift* in *Archaeologia Homerica* III, ch. X. Göttingen.

Hodgart, M. (1969). *Satire*. London.

Horrocks, G. C. (1981). *Space and time in Homer*. New York.

Huxley, G. L. (1962). *Early Sparta*. London.

(1964). 'Studies in early Greek poets II: Alcman's *Kolymbōsai*', *G.R.B.S.* 5: 26–8.

Jacoby, F. (1941). 'The date of Archilochus', *C.Q.* 35: 97–109.

(1956). *Griechische Historiker*. Stuttgart.

Janko, R. (1982). *Homer, Hesiod, and the Hymns*. Cambridge.

Janni, P. (1965, 1970). *La cultura di Sparta arcaica. Ricerche* I, II. Rome.

Kirk, G. S. (1962). *The songs of Homer*. Cambridge.

(1976). *Homer and the oral tradition*. Cambridge.

(1977). In *Archilochos* by Michael Ayrton. London.

Kirkwood, G. M. (1953/4). 'A survey of recent publications concerning Classical Greek lyric poetry', *C.W.* 47: 51–4.

(1974). *Early Greek monody*. Cornell Studies in Classical Philology XXXVII. Ithaca & London.

Köhnken, A. (1971). *Die Funktion des Mythos bei Pindar*. Berlin & New York.

Labarbe, J. (1948). *L'Homère de Platon* (= Bibliothèque de la Faculté de Philos. et Lettres de l'Université de Liège, fasc. CXVII).

Lasserre, F. and Bonnard, A. (1958). *Archiloque, Fragments*. Paris.

Lefkowitz, M. R. (1968). 'Bacchylides' *Ode* 5: imitation and originality', *H.S.C.Ph.* 73: 45–96.

(1975a). 'The influential fictions in the scholia to Pindar's *Pythian* 8', *C.Ph.* 70: 173–85.

(1975b). 'Pindar's Lives', in *Classica et Iberica*, a Festschrift in Honor of the Rev. J. M. F. Marique, S.J., ed. P. T. Brannan, S.J., Institute for Early Christian Iberian Studies (Worcester, Mass.), 71–93.

(1978). 'The poet as hero: fifth-century autobiography and subsequent biographical fiction', *C.Q.* n.s. 28: 459–69.

Lloyd-Jones, H. (1966). 'Problems of early Greek tragedy', in *Estudios sobre la tragedia griega, Cuadernos de la Fundación Pastor* XIII 11–33.

(1971). *The justice of Zeus*. Berkeley & Los Angeles.

(1973). 'Modern interpretation of Pindar: the Second Pythian and Seventh Nemean Odes', *J.H.S* 93: 109–37.

(1975). *Females of the species: Semonides on women*. London.

Lobel, E. (1925). Σαπφοῦς μέλη. Oxford.

(1927). Ἀλκαίου μέλη. Oxford.

McKay, K. J. (1974). 'Alkman Fr. 107 Page', *Mnemosyne* 4.27: 413–14.

Marzullo, B. (1964). 'Il primo Partenio di Alcmane', *Philologus* 108: 174–210.

Mazon, P. (1948). (ed.) *Introduction à l'Iliade*. Budé. Paris.

Merkelbach, R. (1974). 'Epilog des einen der Herausgeber', in R. Merkelbach and M. West, 'Ein Archilochos-Papyrus', *Z.P.E.* 14: 97–113.

Nagy, G. (1973). 'On the death of Actaeon', *H.S.C.Ph.* 77: 179–80.

Norwood, G. (1945). *Pindar*. Berkeley & Los Angeles.

WORKS CITED IN THE TEXT

Page, D. L. (1951a). *Alcman: The Partheneion*. Oxford.

(1951*b*). 'Simonidea', *J.H.S.* 71: 133–42.

(1955). *Sappho and Alcaeus*. Oxford.

(1956). 'Greek verses from the eighth century B.C.', *C.R.* n.s. 6: 95–7.

(1959). *History and the Homeric Iliad*. Berkeley & Los Angeles.

(1964). 'Archilochus and the oral tradition', in *Entretiens Hardt* 10: 117–63. Geneva.

(1973a). 'Stesichorus: The Geryoneis', *J.H.S.* 93: 136–54.

(1973*b*). 'Stesichorus: The "Sack of Troy" and "The Wooden Horse" (P. Oxy. 2169 and 2803)', *P.C.Ph.S.* n.s. 19: 47–65.

Panofsky, D. and E. (1962). *Pandora's box*. 2nd ed. Princeton, N.J.

Parsons, P. J. (1977), 'The Lille "Stesichorus"', *Z.P.E.* 26: 7–36.

Pavese, C. O. (1967). 'Alcmane, il Partenio del Louvre', *Q.U.C.C.* 4: 113–33.

(1972). *Tradizione e generi poetici della Grecia arcaica*. Rome.

Penwill, J. L. (1974). 'Alcman's Cosmogony', *Apeiron* 8: 13–39.

Perrotta, G. and Gentili, B. (1965). *Polinnia*. Messina & Florence.

Podlecki, A. J. (1971). 'Stesichoreia', *Athenaeum* 49: 313–27.

Pouilloux, J. (1964). 'Archiloque et Thasos: histoire et poésie', in *Entretiens Hardt* 10: 1–27. Geneva.

Privitera, G. A. (1965). *Laso di Ermione nella cultura ateniese e nella tradizione storiografica*. Rome.

Puelma, M. (1977). 'Die Selbstbeschreibung des Chores in Alkmans grossem Partheneion-Fragment', *M.H.* 34: 1–55.

Richardson, N. J. (1974). *The Homeric Hymn to Demeter*. Oxford.

Robertson, M. (1969). 'Geryoneis: Stesichorus and the vase-painters', *C.Q.* n.s. 19: 207–21.

Rose, H. J. (1932). 'Stesichorus and the Rhadine-Fragment', *C.Q.* 26: 88–92.

Rosenmeyer, T. G. (1966). 'Alcman's *Partheneion I* reconsidered', *G.R.B.S.* 7: 321–59.

Schadewaldt, W. (1928). *Der Aufbau des Pindarischen Epinikion*. Schriften der Königsberger Gelehrten Gesellschaft. Geisteswiss. Klasse v.3. Halle.

Schlesinger, E. (1968). 'Zu Pindar, Pyth. 12', *Hermes* 96: 275–86.

Segal, C. P. (1975). 'Pebbles in golden urns: the date and style of Corinna', *Eranos* 63: 1–8.

(1976). 'Bacchylides reconsidered: epithets and the dynamics of lyric narrative', *Q.U.C.C.* 22: 99–130.

(1977). 'The myth of Bacchylides 17: heroic quest and heroic identity', *Eranos* 74: 23–37.

Seidensticker, B. (1978). 'Archilochus and Odysseus', *G.R.B.S.* 19: 5–22.

Severyns, A. (1933). *Bacchylide, Essai biographique*. Liège & Paris.

(1963). *Recherches sur la Chrestomathie de Proclos* IV (= Bibliothèque de la Faculté de Philos. et Lettres de l'Université de Liège, fasc. 170).

Sisti, F. (1965). 'Le due Palinodie di Stesicoro', *Stud. Urb.* 39: 303–13.

Smith, A. H. (1898). 'Illustrations to Bacchylides', *J.H.S.* 18: 267–80.

Smyth, H. W. (1900). *The Greek melic poets*. London.

Snell, B. and Maehler, H. (1975). *Pindari carmina cum fragmentis*. BT. Leipzig & Stuttgart.

Stern, J. (1967). 'The structure of Bacchylides' Ode 17', *R.B.Ph.* 45: 40–7.

Svoboda, K. (1952). 'Les idées de Pindare sur la poésie', *Aegyptus* 32: 108–20.

Tarditi, G. (1968). *Archiloco*. Rome.

Thayer, H. S. (1975). 'Plato's quarrel with poetry: Simonides', *J.H.I.* 36: 3–26.

Thummer, E. (1968–9). *Pindar, Die Isthmischen Gedichte*. 2 vols. Heidelberg.

Tigerstedt, E. N. (1965). *The legend of Sparta in classical antiquity*. Lund.

Treu, M. (1968a). 'Alkman', *RE* suppl. XI 19–29.

  (1968b). 'Stesichoros', *RE* suppl. XI 1253–6.

Vallet, G. (1958). *Rhégion et Zancle*. Bibl. d'Écoles françaises d' Athènes et de Rome CLXXXIX. Paris.

Van Groningen, B. A. (1935/6). 'The enigma of Alcman's Partheneion', *Mnemosyne* ser. III, 3: 241–61.

Vernant, J.-P. (1980). *Myth and society in ancient Greece*, tr. J. Lloyd. Brighton.

Vernant, J.-P. and Detienne, M. (1974). *Les ruses de l'intelligence. La métis chez les grecs.* Paris. (Engl. tr. *Cunning intelligence in Greek culture and society* (1978) Hassocks.)

Voigt, E.-M. (1971). *Sappho et Alcaeus*. Amsterdam.

Vürtheim, J. (1919). *Stesichoros' Fragmente und Biographie*. Leiden.

Wace, A. J. B. and Stubbings, F. H. (1962). (edd.). *A companion to Homer*. London.

Wade-Gery, H. T. (1952). *The poet of the Iliad*. Cambridge.

Webster, T. B. L. (1968). 'Stesichoros: Geryoneis', *Agon* 2: 1–9.

  (1970). *The Greek chorus*. London.

West, M. L. (1963). 'Three Presocratic cosmologies', *C.Q.* n.s. 13: 154–76 (154–6 on Alcman).

  (1965). 'Alcmanica', *C.Q.* n.s. 15: 188–202.

  (1966). *Hesiod, Theogony*. Oxford.

  (1967). 'Alcman and Pythagoras', *C.Q.* n.s. 17: 1–15.

  (1969). 'Stesichorus Redivivus', *Z.P.E.* 4: 135–49.

  (1970a). 'Melica', *C.Q.* n.s. 20: 205–15.

  (1970b). 'Corinna', *C.Q.* n.s. 20: 277–87.

  (1971a). 'Stesichorus', *C.Q.* n.s. 21: 302–14.

  (1971b). 'Further light on Stesichorus' Iliu Persis', *Z.P.E.* 7: 262–4.

  (1974). *Studies in early Greek elegy and iambus*. Berlin & New York.

  (1975). 'Cynaethus' Hymn to Apollo', *C.Q.* n.s. 25: 161ff.

  (1977). 'Notes on Papyri', *Z.P.E.* 26: 38–9.

  (1978a). (ed.). *Hesiod, Works and days*. Oxford.

  (1978b). *Theognidis et Phocylidis fragmenta*. Berlin.

Wilamowitz-Moellendorff, U. von (1903). *Timotheos: Die Perser*. Leipzig.

Wind, R. (1971–2). 'Bacchylides and Pindar: A question of imitation', *C.J.* 67: 9–13.

Wolke, H. (1978). *Untersuchungen zur Batrachomyomachia*. Meisenheim am Glan.

Woodbury, L. E. (1967). 'Helen and the Palinode', *Phoenix* 21: 157–76.

  (1979a). 'Gold hair and grey, or the game of love: Anacreon fr. 13: 358 *PMG*, 13 Gentili', *T.A.Ph.A.* 109: 277–87.

  (1979b). 'Neoptolemus at Delphi: Pindar, *Nemean* 7.30ff.', *Phoenix* 33: 95–133.

Young, D. C. (1964). 'Pindaric criticism', *Minnesota Review* IV 584–641; repr. in W. M. Calder III and J. Stern, edd. (1970) *Pindaros und Bakchylides*, 1–95. Darmstadt.

Zuntz, G. (1971). *Persephone*. Oxford.

INDEX

Main references are distinguished by figures in bold type. Main references to the Appendix (which should normally be consulted for basic details of authors' lives and works, and for bibliographies) are given in italic figures.

Aelian (Claudius Aelianus): on Stesichorus, 151 & n. 6, 221–2; cited, 127, 145, 177 n. 2

Aeschylus: works: *Oresteia*, 155–6; (*Agamemnon*), 66, 150 reputation, influence and popularity, 1, 175; and Simonides, 228; and Tynnichus of Chalcis, 181

Aesop, 115, 151

Aethiopis, 66, 209

Agias (Hegias?) of Trozen, epic poet, 209

Alcaeus, 161, **168–73**, 181, *224–5*; Alcaic stanza, 172; and Anacreon, 177, 178; audiences for, 173; Bacchylides and, 195; choral works, 125; on friendship, 180; on Helen, 150; and Hesiod, 64 n. 1, 115; Homeric language, 149; love songs, 172–3; skolia, 179, 228; and Stesichorus, 145; use of dialect, 128

Alcibiades, Euripides' epinikion for, 201

Alcman, 89, **127–44**, *219–21*; and choral lyric, 124; composing for local festivals, 182; and dance, 125; horse imagery, 176; Laconian dialect, 125; monodic poems, 125; and Stesichorus, 145; on *Tekmor* and *Poros*, 55, 138; theological and cosmological speculation, 138–9

Alexandria, Library, Museum and scholarship at, 205; subjects of study: Alcaeus, 172; Archilochus, 87; biography, 195; canon of poets, 199; Corinna, 199; epics, 68; Hipponax, 117, 218; Homer, 1, 70; Ibycus, 226; lyric poets, 232; Sappho, 162; Theognis, 117; *see also under individual authors*

Ameipsias, comic poet, *Sappho*, 162 n. 1

Anacreon of Teos, 125 n. 2, 133, 136, 161, 173, **175–9**, 181, *227–8*

Anaximander, 138

Antigonus of Carystus, 70

Apollodorus of Athens, scholar, cited, 129 n. 2, 194 n. 1

Apollonius Rhodius: and Eumelus, 67; scholia on, 67

Archilochus of Paros, **76–87**, *211–13*; and Callinus, 88; dithyrambs and paeans of, 125; emperor Julian on, 117; and Homer, 88, 117, 149; invective of, 82–6; life and career, 76–7, *211–12*; and literacy, 4, 64, 87; metres, 79, 87, 88, 92, 110, 112, 118, 238; and monody, 161; personae, 77–8, 80, 86; and sack of Cimmerians, 88; and Semonides, 115; social and political aspects, 80–1; as soldier, 80; style, 78–87 *passim*

Arctinus of Miletus, 204, 209

Arion of Methymna, 127, 141, 161

Aristarchus of Samothrace, scholar, 205, 225, 227

Aristeas of Proconnesus, poet, *Arimaspeia*, 142

Aristophanes: works: *Frogs*, 202; *Wasps*, 179, 180; lost or fragmentary, 179, 201; character of drama: chorus and lyric, 128; language, 176; literary allusion and parody, 201; (Euripides), 202

Aristophanes of Byzantium, 225

Aristotle: works: *Constitution of Athens*, 216; *Poetics*, 238; *Politics*, 225 philosophy and opinions: on Archilochus,

INDEX

INDEX

Ibycus of Rhegium, 125 n. 2, 133, 144, 151, 161, **173–5**, 177, 181, *226*
Iliad, Little, 66, 209
Iliou persis, 66, 209
Instructions of Ninurta, 60
Instructions of Suruppak, 60
Ion of Chios, 96, 201
Ionian philosophy, 55
Ionic dialect, 110, 117, 120, 128, 145, 161, 204
Isocrates: cited, 99 (Theognis), 150 (blindness of Stesichorus), 186 (Pindar)

Julian, emperor, 117
Juvenal, on women, 114

Lasus of Hermione, poet, 181, 229
Lesbian poets, 117, 150, 161, 177; *see also* Alcaeus, Arion, Sappho, Terpander
Lesches of Mytilene, epic poet, 209
Library of Alexandria, *see under* Alexandria
Licymnius of Chios, dithyrambic poet and rhetor, 202
Linear B, 5, 7
Little Iliad, see *Iliad, Little*
'Longinus', judgements, 10, 204 (*Odyssey*), 147, 160, 222 (Stesichorus), 164–5 (Sappho), 184 (Simonides and Sophocles), 186, 194 (Pindar), 194 (Bacchylides)
Lucian of Samosata, on Semonides' *bête noire*, 113; Ps. Lucian, 227
Lycophron, 150 n. 1
Lycurgus, orator, 91

Margites, 68–9, 204
Marmor Parium, 146, 151, 221, 223
Maximus of Tyre, 175, 223
Melanippides, dithyrambic poet, 201, 202
Menander, 1
Milesian philosophy, 138; *see also names of philosophers*
Mimnermus, 87, 93–5, 96, 112, 115–16, 117, *214–15*, 215
Mnesiepes, inscription of, 76
Museum, *see under* Alexandria
Myrtis of Anthedon, Boeotian poetess, 198, 200

Nostoi, 66, 209

Oedipodeia, 65 n. 1, 209
Olen of Lydia, writer of hymns, 127

Olympus of Phrygia, inventor of musical scale, 127
Onitadai, professional chorus, 124 n. 1
Ovid, 223

Palatine Anthology, see Greek Anthology
Pamphos of Lycia, writer of hymns, 127
Panyassis of Halicarnassus, 68, *209*
Parian Chronicle, *see Marmor Parium*
Pausanias, citations, remarks, etc., 53, 59, 207 (Hesiod), 67 (*Corinthiaca*), 74 (temple of Trophonius and Agamedes), 118 (Bupalus), 128 (Alcman), 129 n. 2 (Heracles and Spartan kingship), 154 (Pallanteum), 156 (Iphigenia), 166 (Sappho), 172 (Alcaeus), 199, 200 (painting of Corinna and Pindar)
Peisander of Rhodes, epic poet, 68
Pergamum, 1
Petronius, Hipponax as model, 122
Pherecrates, comic poet, 201
Philochorus of Athens, Atthidographer, 213
Philoxenus of Cythera, dithyrambic poet, 201, 202
Photius, 221
Phrynis, poet and musician, 201
Pindar, 181, 182, **185–94**, 201, 202, 203
  works, 186, *229–31*; *Olympians*, (1), 186, 187, 195; (2), 186; (3), 186; (6), 184; (9), 185; (13), 155; *Pythians*, (1), 136, 182, 183, 187–90; (2), 183; (4), 182, 191; (7), 185; (8), 203; *Nemeans*, (1), 184; (7), 150, 191 n. 1, 198; *Isthmians*, (7), 136; (8), 184; *Paean 6*, 150, 191 n. 1;
  Aeolic forms in, 126; allegorization, 190–1; and Alcman, 130, 131, 135–6; on Archilochus, 82; and Bacchylides, 194, 195, 196, 197–8, *231*; and Corinna, 199, 200, 232; dramatic use of direct discourse, 148; formulas in, 190; 'gnomic bridge passages', 130; and Hiero, 183, 197; on Homer, 204; on Homeridae, 6 n. 3; imagery, figures of speech, 136, 187, 192, 195, 196; and Ibycus, 175; 'kenning' of, 136; on man, 131, 198; metre, 239; morality, 130, 131; and myth, 130; and Neoptolemus story, 150; religious element, 126, 193, 198; and Simonides, 182, 184, 185, 192–3; on Spartan choruses, 128; and Stesichorus, 146, 147, 154, 155, 159; and symbolism of gold, 135; unity of odes, 186–7; view

249